CHALLENGING

THE GIANT, VOL. III--

Other books by the author:

Jessica Dragonette's Fiery Breath
Love Songs for the Irishwoman
Rushing to Eva
Looking for One's Shadow at Noon, vols. I & II
The Flying Bird Brings the Message
India Journal
Challenging the Giant, vols. I & II

CHALLENGING THE GIANT, VOL. III--

The Best of ΣΚΟΛΕ,
The Journal of Alternative Education

Mary M. Leue, editor

Down-to-Earth Books
72 Philip St.
Albany, New York 12202

CHALLENGING THE GIANT, VOL. III,
The Best of
ΣΚΟΛΕ
The Journal of Alternative Education

Down-to-Earth   Books
72   Philip   St.
Albany,   New   York   12202

First   printing: October,   1996
Printed   in   the   United   States   of   America

ISBN : 1-878115-11-1

TABLE OF CONTENTS

SCHOOLS AND SCHOOL PEOPLE

TEACHING AND LEARNING

TEACHING AND LEARNING AT HOME

HISTORY OF INNOVATIVE EDUCATIO

STUDENT WRITINGS

SOCIAL CHANGE AND COMMENT

BATTLE OF THE TITANS

THE PLIGHT OF OUR CHILDREN

COMMUNITY AS SCHOOL AS COMMUNITY

REVIEWS

EDITORIAL COMMENT

During the Middle Ages, because of the prevailing value system of feudalism, direct information about the world became unavailable to most people of substance except what they could find by reading Aristotle. If you wanted to know how many teeth a horse had, it wouldn't occur to you to go to a farm and look inside a horse's mouth, you would go to Aristotle! Myths about anything beyond one's immediate surroundings were the norm, and tales about unicorns, "green men"—all sorts of fantasies—were accepted as reality.

We Americans have always prided ourselves on our pragmatism, particularly in contrast with Europeans. Our schools were thought to be the cornerstone of that grounding in empirical reality. Well, something has changed in the last decade or so and I believe we need to take another look! It strikes me that as a society, we are becoming more and more dependent on myths—in this case, the myths dispensed by the media rather than the Classics. It's as though we've lost our anchoring, commonsensical instincts. Children no longer listen to what is being taught in our schools, because it's all gotten lost in the mists of our mythologies. We've gone adrift.

These are parlous times! Perhaps transitional periods always are—particularly millennial ones. Be that as it may, life goes on and we struggle to make sense of our lives, to do the best we can. For this purpose we need a lot of support from many divergent sources. It becomes harder and harder to decipher information, to sift the good myths from more destructive ones, unless you have some pretty good empirical evidence to fall back on. That's what this volume endeavors to offer. Actually, we are told that we are one of the very few sources of information about schools of many sorts that comes from direct experience—right from "the horse's mouth," as it were, that are available to families with kids.

Thousands of very good people, good families, are agonizing over decisions about their children's education. The stakes seem very high, especially in a time when the cost of living rises steadily. Questions mount. Will these children lose out? If they stay in public school, will they suffer lifelong consequences? If we make the wrong choice, will they blame us? How can we be sure we know best what they need? What happens if we let them quit regular school and do something self-chosen, like an alternative school or be schooled at home without external compulsions laid on their backs? What will they be like when they are grown? Will they fall back into the poverty classes, unwanted by the corporate or the professional world? Or will they simply "turn on, tune in, drop out"? Something new has been loosed into people's lives. Daily life used to be pretty-well prescribed at every age by our compulsory institutional expectations and the laws that were created to back them up. But failures built into these systems which were allegedly for misfits only are now affecting more and more families adversely, and choices have to be made concerning how best to deal with these issues amidst a thicket of dangerous possible consequences. Why is this? Something has happened to change the nature of what we used to think of as our support systems. They have become managerial, intrusive into our lives. The "revolution of rising expectations" has rendered them not only obsolete but actually damaging to too many parents and children! We're no longer dazzled and intimidated by the wizard. The "little man behind the curtain" we weren't supposed to notice is out in the open, frantically twirling dials and hoping we won't see him!

Our social institutions which have borne the overall responsibility for the lives of people have become, as John Taylor Gatto says, solely concerned with their own survival, and have forgotten the purpose for which they were originally established. This has happened, in my opinion, because we do not teach democracy—peer-level selfhood, or self-regulation—choose your own term for this process—to our children—and so when they become parents, they do not pass on a capacity for real democracy to their children through their personal examples. The failure to address the underlying problems gets passed on from generation to generation.

Having abandoned our own initial purpose as a democratic nation with "liberty and justice for all" has created a pattern of extremes between the very rich and the very poor which is utterly shameful for such a rich country! We have all invested ourselves in believing in the potentiality of a cultural/economic system of unchecked industrialism—"free enterprise"—the belief that "the business of America is business." Following our national birth in the American Revolution, we set about to create a culture based on a belief in freedom of personal aspiration leading to universal prosperity. It was the American Dream, and has been our national myth.

We believed in the gradual evolution of a society with no classes, with prosperity and good fortune shared equally by all who are willing to work for it, only the lazy, the morally unfit or the stupid being deprived of this general well-being. Universal education was considered by all to be the means whereby this goal was to be achieved. That myth has gone sour, has developed into a kind of institutional cold-heartedness that is downright *un*-American! And still, the myth dies hard, even though its headlong pursuit is destroying many of our planetary resources, overrunning the earth with far more people than it can sustain, and damaging our climate and our habitat in lethal ways!

We Americans bear a tremendous responsibility for promoting this way of life among the pre-industrial countries as a solution to difficulties, supplanting their simple way of life with its focus on survival by work with our quick-fix, instant gratification through easy and mock-heroic but illegal or morally infantile patterns for acquiring money to play the game with, as promoted by so many stories on TV or in the movies.

Our initially American style of "entertaining" children and immature adults is now world-wide, along with the much-admired Coca-Cola/McDonald's syndrome for addicting people to a belief in instant gratification. We have taught the nations of the earth to drive out or destroy their own native cultures in exactly the same manner as we have destroyed our own Native American, Black, immigrant and underclass cultures.

The hidden destructiveness of our culture is the best-kept "secret" we have—and its hiding place is right out in the open, which is the best way ever devised for hiding something! By our method of acquainting ourselves with the fact of its existence while withholding the living reality of its destructive effects on thousands of people, we desensitize our people. We either ring the changes on it as drama (via the media) and then cut away to some advertisement—or turn it into statistical data to be memorized from a textbook—punctuated by the bell that ends the class—to be later regurgitated on a test. In either case, the end result is a discontinuity of one's ability to think concretely and effectively. This way, it is possible to know and not know—simultaneously!

The task of creating a new and truly supportive culture is neither an easy nor a rapidly achieved goal. It will take more than one generation to accomplish, as John Taylor Gatto has warned us. We need to begin taking it on seriously as our main task in life. Hey, it's not such a bad way to spend one's life. I can personally recommend it highly! Maybe you can start by reading what other people have been doing and thinking.

THE BRIDGE
by Ted Strunck

Ted Strunck is too modest to toot his own horn, but his superb achievement as a teacher can only be matched by the superb accomplishment of his students! Truly, this is a miraculous achievement, and richly deserves to be the lead article in this collection. It is principally a teacher's account of a class project—but strikes us as, by extension, about a school as well, since in our view, schools are made up of the people who live and work in them—which is why this section is called "schools and school people."

> *It's a story of having kids learn by doing real things, learning to use tools and working as part of a team, learning that accomplishing a great task requires making many mistakes and going on from there.*

The following article is about building a bridge. A class of 7th and 8th graders at Upland Hills School in rural Michigan, over a period of 2 school years, completed a 175' long span across a 20' deep gully behind their school. It's a story of dreams and doing the impossible through cooperation and planning and steadfast determination. It's a story of having kids learn by doing real things, learning to use tools and working as part of a team, learning that accomplishing a great task requires making many mistakes and going on from there.

Just yesterday, July 12, 1994, my group and I finished a 2 year long project—we finished our bridge! This is no namby-pamby bridge either; this one stretches 175' across a gully that runs between our school and our Ecological Awareness Center which we use for theatre, recording etc. It stands a good 20' off the ground at center and weighs approximately 28,700 lbs. It was designed and built by 13 -15 year olds in the oldest group and it cost nothing. (We had to pay the local building inspectors about $150 for their building permits and inspections). But yes, that's right, we used all salvaged material.

When I was first asked to teach by the oldest group at our school, I felt they needed some kind of outdoor, physical enterprise to use up some of that incredible energy young adolescents have. I couldn't see myself sitting in a classroom for very long with all this roiling energy just beneath the surface, ready to explode.

Now just behind our school there's this gully we call "Toboggan Hill" because every winter we all sled down its very steep slopes. It's great. But also we all have to tread these same slopes in Fall, Winter, Spring and Summer, carrying armloads of costumes, papers, files, props and musical instruments, and it can get treacherous. The very first time I walked that gully I thought it would be a great place to build a bridge. After walking it 2-300 times, I felt rather strongly about it.

Anyway, I approached my director about the idea and much to his credit, he gave me the OK with only one stipulation—no money for the project. Well I've never been one to let that sort of thing stop me, so I set off thinking about what kind of materials were available for free that we could build a bridge with. Lo and behold! Right under my nose and all around me— utility poles! I called our local utility company and found out that yes, they have plenty of discarded poles we could have if we could haul them away. Okay! Step one. A source for possible materials.

That fall as the oldest group sat attentive and wide-eyed before me, I told them about the idea to build a bridge across "Toboggan Hill". They didn't know what to think. One outspoken 15 year-old was skeptical—said it was impossible and I was dreaming. I agreed. I told them I was dreaming, but why say something's impossible before you even try it?

I had a blank bulletin board at the front of the class with the heading, "Kinds of Bridges". I had each of them go home and draw pictures of bridges they could think of. I got sketches of suspension bridges and simple post and beam. One girl drew a beautiful sketch of the Bridge of Sighs in Venice. We hung them up and looked at them for awhile.

Then I asked them to draw a design on graph paper for a bridge going across "Toboggan Hill". Most of the kids drew suspension bridges so I called our local utility company and asked if they had any cable. Sure enough! They had enough to redo the

Mackinac Bridge and yes we could have it. I was elated and began envisioning a swinging suspension bridge behind our school.

At this point my director suggested calling a local university and asking them for help in the way of design. I called the University of Detroit and talked to their Structural Engineering Dept. They were more than willing to have my group (17 kids and 3 adults) come down to their campus and attend a class on bridge design. I love being on a college campus so was quite enthused about this prospect. We'd go down to the college, attend the class and then go eat lunch in the student cafeteria.

It was great fun, the kids loved it and we learned an important formula—the relation between the length of a span and the width of a truss. Now we were armed and dangerous. The professor we met there, a young African—we called him Dr. David— came out to our site to see what we were trying to do. I asked him if he thought it was possible. He smiled broadly and said, "For an engineer, nothing is impossible." He also gave us some great advice: keep it 1) simple and 2) easy to maintain.

We scrapped the suspension bridge design because it wouldn't be simple to build or maintain. It would require much less material, which was a very attractive advantage, but require very skilled workers and an almost constant maintenance situation. We decided on a simple post and beam arrangement with a supplemental truss system designed to use the materials we were getting from our utility company.

By the time winter rolled in we were busy constructing models of the design we had come up with. I wanted the kids to go through the process of constructing the bridge on a scale model, so they could see what had to be done and in what order. It was great fun. I divided the group into 5 groups of 3 and one group of 2 and made it a cooperative experience. I got to build one too!

From the very beginning of that year, we had been studying architecture with an emphasis on bridges. We were familiar with the columns of Greece and Rome and the arches of the Etruscans. We read the histories of some of the great bridges and some of the great tragedies that befell them. It became almost an obsession with me. I looked at every bridge with new eyes. I studied its structure and design and materials and aesthetic. I began to appreciate these artifices that combine science and art in a most practical way. They became things of wonder and grace.

Sometime that winter, I mentioned the bridge project to someone in our school community. He told me his father had recently retired from the utility company after working there all his life planting poles. Aha! I called him immediately. He agreed to come with me to look at the poles and help me pick out some good ones.

We went down to the salvage yard and there was this mountain of poles—about 1500, all piled willy-nilly. We knew we needed them at least 30' long and fairly straight. No prob. We had an easy time finding our quota.

Someone else in our community knew someone who had a flatbed semi and would be willing to give us one haul. We went to the yard and there was a crew there with a crane for lifting poles. We asked for help. They gave us about 4 hours as we weeded through the pile. We managed to get 26 poles loaded just before quitting time. I had wanted to take about 32-36 just so we could pick and choose on site, but we'd make do.

And so, on a cold crisp late February morning, I came riding into the school parking lot on top of this semi trailer full of poles. We brought them on a Saturday to avoid the crowds of kids that just might complicate things a little. We had set up an unloading spot with railroad ties, and once the poles were untied, just give a kick and off they rolled into a neat pile. I can remember sitting on that pile sipping on a cup of coffee with my good friend Nome, and watching a flock of pure white snow geese fly overhead in the bluest morning sky. I'd never seen that before. I took it as a sign.

That Monday morning the kids all ran out to look at these huge poles. Some of them as long as 45' and weighing about 1600 lbs. I remember seeing a couple of fathers pointing and whispering and later learning of their concerns about the dangers of working with such huge things. Yes we would be careful.

We had recently watched a documentary on the building of the pyramids. Not only to see how they moved those 2000 lb. stones but also to get some ideas about how to make a documentary video. Our school had recently purchased a fine High 8 camera and I thought a video of the bridge project might be an interesting side project for some of my kids.

In the pyramid video, the ancient Egyptians moved those huge stones by placing them on rollers. We did the same. That first morning, I put the number 1 on the chalkboard and said that was my goal for the day—to move one of those poles from where the truck dumped them, about 100' to our construction site. We went to work.

One of my boys knew how to tie a timber hitch. We laid down some old logs we found lying around as our rollers and everyone grabbed hold of the rope. The pole flew along the ground almost effortlessly. That first morning the kids moved 4 poles and were elated. We were off to a great start.

Each morning I upped the goal and the kids always beat it. By the end of that week, we had moved all 26 poles to our site and had logged each one as to length.

Our original design had called for a span of 20' between each upright. That would've required 32 poles total. We only had 26 poles so we had to change our span to 25' between the verticals. We had to use each pole wisely.

We had decided on our site in late fall. It was the least environmentally disruptive. We only had to cut down one 3" diameter sapling and some brush. The course of the bridge afforded a sweeping curve as it ascended ever so slightly (1 foot every 25' span). The mental picture was quite beautiful.

Bud, the retired guy from the utility company who knew how to dig a hole and plant a pole showed up the next week with some strange looking tools. He called them a spud and a spoon. The spud was a 10' long flat shovel and was used for just breaking up the ground. The spoon, also 10' long, was a real exaggerated shovel for scooping out the broken ground. Bud demonstrated how to dig a perfectly round, smooth 4' deep hole. The kids got to work.

Planting those first poles was easy. We were going downhill and they just sorta slid into place. By the time the warm spring weather arrived, we were dealing with some pretty big poles. We were out to the middle now and needed to plant our largest uprights. These were the mothers of all poles. They needed to be at least 28' long. We made a kind of rough sluice by laying two logs together, and ran these big guys down the hill on that. Now to raise them up.

I won't go into all the details, but we learned some pretty fancy tricks with ropes and pulleys. Raising these big poles required the combined efforts of both our oldest groups—about 35 kids—stretched out on a 100' rope outside the fall line of the pole. One, two, three, pull. Up, up it went, but over, over it fell. Our side guides couldn't hold it from falling to one side. Undaunted (and I mean undaunted; these kids didn't blink an eye at our obvious failure) we moved the big mutha back into position and tried again. This time, she fell into place.

And so it went. By the time summer was pressing her presence upon us, we had planted all the poles and started to construct the horizontal beams. Now it was beginning to look like a bridge!

In addition to the poles, the utility company had given us those cross members that actually support the wires. They're 8' or 10' long and are essentially 4x4's. They worked perfectly for our deck boards. Now the deck was designed to be 4' wide so we just laid down a bunch of these 8' 4x4's and cut them in half with a chain saw. Voilà! We had deck boards.

At the end of our school year for '92-'93, we had completed 2 25' sections with decking. We could actually walk out on it and stare at the poles just waiting for their load to be laid on them.

Now that we had deck boards in place, all the kids in our group were able to carve their names into them. We put the years down and then Bud's name on the first, mine on the second and all 17 of my kids' following after. It was a significant gesture. They were a part of the structure themselves. We all felt a sense of immortality, somehow.

Just as a side story: On the morning before our Grandparents day, when everyone would be visiting the school and all the kids would be showing their parents and grandparents the bridge, I was walking out on our 2 completed sections and noticed a cracked support arm. This arm goes across the 4' between the uprights and our horizontal beams rest on them. Well, here was one cracked pretty seriously. I panicked. I didn't know what to do. I worked most of that morning on it by myself trying to repair it to no avail. The next morning, I discussed it with the group. They presented various ideas and we decided to try one. It involved everyone. The entire group had to play a part. We decided to lift the end of the section that rested on that arm, and while the group held it in place—we only needed 2"—we would try to replace the cracked arm with a good one. Well, we set up a double-snatch jig with our pulleys and yes, up she went, first one side, then the other.

We finished our repair job with less than an hour to go before the visitors would arrive. My feeling of relief was tremendous, but also I'd learned a lesson in community. I couldn't have fixed that cracked arm myself; I needed the group.

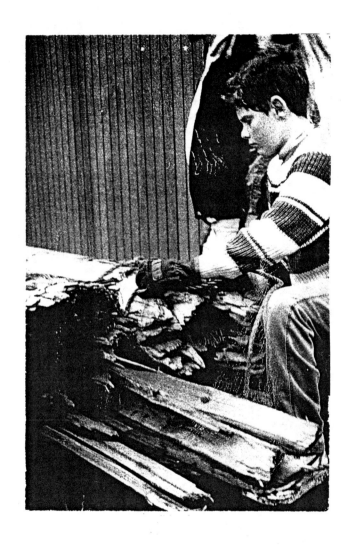

We ended our school year by watching the unedited version of our documentary. It was great. The kids sat there transfixed, watching themselves doing the incredible. There were moments of hilarity we rewound and played again and again. But most of all, they saw themselves working together to accomplish something much bigger than any one could do by themselves. It had been a tremendous experience for all of us. I had hoped we'd finish the bridge, but all in good time.

About a week after school was over, we had a parent-and-child workday. It was wonderful watching the kids. They were so proud of all they'd done and so eager to share what they knew. And the parents who hadn't seen the bridge yet were amazed at its size.

It went well. We managed to finish a whole section—put up two horizontals and decking! The parents seemed to really enjoy rolling those huge poles out across the finished sections and hoisting them into place. There was a lot of self-pride floating around that day.

By this time the whole community was into the bridge symbolism. A beautiful black-and-white photo taken and processed by a girl in my group appeared on the cover of the final edition of our school newsletter. Our school's auction committee asked if they could use the bridge as the theme for next year's fundraiser. "Bridge to the Future" became the theme for our Annual Giving Drive and people were able to get their names on plaques that will be placed on the planks of the bridge. Elisabeth Kübler-Ross bought the first section of handrailing with her donation of $500. The bridge had become a focal point for our community and it wasn't even half done yet. It was a powerful symbol—not being done. One could look at it and see all the uprights standing in their place. The course of the bridge was obvious. The vision was unfolding and had an air of necessity and inevitability.

The next September brought me a new batch of kids. Because our school is arranged in a way that allows most kids to be in the same group for 2 years, I was lucky enough to get some of my best workers from last year back.

It started out slow and painfully. We had lots of rain for one thing, and were now working at the bridge's highest point. It was extremely difficult. We'd go out in the morning and try to place a horizontal beam across the next section, and one end would fall. Then we'd get one end up and the other would fall. Everyone was frustrated. We just couldn't find the process. And the kids from last year lorded it over the new kids. And the new kids didn't feel it was their bridge. And one girl thought it was the ugliest thing she'd ever seen and it was highly dangerous and someone was going to fall and break their neck for sure. I was offended and angry and perplexed and didn't know how to deal with it.

It was a tough fall. By the time the snow made it too dangerous to continue, we'd finished sections 4 and 5 out of 7. We were beginning to climb the hill beyond and work would be much easier come Spring.

One of the new jobs we had begun that Fall was the installation of our truss system. We had originally designed a simple Warren Truss that would also serve as a handrail. We built a prototype. It was a failure. It failed because of the materials we had to work with. We had to come up with something else. In the middle of one of my many sleepless nights, I saw it—the simplest of the simple—a King Post Truss. And the materials had lent themselves perfectly! It would be integral and lightweight and a triangle. You just can't beat that combination.

The old Warren Truss idea involved building the truss itself away from the bridge and then hauling it into place. Our prototype was heavy and cumbersome. The new King Post Truss could be constructed in place and each of the components was easy to manage. We designed a jig where we could precut all the pieces. We installed a Truss system on our first section. It decreased our flex to almost nothing! It made the bridge rock solid. We were elated.

As soon as the snow would allow, we were back to work. We had a crew setting the big horizontals in place, a crew putting the decking boards on, a crew constructing the truss assemblies, a crew putting up the handrails and a 3 stage assembly line cutting and nailing our handrail sections together. Now the last stage of our assembly line operation could be done by children of all ages. After the boards were cut to the proper length, the kids could nail the sections together. We needed 112 sections in all. Plenty of work for all the younger children who came to my bridge class every Thursday afternoon.

Work on the bridge progressed steadily. The end of another school year was fast approaching. Would we finish the bridge?

Along about mid-May, my wife suggested we have a Bridge Camp sorta thing and invite all the kids from last year

and this year to finish the bridge together. Well, I'd promised last year's crew a chance to be there for the final moment, so the idea became reality. Dates were set so everyone could be there, invitations were sent out and the pressure to finish the bridge by school's end was gone. As a matter of fact, one of the kids remarked we'd better slow down a little or there wouldn't be anything left to do at camp.

I remember sitting in a staff meeting and one of the teachers brought up the fact that some of the kids were walking across the bridge to get to their theater classes and because there were no handrails on most of it, we'd better not let that happen. I sat back in my chair and let that sink in.The kids had begun to cross the bridge! It was being used to get from one side to the other. Sure you had to jump a little 2' jump at the end, but still, all the way across! We'd have to make an announcement that no one is allowed to cross the bridge until further notice. I thought it was a glorious issue.

Well, school ended. The kids carved their names into the bridge and we watched our unedited video of the past year's efforts. The goodbyes on that final day were softened by the thought of Bridge Camp coming up soon and the wondering about who would come.

Doing something for the first time is always a perilous proposition, and so it was with Bridge Camp.

A couple of days before it was to start, Phil asked me how many adults were going to be there to help me. Gee, I never thought of that. He wanted to know about safety goggles and work gloves and supervision. I became apprehensive and made a few calls to some parents inviting them to come and be a part of the crew. All answered noncommittally, that sure they'd like to and maybe.... I was worried. What if 35 kids showed up? There wasn't that much work to keep them all busy. Well, we'd have to wait and see.

Monday, first day of camp, I drove out with 5 guys in my van. Now this would be great! We got to school; a student from last year was there waiting. As the morning rolled on, more kids showed up and by lunch time we had a good, manageable-size crew of 11 .

Tuesday was hot. The crew size increased to maybe 12-14. We worked hard and knocked off at 2 and went swimming.

Wednesday, crew size up to 15-18. Lots of socializing and hanging out. Some kids from 2 years ago show up with fire crackers! Great! I feel overloaded. Phil calls from his sanctuary up north and asks how things are going. I dump. I realize I've provided a FREE! week-long, meaningfully-engaged activity for young adolescents and it was growing like the Blob. That night I called more parents and got some commitments. Hurrah! Adults with power tools!.

Thursday came. The crew had grown to 20-22 kids, but I was ready. There was something for everyone. More adults enabled me to have more work stations. We got tons done. It looked as if tomorrow would be the last and final day of bridge building. It would be done tomorrow!

Friday. RAIN! It was raining! Steady—that kind of soaking rain that goes on and on. The phone rang. "Well, are we going to work on the bridge today?" I decided to go.

When we get to school, it had stopped raining. The weather had actually helped in that it limited the number of workers to just 5 or 6. We got to work as fast as possible. We covered the areas we were working in with tarps and wrapped the electrical connections with baggies. We worked right through lunch. We were getting very near the end. A few more boards to go and a downpour came. We had to stop. I couldn't believe it. About an hour's worth of work left and we would've finished on time. Oh well, just another one of those setbacks.

We had one last work day a couple of weeks later and finished it. It was a rather anticlimactic event. No drums, no fanfare; just a simple "That's it."

We looked at each other, shook hands and deep, deep down we knew what we had done.

On Sept. 25, 1994, we had a 'Bridge Dedication Day'. The community shared in the celebration. We thanked all the people who contributed labor or materials and recognized those to whom we were grateful. It was a glorious day. I was a little nervous—the bridge had never held that many people before. It did fine.

There's a documentary video available for $10 from Upland Hills School that chronicles the entire project. You may obtain a copy by calling the school at (810) 545-4549 or you may write Ted at 727 Golf, Royal Oak, MI 48073.

Rockland Project School:

This is a thoughtful account of a school that began with idealistic principles and aspirations and ended when the cold realities of economics combined with the fears of families for the futures of their children clashed with these ideals. There are good lessons to be learned from Alice Gerard's experiences and her after-thoughts about them.

REUNION
by Alice Gerard

Twenty-three years ago, in the fall of 1969, I was one of four public school teachers who quit their jobs to open an alternative school in Rockland County, New York. We were heavily influenced by A.S. Neill's *Summerhill* and George Leonard's *Education and Ecstasy*, and we designed a school full of learning environments where nobody had to attend classes unless they wanted to. By Christmas of that year we had forty students, and we were learning as much as they were.

I think I had had a mental picture of happy students doing school-like things because they wanted to, not because they had to. Instead, the kids spent a lot of their time running around and playing, sometimes getting into fights, destroying school materials, and being mean to each other. Sometimes they asked for classes with us but often they decided at the last minute that they didn't really want to come. Occasionally we all got involved in projects that led to real learning and good feelings. One example was a local history class which excavated a lost nineteenth century community, with proper archaeological techniques. Their records were used later by a Columbia University graduate student writing her thesis on the same community.

We played a lot of music, and sang together often. Norman, one of the teachers, built a playhouse with kids. All of us went on countless hikes, and every June we camped for a week with the whole school. We had school newspapers and made things out of clay and wood. There was a yearly Fair, and wonderful plays written by the students.

At the beginning we had daily morning meetings where each student and staff member had one vote, and a different child chaired the meeting each time. This itself was a powerful learning tool, as was our "Stop Rule." This rule, a child's version of the Golden Rule, stated that if someone was bothering you, in any way, you had a right to say "Stop" and they were supposed to stop. If someone hit you, you were not allowed to retaliate physically. Instead, you were supposed to say "Stop" and tell them what you wanted them to stop and why you felt that way. Our students became skilled at problem-solving with words instead of fists, because we cared so much about this rule.

Our academic curriculum, however, was a real hodge-podge because we were always trying to entice kids to come to class by thinking of something new and interesting. Since they didn't write unless they felt like it, many kids had poor skills in this area. We all had a wonderful time, most of the time, but there wasn't a great deal of academic continuity.

Over the years Rockland County, where we were located, became more conservative. Our parents were not wealthy, and they began to want assurances that their children would learn enough skills to be able to support themselves as adults. At the beginning, our students had been middle class kids, mostly from intact families, who already had many of their basic math and reading skills. With time, that changed. More students came from broken families, and were lacking a core of common knowledge that earlier students had had. They read less and watched a great deal of television. Some of them, when unsupervised, were really destructive. Gradually we took away choices for students. By 1980 we were asking students to go to math and reading classes, and later we scheduled them for all classes, although they still had an hour and a half of free play time a day. By the end, the free time was down to about an hour a day. It was still a special, happy place, for children and for teachers.

All three of the other original founders eventually left, for a larger arena and higher salaries. The school, which had been dependent for many years on a small endowment, ran out of money and students in 1990, after twenty-one years, and closed in June of that year.

In early 1991 I started working on a book about several alternative schools from the same period. This gave me a chance, after twenty-seven busy years of teaching, to read, think, talk to teachers, and visit schools. Much has happened in the field of education since I was a student at Bank Street. I have had to reexamine my beliefs about teaching and learning and to develop a much larger perspective.

Two of the schools I am writing about, the Barker School (later Collaberg) in Stony Point, and my own Rockland Project School, are now closed. Visits to the other three: Meade, in Greenwich, Connecticut, the Free School in Albany, and Sudbury Valley in Framingham, Massachusetts, have been heartening and exciting. Alternative education is still alive and well in a few places, and has now been in existence long enough to evaluate the experiences of some of the early graduates. Sudbury Valley has been working on an exhaustive follow-up of graduates, and promises to publish soon.

One of the things I began to wonder about was what had happened to the Project School students from the early years, the ones who seldom went to class. Were they able to function in "real life" even though they had spent a large part of school playing and hanging out with friends? Had they been academically handicapped?

In June, 1991, I arranged for a Project School reunion, a weekend at a camp in Harriman Park. Over a hundred people came and it was a great success. The most valuable part for me, however, was to meet again those students from the first few years, when no one had to go to classes. I should have known that they would be capable, interesting, responsible people. They had managed the transition to other schools and often gone on to college. Valerie, after the University of Michigan, became a private investigator who handles everything except matrimonial cases. Steven J., a wiry kid who was always jumping from windowsills, was a competitive gymnast in college and now runs a fitness center. Sam G.is an artist who works at a gas station and sells decorated T shirts to survive economically. Jeremy has a job teaching at an alternative school, Rachel is finishing up a graduate degree in holistic medicine, and Josh R., over whom I agonized because he didn't complete things, has just moved upstate and started a new job in a recording studio, continuing an interest in music which began at the Project School.

All of the young people who showed up looked back to their years at the Project School as having been a special, wonderful time. This quotation from Michele Mark, who wrote instead of attending the reunion, is typical of the feelings they expressed. "At the conclusion of my first semester in the graduate program, I await grades and wistfully remember classes without them. Project School played such a vital role in my life, and I am often struck by how differently I view learning, teaching, and authority than my peers of more traditional backgrounds. As naive as it sounds to so many, I honestly believe that people do learn when they are ready. 'Despite' (because of, perhaps) three and a half years of unstructured education, I have never been behind my peers in public schools, and my ability to constructively structure my own time and activities has given me an advantage in every school and job I've been at since Project School."

The stories of two students, however, were particularly meaningful to me. One was Jeff R., now a tall, good-looking young man in his early twenties. Jeff transferred to R.P.S. when he was nine and having difficulty in public school with the work itself and with his teachers. By the time he came class attendance was mandatory for some subjects. I was Jeff's Language Arts teacher and I had a terrible time with him. I couldn't motivate him to work and his behavior in class was sporadically extremely disruptive, although we got on fine outside of class. He behaved much better for Norman, who taught him math, and this was frustrating for me because I felt I must be doing something wrong. When Jeff told me about his life after the Project School, however, I realized what a limited perspective I had had.

He left us when he was twelve and went to a nearby private school, from which he was expelled at the end of the first year. He spent his public high school years cutting classes and getting poor grades, and left school for good as soon as his parents allowed him to. After a succession of unsatisfactory jobs, both for him and for his employers, he accidentally discovered something he could do well. This was sheet metal work, a profession which takes strength and a high level of intuitive mathematical skill. Jeff told me, "I discovered I was a math genius!" He'd always hated reading, writing, and anything to do with language because he couldn't do it well enough. Conventional math was hard for him also, but he told me that the first time he realized he could do something well was when Norman built the play house by the back door of the school with the boys Jeff's age. Jeff, because of his interest and ability, became Norman's right hand man on the job.

I don't know whether his experience with language skills would have been different if he had come to our school earlier.

It's clear to me now, however, that Jeff was someone who didn't fit into conventional schooling at all, and our attempts to get him to, no matter how humane, were bound to be unsuccessful. He'd have been better off with more freedom in school from the beginning.

Brian was the other student whose story taught me something. Now twenty-five, he was at R.P.S. during the years when he could actually play all day instead of attending classes. He was bright and did go to some classes, but not many. He came to us at seven, after a bad beginning in public school, mainly because he was so lively. Now he would be called hyperactive, but in those days he was just considered a bad kid by his public school teacher and by his father, who tried to change his behavior by physical punishment. Although slight in build, he was wiry and aggressive, as well as being smart and manipulative. We all worried about what kind of person he would become as an adult.

When I talked to him, the first thing that surprised me was how important the school had been to him. Although he didn't remember a great deal from those years, he goes back there often. He told me, "It was a lot of fun—it was great. To go on trips, and see all those places, plus to have the whole park to walk around in. We'd go down to the lake, and go up to see the remnants of the old houses—I still go up there all the time.

"The department of Social Services where I work, every August they have a picnic, and they do it at Rockland Lake, right down the street from the school.

"Last year was my first year, but I brought my bicycle, and I cycled up to the school. It was a lot of fun. I always go back there, see my name on the back of the school, my old phone number. It's still there.

"I remember that we didn't have to go to classes, and for a kid, you know, that's a whole world of freedom. I remember the transition back to public school was really rough. I was like bawling and crying and I didn't want to go to school. I guess having restrictions was hard, having to go to class and do all kinds of homework, stuff like that. When you're not used to doing that kind of thing, it can be rough. I think I went back in eighth grade. I did pretty well. When I got to high school I attended most of my classes, but there was a lot of hanging out with your friends, cutting out of class; I still wanted to be free in terms of the restrictions.

"When I got out of high school I went to college but I was pretty well forced, you know, and I didn't want that. So I didn't do so well my first semester and then I stopped. I went to on the job of life training for several semesters and then I went back of my own choosing. Since then I've done well, and maintained at least a 3.3. I had no problems with my math skills and my English skills—in fact I did pretty well in college, I mean with my English skills. I'm pretty proud of myself in that respect. I don't think it's hampered me in any way.

"I tend to get restless still. I play volleyball at home. I've done many things, had many jobs. I don't think I've ever been fired, what I do is I get a job and I like it, and then I just don't like it any more—I get bored and I quit, get a new job. This one—it's the first job I've had full time, I get up in the morning. and I say 'All right, I'm going to work.' And I'm almost excited about it. So I'm very happy in that respect. I run an offset press and a high speed copy machine, and I'm in charge of keeping all the forms, so when they call me, I print them up. I also have that 'Other related duties' clause which can cover anything from fixing a chair to taking someone to the airport. It's a big building—say about 150 people that work in the building I'm pretty lucky. I have a job where I can be anywhere in the building fixing something and nobody's going to say I can't be there. So sometimes I'll just get up and walk around the building and just talk to people, whether or not I'm actually supposed to be doing it. I just do it, and in that respect I really like it. A desk job does't appeal to me."

I think we gave Brian what he needed. His whole story shows that things work better for him when he makes the choices. He's still a restless, lively person, but he's happy and productively employed. I 'd been afraid that Brian and Jeff might have been harmed by the freedom we gave them. On the contrary, I now feel we should have given Jeff more, and that Brian only benefited from freedom, however hair-raising it was at times for us. If the school was still in existence, I 'd want to go back to the old days when class attendance was voluntary. Jeff and Brian are individuals who clearly didn't fit into the usual school patterns. But this is true to some degree of every student. Each is unique and benefits from freedom of choice and an individualized curriculum. To be part of a democratic learning community teaches skills and confers benefits that last a whole lifetime.

East Hill School:

Jonathan Bliss tells us with a great deal of affection about his father's school, East Hill in Andover, Vermont, which was also his. He and his wife Laura have reopened East Hill School, and at last report had gathered a small group of teachers and a goodly gaggle of kids and were deeply involved in running their school. They may not have quite decided whether or not they're doing a good enough job (Dick is a hard act to follow!), but it sure sounds good to an outsider! I hope we'll be hearing more about their school as time goes by.

SCHOOLING AS IF CHILDREN MATTERED:
Thirty-five years on East Hill
by Jonathan Bliss

My father [Dick Bliss], in a question aimed more at himself than at his audience, once asked a group of East Hill parents, "Why school?", which some of those present took to mean: What could we possibly teach children that would help them live in this strange and often pathological world?

Being a provoking man, he might have responded to his own question a number of ways, but the answer he lived for 35 years was East Hill Farm.

In 1957 my parents bought 300 acres in Andover, Vermont, and the following year opened a summer program with four children, only two of whom paid tuition. The kids swam in a muddy pond, rode a borrowed horse, and built their own cabins. My father liked to remember that when the farm had visitors, he'd tell the four kids to slip from one activity to another, hoping the guests would fail to notice that all the children looked alike on what he called "this pimple of a place."

The birth of my older brother Andrew in 1960 lent an urgency to my parents' work. Significantly "retarded," Andy would clearly require something more than the local public school. My parents were appalled by institutions for the retarded and mentally ill, and I doubt this approach was ever a real option in their minds. They were told he might not live past the age of twelve, but they sensed Andy had a chance if they could give him useful work and membership in a safe and thoughtful community.

Word of East Hill's summer program spread during the sixties, but in an early letter to his sister my father speaks of wanting "a total approach to the problem of growing up." The decision to open a school evolved —among other things —out of my parents' realization that a working school community might help them raise their own family well. By the same token, the process could involve other children in a "small society," one with its share of problems and possibilities.

An East Hill day began early, with chores: milking, making breakfast, cleaning, cutting wood. Everyone participated. The person In Charge for the day assigned the jobs. As on many farms, breakfast was a respite and a breathing space. The food was simple, whole, and usually plentiful—barring a major error by the cooks! As the day students arrived, everyone gathered for circle dances; "Hora" from Israel, "Zimmeratik" from Greece, "Road to the Isles" and "Going Down to Cairo" from the British Isles and America.

Next came singing and morning meeting, a time for the group to take stock of itself and its responsibilities. Between songs we heard from the inspectors, two kids who had looked the farm over for cleanliness and orderliness. Volunteers went to tidy up areas that fell short. A student read the rule for the day: "When going into the woods to work, there should be at least three people..."; "Pots and pans should be washed in the large sink..." Announcements were made and concerns aired.

My father regularly used this time to re-focus the farm community. "Dick's lectures" were always sparked by—but never confined to—things directly at hand. Was the farm working together? Were individuals treating each other with respect? He called these surface indicators "tone," and was more concerned about them than almost any other element in the day.

It was sometimes hard for visitors to see the connection between my father's leadership style and the intensely independent culture he was nurturing. In a school more democratic than most, his central role sometimes seemed a contradiction to outside observers. In fact, he knew that democratic principles, however high-minded, can always be manipulated by cynics, and he spoke more often of justice and compassion than of votes and the ruling majority. He was something of an heir, albeit a skeptical one, to the great headmasters of the late nineteenth and early twentieth centuries, in that "head" connoted moral center, steward, facilitator, counselor, and goad. His influences included Gandhi, Jefferson, and Eugene Debs, and he often quoted St. Benedict's Rule to the effect that a good Abbot listens as closely to the junior monks as he does to the seniors. He had large ears for the difficulties of growing up; he also had plenty to say, and often said it. When asked about his attitude toward kids, his response might be: "they need to know where I stand."

He understood the power of metaphor, and balanced every direct confrontation with a story. There was the Enoch Puffer saga, about a young boy from Andover who explores America during and just after the Civil War; stories from my father's own history, of World War II and his coming of age; and the legendary Hunt Carlyle, an Andover boy who did not leave town, but remained behind to know and love it. Somehow—I things it was partly a strain of skepticism that complemented his idealism—my father managed the trick of dealing with morality without seeming above his own rhetoric. And Hunt and Enoch worked their way into farm tradition as touchstones for generations of East Hill kids.

"Hot blood is better than cold blood" was one of his favorite sayings, and somehow, paradoxically, this was a guiding principle for a man who called himself a pacifist. His critique, whether gentle or urgent, was always on target. He could (and often did) exasperate us all, but you could not dismiss him. People have spoken of his "passion," which it was, but informed by close observation and a good sense of timing. "There were times when I wanted to kill him," a former student said not long ago, "but as I think back I understand exactly why he was the way he was. Of all the influences in my life, he and East Hill are at the head of the list. His example of involvement, the way he insisted that we care for each other, is something I try to bring to everything I do."

When morning meeting was over, the group separated for classes. This is one of the most difficult aspects of the farm to write about, not because it wasn't important or effective, but because it was integral. A basic notion of my father's was that you couldn't divorce intellectual growth from psychic growth any more than you could physically separate the head from the rest of the body. Consequently, the reader is warned that anything I say about academics in particular will lead to an impression of fragmentation, something we tried at all costs to avoid at East Hill.

The structure of the farm's academic life was never rigidly set, and took many forms through the years. By the mid-80s, though, a general daily routine had been established. Class groups were composed so that group dynamics interfered as little as possible. This meant they were inter-aged, mixed-ability groupings, usually of from 6 to 10 kids. The curriculum was based on the Core idea, with the defining subject changing yearly—the Greeks, then Native American culture, then medievalism, then the Arabs, then discovery and trade, then industrialism. On Mondays, Dick or another teacher presented the older students with a lecture-story on that year's subject. Those of us who gave Core lectures tried to make our expositions visual and dramatic. It took only a few days at East Hill for a teacher to realize that kids respond to people, not discrete "facts."

For the rest of the week, the individual groups explored material presented in the story-lecture session, and followed students' interests. The idea was that looking intently at the Native Americans, for example, opened a door through which you gained access to a wide range of subjects: sacred ritual, hunting practices, building techniques, modes of travel, botany and the natural sciences, art, warfare, the dynamics of language, inter-cultural experience, mythology. Often, there were almost too many possibilities, and class groups faced the challenges of focusing.

As much as possible kids were given a role in directing their own work. Pacing was individual. In a small, inter-aged, mixed-ability group, it was clear when one student was ready for an essay, and when someone else needed more time to draw. The job of the teacher was to help kids find materials, to lead discussion—and to know when it was time for recess! Math practice took place in tutorials or on work jobs. I learned fractions from Mike at the end of a two-by-four. We were building a shed, and I needed a board three feet nine and a quarter inches long. "Look," he said, "just find the half-inch mark, then divide it—this way."

We took flak from skeptical academicians and nervous parents because we placed academics in context, rather than allowing this part of a child's school experience to dominate. Most people—including the participants—agreed that kids here were, with a few exceptions, interested in being on the farm and alive to the possibilities it offered. I remember my amazement when I first talked to survivors of other high schools, and discovered how it had been for them. I had never liked all parts of my academic experience equally, but it had never occurred to me that being in school could be boring.

Wednesday, at mid-week, was music day. All morning kids gave and received lessons in recorder, guitar, piano, and violin. Every corner of our venerable Main House echoed. It was not literally true, as we often said, that everyone on the farm played an instrument. No one was coerced, and a few kids opted to work in the shop or at outside jobs on music day. But better than two thirds of the group usually played. The noon meal divided indoor activities from the wider, freer scope of the farm outside. Following reading aloud and a wild half-hour of active and (mostly) non-aggressive games, the afternoon was devoted to outdoor work—weeding in the garden, fencing, cutting wood, carpentry—and wood working, hiking, and art. Older kids led crews. The general theme was stewardship: the work of caring for the land, preparing for winter, or getting ready for the next farm festival. Balance was crucial. As on most farms, there was always more labor to be done then there were qualified workers, but for many eight year olds, finding the best climbing tree is work. Equally important, eight year olds need sixteen year olds to guide them—and vice versa. In the end we had to hold all work against a common standard: did it advance a positive farm tone, and was it creative?

From the beginning, each person over 14 took her or his turn being In Charge. This was a student's most hotly anticipated (and dreaded) responsibility. Visitors who suggested it was ceremonial—"Dick runs the farm, after all"—missed the point. Kids were responsible initially to Dick for every aspect of the day. As they grew in the job they responded to challenges implicit within any group or community, challenges no teacher could or should manufacture. Everyone had to be awakened thoughtfully, to get the day off to a good start. If you wanted a decent meal, you couldn't have two rivals on the breakfast crew. The guitar player for morning singing had to be right for the day—a strong leader for visitors, otherwise perhaps a novice and her teacher. If you wanted a successful afternoon, you began setting it up in the morning, finding crew leaders, checking materials. You talked to people before you asked a favor of them, you got a sense of the mood before you took command. You were consistent. In other words, you learned that respect is earned, and you learned to honor the possibilities and limitations of power.

If this was empty ceremony, it didn't feel like it at the time.

Over the years we observed a number of festivals and occasions, and by the late 80s had settled on five major celebrations: Halloween, Advent, Christmas, Passover, and May Day. Each one had its own rhythm, a mixture of tradition and innovation. The common thread was an attempt to give a part in the celebration to each person on the farm. A good festival has room for actors, cooks, carpenters, musicians, and spectators. As a group which varied widely in age and ability, religion and temperament, we were each obliged to take seriously the task of making traditional festivals our own. When an East Hill celebration worked, we saw a critical element of folk culture in action: a feast day allows a participant to play a part, and a part can work its way into your blood. The jester mugs for the crowd, and discovers his own humor and frivolity... the King Of The Day revels in his power, and is shown its responsibilities... Lady Marion speaks her lines from the text of the play and suddenly it is not a play, but a moment full of vitality and consequence.

In many ways, our attempts to make a festival work reflected East Hill's core: everyone had to be **engaged** for the enterprise to sustain belief, and adults could claim little credit for the most significant personal transformations.

The farm closed as a school in 1989 during a bad period in my father's last illness. Since then, we have had time to think about thirty-five difficult and exhilarating years. What did East Hill accomplish? It's hard to say. The things the farm stood for can't be measured in test scores and surveys of conventional achievement. On the other hand, people who spent time here can speak about things which matter to them now: success in relationships, fulfillment in work, clarity. They alone can say whether East Hill proved helpful in these areas. As I think about what we were and what we still are, it is clear that the farm offers room to breathe, and time. Visitors used to ask if we minded being cut off from the "real world"—as if there is such a thing, and as if you can be cut off from it! The farm was, and is, a microcosm; with all the challenges of the society beyond its borders, it brings reality close, and helps focus our lives.

What's ahead? More than ever, we need to engage children in bringing their own society into being. It hardly needs to be said that vital kids reflect our hope for a better world, and are the means of its achievement.

As for my brother, Andy can work the farm from the milking barn to the hay field, and on vacation he explores Long Island's Hallock's Bay in a 12 foot outboard skiff.

He calls her "Victory," a name which says it all.

New School of Northern Virginia:

John Potter, the founder-director of NSNV, was for a number of years the founder-director of the highly successful interracial Somerset School in downtown Washington, D.C., grades 7-12. His address to the Small Schools organization he was hosting at that time appears in volume I of Challenging the Giant, *pp.75-82.*

John was educated in English public schools and Nottingham University before coming to this country.

FROM AN ASSISTANT DIRECTOR'S DESK:
WE'RE TALKING SERIOUS OWNERSHIP HERE:
by Vic Kryston

On a recent Saturday night my eighteen year old son Jason called home, saying that he and some schoolmates, knowing a teacher had been deserted by his fiancée for the weekend, decided to rent some movies and keep him company.

I love my ICIA and I am certainly in favor of kindness to teachers, but this is a young man who has always hated school. He was apparently a victim of one of those diseases invented by ambitious psychiatric hospitals: the dreaded School Refusal. Wanting to spend a Saturday night with an (ugh) teacher suggests some kind of paradigm shift!

Several years ago, when it became clear to us that public school had little to offer Jason, our ultimate solution became a small, alternative school in Fairfax, The New School, headed by an ex-Fairfax County teacher, John Potter.

I knew John from the days when my older son, Jason's brother, Sean, was able to work through his angst in another school run by John Potter, Somerset, in Washington. D.C. Sean really flowered there. I had similar hopes for Jason.

John Potter's model for his innovative ideas was the famous alternative school in Britain, Summerhill. John established Somerset and later New School based on his sense of what was the best of Summerhill, especially the idea that community building is a basic skill necessary before very much real learning can occur.

John also sensed that a community, an all inclusive community where each person feels a sense of belonging, is necessarily small in number. The New School which includes K-12 has a population of about sixty students. Total.

But the small number is only a given, not a guarantee of success. The New School has built into its basic structure ways to encourage community building. School meetings where staff and students meet as equals are scheduled weekly. During these meetings the usual issues of school administration, decisions, problems and discipline are hashed out. Moreover, anyone, staff or student, is encouraged to request a meeting whenever a need is felt. It is not unusual for my son to report that classes were cut short to accommodate a meeting about...well in general, about behavior or rules or previously made decisions that might threaten the community. This year, my School Refusing son is chairman of the Fairness Committee; he's the one people turn to when they feel slighted and in need of community support. The curing of Jason's "School Refusal" has not been immediate. John Potter has what Hemingway said all writers should have: a "built-in crap detector." The school is a loving, people-oriented place to be, but it's not all marshmallows: I have been really impressed by John's acute perception of what makes Jason tick...and not tick. In a conference earlier this year, John told Jason that while, yeah, his grades had improved, as had his behavior, John felt that Jason had not yet "claimed ownership." Wow! I know about ownership...don't I? Isn't that the magic component that turns "students" into "real writers?" Haven't we been talking for years about ways to encourage ownership?! And here's this...this headmaster...this *administrator*, making ownership a prerequisite for graduation!

The conference went on...and on...and on: pointing out to Jason times he had and had not claimed ownership, giving him guidance, time and encouragement to begin to discover his own internal, though latent, ownership sense.

I thought of Sean, my other son at the earlier school. How I knew he had burst into his own sense of self when he spoke during a school meeting to which parents had been invited: he spoke, this young rebel, of his discovery that he would only get from school what "I'm willing to put into it—and I'm putting in a lot!"—And the cliché rang with new truth. I'm not sure what delighted me more—his passion or his transformation. I should have recognized then that John Potter is, like Project People, an ownership freak....

Jason, now in his senior year, will have to claim ownership for himself and for his education before he will be deemed ready to graduate. Credits have to accrue, of course, but his final dragon remains to be slain: he must, as must all graduation candidates at the New School, write a paper in which he explores and defends his own reasons why he feels ready to move beyond high school—a reflection of his feelings of whatever ownership he has claimed for his life.

Later, that same Saturday night, Jason called back. He and a few friends had indeed swooped up the lonely teacher, bought some pizza and rented some movies. I asked him where they were going to do all this pizza eating and movie watching and teacher sitting. "At the school, dad. School's the most comfortable place."

Sure it is. Once you own it.

Kohl Open School:
From *The Stockton (CA) Record*

KOHL OPEN SCHOOL IN FOREFRONT
OF EDUCATION REVOLUTION
by Dana Nichols

The six soft-spoken teachers at Kohl Open School may be prophets in their own land. For 19 years, Kohl has been an oasis of learning without the bells, drills and regimentation of traditional schools. Classrooms mix students of different ages, and the school's 180 children choose when and where to work on their assignments.

In the last three years, the teaching methods used by Kohl suddenly have come into vogue. Schools across America are scrambling to copy the cozy, homelike atmosphere of the six classrooms at 6324 Alturas Ave. in Stockton. As a result, Kohl phones have been ringing with invitations to speak at conferences and requests from educators eager to visit the campus. In the next month, for example, Kohl Head Teacher Bud West and other faculty will make presentations at California Department of Education conferences on elementary school reform and mentor teachers.

In fact, Kohl has been getting questions and invitations from everywhere in California except Stockton itself. Other than a few teachers who have recently visited from Hazelton and El Dorado schools, Manteca is the closest community to show any formal interest in Kohl's successes.

"It's not uncommon for innovative schools to receive less attention at home than elsewhere," said Herbert Kohl, the school's namesake and a nationally known education innovator. Kohl, who says he is embarrassed that the school was named after him, advised the faculty during the early years of the school's operation. He says that the lack of attention given to Kohl has deep roots.

"It is because Kohl exists despite the district, not because of it," Kohl said.

Education-reform advocates at other Stockton schools said they felt mildly embarrassed to admit they had not visited Kohl. "In the back of my mind, I have had that feeling I've got to get to Kohl School," said Ward Downs, a teacher deeply involved in re-structuring at El Dorado School. El Dorado, in fact, has adopted a system of families designed to break students and teachers into four small schools, each about the size of Kohl.

"I know it's there. I've never paid enough attention to it, but I will be going to visit," said Lou Womble, director of multilingual and compensatory education for Lincoln unified School District.

Officials at Kohl and other schools noted the school's small size and the fact that it is a magnet also make it more difficult for teachers in more traditional schools to see Kohl as a model. As a magnet, Kohl only serves students from families that choose to participate in the program. More fundamental, however, is that the school's methods have only recently been seen as within the mainstream of educational thought, said West.

"We've had a reputation of sort of left-wing oddballs that took a long time to get over," West said.

Students at Kohl see the contrast between what happens at their school and what happens in conventional classrooms.

"You work at your own pace," said Brandon Zulueta, 9.

Katie Frampton, 10, recently transferred to Kohl from Village Oaks School in Lincoln Unified School District. She said she believes it will be challenging for teachers in conventional schools to adopt innovations such as those used at Kohl.

"I think it would be hard for them to understand," Frampton said. But, she added, she thinks the original Kohl teachers also faced challenges. "I bet when they first started they weren't quite into it," Frampton said.

West confirmed Frampton's speculation. It took years, for example, to achieve the right balance between giving students freedom to move around and preventing them from wasting time, West said.

Teacher Janet Ratto, who transferred to Kohl three years ago from a conventional parochial school, said it turned her world upside down when she saw how much more children could learn in an open school.

"It caused me to reorganize my thinking about teaching completely," Ratto said. Kohl, the person, said he is proud to see that his namesake has prospered. And he said he hopes that others in Stockton will take advantage of Kohl teachers' experience. Not to do that would be wasteful," Kohl said.

Arthur Morgan School:

Jeff Goldman writes affectionately about his school, Arthur Morgan. Ernest Morgan, the school's co-founder and husband of its first director, Elizabeth, also writes about the school as community in an article on pages 454 - 460.

ARTHUR MORGAN SCHOOL
AS AN EDUCATIONAL MODEL
by Jeff Goldman

What is it that makes the Arthur Morgan School work? How do we meet the specific needs of today's kids? The most recent debate about the state of education in this country has led me to wonder what role a successful alternative school like AMS has in the process of educational reform, especially at the middle education level.

Initially, the fact that AMS is a staff-run school led me to believe that our educational approach would be modified each year according to the consensus of the staff. In fact, I have been struck over time, not by what has changed, but by how much has stayed the same. Ultimately, I trace the consistency of the school's philosophy to the very fact that what we do is dependent on a group process, rather than on fixed dogma. It is the involvement of the students and staff at AMS with our surroundings and with each other that is the defining feature of the school. I have come to believe that it is this sense of involvement—for both teachers and students—that makes Arthur Morgan School work. As I have been able to define the reasons behind our success, I have begun to see how AMS might be used as an educational model elsewhere.

Now, more than ever, we need schools which allow students to be involved with the world around them in real ways. The lives of most children today, both at home and in school, provide few opportunities for them to do meaningful work. Kids are for the most part, adjunct members of society: at best, unnecessary, at worst, a burden. Television, video games and other forms of electronic entertainment dominate the lives of many children; they are growing up passive, unconnected and uninvolved. While the society values self-confidence, creativity and responsibility, there is little in the experience of most children to help them foster these qualities.

In contrast to the structure of most schools, AMS is set up in a way which facilitates student involvement in all aspects of the school's functioning. The physical work that students do at AMS is perhaps the most significant part of the education here. Through our work program they are both learning specific skills—how to cook, clean, maintain vehicles, split wood, etc.— and they are having an opportunity to do work which matters to themselves and others. The work we do is not arbitrary: the wood we cut keeps us warm in the winter, and the roofs we repair keep us dry. In addition to our own work projects and chores, we try to frequently incorporate community service work into our program so that students find value not only in the work from which they personally benefit, but also from that which helps others. Experiences such as serving food in soup kitchens, picking up trash, and planting trees, give us a feeling of connection to the larger community which, like all of our work experience, translates into a sense of belonging and self-esteem.

Academic classes at Arthur Morgan School also afford an opportunity for students to be actively involved in the learning process. Whereas the instruction in a traditional classroom is controlled and directed by the teacher—often in conjunction with a text and a chalkboard—our hands-on academics allow students to see how the material they are learning relates to the world around them. Thus, in Science class, the steaming of a bathroom mirror provides an opportunity to explore the physics of condensation. Likewise, students in English and Social Studies classes learn how to write because they are encouraged to communicate ideas that are important to them. Math classes seize every opportunity to apply math in the real world: from figuring angles and measurements for a construction project to keeping track of the finances on a group trip. In addition, our hikes and three-week field trips remind us all that education does not have to stop at the school's boundaries. Too many schools treat learning as the transfer of information from the teacher to the student, a process which does not involve the students or value their experiences or interests. At Arthur Morgan School, we try to give students access to their own learning so that they can come to see education as a reaffirmation of who they are and how they fit in—not as one more thing imposed on them by adults.

Our attempt to keep everyone here connected to the basic processes of the school extends to our decision-making process. The non-hierarchical nature of our faculty means that teachers are empowered to create curricula and implement programs, and empowered teachers tend to create an atmosphere of empowerment for students. Our All School Meeting gives students a direct say in the running of the school: they plan activities, deal with interpersonal problems and give feedback on interviews. While there are a few standing rules at AMS, each year students help set guidelines in response to specific problems. This process is not without its difficulties—most of us are more familiar with social systems which use chains of power—and it takes time to get used to a cooperative system. For one thing, it requires us all to take responsibility for one another's actions and see how those actions affect the entire community, and this is difficult for people who are used to living lives in which they are isolated and responsible only for themselves. However, by taking part in group decision-making and problem-solving, every person has access to a community which includes them and values their contribution.

Elizabeth Morgan recognized that the Arthur Morgan School program would be specifically suited to the needs of young adolescents. The outcome of such an environment is that students not only show marked changes when they are here, but, as I have gathered from numerous AMS graduates, tend to continue to be active, self-motivated people after they leave. Children who take part in an educational process which values them come to value themselves. As their self-esteem develops, so does their creativity, which, by nature, requires a willingness to take risks. And children who have been given the opportunity to be a part of a community and develop solutions to problems will apply these skills to conflicts throughout their lives.

While teenagers are particularly needy of a feeling of "place" in a society which seems to have no use for them, the need to feel necessary and involved transcends age boundaries. All of us need to be given a chance to see that we matter, that we have something to contribute. I can attest to the fact that AMS works the same magic on staff as it does students. The non-hierarchical nature of the staff allows teachers here to experiment, learn and grow in the same ways as students. The result is an environment which models education as a life-long process.

The success of Arthur Morgan School is related to our small size and rural environment but there is much in our experience that would translate to any school. Today's educational system, modeled on the factories of the late nineteenth century, is failing to provide for the needs of students and teachers. The society must come to think of schools and education in a new way. Through physical work, hands-on academics, and shared decision-making, both students and teachers must be allowed to feel connected to the basic processes of their school and their world. The model provided by the Arthur Morgan School has been tested for thirty years and deserves attention.

Arthur Morgan School's address is 1901 Hannah Branch Rd., Burnsville, NC 28714 (704) 675-4262

CHILDREN'S VILLAGE: THE EVOLUTION OF AN ALTERNATIVE SCHOOL
by Kuniko Kato, Principal

When I was younger I spent a year in Norway studying about children's education. I was deeply impressed by the concern for the needs of weak persons in Norwegian society and the practical provisions made by the society for meeting those needs. Each person in the society was considered to be valuable and of great worth in Norway. I found a society in which the government believed in its citizens and was truly concerned about them.

After returning to Japan, I worked for a few years in a kindergarten and nursery school and began to learn more about the government of my own society and as I became more aware of the nature of my government, I was amazed by its contrast with the government and society of Norway. Here I found a government which did not believe in or trust its citizens. Here I found a society which pushes 30 or more children in a class with an exhausted, overworked teacher, often a young teacher who has had no experience in work with children at all. It is a society which thinks children will go wrong unless adults train them by cramming them with facts which adults think are important. It is a society which thinks that children must be kept apart from society in walled prisons and subjected to rigid training in right rules and behavior in order for them to become human beings.

As I worked with children every day, I came more and more to a conviction that this approach to children's education is wrong. I discovered that children have a deep natural desire to learn, and they will work hard and long if they are permitted to learn what they want to learn in their own way and at their own pace but in Japan this natural desire of children to learn is stifled and twisted by our formal educational system

These concerns and doubts led me to form a group with a few equally concerned mothers and teachers to discuss such issues as the independence of women and children in Japan, the causes of the increase in the number of "school refusers," and other educational concerns. We knew that as women we had not been educated to be persons who believe in our own abilities, persons able to make important life decisions by ourselves. We began to reconsider our educational system and our society. We became aware of the work of A.S. Neill, alternative education associations such as the National Coalition of Alternative Community Schools (NCACS) in the United States and the existence of such a country as Denmark where people have the option of starting and controlling their own school with 85% financial support from public school funds, if they can get a given number of families to join together in the undertaking.

Our study and exploration led us to dream of starting a school of our own. This led to our being offered a house in a forest at the edge of our city, and our dream of starting our own school turned into an actuality. Many people helped us with funds, and we started with ten children. We chose the name "Nonami Kodomo-no Mura" (children's village) for our school. However, we could not get the sanction of the Ministry of Education because schools such as ours are not recognized as schools by the ministry. We believed that children should have the opportunity to begin learning in a more free environment as early as possible. Thus, we initially enrolled children from preschool age through the elementary grades. We found, however that many parents who were eager to enroll their children in our kind of school for their children's early years, became anxious later and decided to take their children out of our school and send them to public school, ignoring the children's desires and hopes. So, we seldom admit younger children now, accepting only older (elementary age) children whose parents make the decision to send their child to "Nonami Kodomo-no Mura" rather than to a public school. Unfortunately, such people are few. This year we have only eight children, two full- time staff members, and several volunteer staff members.

Two of the children are six years old, two are seven, one is eight, one ten, and two are eleven. The children are divided into three groups, a younger group, a middle group, and an older group. The younger children spend their school day playing with the natural things in their environment, doing things with water, for example, making dams, playing restaurant (teachers and staff are the customers, supplying things they need). Individual differences among the older children lead to their working separately. Much of the time a child who wishes to learn about some particular topic or issue is helped to develop a term learning plan and then is assisted in carrying out their plan. Most children carry their learning plans through to a satisfactory conclusion, although the plans are flexible and can be changed, expanded, or dropped. We do not give tests or report cards, but we have found that the children become motivated by their intellectual interests and curiosity.

The three groups meet separately each morning to discuss their activities for the day. Periodically, usually once each week, there is a general meeting of all students and staff. During the general meeting, we discuss such matters as daily needs of the school, cleaning, cooking, lunch arrangements, plans for all-school field trips, personal problems, activities which one student wants to do with other students or staff, etc. In the afternoon volunteer staff come to instruct the children in various arts, crafts, and skills such as origami (paper-folding), handicrafts, English, swimming, sports, dance, etc. Children can choose one craft or skill or they can engage in other activities of their own choosing.

Our "Nonami Kodomo-no Mura" support group plays a vital role in the life of the school. This group, which includes parents, volunteer staff, and full-time teachers and principal, meets once a month to discuss matters concerning the school, hear reports from committees and research teams, plan fund-raising projects, etc.

Nonami Kodomo-no Mura is now in its 7th year. We have been able to succeed in accomplishing our dream of making a school which respects and trusts children and in which children are free to learn and grow in harmony with their nature. As the principal, I am deeply grateful for the devotion and dedication of our staff and supporters which has made this possible and for the help, encouragement, and guidance provided by many alternative school people in the United States and other countries.

Kuniko Kato, Principal, Nonami Kodomo-no Mura, 28-341 Nonami Aioi, Tenpaku-cho, Tenpaku-ku, Nagoya-shi, Japan 468

CHILD REARING AND LEARNING
FOR 'THE REAL WORLD'
by Joel Weber

Joel Weber has headed up Contra Costa Alternative School in Orinda, CA as director for more than two decades now! Once each year, Joel delivers a sermon at the church where his school is located. The following was his yearly sermon, given at Orinda Community Church, October 14, 1992.

The inspiration for this sermon came last June in an end-of-year family conference at the school. Every family has a closing conference like this, and some themes come through loud and clear over and over.

The father was expressing deep concern over his son's lack of achievement in math and his weak performance in homework throughout his schedule. Dad felt that doing homework was an opportunity to learn self-discipline, and that this sort of self-discipline was necessary if you were to survive and thrive in "the real world." Another thing he was thinking but didn't say, though many others have said it before him, is this: "You've got to start learning how to do things that you don't want to do," again for success in the real world.

These issues really get me going and could be a grand starting point for a global critique of western civilization. Fortunately for all of us, I will not attempt this critique right here right now. But I would focus this morning on one small and three enormous questions, which are these:

1. How important is homework for school or for life?
2. What is self-discipline? How does self-discipline relate to learning to do things you don't want to do?
3. What is "the real world?" Isn't CCAS a part of it?
4. Overarching all of these other questions, what do we want most for our children? How do these goals fit with what goes on in schools and in families?

The first one is easy for me as an individual and as an educator. Homework is not that important as it's presently understood. Most homework is still rote and as such is pretty useless. Homework that conceptually connects home with school or involves parents—things like field trip follow-up or inventing an artistic representation for the number 100 for little kids, or even analyses of newspaper articles and TV shows for big kids—make a lot more sense.

But how many of you as adults do homework in the evenings and on weekends? I don't. This is part of what keeps me sane and energetic both for my family and for my work. I suspect that most adults do the bulk of their work during the day, or if they don't, their school homework wasn't what trained them to work nights and weekends. Let me take this even further. In the circles of adults that I know, some folks have homework for work—especially teachers—and I think this homework is a health hazard, bad for them, and bad for their families. It keeps them from, in the words of Henry David Thoreau, "approaching work with leisure," and also from approaching their families with leisure.

Now I don't want to prescribe this "no homework" philosophy as an unbendable universal truth, but if I were in charge, I can tell you there wouldn't be very much homework for anybody except college people with class schedules of less than 40 hours.

How does this relate to self-discipline? What is self-discipline? How will kids learn it if they don't do homework? What does self-discipline have to do with learning to do things you don't want to do? Small children have enormous self-discipline. Just watch them play. Watch them learn to speak. Watch them learn to walk. Educator John Holt was fond of pointing out that these tasks that children learn, with their families' help, are far more complex and demanding than anything most of us learn later. And we learn them without school! The job of the schools then is to keep the self-discipline and enthusiasm flowing rather than constricting or stopping them. It enrages me that year after year, when kids fall behind in reading in the first grade, they get labeled and mistaught. Their fire, their self-discipline, gets quenched, and they sometimes spend years being behind and getting more behind. This to me points to one real context of self-discipline—it's there; we've got it; schools and adults must not take it from us; rather they must nurture it.

Well, there's my unorthodox definition of self-discipline, and I'm saying you don't learn it; it's natural but schools and adults can help you to unlearn it. But what does this have to do with learning to do the things you don't want to do? Surely as we grow up our interests narrow. Or what if there's nothing or very little that you're interested in or that you want to do?

Quite often there are things you don't want to do embedded in the things you do want to do. Paul may want to be a great guitarist and make fine music, yet he may not want to do all the practice necessary to get there. If he's to become a great guitarist, though, he breaks the job down and starts practicing what he can. Somewhere along the line, there's a shift. He discovers that he loves the practice. He gets oriented to process rather than just to outcome. He ends up becoming a great guitarist even though he didn't love the practice at the beginning. Or maybe he doesn't become a great guitarist, but he plays well and loves to play. Isn't that okay? Isn't that, in fact, great, and one of the kinds of things that makes life worth living?

This to me gets almost Zen, this loving of the process, as long as there's time for the process; as long as the process isn't rushed. For myself I really love cooking and even like cleaning the kitchen as long as there's enough time to do it. Conversely, no matter how neat the next thing I have to do, if it's crushed together with a million other things in such a way that I don't really have time to do any of them with leisure or to breathe while I'm doing them, then I don't really enjoy any of them. They become chores.

My son Jonah recently quit piano after about six months. I'm very proud of him for the way he made this decision. He can't do it the good way he wants to while he's being a junior high student and playing soccer on a traveling team. He's one of the only kids I know who has a sense of when he's overloaded, so backs off something. On the other hand, I really hope he picks it up again. I get tremendous pleasure from playing accordion and guitar, and I hope he gets back to piano because I think skill and time there will bring him lifelong pleasure. Once again homework rears its ugly head here. If I were in charge, I would decrease his homework load by whatever it took to create mental space and time for piano. I believe that in the long term, piano will contribute much more to his health and happiness than having done more rather than less homework.

I have dealt so far with how you learn to do things you don't want to do. What if there's nothing, or almost nothing, that you want to do? A CCAS father once told a story of his kid learning to tie his shoes. Dad worked hard with him on this, finishing with, "And now you can tie your own shoes!" expecting Gavin to be delighted. Gavin thought for a minute and said, "You mean from now on I'll always have to tie them myself?" A surprising reaction to me, and to his dad. I would expect that most kids would be overjoyed with the independence and the new skill. Once again this points up the tremendous variety in human beings and human response.

But what if somebody really doesn't want to do stuff, or very much stuff? Look to the schools and look to the family. The child has been wounded and probably doesn't have the self-respect to feel like the kind of person who can do things or who even wants to do things. The damage must be healed or repaired. This is actually a good part of the day-to-day work we do at CCAS—in the classrooms, in conversation, in meetings, in tutoring, in counseling. If a person doesn't have a positive self-image, then someone or something or things took it from them. Others must help them get it back.

But here comes another persistent CCAS parent argument—"It's all well and good," they say, "to work on self-image and music and art and this touchy-feely stuff, but when Gwendolyn gets out in the real world, she's going to need some basic skills, she's going to need to fit in, and she's going to need, at work, to do lots of things she flat out doesn't want to do and never will want to do. What about that?

Let's dispose of the basic skills issue first. With wounded kids, they need to heal before they learn all those basic skills, or they need to learn them in a therapeutic healing setting. If they're not wounded, or if they are recovering from their wounds, they'll learn these basic skills just fine when they're ready, in preschool, or elementary, or high school, or in college, or when they're needed.

What are these basic skills anyway? People will automatically think of reading and writing, but in my experience, speaking and especially listening are far more important in most of our adult lives than reading and writing. Think about this in your own day-to-day work and life and see if it doesn't fit. It's certainly true for top executives and many business people.

What about this business of needing to fit in? I submit that it is a sort of hazing like fraternity or sorority hazing. The whole text to me is, "I, your parent, had to submit and fit in, so you have to also." But the real world is not monolithic; the real world of work is not monolithic; just as kids are different, adults are different, and jobs are different. What am I saying about the real world here? I am saying that late twentieth century America is unbelievably varied. There are many places to fit in; there are many ways to fit in. People have choices. And now I really want to shock you, and me, and all CCAS parents. CCAS is part of the real world. It has corporeal existence. It has been around for

-42-

nearly twenty-five years. I'm a real person in the real world and I actually work at CCAS. So do Jeanie and Daniel and Renée. We even get paid. Our students are real people in the real world. So please, parents, give more thought to what you mean by the real world.

Finally, to that overarching question, what do we as parents and a society want most for our children? How do these goals fit with our parenting and our school system?

I cannot speak for you, but I'm pretty sure of what I want for my own kids. I want them to grow up to be happy, to know how to pursue happiness. I want them to know how to be in relationships. I want them, as my friend Jeanie puts it, to know how to use their community as a resource, as a network. I want them to know what their gifts are—we all have gifts—and to cultivate them. I want them to be aware of the world beyond them, politically and ecologically.

As they and I pursue these goals, I believe that their self-discipline will remain intact with their enthusiasm, and that they will do just fine in whatever niches of the so-called real world they find or put themselves. And what I want for my kids is exactly what I want for all the CCAS kids, past and present. I do not pretend that all kids are like mine, or that all school kids are like the ones at CCAS, but in terms of the school system at large, it could certainly use an enormous shot of this outlook of diversity and support. Kids are not clones and they're not robots. We must respect them in their individuality. They need homes, parents, and schools that recognize their variety and that speak to and bring out their passions, concerns, hopes, and dreams.

The Community School, Camden, Maine:

"WHO'S IN CHARGE AT THE C-SCHOOL?"
by Bill Halpin

This year we asked, "Who's in charge?" Black-and-white thinkers said, "the co-directors." Mythical thinkers said, "the consensus of the staff group." Classical thinkers asked for the organization chart. Colorful thinkers said, "the students, the time of day or term, the mood of the staff on duty, the chemical ingredients of the dinner menu, the daily personality of the administrative assistant" or even whether the Board had good pastry and coffee for their meeting, whether the tutors on their night liked what they were wearing. The paranoid thinkers among us stared and believed they were the only ones who didn't know the answer.

The question "Who's in charge?" is as testy as it is a genuine inquiry into the underlying philosophical dynamic that drives the School. The question led to making a list of the various "authorities" functioning at the School. The list was long. Staff were surprised. It ranged from one staff on duty alone to all staff together at Thursday meeting, from one co-director alone to two co-directors together, from a group of students on a wilderness camping trip with two staff to all the gathered at Group Rap voting on a community issue, from the Board in its overview to a few students in the music room with a good idea. The list led management thinkers to suggest a situational and eclectic authority. Anarchistic thinkers already suspected chaos and random whimsy determined what got done. Indigenous thinkers doubted whether any decision would last even a few weeks.

What is the authority of the C-School? Can it be named? What label affix to it so to own and tame it? The year went by, and the 20-year-old School could not settle on any word to capture what has worked well in the life of the School and those touched by it. Poetic thinkers try two suggestions:

1. It is nameless. Moses got no name but a vague response when he asked Divinity its name. The response Moses heard might be adapted to suffice the C-School's search: "You shall be there, as who you are, shall you be there." I suggest that the authority structure of the C-School is continually co-created and

demands everyone be present in all manifestations of their character. What this means concretely at the School for students and staff, Board and tutors, employers and families, friends and enemies is: Show up, present yourself as you are there and then, and co-create the reality of the School. If you are angry, be so there. If you are enthusiastic and optimistic, fine. If you are depressed and sad, be that there. If creative, yes. If disillusioned and disappointed, yes again. If mistrustful and wounded, please. If bossy or cranky, mellow or funky, organized or lost— welcome! These varied manifestations of who and how we are gives the School its authority.

2. It is fantastic. The Greek word πηανταζειν (phantazein) means "appearance, imagination, to present to the mind." The reality of the School is determined anew each term by whatever experience is brought and whatever intelligence is found there. It is never the same. It is not a system. It is individuals.

I suggest the School's reality is *delabelized authority.* I suggest the answer to "Who's in charge?" is "Who is there, really there!" It is a matter of *presence.* As such, all are invited to come as they are, to show their face.

ANNUAL REPORT FOR 1993
Report from Co-Director Dora Lievow

The Community School's twentieth anniversary year has come and gone. It seems a time for telling stories of where we've been and where we're going and thinking about what we do. It was a perfectly timed year for the publication of the first book about the School, a collection of interviews with former students. In her foreword, Deborah Meier enhanced my own understanding of our work. She answered a question I've been living with for many years asked of me and Emanuel by Jean Bamberger: What is the connection between the cognitive development fostered at the School and the psychosocial growth achieved by students? How does the kind of teaching and learning we do in classes contribute to their development in other areas?

We understand more readily how attentiveness to interpersonal issues frees up students academically and how the program's structure enhances students' ability to learn.

We know from Piaget that, developmentally, "thinking" occurs in actions long before it occurs in language. As Eleanor Duckworth explains, one of the essential aspects of pre-verbal cognition is the seeking of consistencies. "Human beings are born with a guiding intellectual rule that might be stated: 'All else being equal, things will turn out the same.'" Luckily, we inhabit a physical universe where this is generally the case, but the physical world is perhaps the only world we can count on in this way. Our interpersonal environment can be very different.

If consistency is an essential condition of thinking, then learning to think about things requires order in the most profound sense of the word. When a student improves her reading comprehension by three levels in fifteen tutoring sessions and when another student is unable to make any progress in classes for two months and then suddenly "gets it" the month after she finds a steady job, we smile at each other during staff meetings and say facetiously, "Boy, are we good!" What we mean is just the opposite. We know no teachers can attribute change of this magnitude to their own gifted teaching. It's the School as a structure— an orderly, comprehensible arrangement of people, process, and purpose—that gets the thinking going again.

Debbie Meier notes the feedback loop of this process: "What shines through (from the stories of formers) is that they have developed the habit of being unsentimentally reflective....They have a past to tell about and...their way of putting the pieces together gives them strength, endurance, and...two unshakable beliefs: the power of intelligent thought and the importance of being responsible."

It's exciting to see students master math and reading skills and engage in conversations about literature, history, and science. It's even more gratifying to imagine that the habit of reflective thought fostered in classes at the School can inform the lives of students long after their formal classwork is over.

How the School Works

The Community School is a residential School for 16- to 20-year-old high School dropouts. Eight students live at the School for six months during which time they must hold jobs in the community, pay room and board, and attend classes six evenings a week.

Established in August of 1973, the School is state approved and designed to teach students not only academic skills but skills that will help them to take care of themselves in a practical sense. Most importantly, students relearn ways of relating to adults and to each other that enhance both community life and individual potential. Those who complete the program successfully are awarded a high School diploma.

After a two-week trial period students are assigned a staff member called their "one-to-one." Students meet with their one-to-ones weekly to discuss personal and practical issues. This experience often forms a close and enduring connection between student and staff member.

Students work a minimum of 28 hours and pay $55 for room and board weekly. Although their jobs may be physically hard and the pay low, they learn the connection between earning money and the pride of supporting themselves and a job well done.

One-to-one tutoring in the School's informal setting often restores a positive attitude toward learning. Each student's academic history, learning style, and interests are considered. In addition to the mandated academic subjects, the School's curriculum covers many challenging areas of personal growth and learning. Students attend classes in parenting, substance abuse prevention, conflict resolution, sexuality, and self esteem and may choose electives in assertiveness, nonviolence, and relapse prevention.

Cooking, cleaning, and menu-planning are required courses. Students wake up with their own alarm clocks, budget their own money, launder their own clothes, and arrange their rooms. Once a month they go camping. Trips include climbing, canoeing, hiking, ropes courses, and participating in outdoor science and geography labs.

Students deal with interpersonal issues and rule violations at Thursday night Group Raps with the School consultant and staff. Consequences for rule infractions are suggested, usually by students, and everyone votes on the outcome. Group Rap is also a forum where students can discuss their feelings and air personal concerns.

REPORT FROM CO-DIRECTOR EMANUEL PARISER

Funding:

1993 was an extraordinary year for the School in terms of finances. As the State of Maine grappled with a billion dollar projected deficit, the School faced a season in which nearly a third of our parents were unemployed, School Districts had run out of funds for alternative education placements, and cascading interest rates resulted in less scholarship aid from our endowment funds. As more applicants joined the waiting list, less public support became available to them.

In the face of these hardships many people and organizations rose to the challenge—the many families of students who re-arranged a large part of their finances to support their children, the foundations which came through with emergency scholarship support and the members of the legislature who helped restore 2/3 of our funding from the Department of Corrections which was again threatened and cut for the third year in a row.

Without the ongoing grants and scholarship support from our individual annual donors ... the School would have plunged deeply into the red. Even with this support we had to delay acceptance of several total scholarship students by six months, in one case by a year!

Finally, as this year pulled to a close we received two special surprises—employees of a local company chose the School to be the recipient of their annual fund-raising donation and another company gave a generous gift towards refurbishing and renovating our home.

Getting the Word Out:

Our biggest news is the long-awaited publication of our book by the University Press of America, Lanham, MD. *Changing Lives: Voices from a School That Works* was written by Jane Day with photos by Maryanne Mott, foreword by Deborah Meier, and copyediting and layout by Marty King. Along with interviews of 40 graduates, the book presents a brief history and philosophy of the School which I wrote.

One of the most gratifying aspects of putting this work together has been the response by readers who submitted "blurbs" for the book:

Senator George Mitchell, "The common sense and the uncommon compassion of the Community School has improved hundreds of young lives and enriched the surrounding neighborhoods;"

Dr. Robert Coles, Harvard, "I was moved and most impressed by those life stories exactly what all of us need to learn from those we teach, who in turn teach us;"

Herb Kohl, "I urge educators and parents to read this unique and intimate book which provides a multidimensional look at a successful School and the students who benefited from its work;"

Dr. Julius B. Richmond, former Surgeon General, "The stories of these young people have much to teach us concerning resilience and hope. And the program of the Community School suggests options which the nation should be applying on a much wider scale;"

Lisbeth B. Schorr, Harvard; "These stories ... provide encouragement to those who are engaged in the daily struggle of supporting high-risk youth and challenge those who maintain that no intervention from outside the family can help;" and

William Ayers, University of Illinois, "The experiences of these students...demonstrate again and again that what young people want and need is relatively simple...a community to belong to, something worthwhile to think about and to do, responsibility and acceptance, someone to love them, and others to care about."

See also an article by Emanuel Pariser on "Intimacy, Connectedness and Education," on pages 434 - 448.

The article below was reprinted from the FEAA (Folk Education Association of America) Journal Option, vol. 17, No. 2, Fall, 1993. The issue is titled, "Pioneers and Heroes: Part II from the Americas.

MYLES HORTON (1905-90) OF HIGHLANDER
Adult Educator and Southern Activist
by Franklin Parker and Betty J. Parker

Introduction

Who was Myles Horton and why is he worth our time? As a leader of social change in the South, Horton was significant because:

—his Highlander Folk School in East Tennessee helped unionize southern textile workers and coal miners in the 1930s and '40s; and helped advance civil rights in the '50s and '60s;

—early black leaders (Martin Luther King, Jr., Rosa Parks, Andrew Young, and others) attended Highlander workshops before the Montgomery, AL bus boycott, lunch-counter sit-ins, student freedom rides and school integration;

—Highlander first popularized "We Shall Overcome," the civil rights song;

—Highlander-initiated Citizenship Schools helped some 100,000 blacks become literate and thus qualified to register to vote.

To critics he was a rabble-rousing "red," a "communist," a threat to American institutions and traditional values. Huge billboard photos in the South in 1965 were captioned, "Martin Luther King at a Communist Training School" (Highlander).

He challenged entrenched power and privilege (like India's Gandhi), helped workers form unions and (like labor organizer Saul Alinsky, 1909-72), helped empower dispossessed people (like Brazilian adult educator Paulo Freire), and helped people realize and achieve their legal rights (like consumer advocate Ralph Nader) .

But what in Horton's background and upbringing foretold what he was to become?

Youth

He was born in Savannah, TN July 9, 1905, eldest of four children. His parents, Perry and Elsie Falls Horton, were Tennesseans, Scotch Irish, and poor, although a paternal forebear had received the first land grant (c. 1772) in northeast Tennessee. His parents passed on to Myles their Cumberland Presbyterian Church's Calvinistic values, independent spirit, belief in helping others less fortunate regardless of race, and a respect for education (both parents, with grade school education, having been schoolteachers).

The Hortons moved from Savannah to Humboldt (near Memphis), where Myles went to high school, and worked summers. Becoming skeptical about religion, he questioned his mother, who advised, "just love people." He majored in English literature at Cumberland University, Lebanon, TN, 1924-28, refused to be hazed himself and organized other students to resist hazing. Working in a Humboldt box factory in the summer of 1925 and reading about the Dayton, TN trial on teaching evolution, he supported John T. Scopes to the shock of fellow workers. President of his campus YMCA in his junior year, 1927, he attended a southern YMCA conference on Nashville's Vanderbilt campus and had his first contact with foreign and black students. He resented not being able to take a Chinese girl to a restaurant or enter a public library with a black acquaintance. Then Cumberland University trustee John Emmett Edgerton, a woolen manufacturer and president of the Southern States Industrial Council, lectured the student body against labor unions. Upset, Horton, on impulse, went to the Edgerton textile mill in Lebanon, was dismayed at the unfair practices he saw, and urged the workers to organize. University officials threatened to expel him if he visited the mill again.

Ozone, TN: Summer 1927

In summer vacations, organizing vacation Bible schools for the Presbyterian Church, Horton in the summer of 1927 got his assistants to teach the young people at a small Ozone, East Tennessee church while he invited their parents to discuss their problems. They asked about farming, how to get a textile mill job, how to test wells for typhoid, and other problems. Myles said he'd get experts who knew the answers: a county agent, a health officer, and others. He realized for the first time that he could lead a discussion without knowing all the answers. He sharpened their questions, got them to talk about their own experiences, and found that they already had many answers. Ozone people liked these discussions, attendance increased, and a woman who liked what he was doing said that she would be willing to turn over her home to him for such programs.

Horton, grateful, said he would think about it and would return when he had something to offer. "O" for Ozone in his later notes stood for the kind of school he wanted to start. The Ozone experience, he later said, was the genesis of Highlander.

Union Theological Seminary: 1929-30

Crisscrossing the state as Tennessee YMCA organizer, Myles found a sympathetic listener in Congregational minister Abram Nightingale, with whom he sometimes boarded. Nightingale encouraged Myles's intent to establish a school, saying: "You need more learning, more experiences, more contact with freethinkers away from the South". He encouraged Myles to attend Union Theological Seminary, New York City, and shared Union Seminary ethics professor Harry F. Ward's (1873-1966) book, On Economic Morality and the Ethic of Jesus. Ward held that extremes of wealth and poverty were the Achilles' heel of U.S. free enterprise, that the profit motive hindered Christian brotherhood and equality in "a just and fraternal world."

As the stock market crashed, businesses failed, and the jobless formed bread lines, Myles at Union met probably the most socially activist academics in the U.S. Seeking a philosophy to guide the school he envisioned, he took theology courses, read widely at Columbia University Library near Union, worked in a Hell's Kitchen ghetto boys' club, visited Greenwich House and Henry Street Settlement House, and helped organize an International Ladies' Garment Workers' Union strike. He went to observe a Marion, NC textile strike; visited Brookwood Labor College, Katonah, NY, which trained labor union leaders (Ruskin College, Oxford, England); observed remnants of the utopian Oneida Colony in upstate NY, and the cooperative communities at Rugby and Ruskin, TN and at New Harmony, IN. He sadly noted that these had turned inward and away from active involvement in society. His envisioned school would be loosely structured and adaptable to involve, serve, and help poor people in labor and racial strife, help them find ways to gain dignity, freedom, and justice.

Unconcerned with credits, grades, or a divinity degree, he read the Fabian socialists, John Dewey, George S. Counts, and others. Observing a New York City May Day parade while unwittingly wearing a red sweater, he was rudely awakened to reality when a mounted policeman clouted him for being a "goddamn Red."

Most influential was liberal theology professor Reinhold Niebuhr (1892-1971), a passionate advocate of the social gospel. Niebuhr had come to Union the previous year, 1928, from a small Detroit church. His Christian ethics seminar, which Horton attended, was the basis of his 1932 book, *Moral Man and Immoral Society*. Niebuhr questioned the generally accepted notion of inevitable progress, was sad that the poor were oppressed and exploited by the economic and political system, and headed the Fellowship of Socialist Christians, which wanted progressive churches to ally with labor to achieve fundamental reform. With socialist Norman Thomas, Niebuhr cofounded a journal, The World Tomorrow, dedicated to "a social order based on the religion of Jesus." Niebuhr saw the reformer's problem as how to achieve equality and justice peacefully; that is, how to nonviolently pit the power of the oppressed against the power of oppressors. Niebuhr's thesis fitted the aim of Horton's southern adult education school—to help downtrodden people find ways to solve their own problems. To Horton, Niebuhr was sympathetic and encouraging.

University of Chicago, 1930-31

Interested now more in sociology than in theology, Horton went to the University of Chicago. He was impressed by sociology professor Robert E. Park's (1864-1944) theory that antagonistic individuals unite when they see they can attain common goals by working together. Through Park, Horton saw that conflict is inevitable; the thing to do is to use conflict creatively to move people away from the status quo and toward a better economic, political, social and moral position. Horton was also influenced by Lester F. Ward's *Dynamic Sociology,* which argued that education requires action and that social progress is possible only through dynamic action. He talked with and was encouraged by Jane Addams of Hull House. In the spring of 1931 he met two immigrant Danish Lutheran ministers who, when they heard him describe his school ideas, said that it sounded like the Danish folk school and urged him to visit Denmark.

Reading about Danish folk school history and accomplishments, Horton compiled a pertinent bibliography for the university library. He also read *The Southern Highlander in His Homeland* by John Charles Campbell (1867-1919), written with Mrs. Campbell who in 1925 had established the John C. Campbell Folk School near Brasstown, NC, along Danish folk high school lines. Horton earned enough money for travel to

Denmark by returning to New York City as researcher for a professor he had met at the University of Chicago.

Denmark Folk Schools, 1931-32

Visiting Danish folk high schools, Horton appreciated 19th century founder, Bishop N.S.F. Grundtvig's (1783-1872) "Living Word" sermons, and admired disciple Kristen Kold's folk schools, which had awakened oppressed peasants' patriotism and civic responsibility, helped restore Denmark's economic prosperity, and led to cooperatives and a broader based democracy. He liked the newer folk high schools for industrial workers and admired their informality, close student-teacher interaction, highly motivated learning, and clear objectives.

Christmas night, 1931, Copenhagen

Unable to sleep on Christmas night, 1931, Horton wrote about his future school: it should be located in the South; have white and black students and teachers working together, give no credits nor exams; face problems, propose solutions and try out those solutions in conflict situations in the students' home communities.

Highlander at Monteagle: November 1,1932

Horton returned to New York in May 1932, outlined his school plan to Reinhold Niebuhr, who wrote a finance appeal letter for a school in the South to train "an educated radical labor leadership." At Niebuhr's suggestion, Horton got his school's first $100 contribution from International YMCA Secretary Sherwood Eddy (1871-1963) and had promise of two Niebuhr graduate students as teachers: one who stayed less than a year, and James A. Dombroski (1897?-1983), son of a Tampa, FL jeweler, who stayed nearly a decade.

Searching for a school site, Horton contacted Will W. Alexander (1884-1956?) of the Commission on Interracial Cooperation, who mentioned Don West, who also wanted to establish a southern Appalachian folk school. West (1906-), a rural north Georgian and Lincoln University (Harrogate, TN) graduate, was, like Horton, campus YMCA president, Bible school organizer in mountain communities, and a Danish folk high school enthusiast. Horton learned that this Vanderbilt Divinity School graduate and Congregational church pastor near Crossville, TN was attending the YMCA's Blue Ridge Assembly, Black Mountain, NC. Horton hitchhiked to North Carolina, met and shared common interests with West and, by one account, learned through the Rev. Abram Nightingale that retired college president Lilian Johnson (1864-1968) wanted her Monteagle, TN farm used for community uplift.

This daughter of a wealthy banking and mercantile family had a Cornell University doctorate in history, had been president of Western State College, Oxford, OH, was a leading southern suffragist and a member of the Women's Christian Temperance Union. She had gone to Italy to study cooperatives and returned to spread the idea in the South, working from her house and farm in Summerfield, near Monteagle, Grundy County, TN. Horton and West, with meager financial backing and a small staff, got Lilian Johnson to lease her property for a year and, subject to her satisfaction, perhaps longer. Highlander Folk School, as it was named, opened November 1, 1932. Only eight students enrolled in its first residence term, November 1932-April 1933, a small beginning. But with the Wilder, TN coal mine strike 1932-33, 100 miles north of Monteagle, Horton and Highlander became involved for the first time in mineworker-union conflict.

Wilder, TN Mine Strike, 1932-33

The Wilder strike began in the summer of 1932. Mine owners refused to renew a United Mine Workers (UMW) contract unless union members took a 20 % wage cut. Long critical of mine conditions and company store prices (they were paid in scrip redeemable only in company stores), union miners struck, closing the mines to mid-October 1932, when non-union scabs and some union members resumed work under armed guards. Violence flared. The state governor sent in some 200 national guardsmen, whose inexperience, drinking, and partiality to scabs and mine owners hardly kept the peace.

Myles Horton went to Wilder in November 1932, took notes on the strike, ate a meager Thanksgiving dinner with UMW local president Barney Graham and, waiting for a bus the next morning, was arrested, jailed, charged with "coming here and getting information and going back and teaching it." He was released next morning.

To Horton the strike was a conflict situation from which Highlander students and the miners could learn. He and Highlander students distributed emergency food and clothing. Some strikers thought him a "Red." Others appreciated his and Highlander's help and good intentions. Violence continued.

Horton heard of and told state officials of a plot to kill union president Barney Graham. Horton's warning was ignored. Graham was shot to death April 30, 1933. Their leader dead, strikers returned to work without a contract and under near starvation conditions. Said Horton, "If I hadn't already been a radical, [Graham's murder] would have made me a radical right then." The strike helped shape Highlander's labor education program, which thereafter examined the roles played in labor conflict by newspapers, churches, the power structure, and other community factors. Wilder also confirmed for Horton what he already knew: the power structure's determination in the 1930's and 40's (omitting the war years) to cripple labor unions. He later saw in the 1950's and 60's the power structure mobilize to stem the tide of racial integration.

Zilphia Mae Johnson (Mrs. Myles Horton): 1935

She was from Paris, Arkansas, attending a two-month Highlander winter session. This privileged daughter of an Arkansas coal mine operator and College of the Ozarks graduate was a talented, classically trained musician. Influenced by radical Presbyterian minister Claude Williams, she wanted to use her musical and dramatic talents to advance labor unions. In this, she clashed with and parted from her father. A friend got her to Highlander to learn about the labor movement. She and Myles fell in love and married March 6, 1935. She then studied about workers' theater at the New Theater School, New York City. At Highlander, she taught drama, play writing, public speaking, wrote and directed plays based on labor strikes, and led square dancing and singing.

Zilphia Horton had a gift for using music, drama and dance to advance labor union concerns and civil rights. She united people, mellowed differences, and lifted spirits. By collecting songs and encouraging Highlander students to collect and sing them, she involved communities around Highlander, helping heal wounds, lessen suspicion, and foster cultural pride. Through Zilphia, Highlander's cultural programs gained national and even international renown when the BBC presented a cultural program from Highlander in March 1937.

She also helped give "We Shall Overcome" national and international renown. Originally an Afro-American folk song, "We Will Overcome" became a Baptist hymn and was sung by union members to maintain picket line morale at a Charleston, SC CIP Food and Tobacco Workers strike. Two women members from that union sang it at Highlander in 1946. Zilphia recognized its emotional appeal, slowed the tempo, added verses and sang it at meetings. Pete Seeger (1919-) learned it from Zilphia in 1947, altered its title to "We Shall Overcome," added verses and sang it at 1950s folk song concerts around the country. Folk singer Guy Carawan (1927-), who with his wife Candie worked at Highlander, further refined it, and added the verse, "We Shall Not Be Moved," during a police raid on Highlander, the night of July 31, 1959. It was sung at Highlander workshops, at civil rights gatherings from the 1960s and became the freedom song heard round the world.

Zilphia and Myles Horton were married 21 years, had a son and daughter, when she tragically died. Reaching for a glass she thought held water, she drank some carbon tetrachloride, realized her error, induced vomiting and phoned her physician, who assured her that she had remedied the accident. But the poison aggravated a kidney condition discovered at Vanderbilt Hospital, Nashville, where she died of uremic poisoning, April 11, 1956.

Citizenship Schools for Voter Registration: 1957-61

Two South Carolina blacks attended Highlander's August 1954 workshop on "World Problems, the United Nations, and You," comparing discrimination in the South with discrimination elsewhere. Esau Jenkins (died 1972), a businessman and community leader from Johns Island, SC, accompanying Septima Poinsette Clark (18981987), a Charleston, SC teacher, was more interested in adult black literacy than in the United Nations. Esau Jenkins wanted his neighbors to learn to read and write and so qualify to register to vote. Highlander's staff hesitated, then busy training black leaders for the school desegregation movement. Jenkins and Clark convinced Horton that Johns Island blacks needed adult literacy classes. These began on Johns Island, spread to other Sea Islands, and then through the South. It was Highlander's most successful training program and significantly increased black voter registration, black political awareness and involvement, and helped elect black mayors, sheriffs and other officials in the 1970s and '80s.

Johns Island, six miles south of Charleston, SC, with a 1954 population of 4,000, is the largest of the Sea Island chain along the South Carolina and Georgia coast. Inhabitants, 67% black (other islands had higher black proportions), lived just above subsistence. Some owned farms and small businesses.

Most worked on large truck farms or in Charleston as servants or as factory and shipyard hands. Gullah was their home language, a dialect from their African slave ancestors. Until the WPA built bridges in the 1930s, they went by boat to Charleston. Jenkins, a Johns Island leader, had supplemented his fourth grade education with night classes. Converting his small cotton farm to truck farming, he learned enough Greek to sell produce to Charleston Greek vegetable merchants. He was PTA president, church school superintendent, assistant pastor in his church, and also ran a small bus line to the mainland. During the 45-minute drive, he distributed, explained and discussed the South Carolina state constitution and voting laws, thus encouraging passengers to learn to read and write to pass voter registration literacy tests.

Black islanders were suspicious and white authorities were hostile to outside do-gooders. Myles Horton decided to train potential black island leaders at Highlander and send them back to conduct Citizenship Schools. The schools were thus all-black, local and largely self-taught. Septima Clark sent field reports of progress and problems to Highlander, whose staff were seldom seen and thus avoided adverse newspaper publicity for three years.

Horton deliberately chose a black beautician as the first Citizenship School teacher on January 7, 1957. A black beautician with black customers was not dependent on and hence not intimidated by the white power structure. Her parlor was a community center and she was a natural community leader. Bernice Robinson (1917-), born in Charleston, earned her high school diploma through night school in New York City, where she went to better herself. Returning to Charleston in 1947 to help her ailing parents, she actively advanced race relations through the YWCA and the NAACP, finding work only as a self-employed beautician and dressmaker.

Esau Jenkins formed a Progressive Club in order to purchase a building (with a loan from a Highlander grant), sold gasoline outside and groceries inside while citizenship classes were held in the back. Bernice Robinson discarded elementary school teaching materials and child-size school furniture. She taught islanders such practical things as how to write their own names, read and understand a newspaper, fill out mail order and money order forms, and do some arithmetic. The class met two hours a night, two nights a week, for some three months. She tacked up a large UN Declaration of Human Rights poster

Citizenship School teaching materials were collected into booklets, distributed in South Carolina, and later revised to fit voter registration requirements in Tennessee and Georgia. Guy Carawan, in Highlander "singing schools," improvised lyrics for spirituals and folk songs that urged people to learn to read, write, register and vote. Citizenship Schools spread to Huntsville, AL and Savannah, GA, 1960-61, straining resources at Highlander, in debt in 1961 and about to be closed by Tennessee authorities. In August 1961, Highlander handed over its Citizenship School programs to the Martin Luther King-led Southern Christian Leadership Conference (SCLC). Septima Clark, who continued working with Citizenship Schools under SCLC, estimated that between 1954 and 1970 they helped some 100,000 blacks learn to read and write.

Highlander Attacked: 1953-61

As Highlander's civil rights activities increased, so too did segregationist attacks. Fear of communist internal subversion pervaded the U.S., aggravated by Wisconsin Senator Joseph McCarthy's Communists in government charges. Alarmed, segregationists mobilized state authority and police to try to roll back the effects of the May 1954 Supreme Court "Brown vs. the Board of Education" desegregation decision, the 1955 Montgomery, AL bus boycott, the 1957-56 Little Rock, AR school desegregation crisis, the 1961 black college student lunch-counter sit-ins (begun February 1, 1961, Greensboro, NC) and the 1961 white and black freedom bus riders' challenge of southern segregated facilities (begun May 4, 1961).

Attacks on Highlander were based on Communist conspiracy charges, going back to the 1930s. Paul Crouch told a Chattanooga reporter that while he was Tennessee Communist Party head, 1939-41, Highlander had 25 Communist Party members. Crouch had been courtmartialed in the U.S. Army, served two years in Alcatraz, and was a known paid informer for red-baiting groups. In the 1954 U.S. Democratic Senatorial campaign, Pat Sutton, running against Senator Estes Kefauver, cited Paul Crouch's testimony that Highlander's Dombroski and Horton were Communists. Sutton lost two-to-one to Kefauver, a friend of Horton's, who avoided mentioning Highlander.

In the spring of 1954, Mississippi Senator James O. Eastland (1904-86), white supremacist planter and Joseph McCarthy imitator, headed the U.S. Senate Subcommittee on Internal Security, investigating "subversive" southern liberal or-

McCarthy imitator, headed the U.S. Senate Subcommittee on Internal Security, investigating "subversive" southern liberal organizations, including Highlander. Believing that a well publicized investigation would help his 1954 Senate re-election and convinced that Communists promoted racial equality in order to disrupt and take over the U.S., Eastland tied Highlander to a conspiracy web that included Virginia Durr (Highlander trustee), sister-in-law of U.S. Supreme Court Justice Hugo Black and wife of Clifford Judkins Durr (1899-1975), New Deal official, Progressive Party Senate candidate in 1948, and an anti-polltax activist. The March 1954 hearings, dealing with alleged Communist activities of Highlanders Dombroski, Mrs. Durr, Horton and others, ended in raucous disorder with Horton physically dragged from the committee room.

The Internal Revenue Service (IRS) revoked Highlander's tax exempt status three times between 1957 and 1971, restored on appeal each time. Horton believed this harassment was aimed at stopping Highlander's school integration efforts.

In 1954 the Georgia legislature created a Commission on Education designed to resist school desegregation. The Commission used undercover agents to probe Koinonia Farm, Americus, Georgia, which had jointly with Highlander sponsored integrated children's camps in Tennessee in 1956-57. On Labor Day weekend, 1957, as Highlander was celebrating its 25th anniversary, Georgia Commission agents photographed Martin Luther King, Jr., Rosa Parks, Horton and a publicly acknowledged black Communist who, he later admitted, had conspired with the agents to be in the photo. In October 1957 the Georgia Commission published a four-page paper titled "Highlander Folk School: Communist Training School, Monteagle, Tennessee," with photos of Highlander's interracial meetings. The Georgia Commission distributed 250,000 copies, and White Citizens' Councils and the Ku Klux Klan distributed over a million copies by 1959. Southern newspapers, including the Atlanta Constitution, published articles on Highlander, labeling it at worst Communist and at best pro-Communist. The photo of Martin Luther King at Highlander was displayed by Mississippi Governor Ross Barnett, printed as a postcard by the John Birch Society, and appeared on 1965 billboards across the South titled, "Martin Luther King at Communist Training School." When Highlander's fire insurance was canceled in 1957-58, Horton suspected that segregationists were using economic pressure against the school.

Several southern state legislatures formed investigating committees during 1957-59 on the causes of racial unrest. Arkansas' committee, headed by its Attorney General, tied Highlander to the Little Rock disturbances. He offered to supply evidence to the Tennessee legislature to help them close Highlander.

On January 26,1959, the Tennessee legislature appointed a committee to investigate Highlander, using evidence collected by the Georgia Commission. The charge was that Highlander was integrated, promoted integration, was subversive, promoted Communism, allowed free love between the races; that it was not a school approved by state authorities, had no qualified faculty, and awarded no diplomas; that Horton operated Highlander for personal profit, since the trustees had given him his house and 76 acres; and last (after a July 31,1959 police raid on Highlander which found beer and a little whisky), that it sold spirits without a license.

Horton repudiated each charge. Yes, Highlander was always integrated and this was implied in its charter. No, Highlander was not subversive but allowed all points of view to be discussed, disavowing Communism because Communism was authoritarian and against Highlander's spirit of open inquiry. No, Highlander did not condone free love, but in square dancing and folk dancing hands were held and bodies sometimes touched. No, Highlander on principle did not issue diplomas and taught by discussing problems and issues, as did many adult education institutions. Yes, Highlander did give Horton his house and 76 acres in lieu of over 20 years without salary for himself and Zilphia Horton. Yes, beer was kept at Highlander because nearby cafes would not serve racially mixed groups and a money kitty was kept to replenish drinks.

Tennessee authorities found Highlander guilty of selling beer without a license and guilty of questionable financial practices (citing the gift of Horton's house and land). Other charges were dropped. The trial sapped Horton's and other Highlander staff's time and energy, yet their programs continued. Appeals delayed the closing of Highlander at Monteagle until August 1961. By then Horton and legal advisers had obtained a new charter meeting Tennessee regulations. A re-named Highlander Research and Education Center began in Knoxville, 1961-71, and still continues at New Market, near Knoxville.

Highlander in Knoxville, 1961-71 was frequently harassed. The City Council, dominated by wealthy grocer Cas Walker, passed an ordinance that all educational institutions must be approved by the Council. Police came with warrants which Highlander staff ignored, knowing that such legislation was not retroactive and hence not binding. But the KKK marched in front of the school; there were phone threats and crank calls. Once, in a Maryville, TN restaurant, Horton and a Highlander lawyer were badly beaten while their wives watched. Horton kept on. The lawyer had to close his office and move to another state.

Last Years

Horton retired as educational director in 1971; continued to live and act as consultant at Highlander, traveled to talk about the Highlander idea to adult educators in China, the Philippines, India, Malaysia, New Zealand, Australia, and Nicaragua. He was frequently interviewed, most notably on *Bill Moyers' Journal*, "Adventures of a Radical Hillbilly," Public Broadcasting System, WGBH, Boston, June 5 and 11, 1981. Still, he remained obscure to the general public, a minor figure except to those who valued him as a fighter over *The Long Haul* (title of his 1990 autobiography, indicating the simmering anger he sublimated by a lifelong fight for justice).

Horton died at Highlander, January 19, 1990.

Conclusion

Horton failed to get a fair contract for Wilder, TN coal miners. He was asked to start a Highlander in New Mexico, which failed, and a Highlander in Chicago, which failed. He later came to see that the Highlander idea fitted third-world conditions and succeeded in Appalachia only because Appalachia, exploited and owned by outside business interests, has third-world characteristics. He did anticipate two major social movements in which Highlander had some success and made a contribution: unionized labor in the 1930s-40s (Highlander trained early southern CIO leaders); and race relations in the 1950s-60s (Highlander trained major black leaders; its Citizenship Schools helped enfranchise many blacks).

At Highlander, private, small, fervently committed and with clear goals, Horton taught adults what ought to be. Public schools, which teach what is and so perpetuate the *status quo*, follow and seldom lead in re-shaping the political, economic and social class systems. In challenging and trying to re-shape those forces, Horton was a social reconstructionist like George S. Counts, who wrote *Dare the School Build a New Social Order?*,

Harold Rugg, who wrote social studies textbooks, and Theodore Brameld, defender of a reconstructed education for a reconstructed world. Horton, close to both Counts and Brameld, was a revolutionary reformer who knew that he had not ushered in the secondary American revolution, had not brought full justice and dignity to those denied them. He knew but never condoned that injustice exists in all societies, especially free enterprise ones. But we credit him, honor him, remember him for caring enough to fight for a better world.

PARTIAL BIBLIOGRAPHY

Adams, Frank, and Myles Horton. *Unearthing Seeds of Fire: The Idea of Highlander.* Winston-Salem, NC: John F. Blair, 1975.
Alinsky, Saul D. *Reveille for Radicals.* NY: Vintage Books, 1969.
Bledsoe, Tom, ed. *Or We'll All Hang Separately: The Highlander Idea.* Boston: Beacon Press, 1969.
Brameld, Theodore, ed. *Workers' Education in the United States. Fifth Yearbook of the John Dewey Society.* NY: Harper Brothers, 1941.
Carawan, Guy, and Candie Carawan. *Voices from the Mountains.* NY: Alfred A. Knopf, 1975.
Clark, Septima Poinsette, & Le Getta Blyth. *Echo in My Soul.* NY: E. P. Dutton, 1962.
Draves, Bill. *The Free University: A Model for Lifelong Learning.* Chicago: Association Press, 1980.
Durr, Virginia Foster. *Outside the Magic Circle: the Autobiography of Virginia Foster Durr.* ed. by Hollinger F. Barnard. University: Univ. of Alabama Press, 1985.
Glen, John M. *Highlander, No Ordinary School 1932-1962.* Lexington: University Press of Kentucky, 1988.
Horton, Myles. *The Long Haul: an Autobiography of Myles Horton,* ed. by Judith Kohl and Herbert Kohl. NY: Doubleday, 1990.
Peters, John M. and Brenda Bell. "Horton of Highlander,"*Twentieth Century Thinkers in Adult Education.* ed. by Peter Jarvis. London: Croom Helm, 1987, pp. 243-264.

Joining the FEAA (individual $15, senior /student $12.50) entitles you to both the Journal Option, which comes out twice a year, and the newsletter, which comes out three times. Write for membership and/or a subscription to Janet Trader, 2606 14th St., Two Rivers, WI 54241, or to Chris Spicer, chair, 107 Vernon St., Northampton, MA 01060.

For readers who are not yet acquainted with the first two collections of educational writings we've called Challenging the Giant, *it may appear highly unlikely that TWO writers named John Potter appear on these pages, especially when they learn that BOTH John Potters are Brits, both are teachers, both subscribe to the "alternative" philosophy of education, both are splendid human beings! It's true, though (see the account, on pages 27-29, of JP 1's directorship at the New School of Northern Virginia)!*

THIS John Potter taught at Summerhill in England, and now lives and teaches in Japan. His article below describes the work of the American Homer Lane, toward whom Neill of Summerhill acknowledges a deep debt, as JP 2 tells us.

HOMER LANE AND SELF-GOVERNMENT
by John Potter

Homer Lane's work with delinquent children in the early part of this century is little known In England and perhaps even less known in his own country, America. If Lane's name is all but forgotten he has nevertheless left a legacy of valuable work and ideas in the area of delinquency and has in addition had some influence in the adoption of forms of self-government in some of the progressive schools, particularly in England, following his own experiment in self-government at the Little Commonwealth in Dorset.

Lane's experiment with self-government did not begin, however, at the Little Commonwealth but in his work at what became the Ford Republic in Detroit some six years before he came to England. The Ford Republic (named after the family who donated much of the money to rebuilding the school following a fire) was primarily a reformatory for delinquents which Lane took over as Superintendent after its move into the country. He changed the system in which the school was run from a "benevolent despotism" into a largely self-governing community with a citizens' court and a supreme court over which he, as Superintendent, presided.

The idea of Junior Republics was one that had been associated with W.R. George. His Republics spread, not only across the United States, but to influence schools, clubs and prisons in other countries. Lane, however, claimed to have been unaware of George's work when he reached his own conclusions on self-government at the Ford Republic and said that he had, in fact, been more influenced by his own early experiences with the Sloyd method. This was a theory that working for some practical end would help to gain the interest of the student.

Certainly, Lane's ideas on self-government were in advance of those of W.R. George, who had accommodated a system of punishment into his own Republic—at first thrashing and disciplining the boys himself, then handing over these matters to the community as a whole. Lane also punished at first at the Ford Republic but came to a realization that punishment was useless. Where George had used self-government as the solo method—and in a very crude form—Lane began to understand that he had another weapon which was unique to his own school. This was the "power of affection." It was not until after he had left the Ford Republic, just before he came to England In 1913, that this idea took proper root in his thinking. According to Lane's biographer, David Wills:

> He discovered that, although he had been using a conscious technique that was novel and which few others had used, his work was unique because it was permeated by a spirit which was wholly his. He had vaguely realized... that the George Junior Republic, superficially so similar to his own, lacked something which his had. He began to see that, whereas other workers in this field conducted themselves as if they were in a different camp, a different category from those they sought to "save", he himself belonged to the same camp, was one of them. How far recent events contributed to this revelation we cannot guess; but certainly now he began to realize that he was, as he was to put it later, "on their side".[1]

Anti-social behaviour was simply a case of "positive virtue wrongly expressed", to demand obedience was futile. and

---

1. Wills, David, *Homer Lane*, Allen & Unwin, 1964. p. 123.

juvenile crime he saw as a kind of play. In *Talks to Parents and Teachers* —the only collection of Homer Lane's ideas, as reproduced from lecture notes—he says:

> If schools would forget the ritualizing of games and books, and would allow children absolute freedom to sort themselves out and to develop their own activities, we should have a very different type of adult, more love of country and less patriotism.[2]

The fruition of these ideas came about at the Little Commonwealth which Lane was invited to start in England in the Autumn of 1913 and which was closed in 1918. The Little Commonwealth was a self-governing community of children and adolescents up to the age of eighteen. The vast majority were difficult and delinquent, many being sent direct to the Little Commonwealth from the law courts. The community contained both boys and girls, unlike the Ford Republic which had born for boys only. The self-government was introduced very gradually. Lane's idea was for the community to come to their own realization of the need for rules end order following what must have been a lengthy and grueling period of chaos and aggression. Out of all the noise and turmoil there did evolve a system of self-government, which by 1916 was complete.

Lane claims to have stood aside and watched these developments without interference, in fact encouraging members of the community in both good and bad actions.

An important feature of the self-governing community was that a system of payment for work was introduced. Members of the community helped in building and other outside work as well as attending lessons and each member of the community was paid a wage in Commonwealth currency for their work in the various departments. With this wage the community member had to support himself or herself and pay for food, clothing and recreation. A small tax was also paid and from the collection of taxes the idle or destitute members were supported.

Lord Lytton, one of the Executive Committee of the Little Commonwealth, has outlined what he saw as the three main principles of Lane's work there, which could be of universal application:

---

2. Lane, Homer, *Talks to Parents and Teachers*, Allen & Unwin, 1928. p. 99.

1. The "law of love"; Lane was on the side of the child, and "badness" was simply misdirected goodness.

2. "Absolute freedom" is never really absolute. We can never escape the consequences of our actions. The economic lessons of this could be discovered at the Little Commonwealth; also the liberty to discover that the community disintegrates if it doesn't discover how to maintain itself.

3. Self-government. The community at the Little Commonwealth made their own rules and enforced their own discipline.

Lane, in *Talks to Parents and Teachers*, says that it is a common mistake to think that man is composed of good and bad in fairly equal parts—that the good can be encouraged by favour and rewards, the bad stopped through punishment. It cannot. All of his experience at the Little Commonwealth convinced him that these assumptions were wrong. On the contrary, he found that:

> *...almost all delinquent children will resolve their difficulties in an atmosphere of freedom and encouragement.*[3] *and,*
> *The authority that is based upon force will transform love into hatred and hope into fear.*[4]

While these ideas of Homer Lane's on the treatment of delinquency may be even now seen as radical, the idea of self-government—at least of a very early and primitive kind—was in existence as early as the mid-eighteenth century. William Gilpin in England introduced into his school an early system of jury and appeal, a forerunner of the idea of self-government. David Manson, in Belfast, had a form of self-government in his school based on the complex gradation of rank. It seems, however, that they were motivated by quite different reasons from later concepts of self-government. Their motives were mainly to attempt to give teachers an easier time by manipulating the pupils in more effective ways. Later pioneers such as David Williams introduced forms of self-government, while Robert Owen introduced a Rousseau-influenced system involving no rewards or punishments. In the Co-operative schools of England the top classes had a vote in the running of the school, and the Hills and

---

3. Lane, Homer *op.cit.* p. 162.

4. Lane, Homer *op.cit.* p. 177.

classes had a vote in the running of the school, and the Hills and Hazlewood School, in the early nineteenth century is reported to have had "complete self-government for the boys."

However, it seems that there was no one until Homer Lane who was prepared to introduce such radical forms of self-government based so much on faith in children and in their finding their own ways to work things out. W.A.C. Stewart, in his book, *Radicals and Progressives in English Education*, compares Lane with another, more famous pioneer, Maria Montessori. He notes that Lane's teaching prescribed very little: money had to be earned, the school community had power. Montessori, on the other hand, had many more subtle ways of moulding children's learning, and an adult control of disruptive factors. Stewart says that the key question is this: "To what extent do children know what is best for them?" This sorts out the Montessorians from the Laneites.

The Laneites were and are, of course, very small in number. The direct influence of Lane was felt in particular by a small band of educationists who were his contemporaries or near-contemporaries. Norman MacMunn, who wrote *The Child's Path of Freedom* (1928), was one who acknowledged Lane's influence. Later, David Wills was another who attempted to follow Lane's path.

Two of the men who were most affected by Lane and who went on to follow his self-governing principles in their own independent schools for "normal" children were J.H. Simpson at Rendcomb and A.S. Neill at Summerhill. J.H. Simpson's experiments with self-government were carried out chiefly after he was appointed headmaster of Rendcomb in Gloucestershire, which started on his appointment in 1919. Simpson's background was as a teacher in Public Schools and he had also spent some time as a junior inspector of the Board of Education. During that time he had had some contact with the Little Commonwealth and had been impressed. He called Rendcomb a "self-governing" school and tried to base it loosely on the Little Commonwealth. Stewart states that:

> There was a General Meeting to which boys ages thirteen and older belonged. Offices were held for a term and holders were elected by the boys, as were appointments to the many sub-committees, the Games Committee, the Finance Committee, the House Committee, and so on. There were games wardens, three

boys who were elected for the duration of their school life and who acted as a boys' judiciary.[5]

To this rather complicated organization, was added a fairly complex system of money and grants to be spent by the various officers. As at the Little Commonwealth, a considerable economic responsibility was vested In the community and its individual members. At Rendcomb, after some experiments, it was decided that the staff could not attend the General Meeting as members; Simpson himself sat in as a "non-voting member."

J.H. Simpson left Rendcomb in 1932, the self-governing features remaining. He writes of his experiments and his influence by Lane, primarily in *Schoolmaster's Harvest* (1954). By that time though, he believed only in the "limited value" of self-government, felt that he had not given enough thought to ethical and religious education, and was critical of Lane for handing over all responsibility to the children, something, he felt, that had given them too much trouble.

If we are to find a close contemporary of Lane who followed through Lane's faith in children without wavering, we must turn to A.S. Neill. Neill has continually written of his debt to three men: Freud, Wilhelm Reich and Homer Lane. But it is clearly Homer Lane who, on Neill's own admission, has been the greatest influence and whose ideas of self-government for children and belief in their nature permeate Summerhill to this day. The Summerhill system of self-government has been well-documented in the writings of Neill and others, and it has survived relatively unchanged for over seventy years, outliving its founder. Compared to Rendcomb and other experiments in self-government, the system at Summerhill, based on Ombudsmen, Tribunal and General Meeting, is fairly simple and straightforward and can be easily understood by the children, whose ages have variously ranged from five to seventeen. Neill, of course, having met Lane at the Little Commonwealth during the First World War, had been so impressed with his ideas that he had planned to join Lane in his work there after the war. However, by that time the Little Commonwealth had been closed.

There are many features of Lane's method of dealing with difficult children that are also evident in Neill's style. What Lane

---

5. Stewart, W.A.C., *Progressives and Radicals in English Education*, MacMillan,1972, p. 240.

calls "contra-suggestion" or doing the opposite of what is asked is very reminiscent of Neill's habit of dealing intuitively with problems at Summerhill. Lane felt that the abolishment of prohibitions is the most sensible way to curb behaviour which is anti-social:

> We believe that children develop bad habits by indulging in them; in reality, children develop bad habits if prevented from indulging in them.[6]

This remark, from *Talks to Parents and Teachers*, was made concerning the topic of weaning but the same principle applies throughout both Lane and Neill's philosophy.

However, Neill did not simply copy Lane uncritically. Although only seven years Lane's junior, Neill appears to have broken free of many habits which trapped Lane in a "New England puritanism." While Lane, for all his radicalism, was recommending the use of religion to explain ideas of birth to children, Neill was advocating telling the complete truth at all times.

Summerhill did not, and does not today, have any kind of economic system as the Little Commonwealth had—a small fine of money at the General Meeting being the only thing remotely resembling a financial aspect. Similarly, cleaning and outside work is generally taken care of by other staff and the children have no say in the hiring of teachers and other related matters. Rather than being a weakness, as some critics of Summerhill have implied, Albert Lamb, in his introduction to *The New Summerhill*, sees this as a reason for the community's strength:

> Our (Summerhill) children are given great responsibility over their lives but are still provided for in such a way that they can follow their childhood unhampered by social concerns that are beyond them.[7]

An important aspect of Lane's innovation—not just at Summerhill but at many progressive boarding schools—is the "affective" relationship encouraged by Lane, or the growth of a kind of family feeling. Members of communities such as that at Summerhill are just as likely to attack each other verbally as

---

6.   Lane, Homer, *op.cit.* p. 42.

7.   Neill, A.S., *The New Summerhill*, Penguin, 1992. p. xiv.

they are to utter sweet and soothing words, as indeed can members of any close-knit family unit; without endangering their relationships with each other or to the family. David Wills has put it like this:

> Although to the stranger some of its manifestations may seem unpleasant, its background is mutual affection and mutual respect, and humility on the part of the adults. Because the adult does not think of himself as essentially a superior being, he does not say "I forbid you to do such and such a thing"; he says rather, "Don't be such a silly ass" (or even, indeed, "a bloody fool"); "if you do that it will have such and such consequence and you will wish you'd never done it". The effect of this approach is to induce neither unwilling obedience nor rebelliousness but rather, an acceptance of the facts and an acting upon them.[8]

The General Meetings at both the Little Commonwealth and at Summerhill seem to have had a history of being conducted in a very orderly fashion. Fears that children governing themselves might punish wrongdoers too severely have not been borne out. What punishments there have been have proved to be remarkably lenient, and the patience and eventual wise authority of the meetings has become well-known. Despite fears also that Lane's methods could only be applied by him because of his own charisma, others such as Simpson and Neill have found that given the right conditions self-government can work very successfully. Indeed, similar fears about Summerhill being a "one man show" and about the future of self-government were expressed following Neill's death, but almost twenty years later the system is flourishing. The Little Commonwealth—and Summerhill—as boarding communities of more than one hundred members are in the most favourable position for the introduction of meaningful self-government. It might be more difficult for day schools to adopt such a full and thorough system. In addition, where there are large numbers, or groups of very young children, say, of children exclusively under the age of twelve, it might be difficult to generate the same degree of social responsibility. However, there seems no reason why modifications of Lane's system should not be introduced if thought desirable. Various

---

8. Wills, David, *op. cit*. p. 139.

forms of self-government are now in existence, not just in progressive or radical independent schools, but in the form of "school councils" in some government-run schools.

Despite Lane's troubled life, the scandals and the eventual closure of the Little Commonwealth, it cannot be seriously denied that his methods achieved considerable success and have interested and influenced a number of people, especially in education. That his methods have been adopted and developed by so few seems less because of doubts about their viability than with the inclination of societies that still prefer to repeat the mistakes of the past. The former psychoanalyst, Alice Miller, writing in *Banished Knowledge*, says that children who have been loved and respected, given responsibility and freedom, will store this knowledge within and cannot help but protect the weak and raise their children in the same loving and respecting way. Unfortunately, most of the people in charge of children's' lives today had very different kinds of experiences in their childhood:

> ...and they still believe those were correct. They can seldom empathize with children or summon any feeling for their own childhood fate.[9]

Neill, who regarded Lane as the most influential factor in his life, asked:

> Why does humanity choose a Hitler end not a Homer Lane? Why does It choose war and not peace, inhumanity towards criminals rather than psychological and social treatment? Perhaps because it is afraid of love, of tenderness.[10]

In the limited life of the Little Commonwealth, Homer Lane was able to demonstrate at the very least that self-government was a possibility for even some of the most hardened delinquents. If such successes could be achieved over seventy years ago a great chance is being missed if his ideas on self-government are not championed by many more of us.

---

9. Miller, Alice, *Banished Knowledge*, Doubleday, 1990. p. 174.

10. Neill, A.S., *op.cit.* p. 215.

Zoë Readhead carries on her great father's tradition at Summerhill as one to the manor born—which she was! We are grateful to the Newsletter of the National Coalition of Alternative Schools *(NCACS) for permission to reprint Zoë's tribute to her father. Summerhill is alive and well under her banner.*

A.S. NEILL AS A FATHER—A PERSONAL MEMORY
by Zoë Neill Readhead

Being the daughter of the great educator A.S. Neill is probably the most difficult thing I can think of to write about. Many people are keen to know what sort of father he was and what my life as a child in Summerhill was like. I am often asked about Neill by school visitors and I do my best to give them a picture but the memories are very personal and therefore difficult to convey without it sounding either smug or totally uninteresting. I tend to remember things like his morning cold baths, watching "Wells Fargo" (which he loved) on TV and our imaginary friends, Rosie and Posie, who got up to all sorts of nonsense and eventually disappeared down the plug-hole of my bath.

Neill's ideas on child-rearing and education did not enter my life on a conscious level until I was in my teens. In other words, although I lived a special and unique childhood because of his ideas, on a day-to-day basis I was not really aware of the significance of it all. He may have been a champion of children, a hero throughout the world to those who care about children's rights, but to me he was just my Daddy.

As a father Neill was warm, witty, patient, and possessed an almost unique ability to keep out of the way. This was true of his life within Summerhill as well. He was able to let life pass by without feeling the need to interfere in any way. Some people think that he cultivated this quality to help the children in the school to grow away from adults and strengthen as individuals. I think this may be partly true, but I also think, knowing Neill as I did, that he was often so engrossed in his own thoughts that he really didn't notice things going on around him. My childhood memories of Summerhill seldom include my father. My mother took a much more active part in the community while he tended to keep his distance and get on with his own affairs. That isn't to suggest that he was not involved. His keen eyes watched all the children; he made very accurate assessments about their problems and development. But there is a mythical view of Neill, lover of children who played with them and ventured off into the bushes with them to build huts or have tea parties which is not true. He may have been like that in his early years before I was born, but later, he behaved like a normal adult and got on with his own business—except for special occasions when he needed to counsel a child for a particular reason.

Somehow he was not part of our lives at school while at the same time he was always THERE if we needed him. Of course he also had a lot to do with all of us on an "official" basis, e.g. discussions, meetings, spontaneous acting (he set scenes for us to act out in whatever way we wanted) and of course his famous stories on Sunday evenings. In meetings he spent a lot of time complaining about us using too much electricity or wasting too much food. He was a true Scot and never left an electric light burning if it wasn't needed, often walking along the top corridor at school and flicking the switch while you were sitting quietly reading a comic. He never saw you but was very apologetic when you shouted "Hey! Neill!!" To this day I cannot leave a light burning in an empty room.

Neill was a very "adult" person. He never tried to behave in a child-like way in order to gain ground with us kids. He could not bear Rock 'n' Roll music nor understand our teenage culture. He read "good" books and often complained to me about my taste in literature. He seldom swore and when he once used the word fuck to describe two ducks having sex it shocked me deeply. He loved Wagner and wished that I would listen to it with him. He once said to me that if you love a piece of music or prose it is no use unless you can share it with somebody. At the time I did not appreciate what he meant but now I often want to share things with my children. They, like me at the time, are not always interested!

Poor Neill, my biggest regret is having lost him at the age of twenty-seven when there was so much more to share with him. As a young thing, I was too busy growing and learning to spend much time with him in the sense that I would now. There are so many things I would like to discuss with him now that I have reared my own four children—some small disagreements too, I expect!

All of my childhood I was aware that he would die long before other kids' fathers would. He was sixty-four when I was conceived. Although I never worried about him dying prematurely, I used to have nightmares about his death and was always aware that I did not have him for long. When I was around six years old I had a dream about him being buried alive and a machine counting the time he had left. I woke up distraught and the dream hung over me for a long time. But being young you don't prepare for a parent's death, you live for today and probably just as well too. Now I feel that I should have spent more time with him so as not to waste a moment but, of course, I could not have spent more, nor would he have wanted me to. He lived to see Tony's and my daughter, Amy, born and grow into a lively toddler and our son, William, was born a few weeks before he died so he had a chance to hold him in his arms as well. I dearly wish that he could have known Henry and little Neill and that he could have watched them all grow up in the way that he pioneered—watched them go through his wonderful school and emerge as fine, gentle, strong individuals of whom he would be so proud. Those fine characteristics which they have they owe directly to their Grandfather, for without his foresight, compassion and tremendous energy Summerhill would not have existed for them.

Matt Appleton is a "house parent" at Summerhill—and a very good one! We are grateful for permission to reprint his account of Summerhill.

SUMMERHILL: A CHILDREN'S CULTURE
by Matthew Appleton

A visitor to Summerhill, if s/he were to return five years later, would find that there were many faces, and only a few that s/he recognized. This is due to the large turnover of both staff and children.[1] Of those familiar faces most would be amongst the older kids, though they would have changed a lot in five years, from scruffy, dirt-streaked House Kids, running around doing their own thing, to well groomed, sociable adolescents. There would be some familiar faces amongst the staff, but these would be outweighed by the new ones, some enthusiastic and eager to talk about their fresh experience of Summerhill,

---

1. There are various reasons for this high turnover. With the kids it may be the child has been disruptive at home or at school and when they begin to 'improve' at Summerhill they are taken out again, so that they may have "a proper education". These are the kids who were sent to Summerhill as a final resort rather than a first choice. Some kids are taken out because their parents have become anxious as they are not going to class. Often such parents have an intellectual attraction to Summerhill, but in their hearts they do not have the trust in their children that the school does. Other times the concerns may be purely financial and the parents find they can no longer afford the school fees. The high turnover of staff also has many reasons. Summerhill is not an easy place for adults to live. It is noisy, demanding and offers little adult privacy. It requires a great deal of self-motivation, as there is no career structure that offers rewards or promotion. The pay is low, and many adults find it difficult to let go of their preconceptions and relate to the children as equal members of the community, without losing their own sense of adult identity. However within the staff there is also a strong core of long-standing adults who help new staff integrate.

others more reserved, as they struggle with their own emotional reactions to the place.

Summerhill has been described elsewhere as "the bare minimum of a school". The description is a valid one in the sense that it has been designed to accommodate the needs of the children, rather than impose unnecessary restrictions and adult ideology upon them. Teachers are available to teach their various subjects if the children are interested. Houseparents provide first aid and wash dirty clothes, and the staff as a whole are there as adult members of the community to whom the kids can turn if they want adult company or advice. Cooking and cleaning is provided by the day staff. Zoë,[2] and her husband Tony, with the help of Sarah, the school secretary, deal with the administrative aspects of school life, such as finances and dealing with outside bodies.

The staff are responsible for deciding which rooms children should sleep in, with the exception of the older 'Carriage Kids,' who make their own arrangements. It is also a staff decision as to when children move from one area of the school to the next, for example from the San to the House, or the Shack to the Carriages.

Within this basic adult arrangement, which has been provided to give the children a safe space in which to live their lives, there is no adult imposition, only various adult opinions which carry no more weight than any other voice in the community.

The weekly meetings are an established part of community life. With the exception of a few health and safety laws the meeting decides upon what laws the community shall live by, and in making these decisions the adults have only one vote, just the same as the children. But this lack of adult authority or guidance does not mean that the children live in a vacuum. Although there will be some adults who are active and powerful members of the community, by and large the guiding light of community life will come from the older kids. They are, so to speak, the "elders" of the community, many of whom have been at Summerhill

---

2. Zoë Readhead, the daughter of A.S. Neill, who now runs the school. [See her article, preceding this one, on being her father's daughter.]

longer than most of the staff, and will have much deeper understanding of its processes.

In my first term there was the unusual situation of the school having a large intake or new kids, while at the same time almost half the staff were new that term too. Of the remaining staff, many had only been there a few terms themselves, and there were many conflicting opinions about how best to handle situations. Zoë, who does not actually live in the school but at a local farm, came in daily, and I would often discuss problems that came up for me with her. I always found her advice helpful, and her insights deep. But apart from Zoë my main source of understanding came from talking to the big kids and listening to their impressions and feelings. This is something that I have seen many new staff struggle with, for they find it difficult to let go of the notion that adults should know best, or at least be seen to know best. It turns their sense of hard earned "professionalism" on its head and appears to them topsy turvy, which is a shame, as there is a lot to be learnt there.

The big kids are mostly very active in community matters. It is usually one of the big kids who chairs the meetings. whilst another acts as secretary, taking the minutes. The older kids are also a strong voice in the meeting, drawing from their years of experience of community life and understanding of the younger kids. They also take on more normal roles, which they are voted into by the community as a whole. These include the Fines officer, who keeps a record of what people are fined in the meetings and makes sure they pay up. The Beddies Officers enforce the bedtimes each night. Ombudsmen deal with problems between people that are either too trivial to justify a meeting case, or cannot wait until the next meeting.

There are also various committees, which are also voted in by the community, and consist largely of the big kids. There is the Gram Committee that looks after the school's disco equipment and acts as D.J.s on "Gram nights" and for parties. At various times there has been a Social Committee, that organises social events, such as games and entertainments, a Table Tennis Committee, to ensure that the Table Tennis equipment was kept in good repair, a Bike Committee, to help the younger kids keep their bikes in repair, a Food Committee, to keep a good relationship between the kitchen and the kids, a Swindling Committee, to make sure none of the small kids were being cheated by some of the more devious characters in the community whilst swapping or buying things, a Visitors Committee to show visitors around. These have come and gone as the need arises, and are only the handful that come to mind as I think back over the seven years I've been at the school.

There are committees created to raise money and organise special events, such as parties at Halloween, Guy Fawkes, St. Valentine's Day and End of Term. On all of these there will also be an occasional staff, and a handful of younger kids working alongside the big kids. But it is the big kids who are most active in organising things and are passing on traditions that have developed within the school to its newer and younger members.

There will be certain games that are traditionally played at the party, or ways of celebrating, such as on the stroke of midnight, on the eve of St. Valentine's Day, a large crowd of kids running around the school kissing whoever they can find. Even though the bedtime laws are being broken the Beddies Officers take no notice, as it is an accepted, albeit unspoken exception to the law. There is also the Midnight Walk to a local beach at Summer half term. This is organized by the Half Term Committee, who arrange wood for a fire, soup and marshmallows to roast, and transport for the younger kids if they are too tired to walk back.

The single most important event of the term is the end of term party, when the lounge is closed and decorated by the End of Term Committee. They decide amongst themselves on a theme and the walls are covered in paper and painted to depict that theme. In recent years it has included such themes as madness, black and white, inside the waste bowl (this being the bowl into which unwanted food is emptied at mealtimes), Batman, the history of music, the Jungle Book, the school meeting, cities, a carnival, a haunted house, to name a few. Nobody else is allowed to see the lounge or know what the theme is until the party begins and the lounge is opened again.

The end of term party is an emotional affair, not only because everyone is preparing to go home and will not see each other for several weeks, but also because it is when the community says goodbye to those who are leaving and not coming back. At midnight everyone links hands and gathers in a circle around the people leaving. "The Gram" begins to play "Auld Lang Syne" and everyone sings along. When the music ends the circle breaks up and closes in around those in the middle. Friends hug each other, often with tears running down their faces and sobs shaking their bodies, maybe for the last time, as some will return to countries across the other side of the world.

Certainly they are saying goodbye to a way of life they have been a part of and shared together, sometimes for many years.

It is difficult to express the emotional intensity of such partings, and even as I write about it I find my eyes are welling up with tears. Living in Summerhill is like being part of a huge family. As one girl said, "The boys are all my brothers and the girls are all my sisters. I love them very much." Another girl told me, "I feel closer to the people I know least well here than I did to my best friend in my old school."

Many of the younger kids feel the loss of older kids leaving acutely. In fact I have seen more emotion generated by big kids leaving than by many of the staff who have come and gone (although kids do form very strong attachments to individual staff, and are upset when they leave. But the fact is that many staff do not stay as long as the kids who have gone through the school to become big kids, nor are they necessarily as involved in the life of the community, although, again, some are very active and involved[4]). Sometimes there have been obvious friendships whereby one of the big kids has taken one of the younger kids under their wing, or maybe there have been less obvious links, but one to which the younger child has attached a lot of meaning. It could be a certain compliment, or show of affection or perhaps a moment when the bigger kid helped them accomplish a task or deal with a problem. Such events may seem of little importance to an adult, but to the younger children to whom the big kids are cool and powerful people, and closer to their own age and immediate future than the staff, these can be

---

4. *Editorial note: My own impression is although the big kids do essentially play the role of being the 'elders' of the community, the consistent presence of a core group of adults who both understand and deeply care about the community and its processes is important. This is as important from the perspective of knowing when to step back and say nothing, as for when to get involved as a caring member of the community. The potential problem that such a community faces with its inherent high turnover of staff is that it may go through periods when such a presence may be rather thin on the ground. My experience of Summerhill is that this has never been acute enough to constitute a real problem, but I believe it is a potential weakness worth acknowledging and being aware of when we are involved in this field of work.*

thrilling, exciting moments. I remember myself as a boy the elation I felt when an older boy paid me some attention. It really made me feel like I was somebody. One of older girls told me once, "When you're a little kid you like the staff, but you don't look up to them. It's the big kids you look up to. You look at them and you think maybe I can be like that one day."

The games that the smaller kids play are often games that they have learnt from seeing bigger kids play them, such as "Kick the Can" or "Touch Prisoners". Sometimes one of the big kids will organise "The Murder Game". This is a game that was devised by one of the big kids some years ago. Usually most of the school will sign up for it. It consists of various people being murderers, private detectives, and undercover private detectives. Everyone else is normal, but no one knows who the undercover P.I.s or murderers are. The murderers have to be killed themselves. They must carry 'murder notes' with them at all times, with the names of all the normal people on, and can be searched by the P.I.s if they are acting suspiciously or have been seen killing someone. It is an exciting game, with lot's of mutual suspicion, and can last for days. More recently one of the older kids devised a variation on the theme called "The Cold War Game", with the players being split into two sides and various people playing the roles of generals, lieutenants, spies, and military police etc. The object of the game is to find out who the other side's general is and kill him. Even though the inventors of both games have now left, the games continue to be played by kids who will never know them.

As the kids move up through the school from San through to Carriages, each stage has its own sense of being a rite of passage. The youngest kids, the San Kids, have the earliest bedtime and the community has a strong feeling of protectiveness towards them as they are the smallest and most vulnerable kids in the school. There are even some special laws specifically to look after the needs of the San Kids. The next age group up are the House Kids. These are the kids that Neill called the school "gangsters". They are more independent than the San Kids, spending a lot of time playing off on their own away from adults. They also tend to be more daring, breaking the school laws in various minor ways. Then there are the Shack Kids, who are beginning to get a sense that they are not House Kids anymore and will soon be the big kids. Lastly the Carriage Kids, who have finally become "the big kids" and start to feel a sense of their power in the community and the responsibilities that go along with it.

There may be time when a group of big kids has just left and the school is quite young for awhile. At such times the self-government may be weak, and the staff have to take more of an active role in things. There may also be times when some of the staff harangue the big kids to "get their act together" because they are being kept awake at night or the meetings are sloppy. But the bulk of social traditions and responsibilities within the community are not dictated by adults, they are handed down by example and interaction from one generation of big kids to the next. So although Summerhill is "the bare minimum of a school" it is not just a vacuum but a self-perpetuating, self-regulating children's culture in which kids feel they can belong and be themselves at the same time.

TEACHING AND LEARNING

Bill Kaul lives and teaches in or near Waterflow, New Mexico. He is a frequent contributor to ΣΚΟΛΕ, the Journal of Alternative Education. Some day he may tell us more about his background/life—but for now, all you need to know is what a magnificent person he is, as you can see for yourself by reading his articles. In addition to this one, we've included two under the heading of "Social Change and Commentary," beginning on page 368, and a third under the heading of "The Plight of Our Children"—my favorite, actually—which begins on page 420.

SOME NOTES TOWARD A PRACTICAL IMPRACTICAL CURRICULUM
by Dr. Bill Kaul

I. Flexibility

   A. A curriculum must bend to meet the needs of the students it is designed to serve. Involving students in the writing of a curriculum is seldom a bad idea. (Diagnosis always involves input from the patient's own perspective.)

   B. A curriculum should be based on community as well as global needs; it needs to be able to move between global and local realities, building bridges between the two. Involving the community in the writing of a curriculum is seldom a bad idea. (Global involvement is usual, handed down by pundits.)

   C. A curriculum must not be more than a plan nor less than a plan. Expectations of outcome from a curriculum must leave room for unexpected pathways, unexpected (not necessarily undesired) outcomes. Plan ahead, but don't plan *all* the results.

   D. Small is beautiful—where people can talk and work together openly and honestly (students, faculty, community, parents, administration), there is a synergy of effort which cannot be matched by any written plan of action. (Examples abound: common law, unwritten constitutions, etc.) (Even written constitutions are mutable.)

   E. One would hope that the writers of the curriculum are as flexible as the recipients: Piaget's notions of assimilation and accommodation flow both ways: curriculum changes not only students but also teachers, parents, community, etc., both ways.

accommodation flow both ways: curriculum changes not only students but also teachers, parents, community, etc. in both ways.

II. Effectiveness

A. The effectiveness of a curriculum is determined by the visible evidence resulting from its implementation. Some questions:

—What was learned?
—How was it learned?
—Who learned it?
—When was it learned? Under what conditions?
—How do we know it was learned?
—What are the results of this learning?
—What useful divergences were uncovered?
—What things were *not* learned? By whom? Why?

B. A curriculum's effectiveness is also closely tied to the manner in which it was implemented. (See "Flexibility.")

C. Some things cannot be measured, only described. Descriptions are often more valuable than measurements because they contain their own explanatory keys.

D. Part of the purpose of evaluating the effectiveness of a curriculum lies in uncovering the "hidden curriculum." Uncovering the "hidden curriculum" is also the work of a part of the curriculum itself: critical thinking applied internally.

III. The Dirty Work of Writing a Curriculum

A. Always be guided by the idea that a curriculum is an *open* document with a *closed* purpose; that is, it should be written with *both* the idea of a secure plan and vision and the ability to change as conditions warrant. (Thus the value of close communication between *all* parties affected by curriculum, bearing in mind that the writing of the curriculum is itself *a part of the curriculum*. This is much like the notion that writing of a constitution is a part of government, as the amendment of the constitution is a part of the document that can't be foreseen.)

B. The wording of a curriculum should be clear and accessible. Nothing is more odious than intellectual doubletalk for "I don't know" or "I won't tell you."

C. Complex curriculum issues should be handled as are complex philosophical issues: the drawing of lines, the application of Ockham's Razor.

D. Disciplinary concerns should be addressed in such a manner that the goals of a discipline are exposed in the interconnections it has with other disciplines, as well as its role in the community; e.g., what is the role of communication in history, the role of history in the community, the role of writing in history, the science of writing, the biology of communication?

E. When possibilities are closed off as a matter of practical concern (see "C," above) that shouldn't mean they are buried.

F. People who aren't familiar with the process of designing and implementing curriculum should be taught— this should be a part of the curriculum. In this manner the document is written more quickly and with more input—it tends to achieve "A," above.

IV. The Content of a Curriculum

A. The content of a curriculum should focus on the large issues of life as expressed in the forms of life practiced in the community.

B. These large issues should be addressed in both a local and global context; e.g., the issue of overpopulation as both a local and global concern, overpopulation as it affects jobs locally.

C. A very decent curriculum can be built around the linguistic constants of Who What When Where Why and How as they are applied to broad issues. The domains of various disciplines make themselves manifest in these applications. Bridges are built. Relevance is established.

D. A curriculum's timeline should be flexible, based on outcomes for individuals and communities—if topic A is mastered by person B in two weeks but mastered by person C in ten weeks, so be it. The interconnectedness of a curriculum is both a function of time and readiness. Thus, students must also teach, plan, and evaluate—learning to do these things, learning to take responsibility for one's own education, this is a large function of a curriculum.

E. A good example of this is the Hampshire curriculum design.

F. Another is the design of Fauré or that of Montessori.

G. Chamofsky.

H. Socrates.

I. Etc.

To: Teacher Formation Program
The Fetzer Institute
Kalamazoo, Michigan
From: John Taylor Gatto
Dear Fetzers:

Teachers teach who they are. That's a perspective I've held on teaching for nearly three decades and all the effort I ever spent becoming a better teacher was spent directly on becoming a better me. Anyone willing to reflect on the matter carefully will see that there hardly can exist a service called "teacher training", the idea is based on a military fantasy of Helmuth von Moltke that the method to train a mass army was a rigid plan set down by staff experts which the field command would execute.

Teacher training was a Prussian invention, too; it was supposed to make the educational plan teacher-proof—and it did! The net result is the school world around us. Except for stuff too petty to matter much, no form of collegiate teacher training can help men and women be wise, mature, competent and humane adults. And parents should go to the barricades before they let the State put their children with any other kind.

So I was glad to see you call your program teacher *formation*, because that *may* be a possibility. If you can help human beings become complete you'll get better teachers as a natural by-product of that. A better deal for kids starts with a better deal for teachers, there just isn't any other way.

But don't jump to the conclusion I mean more money because I don't mean that at all, in fact if you redefine teaching to include all those grown-ups, no matter who they are, who have 1) made something of themselves, 2) want to work with kids, part-time or full-time, 3) are willing to forswear force in attracting an audience, and you work to get rid of the phony certification requirements that presently drive the majority of good candidates away from the teaching business, I think you'll find the net bill to society is much *less*. I'm sympathetic to the argument that teachers should be compensated fairly, it's just that government is the last agency who might know how much that would take. As it is, one out of every two people being paid in schools now—many of them as "teachers"—don't see any kids from the start of a week to its finish.

Teachers teach who they are, they can hardly teach much of anything else if you think about it.* If you take that seriously, and I do, it suggests that much of the expensive attention given to prepared curricula, official materials, suitable spaces, testing, various specialized licenses, etc., is misguided.

A better deal for teachers would consist of building social architecture around them with enough room in it to allow them to become whole people. If we were very candid with each other we might begin by acknowledging that the characteristic most prominent among the millions of people teaching school these days is that they are childlike and incomplete. By teaching who they are they inadvertently do a great deal of harm. I don't mean to say there aren't hundreds of thousands of exceptions to that, or that teachers aren't as smart as any other labor category in our economy. In the beginning they're probably a cut or two above most other groups. But the constant confinement with children, the sterility of the workplace, the dependence on routines, sequences, extremely low grade text material, bells and surveillance, the lack of privacy, the relentless isolation from policy-making and colleagues, the implied inferiority, catches up to them quickly. If they didn't enter the business childlike and incomplete—and the nature of going into a job like teaching right out of college almost ensures that they will be—the culture of schools will make them that way or terminate them.

I know there are schools you think are exceptions to that indictment, but in the government sector I'll have to disagree with you; there *are* schools where teachers are given a chance to grow up because of a personal decision (and some risk-taking) by the principal. They don't qualify as exceptions. When your fundamental human rights depend on the whim of somebody else, you have no rights—and surely if you have a brain in your head you know that. All the "pilot" projects in the country aren't much more than some colossal trickery on the part of State schooling, a way to vent pressure that might otherwise build and jeopardize the main part of the business.

---

* The children I had who had the most profound effect on me as a teacher were invariably those who were incomplete in the same way that I had been or perhaps still was. The implications of this are deep.

Around the year 1840 the French philosopher Comte, who had such a great influence on American business and social work, laid down a formula to create a teacher proletariat which could serve the State's purposes best: it would be drawn from people who had light ties to family, to place, to property, to private enthusiasm, to ideology, to religion, to community. Docility above all else was to be sought, tractable men and women. No independent thinkers need apply.

That formula hasn't changed a stick. Who can say honestly that Comte's formula was ignored? Even the humane stream of theory out of Rousseau, Pestalozzi, Froebel, Herbart, Parker and Dewey doesn't bear very close scrutiny—the operation of schools are meant to serve collective, State purposes. No independent thinkers better apply to progressive schools either, and the ones that do are in for a *rocky* ride.

Real people don't ever serve an *idea* without changing it drastically; only cookie-cutter people do that. We don't need to "form" any more teachers like that, the woods are already full of them and state compulsion schooling and television will guarantee an abundance for the future. Our society makes incomplete people a renewable resource.

What regular engagements with single-age children in confinement cells do to public schoolteachers isn't pretty and it isn't easily reversible. A few casual encounters with other grown-ups in the same boat isn't enough ballast to give a life *weight*—teachers threaten to leave the ground at any minute because they are unbearably light. It's not a matter of intelligence or good will. If deliberate or circumstantial training has left a teacher with no genuine skill, no categorical family, no God, no community, no culture, what on earth business has the State *compelling* young people to share the same cell with them?

Parents should ask, "Can you build a house, build a boat, grow food, make clothing, repair things, defend yourself, sing a song? If your answer is "No," then what business do you have with my child?"

My point is you can't form teachers; nobody's that smart. The unstated premises of teacher training are all flatly wrong and would be rejected in horror by all of us if they were brought out of the cellar to be looked at. We've gotten into this mess by linking together a long chain of false assumptions; at some point the economy will suffer because they are so expensive to maintain. You can, however, help to form teachers by deciding what impressive human beings need to get that way and assembling those things for teachers.

Once you set your goal as the vision of a complete human being, then the smaller priority of forming a good teacher will take care of itself. Complete human beings are always drawn on a singular blueprint that is innate in each one of us—time to deep-six John Locke's *tabula rasa* child, and B.F. Skinner's operant conditioning; both. The first is flatly wrong and the second is such a certain scheme to mutilate the complex spirit that its proponents should be regarded as criminals. The minute we begin to think of people as types or classes or as interchangeable in any important way, the game is lost.

If we are machines, the word "education" has no meaning, nor does any form of schooling make the slightest bit of sense. Machines have no obligation to be programmed by other machines. " Purpose" only makes sense in the presence of Free Will. If we're going to fuss about teacher formation at all I'll just assume we're on the same wave length about this, because otherwise you're nutty as a fruitcake; we need to keep a sharp eye out for determinists and slap a "Kick Me" sign on their backs.

If we're going to form teachers, then, or help in forming teachers would be more accurate because the main part of the work is out of our hands since people aren't machines and we aren't God, we have to see that the goal is forming a complete human being, because incomplete people tend to be miserable or angry or indifferent or dependent.

I've found the easiest and least confusing place to start is with a job of sculpture: knocking away the material that keeps the human image from emerging—what constraints keep the teacher in the deadly state of incompletion they find themselves? Once you see the obstacle clearly, you can focus like a laser on burning it away. Think of the chisel setting the innate image free.

If anyone thinks I might be overstating the case of incompletion I'd ask them to consider what other reason could possibly explain the vast silence of millions of teachers on policy matters in education, or in political and social matters generally throughout this and the last century? I don't mean the political activism of teacher unions, because collective institutions are never the voice of individuals but some pale averaging of limited special interest.

Why is this uncanny *silence* not part of the school debate anywhere? What accounts for this terrible phenomenon?—that ought to interest anyone who preserves the Christian tradition of caring, loving, helping which is one of the foundation stones of Western society. Shouldn't these mute millions be given back their tongues? In ancient times slaves who were set to guard a secret or do a horrible deed had their tongues ripped out; it's not good public policy to have silent teachers.

Every now and then you hear an Escalante or a Marva Collins reacting to oppression; usually after they've been driven out of their school. It isn't enough.

And doesn't your intuition tell you that the physical immobility and isolation imposed on teachers is a bad thing, and the regulated time and subordination? Anyone who did these things consistently to his own child would be guilty of child abuse; the effect on teachers is just as bad. After they do their work with children, they have to come out into the light of day and live among us all. The real stinger in the Golden Rule is the inevitable reciprocity that follows mistreatment; the bad energy gets passed around and back to you.

You teach who you are. You teach who you are and were as a son or daughter; that's an important part of completing your humanity and a necessary honoring of the world's most basic institution. You teach who you are as a parent yourself and a relation, and if you aren't these things you teach *why not*, even if never a word is said. I've started with some very human compartments of a complete man/woman because they are the ones we customarily ignore. If you make a list of the parts of a complete life that come to mind, each of them will suggest definite curriculum exercises which involve reading, writing, arithmetic, critical thinking, explorations, rhetoric, science, etc.

I'll make a stab at this without any pretense of being comprehensive; these are what came to my mind after 5 minutes' thinking; a different list or a different method of attack might come to yours.

The Archetype of a Complete Person (Teacher) Has These Dimensions:

Teaching	Neighbor
Administration	Craftsman
Policy-Making	Artist
Learning	Adventurer
Religion	Naturalist
Community Participation	Creator

Private Interests	Entrepreneur
Philanthropy	Servant
Family:	Master
a) as son or daughter	Friend
b) as father or mother	Judge
c) as relative	Priest
d) as historian, respecter of the dead.	Sportsman
Gambler	Lover
Fighter	

And any complete person has a dark side, too; people who seem to be too good to be true *are* too good to be true. That's why children don't trust teachers, although they couldn't put the idea into words. They know we lie because they can look inside themselves and see the dark side: either they are freaks or we are liars.

If we are to re-member our humanity, here are a bunch of arms and legs to sew back onto teachers. Then we need to make these things part of the curriculum so that as the teacher teaches, he/she is able to clearly remember being whole. That's the end I consciously worked for for at least half my teaching career—to make myself whole—and it explains the otherwise shocking confession that I did nothing in the classroom that wasn't directly useful to me. Everything I undertook, without exception, was to fill in a gap in myself. That's not an exaggeration to make a point but a precise description of how I approached my work on a daily basis.

The fallout from struggling to be whole is all I had to give my students, but I was honest and open about that. The hierarchical *ministration* model of schooling,* the gift to the 20th century of G. Stanley Hall, Frederick Taylor, Thorndike, Columbia, Hopkins, the University of Chicago and other mills grinding salt is an ugly and very expensive lie to maintain. You can neither "teach" teachers nor can you order them about without ruining their value. I'm tempted to shout to the quarter of a million teacher trainers who clutter the colleges and schools, "For God's sake, get a job!" but I realize, at bottom, that's everyone's prob-

---

* You cannot be someone else's minister unless they choose you of their own free will, a lesson schoolmen never learned.

lem—building an economy that makes sense so most of us can have real work instead of "make work."

But what if I were in your position, struggling honorably to set up a teacher *formation* program so your Institute can have a worthwhile agenda? Well, I would consider, in light of the above, who might have the most to contribute to a young man or woman thinking about teaching. And I'd assemble the candidates and the counselers together in some retreat where they could interact productively.

Who would the best teachers of teachers *be*? Let me start with old people at the ends of their lives looking back. What could they have been helped to know that now they realize was missing?

Can you see how valuable such information is and yet how ignorant any one of us is in this area because we have allowed a bankrupt vision of expertise guide our thinking? What wise man or expert would be so rash and arrogant to answer this question? It can only be answered at the source. The resource is inexhaustible; it just takes the first Fetzer Institute to show us all how to look.

The second great resource which is never tapped lies in failed teachers struggling to understand. I learned a little but not very much from good teachers, but a world of insight from the despair and self-loathing of bad teachers, and the bitter anger of indifferent teachers. Find these people: some will have quit or been fired, but not many; most will still be in the classroom. Some are honest enough to come forward to talk to candidates.

The most magnificent single resource which the business overlooks deliberately, and all the fancy conferences and institutes and retreats and colloquia, is the huge number of children oppressed by schooling. We ignore them not because they can't be insightful but because we do not dare to face them as equals—the extremity of what we have done to them allows no convincing justification. Children are locked up for the convenience of *a few adults*, not at the collective decision of a consensus. It may appear that way now that they have been so confined for over a century, but the most shallow reading of history will disclose the truth. Hardly ever have a teacher formation meeting without children in attendance! If that seems to be a guarantee that the participants will be uncomfortable, there is your most compelling reason to do it. How can you "form" anything without altering its natural state?

The point of view of the victims of this failed institution is the best and most potent tool to change it, time to put on the back burner the advice of the people who made the business this way in the first place, and the people who make a good living maintaining it as it is.

Only with complete people or those dedicated to the struggle for completion can you realistically begin to talk about what a teacher should deliver. How people are made complete deserves, I think, to be near the center of the initial focus.

TAKE A HIKE: LESSONS IN SELF RELIANCE
AND PARENTAL PATH FINDING
by Robert L. Kastelic, Ed.D.

Robert is a former professor of Education at Pacific University in Oregon. He taught high school social studies for eighteen years in Scottsdale, Arizona. His professional experiences also include supervision and professional preparation of teachers in New York, Arizona, and Oregon. He is presently the Director of Research and Development for Southwest Research and Educational Services, (SRES) Inc., a non-profit educational group, and also serves on the Board of Directors for SRES and The Joyful Child Foundation.

He holds his Doctorate from Columbia University's Teachers College in New York and his Masters from Arizona State University, and is Institute certified in Reality Therapy and Control Theory.

Each summer over the past eight years we have provided an opportunity for a personal and unique adventure for our sons. We have spent the summer in the White River National Forest in Colorado taking care of a Forest Service campground. My wife and I are educators and have the summer break to provide extended educational opportunities for our sons, as well as to get a chance to recharge and relax. For each of us working in the forest during the summer has meant several different things. However, for our children it has meant more than merely being with nature. Over the years they have been provided the opportunity to learn some basic skills in self reliance. Self reliance figures big in this short story because I perceive that many young people are being deprived the opportunities of learning for themselves the value and importance of self reliance except through negative or traumatic experiences. Unfortunately, too many children are learning to take care of themselves because of being abandoned either emotionally, physically, or both.

Each summer we would pack up our travel trailer and head for the Colorado mountains. This kind of vacation was done in an effort of sanity as well as enjoyment. We live in the Sonoran desert and temperatures in the desert were reaching 110 degrees in early May. Our destination in the mountains, on the other hand, was hovering in the mid 60s to 70s degree temperatures. We came upon the campground host situation by simply writing a variety of government offices that dealt with camp services. The opportunity presented a wonderful classroom for us and our children.

Our summer site was located in a glacier valley at about 8,000 feet altitude. Each year it would take awhile to acclimate to the altitude. But that did not mean that we could take it too easy. You see, there were no hookups of modern convenience at our site. This meant that we were responsible for getting all of our water, electric, and sewer needs. Our water was supplied by a nearby well that had a water pump which provided fresh glacier melt water. Our electricity was provided by a series of 12 volt batteries connected to a solar panel setup that I installed on the roof of our trailer. And, our sewer needs were met with periodic runs to a nearby Forest Service outhouse and a portable sewer dolly. Propane served our cooking and heating needs. All of these concerns required a good deal of maintainance time and had to be done. If you didn't follow through with daily chores, then you simply went without. No one was there to fill in the gaps for us. There was no telephone available to us so we couldn't phone in for a special delivery. While it appeared as somewhat primitive, things never really got desperate. Over the years the boys perceived these tasks as jobs that merely had to be done, and they were expected to participate. At first, working the hand pump at the well was fun; however, as the summer wore on, it became work and a task that might easily be replaced with fishing. The boys also saw at first hand the value of conservation of resources. The more water they used, the more work there was the following day. So, for instance, it was silly to leave the water running while you brushed your teeth. Lights were not needlessly left on. The heat was turned off as soon as it was no longer necessary. Other considerations were made too as a real live connection was made between the product being used and the process to obtain it. Sometimes our comfort zones were really challenged.

There was one year that was especially revealing to us as parents. That was the year that we perceived the boys were gaining a personal understanding of the value of self reliance. Our oldest son Ben was 10 and Nathaniel was 7 years old. They had already spent many years in the area. Nathaniel had spent all of his summers in the forest. The boys had just completed listening to the rather long and detailed story, *The Swiss Family Robinson* . It had taken about four consecutive nights, and their attention was glued to the story. Now, parents need to consider that there is a lot of killing of things in the story, so we were a bit concerned that the boys might find it to be repulsive. On the other hand, the killing was done mainly for survival. Yet we did point out to them that some of the animal killing seemed to be glorified, which they agreed was unnecessary. A couple of days following the conclusion of the story, the boys were engaged in making lists, drawing maps and collecting equipment, in earnest'. We didn't find this to be too unusual as they were always creating adventures for themselves. However, this adventure was going to be different, as we soon found out. They presented us with their "plan," which was to go on an overnight backpack trek up the mountain to the next campground area. They intended to do this trek alone. They were prepared to hike up there and spend the night alone at about 10 thousand feet altitude! Funny enough, they thought this was perfectly normal and no big deal. Of course, we, thinking of ourselves as responsible parents found this to be a bit much for two young children. It was a lot....

But then we began to think. Why were we spending the time with them in the forest in the first place? What did we really want them to learn? Weren't they saying that they were comfortable enough with the natural world and confident enough in themselves to hike up the mountain, set up camp, get their firewood, cook their meals, get their sleeping bags out and take care of each other? Wasn't this what we really wanted for them? Sure it was, we said to each other. We just thought it would be nice for them to do when they were 18. After talking it over with each other and with the boys, we concluded that it would be all right to take the adventure. We considered that the conditions were safe. There was a Forest Service Ranger and another campground host staying in a nearby camp area, should any problems arise. The boys agreed on the conditions we set down and gave each other the high five slap of approval when we finally agreed on a plan. After making an extensive list of gear and camp needs, they proceeded to pack and plan activities. They considered the things they would take much in the same way that we would. Actually, it was much in the same way that we did every time we packed the trailer or daypacks for hikes. A food list was generated giving consideration to cooking skills and limitations.

On the day of departure the boys stated that they wanted to get an early start. We agreed.

The distance of the hike was about 6 miles and the altitude change was about 1,000 feet. The trail was one that we family. The trail wrapped its way through a wide canyon of aspen trees and beautiful, colorful meadows. The weather was perfect. It was a crisp, sunny and dry morning. The weather report we got was that it would remain that way for the next few days.

It was difficult to watch them hike off together. They turned a few times waving and shouting for us not to worry. It was difficult to watch them and wonder if we had covered everything with them. It would be even more difficult as the daylight turned to dark. The often heard, "take a hike," was taking on a whole new meaning.

It gets really dark in the mountains at night. With no city lights to create an overglow, the sky comes alive with a sea of stars. But it is still pretty dark in the forest. We thought about how dark it was for the boys. They had a variety of tasks which had to be completed before they went to sleep that night On entering camp, they had to collect fire wood, get the water they would need from a nearby water pump, set their tent in order, cook their meal, and clean up after dinner. The following morning they would have a similar set of tasks. Of course, we knew that they would also spend some time fishing and exploring around the area. While we knew we had to trust all of the years of our work with them it was extremely hard not to get in the car and drive up to check in on them. We stayed up late that night; real late. We wondered how things were going with them and we plotted simple plans of how we might go up and check on them. All of these plans were followed by the fact that they would never know that we were there. You know, the way parents slip into their children's bedroom at night to check on them? The pulling up of their covers and firming the pillow or blanket around them seem to be an act of correct parenting. And not waking the child is a sign of an expert status at the task. But either mental exhaustion or common sense prohibited us from checking on them. While at the time it was difficult I am sure glad we refrained. What we all learned might have been lost had we gone up to the camp.

The following day we had arranged to drive up in the afternoon to meet them at their camp We were met by two proud, confident, and eager looking young campers.While they were glad to see us they weren't exactly desperate to see us. They were enjoying themselves and had just returned from a fishing trip to a nearby glacier lake about 500 yards away from camp. They told us all about their hike up the previous day and how they got a bit lost on the trail but waited for a horsepack trip that they knew was coming through to the same area as they were heading. Pulling in behind the pack horses they finished the hike in good time and considered their problem solving process to be pretty clever. They had prepared and eaten all their meals without any difficulty and had spent a good deal of the night playing card games and telling stories in the tent.

What they had an opportunity to learn from the trek and from us not going up there was an increase in self reliance. They could test and rely on their own skills and not those of adults. The concept of cooperative learning would have an opportunity to manifest its value rather than just be an idea that adults had for kids. The trek provided for a situation whereby two brothers would have a positive and memorable experience with nature. These sorts of learning opportunities do not exist in most schools. Instead, hours of doing rather mundane tasks and sitting in seats lined up in rows, or some other sort of formation provide for a rather pathetic means for teaching lifelong learning skills. Schools tend to spend a lot of time and energy working on the academically *effective* skills—and *affective* concerns are all too often left by the wayside. We believe that experiences such as this trek and other similar projects do more for their self-esteem than any grade or reward in school has done. Among the challenge and work I believe they also continued to find a personal value and appreciation of the beauty and awe of the natural world.

What we learned as parents was in many ways similar to what the boys were learning. "Parental self reliance" might describe the learned lesson. Do we advise this sort of experience for all kids or parents? Well, first consider that I mentioned we had spent a good deal of time in the forest area with the boys learning together and working in self-reliance situations. We see this as a key to a positive experience. However, not all kids are up to this sort of thing, just as all parents aren't up to it. Maybe there are other "experience paths" you could explore with your child. You could build up to the solo trek level with preliminary hikes. The point here is to investigate the opportunities for building self-reliance skills and then listen to what your child indicates that they are ready for. Consider too that we did not approve of this trek without taking the following points into consideration:

a. the boys had spent many years in the area;

b. they were both familar with the terrain, the trail and the destination point;

c. we talked through "what if" senarios with them, checking them for clarity of their understandings of the situation;

d. they knew that there were reliable adults in their camp area if they encountered a problem;

e. they had watched their parents model problem-solving and self-reliance techniques in the forest over the years;

f. they were willing and able to list, prepare, and pack the equipment that they would need.

Of course, sensible and appropriate judgement may find you overruling your child's plans at times. A child may not be old enough or experienced for what they are wanting to do. However, there is also the case of a parent being overheard telling the child not to go near the water until they knew how to swim. As silly as it sounds, we all too often may find ourselves making similar remarks. Yet experience in decision-making and in being responsible makes for an experienced and responsible decision maker, whether it's a child or an adult. It's difficult to consider what is responsible parenting given the fears one may have of things that might happen or go wrong. Thanks to projections and oversensationalism by the media, many parents have been trained in the fear of things which might go wrong. Many parents have unfortunately received their parental training through the eyes of a television program. As parents, many of us spend a good deal of time wondering if we have done everything correctly. Through the "Monday morning quarterback" process, we could probably find a number of ways to have done some parenting task differently. Some parents work at presenting their children with nothing but successful options and thereby hoping to avoid any chance of failure and maybe even challenge. Some wonder if their kids know everything they will need to know. We wonder if they will act in a responsible fashion and make appropriate decisions. However, sometimes it may simply be best to trust your work and rely less on fears. Fear is the greatest obstacle to learning whether you're a child or an adult.

CONCENTRATION
by Chris Mercogliano

Here follow four articles by Chris Mercogliano, chapters taken from his forthcoming book tentatively entitled Making It Up As We Go Along—The History of Albany's Free School. *For over two decades Chris has been a teacher, administrator, parent, plumber, environmental activist and softball afficionado at The Free School in Albany, New York.*

Take three adults and twenty-three city, inner-city, and suburban kids of all shapes, sizes and colors to 250 mountain-top acres about twenty-five miles northeast of Albany, N.Y. Drill 9/16" diameter holes in the south sides of some healthy sugar maple trees. Tap in the spiles and hang lidded buckets from the hooks. Thank the trees. Gasp when you see the first droplets of sap spurt forth from a spile. Pray for the right cy-cling of freeze and thaw, freeze and thaw to keep the sap drip-dripdripping into the pails. Empty them when they're full. Haul the heavy sap in five-gallon plastic buckets to the storage barrels near the evaporator and pour in the precious tree-blood. Repeat all but steps one, two and three as necessary. Oh, and remem-ber to take a long guzzle of the ice-cold sweet crystalline liquid every time you empty the pails (to keep the doctor away).

When the fifty-five gallon drums are nearly full, scour the forest for fallen branches or standing dead trees. Drag them over to the arch. Saw them into lengths with two-person bow saws (a chain saw will ruin everything). Learn how to work to-gether and learn the difference between good wood and rotten wood which yields no heat when burned. Drag more branches over. Trip over the underbrush and scratch your face. Get your boot sucked off by the deep, wet snow. Delete a few expletives. Saw more wood... "I NEED MORE WOOD NOW! DO YOU WANT THE FIRE TO GO OUT? HURRY UP!!" ("But I'm cold, but I'm tired, but she/he's not doing anything, but I can't find my mittens, but... but...")

Take a break and start a snowball war. Play in the huge mud puddle next to the road. Salute the sun when it finally breaks free from the cold grey clouds (no New Age—or Old Age—adult inspired pseudo-rituals allowed, either; just a group of young children off by themselves spontaneously breaking into song when they suddenly find themselves wrapped in the sun's warm embrace). Eat large quantities of good food. Drink some more sweet sap.

Try to get a very big, very hot fire going with a lot of damp, soggy fuel. Discover that the dead lower branches of pine trees make fire medicine, and that birch bark is even better. Learn how to strike a kitchen match without burning yourself. Once the fire's really going, pour ten gallons of the sugar maple sap into a two foot by three foot pan (the evaporator) which rests a bit precariously over the fire on two rows of cinderblocks (the arch). Endlessly debate whether a watched pot ever boils. Come back and sit by the fire and feed it twigs whenever you get too cold (the fire remains at the center of the dance throughout). Watch the patterns in the billowing steam and get smoke in your eyes. Stick a stick into the murky, bubbling mess and then taste it. Ask if it's syrup yet a few dozen times throughout the day and night. Discover that it does indeed take forty gallons of sap to make just one gallon of syrup.

Watch the sun set and the first star appear. Let the darkness gradually creep up to you. When it starts to turn cold again, try to remember where you left your coat and hat. If your feet are wet, go inside and put on dry socks, and if your boots are wet on the inside put plastic bags on your feet before you put your boots back on. Come back outside and discover that dry cattail heads make excellent torches if you have enough imagination. Watch the swarm of excited fireflies darting around the fire in the winter/spring moonlight. Oh yes, and don't forget the moon — get out a good telescope and study her up real close for the first time. And search for Jupiter or Saturn, too. Wonder about the stars and the planets and the universe. Ask all the questions, even the why ones that have no answers. Wonder some more.

Get very tired — the good kind of tired. ("It's still not syrup yet?") Go back inside the old lodge and make up a warm bed as near to the woodstove as you can. If you find that you're missing your mommy or your daddy, notice how that feels in your body, and where. (Is there anyone in the room who can give you the right kind of comfort when you're this vulnerable?) Let someone read you a really good Grimm's fairy tale before you fall into a deep, dreamful sleep.

Wake up in the morning and finish off enough syrup for a victory pancake breakfast on the kitchen stove. Celebrate! WE

DID IT!! That thickened, amber concentrate is its own sweet reward for a long hard day's work and play, with its measure of physical or psychic discomfort. Have another pancake or just keep sticking your finger in the syrup pot and licking it until your teeth begin to ring. Celebrate some more!

*　*　*　*　*

And so ends only a sketchy recipe for education—Free School style. The maple syrup metaphor is a useful one, and I will expand on it later with some stories from our recent adventure at Rainbow Camp, as we call it. But first I want to play with the notion of concentrate, or concentration, which I tentatively chose as the title of this article. I'm not thinking, here, about an intense mental act or the old TV quiz show where you had to remember the location of the other half of the match in order to win the prize. I am thinking about the process of getting to the essence of something, or of getting the most out of whatever you have to work with, to put it another way. It seems to me that there is an ever-increasing gap in our modern world between one's experience and its meaning. This is certainly not a new idea, and I'm not setting out to write about theology; but as the world's children today face an ever increasing level of distraction—increasing in both number and in intensity (to the point of so-called "virtual reality"), I fear that their ability to distinguish between what's important and what's unimportant is ever diminishing. In my mind, this brings us out of the domains of theology or philosophy and into that of education, purely defined, as a process whereby one discovers how to burn off or skim off the dross in order to get to the precious metal underneath; or, to return to my original metaphor, how to boil down one's experience until what's left in one's pockets is essential and meaningful. I was immediately attracted to the label of Essential Schools, but never having visited one, have remained suspicious that it's actually a lot of clever packaging; which, on an institutional level, is so often what happens to good ideas in our society.

This issue of labeling and packaging is particularly fresh for me because for the past several years Albany has been in the process of "magnetizing" its schools, as many other cities have been doing, to avoid forced busing of kids to achieve racial integration.

Just this year, a "Montessori Magnet" was opened four blocks from the Free School. Several million dollars was spent to retrofit this school for about 250 kids, and the other night they had an open house. The next morning, the mother of one of my pre-schoolers, who had attended the open house, came up to me all wide-eyed and said something like, "It was so beautiful and everything was so new and they had so much wonderful equipment. Can't you... can't we?..." Now, I have nothing against Maria Montessori (and I love magnets!); I'm all for kids having access to beautiful things and new equipment; and like John Gatto, I certainly advocate the proliferation of alternatives of every possible kind.

But, I can't seem to dodge the question of what message are we giving ourselves when we expend such huge quantities of material resources for the purpose of schooling young children? Isn't it that basic education is somehow a complex, technological—and expensive—problem? And how much money is being squandered for the dual purposes of public relations and image management? I hope I don't sound jealous or like some well-preserved Luddite; it's just that I'm beginning to understand better why we sometimes have to work so hard at reassuring our Free School parents that our school is indeed a place where their children will learn exactly what they need to be learning at their particular stage of development. But alas, I'm afraid that this, too, is properly the subject of another article.

Our 125 year-old building in Albany is filled with second-hand everything, and more than one friend of ours with regional or even national notoriety has complained to us about our keeping too low a profile. And we don't have any slick labels for our frequent two to five day forays out to our third-hand Rainbow Camp. (We purchased the camp, which is on a small lake, for a very good price because it needed a lot of work; and then, a year later, we were given 250 wooded acres just two miles away. Isn't it amazing how these things happen?) They're not "field trips," or "core curriculum experiences," or anything else that you might invent. We simply load up our fourth-hand Dodge stretch van (originally a state prison van... how's that for irony?) with teachers, kids, and gear and head out of the city, stopping at the grocery store on the way. I guess you could call it instant residential education (IRD)...

Our time at the camp is an integral part of our school program, where I have witnessed personal revolutions occurring in countless children over the years. By now I am quite certain that the secret ingredient is the fact that all of us, adults included, suddenly find ourselves displaced from our familiar (root word family) patterns. There are very few props, either. We heat with wood, and there is no running water in the winter-time. All quickly learn the basic law of water conservation: *If it's yellow let it mellow, if it's brown flush it down.* Water for flushing comes from one of the brooks that feeds the lake, just a short haul away. It's very much like rural farm life. We live like a sprawling extended family, with even the youngest sharing the cooking, cleaning, and firewood and water gathering chores, and the oldest oftentimes reading bedtime stories to the younger kids. It can be a lot of hard work, especially during sugaring season.

There's really no formula for what we're doing because life at the camp is governed by the needs of the moment. Two concepts coined by radical psychotherapist Wilhelm Reich way back in the 1930's and 1940's at least partially describe what we're up to: "self-regulation" and "work democracy." Much of Reich's thinking and practice were aimed at *preventing* mental illness, which he broadly termed character neurosis. His life goal was to create a model of healthy human functioning, as opposed to some systematized analysis of disease states, as is the norm to this day. Having decided on an in-depth look at child development, Reich took his concern with child rearing practices and education to a lecture by A.S. Neill. The subsequent meeting of the two led to a life-long friendship, self-regulation being the cornerstone of Neill's approach at Summerhill. The idea is that if kids can learn at a very early age how to manage their own rhythms, how to make responsible choices (by learning from the consequences of their mistakes), and how to meet their own needs, then they will grow up into autonomous adults capable of authoring satisfying and meaningful lives. Reich was absolutely delighted to discover a school that actually lived by this principle.

A bone that I have to pick with Neill on this subject has to do with his attitude towards work. In *Summerhill: A Radical Approach To Child Rearing*, Neill wrote that if you ever saw a child working, then you were looking at a kid who had in some way been brainwashed by an adult. According to old Neill, work is a four-letter word for healthy, free children. Not that I entirely disagree with him, but my twenty-one years of experience at The Free School have taught me something a little different. Neill was a rebel at heart, and Summerhill has always been populated largely by rebellious middle and upper-middle class

children; and I think that these factors may have colored his conclusions on this score. On many, many occasions over the years, I have observed kids working, both by choice and with great gusto and pleasure. Several factors are necessary to make this so: The work has to have inherent meaning to the kids *on their level*.. Also, they have to be continually free to change the way and the pace at which they go about the job, whatever it may be. Free children certainly hate just about anything when it becomes routine. Sometimes, I have to bite my tongue when I'm tempted to suggest a better, faster, more efficient way to get the job done; and if I do intrude, invariably their enthusiasm disperses as fast as the air out of an untied balloon. Finally, the fruits of their labors need to follow directly from the completion of the task. It's evident how the maple sugaring fits in here: The kids will each take home a small jar of syrup to share with their families, and then will help marketing the rest to raise cash towards the taxes on the new land (kids love making money, even when the money goes to the school and not directly into their own coffers).

Reich coined the term "work democracy" early in his career after attempting to effect mass social change in Europe through the political systems of several different countries. He eventually became disillusioned, concluding that power politics under any banner, no matter how enlightened or "socially democratic," always stands in the way of real solutions to social problems. Work democracy, on the other hand, is the notion that when groups of people organize themselves around common tasks and goals, then natural forms of authority and decision-making which support mutual accomplishment can emerge. Modes of being and of action remain fluid and changeable. This is because they are non-ideological, which is a critical factor since even the best of ideas turns toxic when it is practiced in a rigid, fundamentalistic fashion. In a true work democracy, cooperation rather than competition becomes a core value. I would argue here that M. Scott Peck's more recent model of community is essentially a reworked version of Reich's original concept. (Reich's body of work later became a foundation stone of the new school of the psychology of groups and group dynamics that emerged in the fifties and early sixties, which was Peck's area of early training.)

At Rainbow Camp, life is not always "democratic." Often the situation demands of kids and grown-ups alike that they do something that they would just as soon not do right then.

Sometimes I just put kids to work; we don't have a meeting; we don't take a vote; I just say, "Please do it." On his first Rainbow Camp expedition, when eleven-year-old Rakeem *[not his real name]*, a recent inner-city parochial school cast-off, helplessly decided that he couldn't stuff his borrowed sleeping bag into its generously large sack, I very undemocratically decided to intervene. Rakeem's strategy was to try to force the unstuffed bag back on the much smaller boy that he had borrowed it from.

That boy could have, and in fact probably would have, called a democratic "council meeting," which is our school's preferred tool for conflict resolution, policy making and changing, etc. I happened to have an instinct that this was just the moment for me to put Rakeem, who has a smothering mother and no father, in a bind instead. I simply told him that neither he nor anybody else would get their breakfast until they had all their gear packed up and in order; and even though the bag was borrowed, it was certainly his to deal with. Predictably, Rakeem, who is overweight and a very angry man-child, stomped off upstairs to curse and sulk.

Breakfast time drew near, and as there was still no sign of our boy, I announced to all the other kids that I was ready to bet cash that Rakeem was about to miss a meal. Immediately Isaac, another cast-off from the same parochial school, held out his hand and said, "Dollar bet!" We shook on it and then went about our business. About five minutes went by and there was still no sign of our boy, so I told Isaac that he'd better get his money together because breakfast was just about ready. Instantly, several other older kids went dashing off to find Rakeem to tell him what was going on downstairs. Rakeem appeared within a minute, stuffed the bag and returned it to its owner within another, and a few seconds after that, Isaac had his crisp new dollar, much to everyone's delight!

Interestingly, it was Isaac who had called a council meeting on Rakeem just the night before because Rakeem had bullied him out of one of the camp's cozy armchairs by the woodstove. At that meeting, Isaac got a motion passed that Rakeem, who only sullenly stonewalled when asked by the other kids what was up, would have to sit in the very chair he had taken from Isaac (all night, if necessary) until he was willing to call another meeting to work out the problem. (He eventually did.) So, as I paid off my lost bet, I made sure to point out to Rakeem what a true friend he had in Isaac—on two counts now—one for caring enough to stop him when he was being a bully, and two for believing in his ability to get off it and take care of himself. All of us value friendship very highly at the Free School, and many life-long friendships are forged here.

I tell this story for several reasons. First, though he isn't around any more to check with, I think Reich would cite this an example of work democracy in action. It's important that we all learn to practice self-sufficiency at Rainbow Camp, and that we all pull together as well. I think that this was a most appropriate time for me to exercise my natural authority as an adult and as a parent figure with a kid who gets far too little effective parenting at home. Next there's the fact that at the Free School we try not to adhere rigidly to any ideological precepts, democracy or otherwise. We certain give democratic decision making its due; but above all, we just try to do what works. Every child is different, every situation is different, and we simply don't find that "democracy" is always the answer.

Finally, to return to the maple syrup metaphor, we believe that the process of change always requires some heat. In the case of Rakeem's mini-breakthrough, Isaac and the other kids provided plenty of heat at the council meeting and then I started a little one-on-one fire with him the next morning. Rakeem returned home later that day not quite the same child. While we were driving back to Albany, I asked him whether he wanted to come back out to the camp again. His face lit up with a smile in response and he said, "Yeah; only I wish that we didn't have to work so hard!" Life at Rainbow Camp as well as at our day-school in the city involves fairly frequent conflict which then gets handled, sometimes unpredictably, and always in a myriad number of ways, some of which are "democratic" and some not. The school motto that I coined many years ago is, "Never a dull moment, always a dull roar!"

Several stories remain to be told that further depict the education that takes place at Rainbow Camp... It was Alexandra, a nine-year old who set fire to her bedroom three years ago, that turned up as one of my frequent helpers while I tended the fire in the arch. I remembered that for some time after that near disaster she was absolutely terrified of fire; understandably so. At one point, when the two of us were alone, I found just the right opening for talking through her fire setting experience with her. Her memory of the event was dimming and it seemed to me that some denial was creeping in; and so I think it was important for her to go gently back over that traumatic past event and explore its teachings. It was a very relaxed talk, and all the while she was steadily pushing back the edge of her fear of fire by tending and feeding the one that was boiling off our syrup and warming us against the chilly evening. It seems unlikely to me that that "lesson" would have arisen out of any planned discussion about the dangers of fire, or even by chance back at school in Albany. And no expensive props were needed (there I go again).

Then there is Anton, a six-year-old boy who a year ago was taken away from and then returned to his mother by the Department of Social Services; thanks, in part, to our intervention on their behalf. He was the last one to go in one night while I was pushing to finish boiling off a batch of sap. Anton quietly sat for hours just poking the fire with one stick after another while I sat talking about everything under the moon with Mark, a recent college graduate who has been volunteering three days a week in the school, and who had decided to come out to the camp and really get his feet wet. What was Anton, fatherless like Rakeem, learning while he sat there listening to our impromptu rap session? There simply were two men talking, talking by turns intently and then laughing in low tones—nothing more—and yet there was nowhere else that Anton wanted to be at that time.

Joseph Chilton Pearce says that all children actually learn via a basic modeling process, as opposed to all the other pseudo-scientific and technical, jargon-laden constructs that humans have come up with to describe how learning takes place. I would hazard a guess that Mark and I were showing Anton, among other things, how two men go about getting to know each other a little more intimately.

At the Free School, we place much emphasis on all forms of relationships. The late George Dennison, author of the classic, *The Lives of Children*, which is about his experiences in a wonderful, but short-lived, school on the Lower East Side of New York back in the late sixties, wrote the most eloquent descriptions of the primacy of human relationships in the "educational process" that I have ever seen in print. In the book, George told story after beautiful story to reinforce his belief that all true learning takes place within relationships. Period. So, Free School adults and children alike spend a good deal of time working on and working out relationships, and the ensuing learning is literally the heart of our "curriculum."

When Mark, the aforementioned volunteer, showed up two months ago with absolutely no teaching experience whatsoever, we told him that the water was warm and to go right ahead and jump in if that was what he wanted. He chose to do just that, and he has been nothing but a great blessing to us ever since. Mark is both open-hearted and open-minded, and he is entirely and refreshingly available to "relate" on a variety of levels. The kids both love and respect him. Any day now, I guess I should make up an official-looking badge with the word "TEACHER" printed on it and pin it on his shirt!

The last story to tell here has to do with a story that I decided to read as a bedtime one to the kids one night at the camp when I wasn't running the evaporator until all hours. It was Grimm's, "The Water of Life," a powerful tale about a young prince, the youngest of three sons, whose father was slowly wasting away from some mysterious ailment. As the three young men were walking about grieving one day, an old man met them and told them where the cure for their father, the king, could be found. Known as The Water of Life, it could only be attained after a long journey. The oldest son first won permission to go in search of the cure; and soon after setting out, came across a dwarf waiting beside the road.

When the dwarf asked where he was headed, the prince only sneered at the dwarf, and so the insulted and enraged dwarf placed a very effective curse on him. Ditto the second son, and when he failed to return, the youngest prince begged his dying and reluctant father for permission to go. When he encountered the very same dwarf, unlike his older brothers, he stopped, told the dwarf the whole story, and asked for his help. The dwarf responded by telling the young prince to travel to a certain enchanted castle where the Water of Life could be found, and then giving him exactly the tools he would need to survive the trials to come. Once there, the prince met a beautiful princess who promised him the kingdom if he would free her from a spell she was under and come back in a year to marry her. Then, she told him where to find the well containing the Water, and he filled a cup with it and headed home.

Passing the dwarf along the way, the prince stopped to thank him and to ask if he happened to know where his two brothers were. The dwarf told him about the curse; the prince begged for and received their release; but not before the dwarf warned the young man about his older brothers' bad hearts. Soon enough, the brothers did betray him, each to the point of going after the spellbound princess, who, anxious for the return of her prince, had ordered a road leading to the palace to be built of shining gold. Next, she had instructed her courtiers to admit only the man who rode straight up the middle of the road to her gate, as that would be her true lover.

When the oldest brother saw the golden road, he stopped to admire it and decided that it would be a shame to ride upon it; so he rode to the right of it instead, and was turned away by the castle guards. Ditto the second brother who decided to ride to the left and was also turned away. Meanwhile, the young prince, having now survived a whole year in bitter exile, decided to seek out the princess and was so intent on joining with her beauty that he never even saw the golden road! Therefore, he rode right down the middle, married the princess, and was even reunited with his father who had eventually learned of his older sons' deceit.

This story is a deep one containing many interior meanings, as do all the juicy fairy tales I read or tell to kids whenever I get the chance (Rainbow Camp is ideal for this). For me, "The Water of Life" beautifully brings home the themes of this article—and in a properly mythical fashion: The young prince, despite great hardships and betrayals (and also because of them), is *concentrated*. The heat generated by his troubles and his great yearnings are a very necessary element in his growth. In the end, he is so focused on his love and undistracted by unimportant material details that he reaches his goal—not without help, of course—which he receives because he is open to relationship and is willing to ask.

At the Free School, we believe that the task contains its own reward, and our kids practice open-heartedness, persistence and resourcefulness every day because they are truly responsible for themselves and for each other. We also try never to ignore the mythological dimension of life and of learning. Properly lived, life can be an infinitely magical series of events, if one still believes, and the essential need not be lost sight of. Certainly, nothing is more magical in the everyday world than the process of slowly transforming the water of life of the sugar maple tree into thick, sweet amber liquid-gold.

METAPHORS WITHIN METAPHORS
by Chris Mercogliano

I

Once,
In 1974
my shrink
told me I was
too metaphorical.
Why didn't he tell me
to write poetry instead?

I'm gradually finding some peace in the conclusion that life is just plain metaphorical—or at least mine undoubtedly is. These days, a "New Age" paradigm known as *The Gaia Hypothesis* views the entire planet Earth as a living metaphor of sorts; which leads to my idea that each of us is then free to create, more or less, our own life-metaphors within that grand context, limited ultimately by our own imagination. Of course, practically speaking, we are all shaped by myriad influences such as inherited traits, parental and societal molding, and the political and demographic realities which have a great deal to do with which roads are taken and which are not, to borrow Robert Frost's metaphor from his famous poem. And so, what real value can what we call education (from the Latin word *educare*, meaning to lead out) have if it is anything less than a process whereby we each arrive at the fullest expression of ourselves for the limited time that we have on this good earth?

An episode from Rod Serling's insightful and often chilling classic television series, The Twilight Zone, suddenly comes to mind. The setting was an apparent museum filled with a large number of extremely life-like dioramas featuring people engaged in all sorts of endeavors: astronauts in space, old men fly fishing on perfect mountain streams, elegant dinner parties, families at the beach, and so on. As I remember, a couple of older gentlemen had taken this particular week's "wrong turn through the twilight zone," and found themselves in the very unusual museum where they eventually met up with a mysterious old curator; who after showing them around, asked each of them their ideal fantasy of what they wanted "life" to be like after they died. I forget exactly how it went—I was about seven when I saw the show—but one guy decided he wanted to spend eternity exploring space and the other fishing or something like that. As the curtain falls, the viewers learn that there are now two brand new exhibits in the big museum, each with a single old man happily indulging in his dream pursuit!

Life as Metaphor:

It appears more and more to me as I get older that life before death is a lot like Serling's macabre museum, without the still-popular eerie music which introduced each episode. Don't our lives end up following the scripts that we—with plenty of help from our friends—have written for ourselves? While the never-ending debates over human dilemma/questions like "nature vs. nurture" and "free will vs. determinism" rage on, I have decided to throw in my lot with the Haudenosaunee (Iroquois or Six Nations) people of upstate New York, who have managed to hang onto small corners of their ancestral lands and thereby preserve a majority of their cultural traditions. They simply choose to refer to the idea of God, or Creator, or the Universe as, "The Great Mystery," and leave it at that. It saves a lot of arguing, without suppressing any of the wondering, which is why I like the notion so much. Besides, it has worked very well for them for over thirty thousand years; so it seems to me there must be something to it. Joseph Campbell, the late mythologist who nearly spent his entire life studying and unraveling the underlying meanings and commonalties of the mythologies of a great many of the world's cultures, once said, "God is a metaphor for a mystery that absolutely transcends all human categories of thought." On another occasion he defined mythology as "an organization of symbolic images and narratives metaphorical of the possibilities and fulfillment in a given culture in a given time. Mythology is a metaphor. God, angels, purgatory—these are metaphors."

Giving Children the Space to Invent their own Metaphors:

The intent at The Free School is to allow each child ample time and space to invent, tear down, and experiment with metaphors of their own making. Often this can be quite trying to the surrounding adults who are "holding the container" for them, to borrow a recently coined phrase from Michael Meade, a brilliant modern storyteller/philosopher and spokesman for the current "men's movement." My wishes regarding students' plans of action (or lack thereof) and their own ideas don't always intersect all that well. It's a dance every day. In the end, I would say I practice non-interference more often than not, falling back during troubling moments on my ultimate faith that kids generally know themselves and their true needs better than I do. After a child has been in our school long enough for me to get to know him or her pretty well, I try to begin practicing a "technique" I once learned from nationally-known Oneida Nation author and teacher Paula Underwood Spencer. She calls it "new eyes," which simply means that every day teachers should try to look at their students as though seeing them for the first time.

It can be so tempting and so easy to stereotype kids and put them into categories which govern how we relate to them, with the real trouble beginning when they behave in such a way as to feed us back our fantasies of them. The now classic and oft-referred to study where the performance records of the "smart" and the "dumb" incoming fourth grade classes of a public school get switched without the two teachers knowing is relevant here. After a month or so into the new year, someone tested the two groups and presto-chango, dumb kids were suddenly smart and smart kids suddenly dumb! Practicing "new eyes" is not nearly so easy as it sounds. But if one begins to look at life as essentially metaphorical and education as the fulfillment of possibilities, one can readily see that the impact on children, when adults fixate and stifle them with pre-determined notions about who they are, goes far deeper than the scores on standardized achievement tests. This sobering realization always reminds me to exercise my "new eyes" as often as possible.

How Does a "Real School" Look?:
It is not uncommon for a new visitor at our school to look a bit bewildered. Though certain of the right props are in place: some well-worn desks scrounged long ago from a closing public school, real chalkboards (a recent donation), a long wall of textbooks (all public school cast-offs), a hybrid collection of mostly donated personal computers, etc., etc., the confused guest's unexpressed question in its simplest terms is usually something like, "Is this a real school?" Now this is a very good question, which leads me to ponder, "What is a real school?" Hmmm... I think we're back to metaphors again. In ancient Greece where people still co-existed with their deities, "school"—or in Greek, "σκολη"(skole)—was a locus for the life-long practice and at-

tainment of human perfection, where body and spirit received every bit as much attention as the mind. (At least this was more likely to be the case in classical Athens, as opposed to the rival and militaristic city-state of Sparta, which had a much different agenda.)

"School," then, as it is here today, has essentially been a microcosm of the prevailing cosmology; or, if you will, a metaphor. In pre-Columbian America, life was school and school was life. The transmission of knowledge and tradition was woven directly into the fabric of the culture, where the belief in the oneness of creation was an everyday, living reality. These are oversimplified, romantic notions, to be sure; but then, that's one of the attractions for me of working in metaphor. Today's homeschooling families, it seems to me, are in many ways living out an updated version of the early European-American ethic of well-educated independence and self-reliance. (Prior to the advent of compulsory schooling in Massachusetts, the literacy rate there was 95%, a figure that dropped measurably once kids were forced into classrooms.) Recently at a national alternative education conference, I met a mother now teaching her three children at home who summed up this viewpoint very succinctly: "The schools were trying to take my kids over; but they're MY kids, NOT the school's."

School as Factory:

Recent critics of American compulsory education like John Taylor Gatto have been feverishly exposing the roots of that institution's "family tree." There isn't much Romanticism to be found in the writings of the founders of our modern system of public education, who were most up front about the premises of their design. Urgently needed, they wrote, was an institution for feeding the hungry fires of the burgeoning Industrial Revolution and for rapidly Americanizing the masses of immigrants who would provide the fuel. Today, Gatto calls it "government-monopoly, factory education," and with good reason. Way back in the sixties, Marxist and "New Left" critics were decrying the now unspoken economic motives of our schools. According to this radical view, schools are training centers whose only purpose is to prepare children "for the workforce," where students are taught to be on time, to start and stop at the sound of a bell, to work on tasks that often have no inherent meaning—with the motivation coming in the form of a carrot of some kind attached to the end of a long stick—and to accept being stratified into different status groups. In other words, the metaphor is one of a factory within a factory.

The Need for a New Model or Metaphor:
Now, among others, post-modern educational thinkers like social philosopher Ivan Illich and Dan Greenberg, founder of the Sudbury Valley School in eastern Massachusetts, which is rapidly becoming a model for a number of other genuinely democratic schools around the nation, are suggesting that the factory model is already an anachronism and that a new post-industrial metaphor taking into account developments like the "communications revolution" and the "global economy" is being called for. Neither man can quite spell out how to get there from here; but both have compelling arguments for this being where we need to go. Actually, Greenberg would claim that his school, where a child's individual will and imagination are fully recognized, is already a working example of an educational environment based on human creativity that a post-industrial world will need in order to flourish.

When I take a step back from our school, one image I see is that of a complex molecule with a lot of free radicals (pun intended) dancing around a very active nucleus. This molecule is always in motion, and there is a great deal of exchange between it and its surroundings, because the outer membrane is quite permeable. To spell out this metaphor of mine, the molecule is the Free School in its entirety; the free radicals are the children, of course; and the nucleus is comprised of the various teachers—full-time, part-time, or volunteer. In our school, as is the case with Greenberg's Sudbury Valley, the teachers usually wait for the students to come to them for ideas, assistance and resources rather than the reverse, which is generally the pattern of most conventional schools where adults structure the content, rhythm, rules, etc., etc. We find that our recent public school transfers are often at a loss for a time; but then their self-motivation begins to grow by leaps and bounds as they watch "veteran" students joyfully propelling themselves through each school day, guided by their own moods, interests and initiative.

How Teachers Can *Really* Teach:
Meanwhile, an observer would be likely to find teachers who have not been sought out for one reason or another engaged in their own favorite activities, undertaken for their own satisfaction. When not busy teaching, weavers weave, artists sketch,

writers write, clothing-designers sew, wood-workers saw and hammer, potters pot; and then kids who are drawn to that particular endeavor gather round to watch, and often, to join in and learn. It's much more like the pre-industrial village model, where children learned by being directly involved with the adult life of the community. The prolonged adolescence currently in vogue in our country is a twentieth century, "first world" invention, and something we work very hard at undoing. During a given week, one will find any number of talented volunteers in our school "sharing their thing" with interested children. We also have a very active apprenticeship program which places kids out in the city to work closely with adults who are practicing a skill or a trade that they want to investigate for themselves, and we generally find that professionals who are finding true satisfaction in their work are more than happy to oblige.

> *Again and again we are taught by our students that finding their bliss can have far-reaching effects.*

In addition to metaphor and mythology, Joseph Campbell spoke of the necessity of "following your bliss," unless you wanted to wake up one day late in life and sadly discover that "your ladder had been up against the wrong wall" all that time. Free School teachers try to resist the ever-present urge to race children through a series of academic hoops so that they can feel like successful teachers and at the same time quiet parents' fears that their kids aren't learning enough of the things they should be learning. We recognize the simple truth that no one else can find your bliss for you, and that this process of self-discovery requires a supportive environment where there is both plenty of time and the relative absence of fear, which I will say more about in another place. Again and again we are taught by our students that finding their bliss can have far-reaching effects.

Kids Can Make Amazing Turn-arounds
Since our school has been a "school of last resort" for many children over the years, I have witnessed countless kids begin to make complete turn-arounds once they discovered that one thing they could throw themselves into with abandon. I can readily think of dozens of examples, but Arthur comes to mind as a particularly striking and recent one. He had come to us at the late age of eleven, having previously been thrown out of several

Albany public schools—his last stop being a special classroom where he was medicated with ritalin, a standard drug treatment for "hyperactive" children. My distaste for that label notwithstanding, I must say that Arthur was about as active a boy as I had ever encountered. He literally could not sit still, and his attention span—even when he was doing precisely what he wanted to be doing—was pitifully short. It was not hard to imagine why no previous classroom could contain him. As with all of the others who had preceded him, we gave Arthur the free run of the school; and like the others, his favorite sport, initially, was to generate excitement by trying to disrupt any and everything going on around him. And then he fell in love with Oscar and with drawing; I'm not sure which came first.

Oscar was a small, introverted boy who was already an accomplished artist, often spending the entire day doing nothing but creating powerful action heroes and dragons and castles on his well-worn sketch pad. At first, Arthur could spend about five or ten minutes drawing before he had to run around and let off some steam. Then, ten minutes stretched to twenty; and before long, he was sitting head to head with his "teacher" for an entire morning without getting up, sometimes choosing to work right through a most delicious, hot Free School lunch. The disruptions mostly stopped, and Arthur started showing interest in other activities, too. All was well until he formed an impossible and sometimes hostile alliance with another domineering and aggressive public school "reject" who had come to us the previous year. Adolescence was beginning to rear its sometimes ugly head and the two boys became increasingly disrespectful and sometimes downright abusive towards their female peers and teachers as well, rejecting all efforts to stop their unacceptable behavior. I was at my wit's end and finally convinced the other boy's mother to try him back in public school again before he regressed into the state he was in when he came to us. My hope was that Arthur would come off it if he were separated from his cohort. It was a nice try; but as it turned out, Arthur decided he wanted to follow his buddy to the same public school; and although I did not think he had been with us long enough to "complete the cure" (it had only been four months), he continued to escalate his awfulness until we were only too glad to help him on his way. Much to my amazement, Arthur went back into a regular classroom at his normal grade level—without drugs—and has been doing very well there ever since. He returns to visit us often.

I am quite certain that it was the development of his love for drawing and for his quiet teacher who was half-a-head shorter, that had enabled Arthur to return so successfully to the very place where his history of "failure" had begun. The carry-over from the drawing to other areas was nothing short of miraculous; though again, I have observed the same healing progression taking place countless times in our little school year in and year out. The knowledge that the public schools, in ninety-nine out of a hundred cases, take the chemical shortcut of administering body-, mind- and soul-deadening drugs to render children "manageable" absolutely sickens me. The human damage done is often permanent, and is, as Arthur so quickly taught us, utterly unnecessary.

Looking back, I wonder if *what* Arthur and Oscar were drawing didn't also have something to do with the remarkable and rapid transformation which had taken place. Perhaps working and reworking those same mythical scenes and action figures had the effect of creating some sort of inner repatterning; and perhaps they were inventing just the personal metaphors needed to fill in gaps left in their developing psyches by factors like absent fathers, dysfunctional families and a corrosive popular culture. Much has been said and written about the psychic damage now being done to our children by television and other post-modern media, and I find every bit of it to be all too true. Kids today are totally weighted down, frustrated and often corrupted by the violence, narcissism, and pornographic blend of sexuality and naked aggression that is often such a hefty part of their daily sensory diet at home. At the Free School, we continue to place great value on helping kids find as many alternatives as possible to the stinking garbage being served up by our hyperstimulated society.

Play-acting as a Metaphor:

Nowhere is the experimentation with metaphor more obvious than when children are play-acting and dressing up, and we have an entire room in the school devoted primarily to this purpose. There are two large trunks filled with costumes and accessories of every imaginable kind, including a set of exotic, lacy gowns donated to us by a bridal shop which was going out of business; and of course there is a large mirror on the wall for carefully studying "the look." Inevitably, the costuming inspires the co-creation of some drama or fantasy of one kind or another, and the variety is literally endless. The kids generally do this entirely on their own and often for hours at a time. Only occasionally does a finished product emerge; which then usually gets staged before the school's best guaranteed audience—the preschoolers—who love nothing more than a spontaneous live production and who are most uncritical!

Only occasionally, when the time and the kids feel just right, will I join in and work with a group of aspiring young actors on a more elaborate production. If I reach back quite a few years to a time when we were less confident in our unorthodox approach to education, I can recall a particularly wild bunch of seven-, eight- and nine-year-olds who were under my charge, several of whom were just coming off unhappy public school experiences. These kids seemed incapable of getting along with each other and mightily resisted my efforts to help ease them into the flow of the school. Finally, in near desperation, I decided to give up everything else I was trying to do and just read aloud to any of them who wanted to listen. I selected a juicy and exciting children's classic, George MacDonald's, *The Princess and Curdie*, a turn-of-the-century English romance full of intrigue and magical beings, and with both a girl and a boy protagonist about the group's age. When about half of them began wandering in and out of the room over the course of the first few chapters, I grew a bit doubtful of my choice of novels, which was written in a language and style quite foreign to the kids. My fears were quickly laid to rest when I realized that the student most tuned into the story was Franz, the boy who had been giving me—and everyone else—the hardest time. Somewhat "dyslexic," and still struggling with reading on a first grade level at age nine, Franz was hanging onto every word. His ability to understand the difficult syntax and to follow MacDonald's long descriptive passages was extraordinary, and his enthusiasm was quite contagious. Before long, all eight children were glued to their seats, insisting that I read to them for the entire morning!

As the story drew to a dramatic and happy ending, I was deluged with a chorus of pleas to let them act it out. Still a bit shell-shocked by this crew, I decided to play hard to get. I told them that the story was too complex, and besides, it was a novel and not a play. They responded by saying that I was all wrong and that they would create the dialogue and ask the art teacher to help them make props, scenery and costumes. Before I quite realized what was happening, they had organized themselves into a cast and I was appointed director and told please to write everything down. Here was a miracle in progress and it was my turn to get into the flow! A group of cantankerous kids who previously couldn't even cross the street together without battling for position had just sorted out their roles for the play—with some of them playing three or four parts—with hardly a single argument.

When things quieted down and I had a chance to reflect on just what was taking place, I began to notice that the children each had chosen precisely the right roles for themselves. For instance, Franz, who was not well-liked because of his constant teasing and bugging to get attention, was the unanimous choice to play the leading role of Curdie, who undergoes an important maturational transformation during the course of the tale. When work on the play began, Franz was still fighting learning to write his last name; and here the class was clamoring for an all-out adaptation of a very long and complicated story with Franz responsible for a majority of the lines, including numerous long speeches taken verbatim from the novel. Furthermore, the kids decided they wanted to invite parents, grandparents, friends and neighbors to a gala evening performance of their production, thereby increasing the pressure on themselves (and me) by at least a hundredfold. Franz, to whom the idea of reading or any kind of "schoolwork" had been anathema, went home and studied his lines every night. At one point he was having terrible trouble memorizing one particularly long and difficult speech, so I suggested that we rewrite it in his own words so that it would be easier to remember. He came in the next day able to recite the original word for word!

Then there was Alicia, another struggling new student who was always on the fringe and either choosing to be alone or to play with much younger children whom she could easily dominate. She was also a reluctant reader who generally came to school looking like an unmade bed. So, of course, she was selected to play the female lead, which was a complex dual role of an ancient and mystical grandmother-queen and the beautiful young princess who was the alter ego of the old queen. She demonstrated amazing inner flexibility and control as she alternated between the two parts; and she, too, was absolutely determined to overcome her reading "handicap" and learn every one of her numerous lines. Also, she began coming to school each day, much to the delight of her exasperated mother, I'm sure, with her hair beautifully brushed and parted.

Little Mark, passive, painfully shy and quiet as a churchmouse, elected to play the role of the evil Lord Chamberlain who

betrays Curdie at one point. Before long he was astounding everyone as he really hammed up his part and shouted out his lines to an imaginary back row. Bryn, a diminutive, blond-haired and blue-eyed "good little girl," typecast by the others as the young princess in the play, began to rebel and to assert her own wishes. She refused to sit back and watch the climactic final battle as MacDonald had written, and instead insisted on slashing away with her dagger right alongside the boy-warriors. She also didn't want to marry Curdie in the end, either, and so we changed that, too!

In the course of developing the play, all of the kids seemed to be going through with an inner process that was exactly right for them. They each had chosen precisely the metaphors which corresponded with where they sensed themselves to be in their lives at that time. It was quite uncanny, really. There is a branch of modern psychotherapy called Psychosynthesis which works with all of the various "sub-personalities" that each of us consists of. Therapeutic change is achieved by experiencing and acting out these interior characters out with conscious awareness so that the individual becomes more of an integrated team and can then live more harmoniously and get more of what he or she wants out of life.

As the kids readied their play for the stage, I could see each of them busily exploring any number of their "sub-personalities." Philip, a talented and creative boy who was prone to violent outbursts, chose to play both the roles of the wise king and the traitorous butler who is part of the plot to poison him. In the end, the king manages to harness his rage at being betrayed by those so close to him, and to drive the evil forces from the kingdom. James, on the other hand, who ordinarily kept his anger and aggression tightly under wraps, got into the role as the devious royal physician so much that the audience would hiss loudly every time he appeared on the stage—especially when he attempted to stab the king. Michael was a one-of-a-kind, odd-ball sort of kid. I suspect that he didn't like himself very much, and he reveled in acting weird to win attention. In the play, he cleverly improvised one of the strange, magical monster-creatures that help Curdie defeat the enemy. Creating that role, which he pulled off with aplomb, seemed to be his way of getting at his wounded self-image; and I loved the way in which he turned what might have been considered a weakness in his character into a real strength. Then there was big Tom, a physically powerful and athletic boy who often shied away from any non-physical challenge. He played Lina, Curdie's wolf-like guardian that becomes a centrally heroic figure as the story develops. Though it was a non-speaking role, Tom received one of the loudest ovations at the end. Finally, there was Tyrone, with a hot-tempered father and angry at living in the shadow of an idolized older brother, choosing to play the role of Peter, Curdie's kind and reasonable father. In the play, he arrives in the nick of time to rescue Curdie, having made an entrance so total that it practically carried him into the audience where his big brother sat watching proudly!

It was a magnificent performance, played to a standing-room-only crowd in a makeshift theater in the upstairs of our school. Ovation after ovation provided the kids with well-deserved acknowledgment for their months of dedicated work. It had not been easy, and they had challenged themselves in every imaginable respect. Though there was no shortage of ruffled feathers along the way, especially as the tension of performing before a live audience mounted, they absolutely amazed me with their willingness and ability to cooperate with one another. Reflecting back on it now, I can see what an invaluable experience this was for everyone, containing so much learning and healing on so many different levels.

A post-script to the story involves Franz. A few weeks after the performance he wrote a wonderful poem which he planned to read at an annual event held by the local social justice "community" called Readings Against the End of the World. Then, at the last minute, Franz began to get cold feet, fearing that he would be unable to read his beautiful work in front of a group of mostly strangers. I sat down with him and reminded him of his splendid accomplishments in *The Princess and Curdie*. Reassured by that memory, he reconsidered and went on to read his poem without a hitch!

Children's Poetry:
It goes without saying that poetry is another region where children can mine their own mother-lode of personal metaphors. We have found over the years at the Free School that children will spontaneously come out with the most amazing poems and short stories when writing isn't turned into a measured academic exercise. As was the case with *The Princess and Curdie*, the images that kids elect to write about tell us a great deal about where they are in their developmental process, and most important of all, in their own idiom. Especially when they aren't

forced to write; and when spelling and grammar take a far-back seat to mood, feeling and content, young writers work almost reflexively in metaphor because their identification with animals, colors, sounds, etc., is so natural and so complete. A couple of years ago a bunch of our kids entered a city-wide poetry contest sponsored by the public library. Although we had by far the fewest entrants because our school is so small, we ended up with the majority of the winners, the public and parochial schools being the main "competition." The results were extraordinary.

As I think Joseph Campbell would readily agree, children themselves are metaphors within metaphors, and their healthy growth demands a recognition of this vital dimension of human existence. At least part of the blame for the mayhem and destruction found among our youth today—especially our urban young people—should be laid at the door of our mechanistic, materialistic mass-culture, and particular at the thresholds of our schools which so effectively hammer home its values. Part of the solution, I now know, lies in helping children to discover that they have the power, with a generous measure of help and collaboration, to create a world worth living in.

Now, having begun this chapter with a poem, it seems only fitting to end with one. Written years ago by a former student named Jesse—a boy of six who also lived with my wife and me for a time—this poem has been growing yellow and wrinkled while attached to our bedroom wall. Pretty much abandoned by his Ethiopian father and one of three children of a young welfare mother of southern Italian descent who was struggling with alcohol addiction, Jesse had not been having an easy time of it. At one point, he even lost most of his hair due to stress-related alopecia (it has since grown back and he is now a handsome and happy, very normal teenager). The poem speaks for itself, I think:

ALL OF A SUDDEN I TURNED INTO A RAINBOW

I am all different colors.
When I come out, the people look at me.
They say I look pretty.
I am magical.
I come out every morning
And people see me get happy.

THE THERAPEUTIC SCHOOL
by Chris Mercogliano

Because we appear as such a motley crew, always with at least a few kids looking a little bit wilder than most, people often ask if we are some kind of special school, for, (you know), "special" (problem) children. Of course, I always answer, "Yes!" because damn it, all children are special, and all children have problems. We all have problems for that matter; that's just the nature of the beast.

Actually, we are not a school that is specially designed for anyone. Year by year we simply take on, with little fanfare, whoever happens to show up. And God just always seems to know who needs us the most. Since we are the only non-conventional and affordable alternative to the public and parochial schools in the center of a small metropolitan region with over a quarter of a million people, and since our only entrance requirement is a genuine desire to come every day to be a full participant in the life of the school, some very interesting characters do show up each year. I would guess that we tend to be a "school of last resort" for about a third of our kids, with roughly another third seeking us out because they and/or their parents are attracted to our unorthodox approach to education, and with the remaining third coming because we are simply their neighborhood school. This last group struggles mightily to come to terms with our unusual style, and we try to help them bridge the gap. We all do the best we can with it, but as I learned long ago, try as we might, we just are not for everybody.

So what does it mean, "therapeutic school?" It occurs to me that this is a very tricky notion. Mary, our founder, often says to people that the Free School is like a Rorschach Test, meaning that whatever someone experiences in our school is simply an outward, concretized manifestation of the inner rumblings in that person's psyche. In other words, if one has preconceived ideas about school, or about life, for that matter, then sooner or later one will get reality to bear them out in our school. For this reason, I always tell prospective parents, and often their kids, that if they are coming to us because of problems in the previous school, they can be sure that the very same problems will crop up in our school as well, in spite of the fact that we are so different. And we intend it to be this way, which is one important reason why there are so few fixed rules and policies and why the structure of the school is free to evolve as needed to meet changing circumstances. One of the things that tends to separate us from other schools is the way we then follow problems to their true and hopefully lasting solutions, rather than temporizing with standardized responses and formulaic "discipline" all of the time, as most schools do.

Visitors to our school frequently comment on how "unstructured" we seem to be. What I am gradually coming to understand is that here the participants themselves are the structure. A true community, a concept I explore in much greater detail elsewhere, is an assembling and reassembling of people—not policies, or ideologies, or buildings. Communities consist of relationships among people, and people—with all their quirks and idiosyncrasies—make up communities, each with their own unique structure and identity. Everything else is secondary, or even tertiary, if not irrelevant altogether.

In the absence of a great many prescriptions and prohibitions, and in the presence of a good deal of spontaneity, "shit happens" on a regular basis at the Free School. I am purposefully borrowing that recently popular scatological expression from a bumper sticker that swept the nation for a time. This, I think, is where the idea of therapy comes in, and where, as I said, we part company with a great many other schools. Just as a good therapist would do, we encourage and invite the inner rumblings of the psyche "to come up." Then we work together, or struggle alone as the case may be, to take the drama all the way through to its logical completion, though the logic I'm speaking of here is of the inner kind. This is not a revolutionary idea. Getting away from all the psychotherapeutic lingo, it's simply called learning from your own mistakes; which many would argue is the only way true learning occurs anyway. When we take on kids with serious problems, they usually take full advantage of the available freedom, setting into motion a highly accelerated and certainly imaginative course of study based entirely on personal trial and error.

You might ask, "So what about the other kids, the ones who don't want to raise hell all the time?" Ah, this is another very tricky question. First of all, I firmly believe that it is important, even at quite a young age, for kids to learn to relate to and deal with all sorts of people. That's how they explore the limits of their own personal power and learn who to trust, and who not to trust; when to ask for help and when to go it on their own, and when to fight and when to flee (all of this belonging to an area of human experience sometimes referred to as "the politics of experience"). I have also discussed elsewhere the many tools and procedures available to our kids which enable them to deal safely and non-abusively with one another. When one of our "troubled" kids, having seen whatever pattern they happened to see in their ink blots of daily school life, stirs up the pot at school, we view it as an opportunity for the whole community to learn something about themselves.

I received an important lesson on this subject a number of years ago, when a couple of other men and I took a group of our more unhappy Free School boys with us to a weekend "men's council" held on the ancestral land of a quite elderly clan mother of the Seneca Nation in western New York State. During the course of the weekend, one of our boys—who suffered from occasional volcanic rages—got into it with one of the local boys, eventually going after him with a very sharp pocket knife. Fortunately, a couple of men were nearby enough to disarm Peter before anyone was hurt. The men presiding over the council, a mix of Native Americans and non-Native Americans, were at a loss as how best to respond to this disturbance to the peace of the council. The mutually agreed upon taboo against violence clearly had been broken. Should the boy be punished or sent home? The men from the Free School were advocates for having the whole group of boys sit down together and talk out the entire event, which they all, as it turns out, had a part in. The only problem was that our boy flatly refused. He was still too angry, ashamed and frightened by the power of his own reaction.

Finally, one of the council leaders, the one who had been placed in charge of the kids, decided to consult with Grandmother Twylah, as we called her, who was not actively participating in the council, but at whose invitation we were all there. That proved to be a very wise decision. Grandmother Twylah insisted on speaking to Peter immediately, and I ended up with the dubious honor of nearly dragging a very frightened boy to her sitting room. She instantly melted Peter, whom she had never seen before, with a smile of total acceptance. She told him that she sensed that he had had a problem controlling his temper before, and he nodded his head solemnly. She asked him if he knew that some of the men were suggesting that he be sent home, but that she had said absolutely not. She told Peter that she knew that he had come to her land that weekend just so

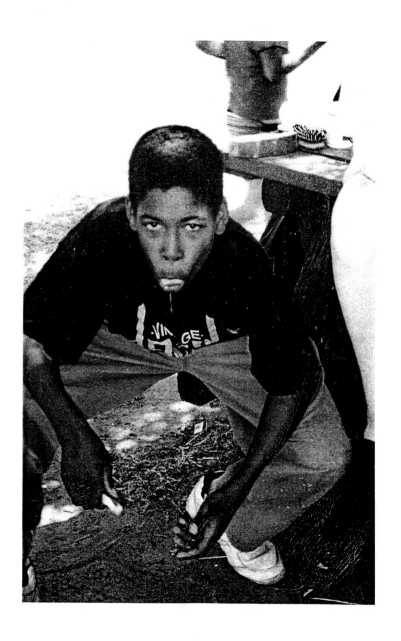

that this very problem could arise and so that Peter would have the opportunity to begin to learn to deal with the force of his own anger. The old clan mother explained to us both that in the Seneca tradition, children are not punished for their wrongdoings because each contains a lesson to be learned. To this day I have posted on my wall Grandmother Twylah's *Ten Lessons for Being Human.* The first one is that life is nothing but a series of lessons; the second is that we repeat each lesson until it is learned; and the third is that when one lesson is learned, it is immediately replaced by another one. You get the idea after that.

At the end of her talk with Peter, Grandmother Twylah asked him if he would be willing to bury his knife under one of the old trees on her property, an act that would signal his willingness literally to begin learning to "bury the hatchet" when he found his rage being triggered. The pocket knife was a recent birthday gift to Peter and he loved it dearly, and so this was no easy decision for him to make. He thought for a long, silent moment before agreeing to do it. Peter was not the same ten-year-old boy when he arrived back home that Sunday evening, and today he is a tall, responsible, and even-tempered sixteen-year-old, and one of the most valued counselors at the overnight camp where he now spends his summers.

What about when the actions of one individual child begin to pull down the rest of the group? A.S. Neill, founder of Summerhill School in England back in the 1920's, addressed this sort of question by differentiating between freedom and license. Freedom, according to Neill carries along with it the responsibility for one's impact on others. For example, one is never "free" to shout, "FIRE!" in a crowded theater. That would be an obvious example of license. At the Free School, we continually walk a very fine line in terms of how much leeway to give an unhappy child to work out their kinks and knots. It is a fact that because our school is so much an intimate, living community, when one person is suffering, everyone else inevitably suffers as well, to one extent or another.

Well, then at what point does it just become plain unfair to the other kids? On certain rare occasions—I can remember two examples in twenty-one years—the kids themselves settled the matter by voting a chronic antagonist out of the school. This drastic action was taken only after repeated warnings and last chances failed to bring about any real change. I can think of three other instances when the teachers got together and decided that it was time for a troublesome student to leave against his will. In the majority of cases where it just hasn't worked out, kids have ended up making their own, I think, necessary decisions to return to the "safety" and predictability of the rule-bound, heavily supervised conventional schools. They somehow sensed inside themselves that they had moved as far as they were capable of moving at that time, and I suspect that they also were picking up on their parent(s)' mixed feelings about them attending the Free School as well. Unfortunately, this type of parental ambivalence freezes a child's willingness to experiment with new behaviors and ways of interacting with other people. At any rate, I make a point of following up on each and every one of the kids who don't stay on with us, and they all seem to manage to come 'round right, usually more sooner than later.

All this having been said, we haven't won any popularity contests with our insistence on including troubled kids. One year not too long ago a respected area psychotherapist who, ironically (from my point of view), specialized in helping Viet Nam War veterans suffering from post traumatic stress syndrome, sent his young son down to visit because he was dissatisfied with their uptown public school. We had two disturbing older boys in the school that year and the therapist ultimately elected not to send his son because of his concern over the level of crisis that he felt he was observing in the school at the time. It's true that there was a lot of uproar being generated by those boys in particular, and I certainly didn't fault that father for his decision. Nevertheless, if I had it to do all over again, I still wouldn't throw the two troublemakers out. Both badly needed us, both later were able to transition successfully back into more conventional schooling situations, and both are now doing very well indeed.

One of the boys, whose name I won't use for obvious reasons, was sent to us because he was that kind of kid who chronically invites the abuse of the entire class in the typical public school environment where there is so often a reservoir of pent-up hostility and frustration on hand. He was large and gawky and very used to playing the role of what I call "kick-me." To make matters worse, his father had serious paranoid schizophrenic tendencies; and furthermore, there was a relatively mild form of sexual abuse slowly being transmitted down the line of six siblings, with our boy being smack in the middle of it all. To make matters worse for us, he was the largest kid in the school, and prone to expressing his anger with definite sexual overtones toward anyone female. And then, to top it all off, he had a history of academic failure and now had no apparent interest in learning or doing much of anything. Free at last, our boy simply chose to sit around all day and bug other kids, both for the sport and for the attention it gained him. And then, one day, the Lord who works in such mysterious ways sent us an old eight-track tape player with a big box of working tapes, all from the sixties and seventies when the boy's father was a real music-loving young, died-in-the-wool hippy. Now, our boy sat around on his somewhat overweight derrière and listened to music all day long—a definite step in the right direction since at least he stopped being such a general nuisance. Still, I was worried about him because he was already thirteen, years behind academically, and very depressed. Getting him to do anything other than play his tapes was like trying to move a glacial New England boulder with a lever made of Styrofoam. All was business as usual until he got it in his eternally earphoned head to hold a dance at the school, with you-know-who as the DJ. Lo and behold, the dance was a great success, with more to follow, and suddenly this budding teenager had a standing with his fellow students that he had never before had in his life. At some point along the way, it occurred to me to ask him if he might want to apprentice with a professional radio disc jockey if I could find one (anything to get him moving and out of the building!) His face lit up at the idea, and miraculously, I was able to find a student at a local college radio station who was willing to take on an eager, but totally inexperienced learner. He had him on the air the first day! Our young apprentice went on to earn his FCC license and then to start his own radio station on the block in his neighborhood, all within three months of his debut!

Eventually, our boy outgrew the Free School in more ways than one and returned to his local public junior/senior high school, a move which was entirely of his own creation, since neither his parents nor I believed that he was ready to make the transition back to the abysmal world of failure and abuse from whence he had come. What actually happened was that one day, entirely unannounced of course, he managed to persuade his aunt to take him to visit the public school nearest his home. While there, he further convinced her to enroll him on the spot, with the aunt claiming that she was his legal guardian! No one was more surprised than me when I received a phone call from his new principal the next day asking for his school records and if I could tell him a little more about his unusual new student. You can imagine what my next phone call—with his mother who still knew nothing about any of this—was like. To complete this very abridged version of the story, his mother and I agreed that there wasn't much else to do at that point but respect her son's determination to escape from freedom. Within two weeks of his cleverly orchestrated "transfer," I learned that he had already started a school radio station and that the principal had him "on the air" every morning broadcasting from his office before the morning announcements! What a turn-around! He's apparently keeping up academically now, is beginning to have girl friends, and is generally turning out to be a very "normal" teenager.

John was the other boy that year that kept things livelier than they might otherwise have been. He had been adopted at the age of three after having been taken away from his mother by the local child protection people due to extreme neglect. This was in an extremely isolated area in upstate New York where they lived in Appalachia-like poverty. John's young mother sometimes worked as a prostitute in order to get by and she frequently left her little boy alone to fend for himself for long periods of time. John's new family was troubled as well. His adopted father was a combat veteran of the Second World War already in his sixties, and was disabled, alcoholic, and still suffering, I think, from untreated Post Traumatic Stress Disorder. To top it all off, he had a slow-growing cancer, and so John was often preoccupied with fears about his new dad dying. John's adopted mother, a sensitive, quiet, and insecure woman, was a full generation younger than her husband, and finally left him a couple of years after the adoption because of his drunken abusiveness, taking John with her.

In school, John's stock in trade was somewhat similar to his classmate, the DJ's. The only way that he seemed to be able to get at his buried grief, anger and despair—so understandable in light of his origins—was to play out a victim scenario, inviting his classmates to tease him and rough him up, all the while adamantly refusing to stick up for himself. He would then spend long periods of time off by himself, feeling abused and neglected—an obvious reenactment of his actual predicament in early childhood. Just the other day, a reporter from a local newspaper spent the day with us, working on a feature-length profile of the school, and near the end of his visit, he shared a very astute observation with me, one that I'd never heard put quite that way before. He asked if I had noticed how in most classrooms in most schools, there are always at least a couple of kids who are loners, who often seem depressed or withdrawn, or who are in some way "out of it." I nodded my head. This thoughtful journalist then went on to say that he was quite taken by the fact that he hadn't seen a single child all day fitting that pattern. All the children in the Free School, he was realizing, seemed to be "in the flow." All seemed to him to be always actively engaged in something, whether alone, in pairs or in small groups. No one appeared to be left out, and he wondered why I thought that was so. I answered that we place a great deal of value and attention on precisely that level of experience, and that we in some ways give it a higher priority than purely academic or other more mental forms of learning. Furthermore, I told him, the kids care so deeply about each other that it's usually not o.k. with them when someone's pain is being ignored—either by themselves or by others. Perhaps this statement could form the basis for a wonderfully unrefined, albeit "therapeutic" definition of "community," a term rendered nearly useless by constant over- and mis-use.

Our kids will inevitably find ways to draw each other out, much the same way that applying a hot compress to a boil slowly brings the trapped pus up to the surface, speeding up the healing process. Their assorted techniques for treating emotional wounds don't follow adult logic and instead are mysteriously intuitive. They often involve conflict and are rich in paradox. John's "abusers" finally stood the situation on its head by calling council meetings on him because he so consistently refused to defend himself. Riding the horse in precisely the direction it was going anyway, they ultimately, after all their caring pleas and exhortations had failed, voted in a motion that John had to sit alone—for as long as it took—until he called his own council meeting and got to work on changing his self-abasing pattern of behavior. The kids' ploy worked like a charm, just as I'm sure they instinctively knew that it would. After two very stubborn days, John finally became so enraged at *having* to be isolated, that demanded his own meeting at which he gave his "persecutors" hell, and then pledged to stick up for himself from there forward. And that was a promise that he kept. Soon after this breakthrough which was largely engineered by his peers, out of the blue one day, John decided to write down his life story. I suggested he use the computer to make it faster and easier, and what followed were tens of hours, day after day, spent by himself in front of a computer screen. It was wonderful to watch his curse of self-isolation turn into a blessing of self-healing. Eventually, John also "outgrew" us and chose to switch to another excellent alternative school nearer to his home in the country where he is now flourishing. Stealing a line from one of my favorite modern Protestant hymns, "Wise hearts find truth in paradox." Amen, I say to that.

One of the most important points that I wanted to get across to the aforementioned reporter was that children, given the space to associate without external constraint, free from adult-imposed judgment and competition and free to be their authentic selves rather than some false school persona, are simply their own best teachers and therapists. The kids are thus entirely unfettered, as he had so accurately observed, not because of any particularly enlightened methodology being practiced by us teachers, but because we trust them to employ their own devices, knowing that they are naturally inclined to have it be this way. Which isn't to say that the adults in the Free School just ignore the kids while they float about in some artificial and exclusive bubble. We are interacting with them all the time— sometimes at their initiative, sometimes at ours—and we seldom hesitate to intervene when there is just outright abuse or dumping of negative emotion taking place. At the risk of repeating myself, we spend much of our time attending to the emotional and interpersonal dimensions of everyday life in the school because we believe them to be the cornerstones of life and of all learning. Our experience tells that when children know themselves, like themselves, and belong to themselves, the areas of learning that conventional schools spend countless thousands of hours going over and over again become practically effortless and require amazingly little time. I suspect that what the reporter was really picking up on, though he didn't use these words, was the surprising degree of aliveness that one usually finds in our school, and this, I am quite sure, is why.

Now it occurs to me that the risk in going on with this notion of "therapeutic school" is that it might suggest to some that we are all actually a bunch of amateur psychologists running around playing therapist most of the time. While I personally have done a great deal of individual and group therapy to repair my inner damage and to strengthen a much too fragile sense of myself—so that I would be both a better person and a better teacher—I recognize its built-in limitations and its potential for fostering dependency. On the other hand, I see many similarities between the roles of teacher and therapist, properly played. Neither good teachers nor good therapists impose their idea of who the individuals they are working with should or shouldn't be. Adroitly keeping their leading and guiding to a minimum, both endeavor only to encourage the growth and unfolding of the possibilities that are already present. Sometimes a little poking and prodding, or a little limit setting is called for, and sometimes it's better to let someone make mistakes and then learn from them. Good teachers and good therapists trust those they work with to know themselves better than anyone else.

I've gradually come to know that therapy doesn't cure anything, nor should it. We are all wayfarers, each on our unique journey in this life, with all its joy and all its suffering. So, the Free School isn't a place where we are always trying to fix kids, though we are certainly guilty (sic) from time to time of searching for psychological explanations—perhaps too often. Such is the temptation of a therapeutic orientation to reality, I guess. We try to avoid this pitfall as much as possible, and in any case, the kids usually protest loudly when they feel that we are over-psychologizing their experience. We then struggle to receive their teaching as gracefully as possible.

What the Free School is, I hope, is a place where all its co-participants can come to find out enough about who they uniquely are so that they can remove any obstacles to the full expression of their particular forms of specialness—be they artistic, intellectual, musical, scientific, poetic, athletic, mathematical, or some rare combination of them all—if that is what they choose to do. One of the cornerstones of our approach to education is that personal authenticity is the ground from which all true learning springs. That does, indeed, sound very "therapeutic," doesn't it? and means, I suppose, that we are a special school after all.

I can no longer count the number of times that children have demonstrated to me their superior inner wisdom regarding choices they have made about what they have needed to be doing in school, and when and how, as well. A few years back, Allan came to us at the late age of eleven, already a budding young man with his mind made up about a great many things. His academic performance in public school had always been poor, as was his overall attitude toward almost everything, and when he began refusing to go to school at all, his parents decided to give us a try. Allan had suffered a lot of emotional abuse and neglect as a young child. Although his mother was

well on her way to making a beautiful and complete recovery from alcoholism and had remarried a man who was a caring stepfather to Allan, he continued to display a number of psychosomatic side-effects such as nervous ticks and so on. Today, he most certainly would have had the absurd label, "Attention Deficit Disorder" stamped on his records, but thankfully it hadn't been invented yet. Allan had tremendous nervous energy and rarely liked to sit still for long, which generally made "progress" in things like math, and certainly reading, pretty much out of the question.

Naturally, there was a lot of concern about his academic standing, although not on Allan's part. His parents were shocked and relieved enough by the sudden reversal of his attitude toward going to school that they were willing to go along with our novel approach to their son's education, which consisted mainly of letting him do as he pleased while he was in our care. In addition to always being on the go, Allan was quite cocky and had little if any respect for anyone female. God, in all His infinite knowing, arranged it so that when Allan happened upon our little school, all six or eight of his age-mates were girls. I told him right up front that this was a curse placed on him to rid him of his prejudice and that no boys his age would arrive until he decided to begin treating girls and women with proper respect, which as it turns out, is exactly what ended up happening.

I discovered at some point that Allan had a fascination for the outdoors, for wildlife and for hunting and fishing. On a five-day trip to what was then our school's wilderness site in the Berkshire Mountains of Western Massachusetts—we have since been given 250 acres of undeveloped land closer to Albany in eastern New York State—Allan spent most of his time trying to catch small animals in homemade traps. His designs were crude and he caught nothing; but lo and behold, he showed up at school on the Monday morning following the trip with a book on animal trap design which he had gotten from his local library. We'd never seen him with a book before, and he proceeded to spend the next several weeks attempting to build the traps in our little school workshop. So much for his short attention span! Before long, he outgrew the book that had gotten him started and began working out his own designs, some of which were quite ingenious.

As paradox would have it, helpless baby animals literally began falling at the feet of our budding young trapper, who now began pouring the same intense energy that had previously been focussed on hunting into nurturing nature's offspring. Allan's first "patient" was a starling hatchling, not more than a few days old, that had probably been pushed out of its nest by the mother. He contacted the State Conservation Department to find out how to feed and care for the featherless little creature. I have seen countless wild baby birds perish while under the hopeful and tender care of well-meaning children, and I certainly didn't expect this tiny starling to survive for very long either. Not only did the bird survive, but with Allan's tireless and loving parenting, including several middle-of-the-night feedings in the beginning, it flourished. When its feathers grew in sufficiently, Allan then helped the bird learn to fly. He was well along in preparing the young starling for its eventual release back into the wild when tragedy struck.

Once again paradox was at work. I had driven Allan out to the State Conservation Department so that he could show some other students the lab where he was volunteering his help a couple of times a week. Allan's relationship with these folks around the bird had led to an exciting apprenticeship with the State Wildlife Pathologist, and among other things, Allan was getting the training there that would lead to his becoming a licensed wildlife rehabilitator. Allan had brought the bird along with him—he generally took it everywhere he went—and we left it in the school van while we went in to tour the lab. Though it was a mild day in mid-spring, I made the common and often fatal mistake of not rolling a window down. The van sat parked in the sun and when we returned a half-hour later the bird was already stricken by the heat. We frantically tried to save it, but we were too late and the little starling died a few minutes later in Allan's trembling hands. It often takes a lot to make an adolescent boy cry, but cry he did; and thankfully without shame. When we got back to school, the sad news spread quickly. Before long, the entire school had joined him in his grief, and elaborate funeral preparations were begun. Allan fashioned a little casket while other kids created grave markers of all kinds. The entire school attended the solemn burial in the school's pet cemetery, which is under an old mulberry tree in my back yard.

Try to imagine the preceding vignette occurring in a conventional, age- segregated classroom. Mind you, this isn't to say that it couldn't or doesn't happen sometimes. There are thousands of gifted, dedicated and creative teachers busy working small miracles in our schools every day, usually against great odds. But it is difficult to imagine, isn't it? For one thing, the ease with which the younger Free Schoolers got into their grief when they saw and touched the little dead bird greatly facilitated Allan's necessary grieving in a way that no textbook or adult figure ever could have. Rather than this being some curricular lesson—or "extra-curricular," for that matter—about death and dying (which in itself would be a rare find in most schools), here was a struggling young adolescent receiving the total support of an entire community at a very poignant moment in his life.

Perhaps it is the inordinate amount of attention that we give to the emotional life and health of children and adults alike that would properly earn us the label of "therapeutic school." We believe very deeply that unexpressed feelings get stuck and then fester in the body and in the psyche, and that this causes breaks in the normal program of learning and development. While we don't do therapy with kids as such, we have developed any number of practices and techniques over the years which encourage the healthy expression of emotions as well as the articulation and exploration of life's inevitable conflicts. Throughout this book I keep referring to our "council meetings," with their often strong feeling content, where problems are often unravelled right to their sources. Also, we have always had a large punching bag available for anyone to let off anger harmlessly at any time. Visitors are sometimes both surprised and amused to see even our preschoolers pounding an over-stuffed chair with an old tennis racket and shouting, "No!" A few years ago, I actually lined a small, windowless interior room in the school with donated second-hand mattresses. Appearing to the uninformed as a veritable "padded cell," we named this unusual space, "the Feeling Room," and anyone can ask to use it whenever they feel the need. It gets quite a lot of good use because it is a wonderfully safe, private place for the release of pent-up emotions of all kinds. We noticed that the amount of fighting in the school dropped off markedly once the Feeling Room became popular. The Fire Marshal, on the other hand, was entirely unamused when he first discovered our new addition, but even he eventually came to understand its value and finally stopped insisting that we remove the mattresses because he thought they were a "a fire hazard."

I want to return to the word, "No," for a moment. Often one of young children's very first words, it carries great power as it plays a defining role in the emergence of their identities as separate individuals. And then, at the age of five, if not sooner, we hustle them into an environment where "no" is virtually *verboten* and where conformity is enforced by all necessary means. Some children have no problem with such a regimen and appear to thrive under those artificial conditions. But what about the ones who don't? We have found over the years that they need to say, "No!" a lot, and without consequences other than ones organically inherent in the situation. Kids who have been spoiled and over-controlled for too long, either at home, or at school, or both, will sometimes say "no" even to spite themselves. When they are allowed to do that, it can then become a source of profound self-discovery. I remember a small group of nine-year-old boys we had once, all public school refugees, who banded together and refused to go on a week-long trip to our school's lakeside "outdoor education center." Now, I knew that these boys—all city kids—loved to fish and to run in the woods. But on the previous trip, they had been furious at the idea of having to gather firewood, and so here was an obvious act of glorified rebellion. I was sorely tempted to force them to go because, first of all, this was just the sort of experience they needed; and furthermore, I knew they would have a ball once they got there. Still, a quiet voice inside told me just to let them be. I will never forget their faces when the school emptied out as all of the other kids departed for the lodge. Their smug looks of victory turned lonely and forlorn within minutes, and then they were one sad sight when the others returned at the end of the week with all of their stories of great adventure. Our newly humble rebels proceeded to pester me for weeks to organize another expedition, and when they did get to go again, there was very little fuss about the chores that belong to camp life. How can we ever expect kids to become skillful in the art of making choices for themselves if they never get to exercise their option to say "no?"

Fortunately, it wasn't long before Allan was back in the saddle again. One morning, while he was on his way to school, he came upon a juvenile pigeon who was in pretty rough shape and unable to fly. And this story had a happy ending when, after a few weeks of Allan's restorative care, the now full-grown bird was well enough to be released successfully back into its urban environment. Everyone saluted Allan for saving the pigeon's life and he wore the hero's mantle with a lot of grace. The cockiness which I described above seemed to have disappeared without a trace. It was plain for anyone who wanted to see that while Allan was so busy healing those little creatures, he was also applying little splints to the broken wing places in himself that were a legacy of his own difficult and uncertain start in life.

After two years with us, Allan decided that he, too, was ready to leave the nest. Even though he previously had been so miserable in public school, the call of that wildly buzzing hive of adolescence—the middle school—became irresistible. I discouraged him from leaving the Free School just yet, only because he still hadn't done much to "catch up" academically. I was worried that he might be labelled a failure all over again and then revert back to all of the negative attitudes and behavior patterns that had led him to us in the first place. But if there's one thing we've learned, it's that once a kid has made up his mind to leave us, then it's important to let him go, with our full blessing. So, leave us he did; and sure enough, my fears were confirmed. After a couple of weeks, I received an irate phone call from Allan's new homeroom teacher. "Didn't you teach the boy anything while he was in your school?" she shouted at me. In my calmest, most reassuring tones, I explained some of Allan's history to her. Next, I patiently recounted some of his amazing accomplishments to her and told her that, while they weren't exactly in academic areas, she would begin to see a carry-over once Allan recovered from his shock at being back in the kind of graded, competitive classroom where he had been such a miserable failure before. I urged her to try to relax and to see if they couldn't get Allan some extra help in some of the basic skills areas where he was lacking. I shared with her my discovery that there was nothing that I couldn't trust Allan with and that he was, in fact, a born leader. Doing my best to steady my rising annoyance, I struggled to find the words that would convey to her that she had a rare treasure on her hands, and that she'd damn well better not bury it in the sand. I assured her again that Allan's desire to succeed would bring him through the narrow place he was temporarily stuck in, and the conversation ended on a hopeful, friendly note.

I'll never know how much of my pitch she bought, but I managed to help buy Allan enough time for him to pull himself out of his slump. They found him some tutoring assistance, and by the end of the marking period, he was passing all subjects. This leads to my favorite Allan story of all. In the second half of that year, Allan's English teacher told the class to write a two-page paper on the book of their choice. Entirely on his own initiative—I don't even know where he learned of the book—

Allan read Rachel Carson's classic ecological warning, *Silent Spring*. He proceeded to write an eight-page mini-thesis that the teacher then read to the entire class, declaring that it was the best composition that she'd ever received. Although the paper was full of spelling and grammatical errors, it had a big, fat "A+" on the cover. I proudly tell this one last story about Allan because it is such a pure example of what can happen when we return the responsibility for the learning process to its rightful owner (assuming someone has taken it away in the first place). Allan read that book and wrote that paper for himself, not for his teacher. The deep meaning which he expressed in his writing, and which thankfully that teacher was able to recognize and acknowledge him for, emerged from within Allan, and from nowhere else. Here was another wonderful reminder that real learning unfolds from the inside out and not the other way around.

Human development is simply not a linear progression. Not unlike dreams, it follows a logic all its own, varying tremendously from individual to individual. Its course is often uncanny and also deeply mysterious. When we remember at the Free School to respect the kids' own growth strategies—no matter how unlikely they might appear at the time—things always seem to come out right in the end. Again, this is not to say that we are "laissez faire," as our dear reporter ultimately wrote in the ignorant and largely insulting story which appeared in the Sunday addition of his newspaper. Teachers in our school often attempt to influence students in one direction or another—sometimes directly, sometimes indirectly; sometimes gently, and sometimes not so gently. With budding adolescents like Allan, though, force of any kind rarely works very well. They just tend to push back and rebel, or become sullen and withdraw. Thankfully, Allan was open to allowing me to give him some guidance and encouragement in a direction he was already inclined.

But then there was Sally. A student in our school for several years, she had been a bright, precocious child and an eager learner. All of a sudden (or so it seemed at the time), she hit adolescence and lost interest in just about everything. I tried mightily to find some inner spark that I could help her fan into flames, but all I ever got was smoke. I was having increasing "bad teacher" feelings and so the situation was slowly driving me a little nuts. There were two things that entire year that Sally spent her time doing, when she wasn't just sitting around, "hanging out." (My innate prejudice against non-doing is beginning to show, isn't it?) One was melting candle wax onto her hands and incessantly making molds of them; the other was weaving a multi-color rope on a small spool loom that she had fashioned—until the rope stretched more than twice around our rather large building. The whole school got caught up in her fascination as the rope grew longer and longer.

Now, I knew that Sally's parents were just completing a lengthy and difficult divorce, and that the combination of her feelings about that situation with the onset of puberty pretty well accounted for her drawn out, intense mood. Fortunately, I was able to relax my drive to feel like a good teacher by inspiring Sally to some great achievement, and instead to "stay off her case" and trust that she was doing what she needed to do (or not doing what she didn't need to do). Sally completed that year still weaving and molding and chose to move on to a public high school the following September. Though a successful student there, she grew dissatisfied with the endless routine and rote learning and so decided the next year to create a modified homeschool program with our school's founder as her primary mentor. The two of them had a ball together and Sally returned to being aggressive and joyful about learning. To make a long story short, upon completion of high school, she ended up earning a scholarship to a well-known private university. Sally came back one day to tell her old teachers what she realized, looking back, had contributed to her satisfying transition into adulthood perhaps as much as anything else: it was that last year she had spent in the Free School, "doing nothing."

FEAR
by Chris Mercogliano

It has been said and often repeated that the only thing to fear is fear itself. Now I don't know about the "only," but fear certainly is frightening; and worse still is the way in which it feeds on itself. The sad fact today is that we are living in a society increasingly run by its fears—the fear of personal violence and crime, the fear of the international political violence we call war, the fear of nuclear holocaust which is receiving increasing competition from the fear of ecological holocaust, the fear of scarcity, the fear of growing old and dying—this list could go on for pages. A substantial segment of our national economy, beginning with the insurance racket, preys on these fears by offering us protective and preventive policies, substances and devices of every imaginable kind. In short, fear has become a growth industry.

Where I encounter this spreading contagion of fear most poignantly is in my work as a teacher and school administrator. Fear-based policy and decision-making from the national level right down to the individual classroom has reached epidemic proportions. While ours is an independent school largely unaffected in any straight-line way by this trend, I still find us struggling daily with its many subtle, indirect effects. Even though we long ago opted out of the traditional reward and punishment teaching methodology which uses fear as a primary motivator, and even though we are up front with our prospective new families right from the beginning, warning them that we will neither bribe nor coerce their children into learning, the distinctive odor of fear remains in the air nonetheless.

It's everywhere, so why wouldn't our Free School parents, teachers and students smell it, too? The entire nation is hung-up these days on academic achievement, or the perceived lack thereof. We used to be falling behind the Russians; now it's the Japanese. Every day a new Chicken Little warns us that something must be done about falling standardized test scores, which don't measure true intelligence anyway. Academic training is foisted on defenseless pre-schoolers at ever earlier stages, and the call for lengthening the school year grows louder and louder. And then comes the blame game. It's the teachers' fault for not teaching or expecting hard enough; it's the students' fault for not studying hard enough; it's the parents' fault for not caring hard enough about their kids' education; it's the country's fault for not maintaining hard enough standards. There's no end to this list, either.

Here is the voice of fear speaking, where the reasoning is always circular. It's like the ancient image of the serpent swallowing its own tail—there's no beginning and no end—and therefore nowhere to break into such a vicious cycle of negative reinforcement. If this were the end of it, if the trouble were just that massive numbers of adults had nothing better to worry about than how their children were doing in school, then there really wouldn't be much of a problem. Regrettably though, kids invariably become infected as well, and their natural, in-born desire and will to learn gets stifled in the process. Children, who live within the boundaries of their parents' emotional bodies, literally smell the grown-ups' fear and this is how it is passed down.

I chose the modality of smell here for a couple of reasons. For one, fear has a distinctive odor, a lesson well-known to anyone who has spent much time around bees or dogs. Secondly, the connection between the olfactory nerve and the brain is a large and evolutionarily primal one. The extraordinary way in which certain smells can evoke powerful images and memories is evidence of this important mind/body interface—all the more powerful because it is an entirely unconscious response. In other words, a parent's fear need not be spoken—though it often is—in order to be communicated. An anxious look, an apparently innocent question about what a child did (or didn't do) in school today, or what isn't being talked about can all be worth a thousand words and do the job of imprinting this kind of low-level fear quite effectively. Oftentimes, parents aren't even aware they are expressing fear, or doubt or insecurity, and unfortunately, the more subtle the frequency of the message—the farther out of the range of audible hearing—often the greater is the impact on the receiver. Then, of course, there is the classic TV sitcom scene at report card time when the overwrought father is berating his failing son and asking him if he wants to end up collecting garbage for a living some day. That kind of parental anger is obviously based in fear; and because it is so blatant, I think it is a bit easier for kids to deal with.

Shifting the "blame" away from parents, for I don't believe for a minute that the problem begins at home, it must be understood that our entire educational system and its methodology are based on fear. Why else would every "learning task" be broken down into tiny bits so that no chewing was required—and then endlessly repeated? Why else would progress and achievement be so carefully measured? Why else would we as a nation continue to spend countless billions of dollars per year to maintain a system that we collectively know is not serving so many children or their families' real needs?

Fear is a powerful emotion. It shunts the brain away from higher-level thinking, an autonomic survival response I will describe in greater detail in a moment. It prevents parents from thinking clearly about their children's growth and development, rendering many unable to question the school system's assessment that their children are not performing up to some arbitrary standard. These frightened parents then proceed to frighten their children, who return to classrooms which are controlled by frightened teachers, who, in turn, are sweating it out under the supervision of frightened superintendents... So it goes, right up to the top of a giant pyramid of fear, with the hapless students trapped somewhere in a thick middle layer, literally, physiologically unable to think their way out of the bind they're in. Instead, they resort to an unending array of defensive maneuvers, each according to their underlying character structures. On one end of the spectrum, you will find passive kids anchoring their resistance in "forgetting" and playing dumb ("Huh... say what?"); while on the other end there are the aggressive types who actively rebel, refuse and eventually opt out of the game, whose odds are constantly rigged against them.

Here is how fear works in the brain, which we now know is comprised of three parts, one enfolded inside the other. As all organisms evolve, the tendency is to hang onto old outmoded structures, adding to and improving, rather than casting them off altogether, which is exactly what happened with the human brain. The innermost core of the brain, located at the base of the skull, is aptly named the reptilian brain. This ancient control center auto-pilots the central nervous system and manages our vast array of survival instincts and behaviors. When we are generally at peace with ourselves and our environment, the reptilian brain plays a supporting role in deference to the higher two brain structures.

Surrounding the primitive reptilian is what is known as the old mammalian brain, sometimes referred to as the limbic system. Here is the source of our awareness, emotions and our intuition—where crude reptilian instincts are transformed into true intelligence which can be applied to complex life situations. The limbic system maintains the immune system and the body's capacity to heal itself. Finally, five times larger than its predecessors combined, there is the newest brain, or neocortex, whose job is to integrate the input from its junior partners. Here is the source of our inventiveness and creative thinking and problem-solving abilities. Again, when all is well, there is a general flow of energy and information from the inside to the outside, with the lower structures working in support of their new master, the neocortex, which artfully sees to a person's continued well-being.

Now, let's bring fear into the picture: introduce a sufficient stress or threat and the brain goes into full retreat. Leslie Hart, author of *Human Brain and Human Learning*, an advocate for what he terms "brain-compatible education," calls this negative reflex "downshifting." I imagine a speeding locomotive thrown into reverse without first slowing down and coming to a halt, with all of that momentum going into miles of wheel spinning before there is any actual change of direction. Suddenly, all of the developmental powers of the higher two brains place themselves in the service of their reptilian core, fueling the individual's territoriality and other primitive drives and defenses. Watching ten minutes of world or local news on any given night will confirm the reality of this basic biological survival mechanism.

Or just observe for a day the antics of a "slow learner" or of a "problem child" in any traditional classroom in America. I am purposely avoiding the use here of any of the new, hyper-specific labels invented to rationalize the epidemic failure of children to thrive in our schools and to throw parents who might otherwise manage to keep their wits about them off of the scent. The now old-fashioned term for this is "blaming the victim." In *The Learning Mystique: A Critical Look at Learning Disabilities*, written as his PhD thesis while at Harvard University, Robert Coles proposes that the whole labeling system, beginning with "dyslexic," then moving on to "learning disabled," and since refined to the point of absolute absurdity, is simply a clever and consciously contrived way for schools to give middle-class parents who are immune to the "culturally disadvantaged" myth a palatable explanation for why their Johnnies can't read yet.

The real problem, however, is that we then have a real-life self-fulfilling prophecy on our hands. The news that their child isn't developing "normally" is frightening to parents, understandably so. Scared parents then scare their kids and we now know, thanks to recent brain research, exactly what takes place inside all of those frightened young minds as they begin to apply all of the resourcefulness and creativity of their modern brains towards the resistance to the learning game being played in the classroom. If you've never watched this totally reflexive mechanism in action, then you've missed out on an important object lesson. All I have to do is close my eyes and remember back to a time years ago when I naively attempted to "teach" subjects like reading or the multiplication tables—humanely, of course—to a group of public school cast-offs. I'll never forget Tommy, in particular, who, ironically, was the one kid who had never been to public school. Tommy's divorced father was from conservative, working-class Irish-Catholic stock, and frequently expressed vocal concern about his first-born son's lack of academic progress. Tommy was a passive resister, adaptively smiling his way through each lesson, yet growing steadily "dumber" by the minute. I patiently employed every creative teaching trick that I had ever learned, but he never did learn those times tables. I was finally rescued by his impatient and critical father, who did not hesitate to fault me and our school for its lack of discipline and academic rigor, and who finally insisted that the boy go to a "regular" school, where thankfully he is now both a reasonably successful student and an accomplished high school athlete. In Tommy's case, the change to a more conventional school resulted in improvement in his schoolwork for two primary reasons, I think. First of all, Tommy's dad was both pleased and relieved at the move, and so Tommy no longer had to carry the burden of his father's anxiety and displeasure. In addition, the atmosphere and ethic of the new public school were more consonant with the father's belief system, where school is work and work is something that you have to do, so you damn well better just do it. No longer allowed the choice not to do it, Tommy just got busy doing what the other kids were doing. This removed a major thorn in the all-important relationship between father and son, which alone made the change in schools a very good thing for Tommy.

The preceding story also brings us back to the question of what role fear plays in a "free school" like ours, where there is no grading or coercion, and where learning is regarded as a natural, joyful process seldom requiring adult intervention. While our informal, organically structured and family-like school environment usually readily defuses the stored-up fear in a child coming to us from public school, we often seem to have the opposite effect on the parent(s). The litany of questions, spoken or unspoken, which reflect their fear goes something like this: Where are

the desks? What about homework? What if he/she just decides to play all day? How will I know my child is learning if there are no report cards? What will happen when my child goes back to a regular school?

Now, I don't mean to say that these are not all legitimate questions, appropriate expressions of concern about the future of a child. I always try to answer them compassionately, sometimes addressing the subject of fear head-on, and at other times coming at it in a more roundabout way, depending on the degree of the fear that I feel is contained in the questions. My twenty-one years of wrestling with this subject have taught me that this corrosive fear transcends all race and class lines. The one determinant that I have been able to recognize that doesn't lead into murky psychological realms—and to levels where I have no "contract" to work with parents—is the parents' own schooling histories. When I can get overly-anxious parents talking about their childhood experiences in school, the seeds of their current worry are often quite obvious. I discover that they went through one form or another of the same struggles that their kids are undergoing, and that they, too, had parents who were anxious about their educational development. Here, then, is a classic example of how the fear I am talking about indeed feeds upon itself; and in fact, lives to see not just another day, but another entire generation.

Long ago at the Free School, we realized, especially where a child's growth has been decidedly interrupted, that our task is as much to work with the parents as it is with their kids—and I mean work to relieve them of their fears about their children's ability to learn. Yes, it's important that parents read to and talk with their children, that they be consistent and non-abusive in their discipline at home, and so on and so forth. But even abusiveness is often rooted in deep-seated fear; and again, it is fear which scrambles and fogs vulnerable young brains, and fear which throws the entire developmental vehicle into neutral or even reverse.

When talking with fearful parents, I always try to keep in mind and in some way to communicate to them something that I once heard Joseph Chilton Pearce, internationally known lecturer on human development and author of books such as *The Magical Child, The Crack in the Cosmic Egg,* and most recently, *Evolution's End,* say at a workshop for teachers here in Albany a few years back. The condensed version is that all children are "hard-wired to learn," which simply means that our in-born programming automatically gears us for learning, a process that we now know begins *in utero*, to a truly astonishing degree. So, it becomes more a question of how we manage to keep a child from learning, rather than one of how they learn in the first place. Pearce's belief, based on extensive new research into the psycho-biology of the mind, is that each child already contains his or her God-given potential, and that what we call "learning" is just the natural unfolding of that potential. This, of course, brings us back to the true meaning of the word "education," which derives from the Latin, *educare*, meaning, "To lead out." Also, Pearce's recent work in synthesizing the theories of quantum physics and the astounding recent discoveries about the functioning of the human brain tends to confirm Piaget's less "scientific" model of the developmental stages that all children pass through, each at her or his own pace.

Chilton Pearce added one important qualifier to his notion of "hard-wired" learning, which was that it will unfold if—and only if—the environment supports and resonates with children according to their individual natures and to where they are in their own developmental processes. It's not hard to see that this is a monumental "if." The learning which is already occurring in the womb, with the fetus responding to all sorts of cues from the mother's body—heartbeat, voice, emotional states, etc.—as well as to the voices of father and siblings, and which is predestined to continue and accelerate right from the moment of birth, is in so many cases crashingly interrupted by the mindless practices of the "modern" hospital. The newborn infant's early developmental surge depends entirely on immediate and adequate bonding with the mother. Recent biophysical research has determined that it is proper skin-to-skin contact, continued contact with the mother's heartbeat, and plenty of loving, non-anxious eye contact that triggers the rapid hormonal and neurological changes which underlie the crucial early development of the neocortex.

Interestingly, this discussion brings me onto my wife, Betsy's, career playing field. Betsy is what is known today as a "direct-entry midwife," meaning that she got her training via apprenticeship with veteran midwives, and has shared with me many of her experiences from the amazing world of childbirth. We are continually finding new parallels and connections between related areas of concern in our work, and if anything, she ends up having to deal directly with the inhibitory and suppressive effects of fear more than I do. My wife began by helping the founder of the Free School, Mary Leue, set up a meeting place for pregnant women, their partners and their children, and this led her to nursing school and then to a job as an obstetrical nurse in a conventional hospital delivery room. Appreciative of the valuable, paid training that she was receiving there, she stuck with that job as long as her conscience would allow her. Over time, she became increasingly appalled by the number of times and ways in which the nurses and doctors interrupted and interfered with the mother giving birth. A distressing but important lesson that was repeated again and again before this midwife-to-be was how fear slowed down or altogether stopped the process of labor. And, it was all too clear that it was the hospital environment itself which was causing much of that fear. Then, even more disturbing to her was the way the newborn baby was treated after it was born, with one invasive routine procedure after another—shots, eye drops, blood tests, exams—all performed with little or no regard for the subjective effects of all this on the baby.

Medical science continues to have little regard for babies as feeling human beings, and childbirth continues to be approached by mainstream practitioners as though it were a pathological, rather than a natural, healthy process; in most cases requiring little if any professional intervention at all. And all of this, in my belief, is due to fear—fear that something might go wrong and fear of malpractice lawsuits perhaps being the chief ones. Then, either underlying or at least accompanying that fear is a deep distrust of the mother. During childbirth, so many of the routine practices are based on the assumption that a woman does not know her own body, and therefore will not be able to accomplish her task without all sorts of "assistance." Once the baby is on the outside, a new unexpressed assumption kicks in that the world is a dangerous, germ-infested place from which the mother might not know how to protect her baby, and so the hospital staff takes over in that department as well.

Call it fear; call it distrust; call it whatever you want—the result is always the same. In the name of safety and prevention, what ends up being prevented is the natural flow of biological events within and between mother and baby, and the "hardwired" (to borrow Pearce's term) mother/infant bond which is the logical outcome of those events. What comes to mind here is something I once heard one of my wife's mentors—French obstetrician-turned-midwife Dr. Michel Odent—say a number of years ago at a workshop here which my wife organized.

Commenting on the horrifying plethora of ways in which a hospital succeeds in obstructing the delicate and all-important mother/infant bonding process, Odent went so far as to claim that this amounts to a conspiracy on the part of the society to separate children from their parents and particularly to suppress the feminine nature in both little boys and little girls. I have since heard John Taylor Gatto, former New York State Teacher of the Year, turned author and nationally recognized critic of compulsory education in the U.S., passionately decry this to be the very same mission being carried out by another monolithic American social institution—the public school system. There are numerous parallels between the hospital's approach to childbirth and conventional schooling's approach to learning—and the existence of a correlation between the high Cesarean section rate and the number of children in special education programs in the U.S. should be sought out—but this is a subject for another time.

According to Joseph Chilton Pearce, a great many children never truly recover from the setbacks caused by the early trauma surrounding their births, which is then reinforced by other harmful cultural practices such as the impersonal daycare system so often called on to substitute for working parents, the image-robbing and mind-numbing effects of television, and the now well-documented stunting impact of premature academic training. He lets teachers and schools off the hook somewhat by saying that their job today is next to impossible because so many kids are "damaged goods," and essentially buries individual blame entirely, choosing instead to focus on the now totally unnecessary perpetuation of ignorance—by the culture as a whole—around basic life processes such as learning. This is important, I think, because blame—though always a temptation easy to indulge in—certainly will never lead us out of the labyrinth in which we now find ourselves almost hopelessly lost.

The way out, I believe, lies in the direction of putting our fears—both individual and collective—back in their rightful places, and then to seat ourselves back in front of our own controls. Trust is the true antidote to fear, and I can recall a recent poignant example which illustrates what I mean. A group of kids asked me start up a math class at the Free School last winter, and at the very beginning of the first session, I noticed that the student whose idea the class had originated with was sitting at the table crying. Tears were pooling up on the old, tattered workbook that she had brought with her, a relic of an earlier time when she had struggled with learning arithmetic and reading, eventually deciding to put the math entirely aside for awhile.

Referring back to brain structure, we also now know that there is an approximate division of labor between the right and left hemispheres of the neo-cortex, which is actually the only part of the brain involved in the acquisition of so-called "academic skills." The left side is responsible for linear and sequential thinking, and therefore is heavily involved in the "Three R's;" while the right side, working in wholes rather than bits, specializes in the recognition of patterns, and is the half most active when we are engaged in art, movement and music. In my experience, some kids tend to be fairly balanced in the functioning of the two halves of their neo-cortexes, while others have tend to favor one side over the other to varying degrees.

Abby is a classic example of a what I call a "right brained kid." She is an accomplished artist, having begun exhibiting an extraordinary talent for drawing and painting at a very young age. She was also attracted to dance and became the youngest member of her church choir last year. Though not uninterested in reading and coming from a reading family, Abby had had great difficulty "breaking the code" in the early elementary grades. This, naturally, aroused concern in her parents, and to a certain extent, in her teachers as well. Thanks to good communication and rapport between home and school, we all did a fairly good job of keeping our fear in check; but unfortunately, the picture was not this simple. As is so often the case, when an extended family member, influential friend, or outside "expert" will add their worry to the mix, Abby's grandmother—a retired remedial reading specialist—became quite alarmed when Abby reached the age of eight or so and was still not reading much. Abby, indeed, was exhibiting textbook "symptoms" of "dyslexia" like letter, number and word reversals, and the inability to transfer what she had managed to retain from one level to the next.

Although, as I stated above, I don't give much credence to labels like dyslexia, I didn't in any way discount the grandmother's feelings. In fact, at one point we invited her to come to the school to give us a workshop on remedial reading, an experience which lessened her anxiety considerably, I think. The real problem that I saw in this instance was the potential for the transmission of fear to Abby both from her grandmother directly and through her mother (who also had a pattern of setting great store by her mother's beliefs),—resulting in everyone's preoccupation with her having "a reading problem" at that tender stage of her development. That, by working together, we were able to resolve a great deal of everyone's anxiety was an important factor in Abby eventually learning to read, I am quite certain. Exactly how she did manage the task I am not at all sure to this day. There were a number of things done to help Abby learn to read, including trying out some of the grandmother's specialized exercises and the employment of a reading tutor (with whom she developed a mutually appreciative relationship!) for a short time. I think it is important to note that nothing was done without Abby's consent and willing participation, so that she was never confronted with having a judgment (except her own!) that she was defective in some way. In the end, she was largely left to learn to read at her own pace and in her own way—aided and abetted by her reading teacher—and learn she did.

To complete this unsolicited sermon on the "teaching" of reading, I want to say that I have no reflexive problem with adults intervening in skillful, creative and caring ways to help a child to learn any new technique. At the same time, careful attention must be given to the spirit in which the assistance is given. Are there any unspoken messages regarding either the competency or the character of the learner hidden in the "remediation" process? Also, how much underlying fear is being passed along, thereby setting in motion the vicious cycle of not-learning described above? I have seen far too many kids who eventually learned to read, but with their desire and joy killed in the process, which was turned into a knock-down, drag-out affair because of all the fear-based urgency surrounding the situation. My current belief is that a team of wild horses wasn't going to keep Abby from learning to read; she simply needed to be ready first. Thankfully, today, Abby is a voracious reader, and due to her ready access to the right hemisphere of her neo-cortex, she is an award-winning young poet and a writer of clever short stories as well.

There is a twin-headed dragon still terrorizing up to fifty percent of the students in our public schools—the ones determined by the school to be "underachievers." One head continues to believe, all the recent reforms and innovations notwithstanding, that children should be expected to learn in the same (always left-brained) way at the same time. The other believes, in true Hobbesian fashion, that children are essentially nasty, brutish and short creatures, who left to their own devices can't be trusted to learn a damn thing. And kids know this, though most can't tell anyone that they do—above all not their parents. Add the bell-curve to those fear-based beliefs and it's no wonder that "special education" has also become a growth industry as we approach the end of the twentieth century.

Meanwhile, back to Abby whom we left in a puddle of tears in our math class. Abby's impetus to request the class had come from her decision that it was time to "catch up" on her math skills now that she was thirteen and considering going on to the public high school in the next year or so. Seeing her crying quietly at the table, I sat down next to her and asked her what the matter was. She answered that she was afraid that she couldn't learn math, that it was just too hard for her. We talked about her earlier difficulties with both reading and math, and I reminded her how quickly she had learned to read once she was ready. In order to reassure her that it was OK that she was just setting out to tackle her math, I told her that she had been wise to wait until the math learning circuits in her brain were completed. We agreed the fear that she couldn't learn math was the big problem, and I suggested that she begin with memorizing the multiplication tables, after which I claimed, everything else would be downhill from there. It only took her a couple of days to do it, and Abby has been sailing along ever since. She will undoubtedly be ready for high school when that day arrives.

The moral of Abby's story—and I could tell many more just like it—is that learning, like childbirth, is a perfectly natural, healthy process, and children can be trusted to monitor and manage their own educational growth and development. Of course they need good role models, occasional guidance and challenge, and access to books, materials, and equipment, but it must be remembered that the best motivation to learn comes from within, the ever-increasing number of self-taught walkers and talkers crowding the planet today being ample proof of that fact. There's an old joke that says if walking and talking were skills that required teaching to children, then there would be an awful lot more silent people in wheelchairs out there today.

The point is that when children are truly extended trust and are allowed to be responsible for themselves, they learn more quickly and more easily, and the learning tends to be for life and not just until the end of the marking period. In a recent and startling book called *Punished By Rewards: The Trouble With Gold Stars, Incentive Plans, "A's," Praise and Other Bribes,* author Alfie Kohn cites study after study documenting the reality that individuals who perform tasks in order to receive extrinsic rewards do far less well than those who are self-motivated and who find their satisfaction in the activity itself. The inhibitory effects of negative reinforcement were demonstrated many decades ago by B.F. Skinner, the inventor of the branch of psychology called behaviorism which continues to provide the rationale for the methodology of conventional schooling; but now Kohn's research reveals that even such simple forms of positive reinforcement as praise can hamper learning and achievement. And the reason, I am convinced, is fear, which we now know, thanks to theorists like Pearce and Hart, is biologically incompatible with learning. All too often, managed, monitored and measured learning environments like most modern schools communicate an unspoken fear-based dependency that says that without all the structured trappings, nothing constructive would happen. Left to their own devices, kids would just goof off all day—plus the "Lord of the Flies" myth for ghetto blacks—and would never be prepared to face "the real world"—whatever that might be. In addition to being very smart, kids are sensitive to these invisible signals. Far too many respond accordingly, only to be labeled as deficient in some way, setting in motion the vicious cycle of "failure" which often follows them throughout their lives.

The fear-based belief that our children must begin performing academically at a young age has a long reach. Antonio's father, an assistant professor at a local university, once asked me in all seriousness how I expected his son to manage as an adult if he could not read. Antonio, a first-grader at the time, was another typically "right brained" kid in no hurry to begin reading on his own, and who, instead would spend hours either building great structures in our woodshop or concocting far-out, imaginative fantasy games with his age-mates. There was Antonio, highly intelligent and verbal, and yet his inability to read at age seven had triggered the most catastrophic of fears in his well-educated father. However, fear out in the open is far easier to deal with than fear that is unexpressed and hidden away; thus, I was able to reassure Antonio's dad in the space of a one-hour conference, predicting that by age ten Antonio's learning curve would begin to match up with, if not exceed his peers. As surprised as I was by the degree of the father's anxiety, I was equally grateful for his willingness to explore it, and then more or less put it to rest.

We are not always as fortunate as we were with Antonio and his family, and we end up "losing" kids whose parents can't find their way to trust that their kids will learn what they need to learn when they need to learn it, given the time and the space in which to operate. And our reluctance to issue what I call conventional schooling's "reassurance policy"—the compulsory classes, the endless repetition, the graded tests and papers, and so on—certainly doesn't help matters much. We've yet to find a universal solution to this year-in and year-out problem; and meanwhile, it's one that we just do the best we can with. We have learned that maintaining open communication is the key. This establishes the trust that enables parents to hang in there while their kids build the kind of permanent foundation beneath themselves that will support them throughout their adult lives. I have had the privilege over the past twenty-one years of watching hundreds of children—of every imaginable shape, size, race, religion and social class—slowly constructing their own authentic selves. The continual beauty, as well as the occasional miraculousness of the process, have helped me to put a great many of my fears to rest, making me a much more relaxed and effective teacher than when I first began. Nevertheless, fear, which behaves much like a radioactive isotope with a very long half-life, often continues to rear its ugly head somewhere deep inside, challenging me, like Max in Sendak's classic, *Where the Wild Things Are*, to stare it down and order it to "BE STILL!" so that I can get on with the joyful business of living and learning.

> *Think of the kind of world you want to live and work in. What do you need to know to build the world? Demand that your teachers teach you that.*
> —*Prince Peter Kropotkin*

Nat Needle, until recently the Dean of the Campus School of Clonlara in Ann Arbor, Michigan, began his educational career as a graduate student at the University of Massachusetts, from whose ivy-covered walls he began striking out on his own, visiting alternative schools and making his plans for his own school in western Massachusetts, which became a reality during the late eighties: New Salem Academy, profiled in Challenging the Giant *volume II on pages 74-78.*

Forced to close its doors because of financial stringencies, Nat's school still stands as a splendid example of his image of life, from which position of integrity and devotion he has not swerved. In fact, he was largely responsible for the founding of ΣΚΟΛΕ, the proposal for which came from him at a regional conference at his school in 1985!

Nat's quite a guy—a born teacher with tremendously varied gifts as well as a pianist, composer, an irresistible comedian and a natural philosopher. Quoting from the conclusion to his NSA article, on the subject of preventing "burn-out":

> Over the years we have set up little tripwires within our schools which remind us of the wonder of our jobs: an all-school meeting, a class in the woods, a hug from a fellow teacher, another alternative schools conference. Then we catch our breath, hit ourselves on the head, try to figure out how we got here, and go back to this amazing work.
>
> We keep on trucking on this long, endless alternative school path, encouraging the growth of young human beings who, just maybe, from their experiences in our schools, will grow to be a little more open, compassionate, wise and free than we are. It's an ennobling task for all of us to be what a Baha'i friend of mine once called "layers of seeds, heralds of the dawn."

Here are excerpts from a letter Nat sent in response to Chris' article on fear:

... Chris' article on fear could not come, for me, at a better moment. This year, there were six teenagers who were really worried about how the freedom of Clonlara was affecting their ability to be productive in conventional school terms. This triggered my own latent fears that I was harming these kids by letting them run their own lives.

What we did was this: the six kids and I formed a "structure club", kind of a program within a program, to experiment with monthly self-chosen "assignments" in reading, writing, math, and research. I told them that I was willing, at their request, to encourage them to work on these projects at certain times of the day, but that I would stop cold if I felt we were getting into "why don't you, yes but.." games or any other form of passive resistance. We also agreed to discuss the various emotions and behavior patterns that came up within this framework. In other words, looking at the process was as important as evaluating products.

We've been doing this for two months now, and the patterns have sure been interesting to watch and discuss. I found myself occasionally slipping back into old public-school teacher modes of judging myself in terms of what they were doing or not doing, as well as judging them as people. This anxiety and anger would surface, and the line between reminding and nagging started to blur on some days. Students began to enact old "sure, in a minute" responses, making excuses to me, erecting defenses. When students would start to produce things, instead of taking simple sympathetic joy in their accomplishment, I would feel critical, compare it to my own rabid school achievement in high school, and so on. Thankfully, I'm sufficiently bored with these tired old tapes that I can't keep them up for long anymore.

In our group, we discuss this stuff as much as we talk about what people have gotten done or not. Recently, it came up for discussion that students were finishing things at home, and procrastinating about "turning them in," as the saying goes. So what's that all about? Ownership? Fear of criticism? Anyway, as we all get down to the nitty-gritty of the games that fear plays with us, it's fun to see all of us in the group, including me, take more ownership for our own learning, and our own lives.

No matter how many times I go around with teenagers on this loop, I keep coming back to the same starting point. This is that the uniform school-style "productivity" demanded of teenagers in society short-circuits, at least for some kids, some other very important internal processes that are crucial to the development of a free person. When kids start to just work because they want to create, or simply to have the peace that comes with concentration, or to fulfill their organic responsibilities to the group (planning menus for a trip, for example), it's beautiful. When they're struggling with defenses, games, and excuses, it's ugly. If I take a break from my fears, I can directly experience the truth of this, and trust it completely. Fear sucks. Of course, it's also a necessary teacher sometimes, as we ask where it comes from.

Our entire educational system is built on fear, and on the isolation of individuals competing with each other. André Houle compares 1940 with 1990, and blames TV and family disintegration for the downward slide. But I wonder if the seeds for the 1990's weren't present in the 1940's. The threat of enemies (Japan and Germany, then the Soviets and Chinese, now the "global competitive market") gets used to keep everyone on the fear treadmill, running on isolated competitive achievement tracks, with the family commanded to adapt to suit (as it still does today in Japan). But the anti-humanity of this kind of so-called order contains within it the makings of its own chaos, as stress overtakes those who "succeed", and apathy grows in those who don't. Japan too will unravel, in its own way. Or the need to "pull everyone together" will find some new outlet in outward national aggression, too horrible to contemplate.

Are creativity and productivity possible without fear? I'll accept that some fear is a natural ingredient of life; after all, it gives us something to grow out of, if nothing else. But we're not talking about fear as a problem in our system, we're talking about its use as the fundamental solution. All the pretty "motivational" posters (NUMBERS ARE YOUR FRIENDS!!!!!) covering it up just make it uglier. Do creativity and productivity have a higher function than making us individually successful, or "competitive in the global marketplace"? Am I willing to give up all the free, rambling discussion, the time to work out personal conflicts, and the road trips in order to keep everyone "on task" through fear?

What happens when we start to replace the curriculum of fear with a culture of conversation? Well, for one thing, a lot of fear comes up, because it's not what society wants from teenagers, or from teachers. When you create your own sub-culture, it can be scary. But perhaps that's the kind of fear that lets you know you're a fish checking out the land. ...

And Nat sent on the following article:

TEN PRINCIPLES OF HOLISTIC EDUCATION
by Nathaniel Needle

These principles summarize the basis for my educational practice as it has evolved over the past 20 years, working with young people and adults in a variety of situations: public school, alternative school, graduate school, youth theater, summer camp, Buddhist religious education. With the recent birth of my first child, I'm starting home education too!

All the opinions herein are open to ongoing revision based on reflection and experience. This is not a blueprint for a particular educational enterprise. I encourage parents, teachers, and students to use these principles as guidelines for experimentation: what kinds of educational arrangements are best suited to putting these principles into action in your specific circumstances? I hope they can provide a touchstone for educators who are not in a position to stray very far from cultural norms as well as for those who are looking to create intentional communities which embody holistic ideals from the start.

I use the term "ecological" in this article to express how different aspects of life mutually reinforce each other to create a self-sustaining system. For example, the educational plan that requires students to be in one building all day, some distance from home, goes hand-in-hand with the economic plan which requires parents to do likewise. Ecological awareness includes not only our natural planetary ecology, but also our social ecology which affects and is affected by it. It means spotting mutually reinforcing connections already in place, and setting new ones in motion.

The term "holistic" refers to a way of seeing the self, others, society, and nature as an interrelated web. Within this web, no one is separate from other human beings and their suffering, nor from our planet and the natural forces which sustain life. At the same time, each person is, uniquely and preciously, a whole expression of the entire web.

A holistic view encourages awareness of the social, emotional, natural, historical, and other contexts within which experience occurs. Although these contexts shape us, we can also act upon them. For example, a holistic view of education pays as much attention to transforming the context of human relationships within which learning takes place as to the subject-matter itself.

These principles describe a spiritual context for learning which does not recommend any fixed "curriculum": courses, classes, tests, or subject requirements. Within this context, learning content and methods may vary according to individual and community wishes.

What remains constant is faith that each person can contribute in some way to the liberation of society from greed, anger and ignorance. The purpose of holistic education is to allow each person to develop profound self-knowledge, and, through it, the skill required to cooperate with others towards social transformation. Teachers and students pursue the various disciplines with an awareness of this larger context.

Holistic education addresses our essential function as awakening human beings. It is an alternative to education which sees people as isolated competitors striving to achieve personal material security and status within a "global market".

I don't think holistic educators need a master plan for the process or the results of personal and social development on a large or long-term scale (master plans tend to encourage masters who plan them). I think it's wiser to have confidence that as people expand their awareness of internal and external realities, and abandon their attachment to ego, they will evolve social forms which befit their capacities. These forms in turn will encourage further awakening among individuals, and so on in an ecological "feedback loop".

Within such a vision, great meaning adheres to our cultivation of mindfulness in small ways: being kind, making friends out of enemies, conserving material resources, and so on. Without such foundation stones, social change efforts risk becoming the same old wine in a new bottle.

1. **Learning wisdom and compassion is the context for learning everything else.**

Wisdom and compassion are the reflective and emotional aspects, respectively, of our liberation from the bonds of egocentrism. Only as people become wise and compassionate can we have peace on earth. Sheer obedience, whether to authority or to the promptings of ego, is no substitute for exercising one's own wisdom eye and compassionate heart. Nor are technical skill, artistic talent, or athletic prowess, as useful or pleasant as these might be.

Any learning activity has two aspects. There is a contextual aspect involving choice, effort, patience, interest, overcoming fear, and the nature of the teaching-learning relationship. Wisdom and compassion on the part of both teacher and student are exercised precisely when working skillfully and mutually with this context.

There is also the content itself, which should engage the student in a direct experience of expanding his or her awareness and capacities. As these increase, so do the complexity and richness of our interactions with and contributions to others. These in turn multiply opportunities for the exercise of wisdom and compassion on a wider scale. For example, a young person making decisions about the bookstore is helped by skill at math and knowledge of books. Someone who is familiar with the history of World War II, and the varying viewpoints surrounding its final days, can contribute more to a wise and compassionate commemoration of the bombing of Hiroshima and Nagasaki.

2. Young and old can learn wisdom and compassion
Often we assume that wisdom and compassion are faculties that come magically with age if at all. We rarely explore what can be done to develop wisdom and compassion in young people, within the natural context of a social group. Skills and knowledge are divorced from situations which would exercise the capacity for wisdom and compassion. Instead we rely upon obedience to authority figures and a set of rules to keep behavior in line with values.

Perhaps the most important source of wisdom and compassion is prolonged engagement with adults and young people who take these values to heart and strive to live by them. Here is a partial list of other gateways: voluntarily sharing in common tasks, making choices without coercion by others, evaluating the results of one's choices without being dominated by fear, being treated with respect and love doing helpful things and having them appreciated, having opportunities to exercise leadership and judgment on important matters, participating in a democratic process. listening to people of varied views, backgrounds, and personalities, any sincere spiritual practice such as meditation.

We also need to hang on to a wise sense of humor, so that we aren't hovering over every action, assessing it for its purity.

How we develop wisdom and compassion is, I think, an experimental matter. Faith that it can be developed, and that it can be distinguished from mere conformity or cleverness, is what this principle is about. May experiments flourish!

3. We exist in an ecological web

Here's a sample list of questions:

Where does our food come from?

What is the daily experience of those who grew or prepared the food for us to eat?

How does what we eat affect ourselves and others?

How do we organize ourselves for production and consumption? What kinds of people are around to influence us?

How do we relate to nature?

How do we treat animals in different cultures?

How does what we possess influence what others possess?

How much and what kind of waste do we produce? Where does it go?

Who makes decisions that affect us and how are the decisions made?

What are the relations of equality, authority and submission in the workplace and the family?

How did we adapt to what our parents told us when we were small?

How do people of different ages learn from each other?

What are our most pressing desires?

What do we think we must do to be happy?

The most important factors influencing our characters and our learning are the easiest to take for granted. Some of these are natural forces (e.g., the needs of our own bodies) to which we can adapt more intelligently. Others are cultural forces which determine how we interact with each other and with nature, and how we perceive ourselves.

If we are determined to learn and grow, we need to have a society which contributes to learning and growth. Therefore we take, as our starting point for education, critical inquiry, practical experimentation, and social activism regarding the web we live in. The ecological awareness-context in which we work frames the motivating question for our educational activity: how do things as they stand affect our growth, the growth of our brothers and sisters all over the planet, and a healthy, sustainable planetary ecology?

Inquiry should come out of each person's capacity for reason and feeling. Experiments must respect each person or group's desire for action. A friendly ecological curiosity is important, not some imposed dogma about method or any preordained set of solutions. There is room for every kind of sincere effort. The danger in articulating and prescribing this kind of overarching purpose for education is that it will encourage Puritanism, humorlessness, and teaching based on indoctrination rather than shared experience. Ecological awareness is about opening ourselves up, not closing ourselves down. No set of concepts or beliefs can substitute for wisdom and compassion as a check on our tendency towards egocentrism in all its various forms, including thinking we are always right.

Learning is influenced by psychobiological forces as well as larger socioeconomic and natural forces. How aware we are of these forces influences our growth as well. Finally, our attitude towards them is also important: do we see them as aspects of our world which are subject to the scrutiny and regulation of a wise eye and a compassionate heart? Or do we try to navigate a "safe zone" in which our cravings and attachments, and their cumulative effect upon our society and our planet, are considered none of our educational business?

4. Growth is an ecological process

On a trip last spring to the Utah desert, a friend explained to me about efforts to slow erosion and desertification by developing pockets of life. Desert plants were introduced which needed little in the way of soil to grow. As these decomposed, patches of fragile "cryptobiotic" soil, only slightly different from the surrounding sand, began to form. Posted signs and local residents implored tourists not to step on this delicate crust. The cryptobiotic soil, in turn, will gradually be able to support a greater variety of plants, which will create hardier soil. This, with vigilance against disruption, will set in motion a reinforcing loop which will become less fragile and more self-sustaining. Eventually, a wall of sturdy life will thwart the encroaching desert.

Holistic education means nurturing a kind of "growth ecology". Influences are evaluated according to how they contribute to a "feedback loop" which generates skill and knowledge within a context of wisdom and compassion. The indispensable "park rangers" of such an effort are the educators (including parents and others without any particular teacher training) who set an example for others by their conduct. They work with the community to establish and maintain standards for human relations designed to remove fear and promote freedom. This is the fragile "soil" in which some people feel moved to make contributions of talent and energy to a community culture of learning. The satisfaction and appreciation enjoyed by some encourages others. Gradually a world of service, inquiry, artistic and linguistic expression emerges.

5. Educators must work on themselves

Holistic educators may be professionals, parents, or others (those supervising in the kitchen or the garden of a residential facility, for example) who are taking on an educational role.

Because growth is an ecological process, the degree of wisdom and compassion of those in positions of leadership has a strong radiating effect on the quality of everyone's learning. Teachers' honesty, openness, service, sense of humor, and spiritual discipline set an example for everyone. So educators must develop their own characters and their skillfulness in working with others. This process should be both internal and collective. For this reason, friendship and trust among members of a holistic teaching team is a great advantage. Teachers should evaluate their organizational roles and structures by how well they foster mutual growth.

6. The culture is the curriculum

Holistic education holds that learning content makes the most difference to our development when it is part of our cultural experience, particularly our daily life in community and our network of relationships. In fact, it holds that the purpose of knowledge and skill is to deepen our experience here and now, with the understanding that, to paraphrase John Dewey, the best preparation for the future is a rich and meaningful present.

Instead of being overly concerned about the content of any particular curriculum, holistic educators are more interested in the nature and quality of the culture for people of all ages. They ask questions like this:

How does our daily life include opportunities and demands for learning which are inherent in the needs of regularly arising situations: cooking, eating, waste disposal, exercise, dealing with conflict, traveling, playing, performing, religious practice, conversation, and so on?

How can most adults in a community, rather than a custodial few, share knowledge and skill with the young people of that community?

How can people in general, without regard to age, share knowledge and skill with each other?

Is the knowledge and skill thought valuable for the future of the young used obviously by adults (especially parents and grandparents) to enrich their cultural lives?

How can we create a variety of learning contexts for the young, besides organizing them into large age-specific groups? Can they explore on their own, play and work with kids of different ages, watch and participate alongside adults, or secure the individual attention of mentors of all ages?

Aren't there many things which a holistic enterprise might expect nearly everyone to learn? Yes, but these things are not set down and handed down as a "curriculum". Instead, effort goes into increasing the variety and quality of, and time available for, learning relationships between people of all ages (including time to be with oneself).

Within a holistic learning community, the knowledge, and skills of our ancestors become the refreshments at an ongoing lifelong party. There is no rush to get something arbitrarily "covered" by a certain age. Facts, skills, and disciplines that are in fact necessary for full participation in the culture are learned through participation in the culture. This includes intimate relationships (e.g., teenager and younger child sitting down with a book) and group activities (like building a house or producing a newspaper). Classes and other prepared study sequences are organized and chosen for the specialized purposes of some, rather than universally required measures of success or failure.

7. Respect individual learning paths

Nature endows human beings with a vast variety of aptitudes and environmental influences. This variety provides a basis for cooperation and mutual respect. When I help out on an exterior painting project at the Buddhist temple, I follow the guidance of those who know more about this business than I do. When volunteer adults at the temple help me to rehearse a play with children, they follow my lead. It's natural for people to have complementary areas of relative expertise and ignorance.

Holistic education invests in a cultural network of activities and relationships in which nearly everyone can be trusted to learn what they need to enjoy further opportunities while respecting others and nature. Put another way, it is the culture which can be trusted to teach people how to, for example, read and write, control their anger, or use and understand the recycling system.

This liberates individuals to make unique and widely varied contributions within a cooperative social framework. We should value everyone for whatever it is that they do know, or can do, or are good at, that benefits others. People who have a great aptitude for anything help, teach, and enrich the lives of those who have less. It is this very quality, even more than a universally shared body of ritual, symbolic, or factual knowledge, which, from a holistic standpoint, makes a culture most worthy of perpetuation.

When people are secure in themselves and their place in the community, they can be persuaded to try their hand at things for which they have supposedly little aptitude, and at different points throughout their lives. I always thought I was no good at fixing things, but since I have been involved in small projects at the temple, watching what materials and tools experienced people use, I've been less shy about taking up small challenges around my apartment.

When all people are allowed to construct a sense of intellectual, social, and creative self-worth based on their individually varied aptitudes and interests, then language, science, history, and mathematics can take their natural place alongside and integrated with other aspects of daily life, without being markers of superiority. When people who are best at writing and people who are best at making tools are not separated by irrelevant distinctions, they can mutually influence each other's cultural world in the fullest possible way.

8. Respect community

It is difficult to put holistic ideals into practice without giving priority to the development of some level of community, however slight at first (always remembering that first cryptobiotic soil!). The development of our individuality relies on community, on a network of relationships built upon loving kindness and compassion. The commitment to creating and maintaining community helps to liberate us from the constant need to protect the ego, to gain some narrow advantage, to defend oneself against others. It also enlists cooperative support for any goals we have which have the potential to contribute to others. This frees us to discover ourselves, and to bring our potential to fruition.

Community provides a tempering influence on our egocentric tendencies. Rather than receiving information on our behavior from a single authority, we get a wider "reality check" with respect to how what we do and say affects others. To the extent that people share community labor, they get a chance to try out a wide variety of tasks over time. Also, when many people are helping with general tasks, it gives us more time for our own specialized pursuits.

Thus a holistic perspective does not see it as an infringement of someone's freedom to expect him or her to contribute to the community, as long as everyone has equal access to the process of deciding what the expectations will be. Sometimes the contribution may be one in which the individual's unique qualities are less important: everyone has to run outside and get the clothes off the line before the storm hits. Or else it may border on the eccentric: strange sculptures in the garden, or bizarre poems sent home from faraway lands. Seen over the long term, each kind of contribution has its season. Common discussion reveals what the community needs from each person, and what each person has to offer.

When a community makes decisions so as to give everyone a voice, no matter how old, then opportunities are multiplied for everyone's exercise of wisdom and compassion. A democratic approach increases respect for the community by making it clear that "the will of the community" is not just a code phrase for the will of a few dominant individuals.

9. Balancing individuality and community is what calls forth compassion and wisdom

By discovering and rediscovering their own proper balance of personal autonomy and social alignment, individuals in a community grow to understand each other and their life together. Prior agreements on this score can be useful, but they should not be used to avoid all conflict, and the learning adventure that comes with it.

If each person's desires were always identical with what promoted peace and happiness for all members of the community, then there would be no need to exercise wisdom or compassion. But sometimes people tell lies, use force, leave dishes in the sink, and so on. Sometimes people put the reputation and integrity of the community at risk through selfish actions. On the other hand, sometimes the community creates so many taboos and restrictions that individual expression is stifled, and fear of criticism dominates the scene.

A holistic approach includes dealing with conflict between individuals, and between the individual and the community, as part of a whole education. It sees each instance as an opportunity to increase awareness of self and also of our interdependence with others. This creates a universal context for the varying content of interpersonal conflicts. Even if the people most caught up in the content of the conflict can't see the forest for the trees at that moment, they can rely upon others who are more detached to do so. Thus the cultivation of a community with the capacity for open dialogue based on mutual respect has a great conditioning influence on particular conflicts which arise. It serves as a reservoir of compassion and wisdom upon which everyone can draw.

10. Aim towards leaving no one out

Holistic education does not rank or sort people by comparing them to each other or to some fixed, narrow set of criteria. Nor does it seek some artificially imposed equality wherein those most qualified to fulfill some function or exercise leadership in a given area are held back so that others less able do not feel slighted. Both points of view stem from arrangements in which honor, respect, and well-being are scarce commodities, reserved for those who make it to the "top", or at least the "middle".

Within the context of a holistic learning community, education proceeds from the calling forth of individual capacities in service to others through the construction of an intelligent culture. Individual development and collective effort go hand-in-hand within such a "growth ecology". Each person is seen as needed, as having something to offer. Sometimes even the most difficult personalities provide useful challenges to the compassion and wisdom of the community! The community cannot afford to waste anyone; it's in its interest to find a way to include everyone.

This may take time. Following our ecological model, no community that wishes to found itself upon open dialogue and free expression can start off by including the full range of personalities who exist on this planet: it will disintegrate.

On the other hand, communities, as well as the individuals involved, may benefit by including a certain number of people who place greater demands on the group. The wisdom and compassion that grow when the strong protect and care for the weak cannot get much exercise in a group which only includes the strong. It is also possible to design communities from the start with certain kinds of members in mind: the sick, the aged, the emotionally disturbed, and so on.

Discerning the point at which variety stretches the fabric of community past a healthy balance is a matter for wise and compassionate deliberation in each case. Each community, following this underlying principle, must find its own way. There is no single perfect model which is right for everyone.

The principle of leaving no one out conditions how evaluation is used. We need to evaluate each other and ourselves in order to know whether each of us has the skill, knowledge, compassion, and wisdom to use a particular set of responsibilities, privileges, and opportunities in a way that will promote growth for themselves and others.

But evaluation should not limit anyone's opportunity to use his or her capacities to the fullest, or to be recognized and supported as a whole, complex, worthy being with unique qualities to contribute to the community. When this is not at stake, evaluation can become far more honest and mutual. Those being evaluated can get straight feedback from others, at the same time that they cultivate their own self-honesty and patience. The principle of leaving no one out, rather than avoiding evaluation, strives to remove irrelevant fears from the process, thus encouraging greater respect for it as a learning tool in itself.

A holistic context encourages forms of evaluation which are integrated with the student's daily life, and his or her personal relationship with teachers and others. One is the completion of complex deeds or projects which, in addition to their intrinsic value, demonstrate the precise kinds of competence one will need in one's new role. The other is the testimony of those who have closely observed someone in prior situations. Through documenting one's deeds in some organized way, and similarly compiling one's references, one should be able to satisfy the need for evaluation on the part of those outside as well as inside the community.

The principle of leaving no one out conditions our use of competition in the same way. There is no problem with making moderate use of competition to stimulate creativity, fun, exertion, and growth in general. Problems arise when competition becomes the context for education (or economics), the dominant motivating factor. When competition is used wisely and compassionately, within a larger context of cooperation, it does not put anyone's essential material or social well-being at risk. People are free to gain just as much in wisdom and experience by losing as by winning. The community is careful not to glorify winners so much as to obscure the true glory that comes from sincere effort and mutual respect on the part of everyone.

"Leaving no one out" completes the circle of holistic thinking that began with our dedication to wisdom and compassion as the basis for all other learning. It means no one is outside the ecosystem of growth, participation in a full human life, and respect for his or her individual nature. It is to orient ourselves towards this goal that we educate ourselves and our children.

11. Recommended books

I ask the reader to forgive the absence of scholarship in this article. As an acknowledgment of the various inspirations for it, I offer this personal reading list. It is by no means a bibliography for the holistic education field.

Bronfenbrenner, Urie. *The Ecology of Human Development*, Cambridge, MA: Harvard University Press, 1979.

Dewey, John. *Democracy and Education*, New York: Macmillan, 1916.

Dewey, John. *Experience and Education*, New York: Macmillan, 1938.

Greenberg, Daniel and Hanna, et al. *The Sudbury Valley School Experience*, Framingham, MA: Sudbury Valley School Press, 1987.

Gordon, Thomas. *Parent Effectiveness Training*, New York: Penguin, 1970.

Illich, Ivan. *Deschooling Society*, New York: Harper and Row, 1971.

Jones, Ken. *The Social Face of Buddhism*, London: Wisdom Publications, 1989.

Miller, Ron. *What Are Schools For?: Holistic Education in American Culture*, Brandon, VT: Holistic Education Press, 1990.

Peck, M. Scott. *The Different Drum: Community Making and Peace*, New York: Simon and Schuster, 1987.

Piaget, Jean. *The Moral Judgment of the Child*, New York: Macmillan, 1965.

MADALYNE
by Holly Engel

This gifted first grade teacher lost her job at the end of the school year in which this article was written! Are we Americans hopelessly self-destructive?

It was the middle of the 1992-1993 school year at Prairie View Elementary School when I first saw her. I knew it would be difficult for her to be accepted by her peers. She was very short, about five inches shorter than the others. Her eyes were crossed and her eyebrows were too thin. It was obvious that her dress was old from the several patches. Her nose was so incredible. It was very long, with a wart on the end. She had a horrible profile because of the nose. Her hair was long and stringy. She had freckles, Also, I soon found out that she had eleven toes— six on one foot.

When I learned that I was going to get a special needs student, I did the usual things that need to be done to have a new student added. I had a special small desk brought in the room and a tall chair to accompany it. I made out her name tag and wrote her name in my attendance book.

The Monday that she arrived was a cold and windy day. Madalyne was the first one there, beating the morning bell by almost ten minutes. I helped her put her supplies away and gave her a crayon so she could start her morning work. But, she did not get far before the bell rang and the other students entered the room.

I went to the chalk board and began writing the date and some notes for the students to read. While my back was to the class, I suddenly heard a lot of laughter. I heard someone yell, "Miss Engel, what is she doing here?"

I turned to see six or seven children surrounding Madalyne. One was pulling her hair. One was pinching her nose. The rest were laughing and pointing. I was shocked to see this. "What are you doing to Madalyne? You leave her alone! She is a new friend in our class." I was very upset and went to see if Madalyne was all right. The other students sat down and began their morning work, buzzing about the new, odd student.

After the Pledge of Allegiance and the National Anthem, I decided it was time to introduce Madalyne formally to the class. She had been stared at and whispered about for long enough.

I rang my brass apple bell to get the attention of the class. As I stood behind Madalyne's chair with my hands on her shoulders, the class grew very quiet. The first graders were very still.

I cleared my throat. "We have a new friend. This is Madalyne Wimple. She will need a lot of help getting used to our school and classroom. I hope you all will be a good friend to her." I heard a few kids snicker.

Over the next months, the class helped Madalyne in many ways. Sometimes she fell out of her chair. A child would carefully pick her up and put her back in the chair. Madalyne would fall asleep in class, too! This stunned the class. Of course, they would look towards me for a reaction. I would calmly ask someone to wake her up. The child did so very gently. The child would give Madalyne her pencil and show her where we were on the page.

Madalyne was assimilated into our class easily. The counselors and other teachers would go out of their way to greet Madalyne. Some would even have to explain to wondering visitors that Madalyne "was part of Miss Engel's class."

Since we did a lot of cooperative learning and buddy work, Madalyne often was chosen as a buddy. It was both intriguing and touching to see the first graders so hard at work with a buddy that seemingly had so little to offer to the task. After all, she was a "special needs" student and needed a lot of help with even sitting at her desk. But the stories that she and her buddy wrote would bring tears to my eyes.

When a child chose Madalyne to partner work, that child felt free to be creative, be different from the way the class viewed him/her. The class clown became a serious adventure writer with Madalyne's help. The shy, quiet child was able to read her and Madalyne's story in front of an audience with Madalyne's help. A boy who was hyperactive became subdued, somber and physically still while working with Madalyne.

Difficult times at home often plague any classroom in this day and age. Some children act disrespectful, rude, and have deviant behavior as a result of this. Some young children become painfully shy and quiet. The children do not understand the fighting, financial problems, divorce, and even drug, alcohol and physical abuse that may plague an unstable home. To live in and deal with this is an awful lot to ask a child of six or seven. Kids know that things are not calm at home. They know it does not feel good and safe at home. But to verbally express these thoughts and feelings is almost an impossible thing.

I was surprised at the times when Madalyne would be dearest to a child. The neediest, most stressed child would often read to Madalyne, buddy work with her, help her to our special class, and make sure she was sitting up straight in her chair. As I walked around the classroom to check on-task behavior and progress on a project, I noticed that the upset child would be holding Madalyne's hand. Some would even carry Madalyne to my desk and softly say, "Madalyne is sad. She is worried that her parents are going to get a divorce." Or a child would tell me that Madalyne is tired because she had to dance last night from 7:00 to 10:00. Madalyne would also feel sad that her mom was going out of town on business.

Madalyne also had physical needs. She would need to go to the bathroom, according to her helper. Sometimes her shoes were too small and she would need to take them off. Sometimes she might just need a big hug from me, along with her friend.

It was surprising to me that the children used Madalyne as a voice to express the hurtful and scary parts of their lives. At one time or another, each child in my class expressed their feelings through Madalyne. Without embarrassment, children told me of Madalyne's weekend fights with her brother and sister and how she hates her daycare center.

I felt extremely lucky that my small class had the ability to express the hurt they felt. Many people who had a difficult childhood grow up to be difficult adults. Usually, adults with problems need a doctor to help them sift back through the past in order to remember and express hard times when they were very young.

I think my class, with Madalyne's help, will be healthier and happier as they grow. They were able to use Madalyne's "tough times at home" to cleanse themselves of the guilt, fear, and pain associated with growing up in the midst of an unstable home, and an ever-changing world.

One day, during her first week at school, Madalyne was extremely late. We were all very concerned. Was she lost? Was she sick? Did anyone see her in the cafeteria getting breakfast? The class was so concerned that I promised I would call Mrs. Wimple at recess to solve the mystery.

The students were so concerned about Madalyne that the first lesson was not a big success. Everyone stared at the door and at Madalyne's seat. I was working along through my lesson plan about Clifford, the Big Red Dog when there was a knock on the door. All of the boys' and girls' eyes widened with excitement. The door slowly opened. In came Madalyne and Mrs. McKee, our neighbor across the hall.

"Madalyne! Where have you been?" asked one student. Another student ran over to help Madalyne to her seat. Expressions of great relief were written across every small face in my class.

Mrs. McKee explained that Madalyne had gotten lost and one of her students helped Madalyne back to the classroom.

I asked the kids to describe how Madalyne looks. At first, they did not want to talk about it. I gently prodded. "What about her dress?" I asked.

"It is a pretty color of purple," answered a student.

"What about her nose?" I asked. The room was silent. "Do you like her hair? Would anyone in here want to have Madalyne's hair?" Several kids squirmed. No one made eye contact with me.

I tried again at a different angle. "Now really, is she that pretty? Personally, I think her feet are too big." I wrote my idea about Madalyne on the chart paper I had on the chalk board. I solicited new ideas.

"Well, her nose is kind of big. But that makes it easier to smell things with," came the first reply.

"Her eyes are crossed, but I think that glasses would fix that."

"Her dress has patches, but it is a pretty color."

Many hands were in the air now. The boys and girls gave words or sentences to describe Madalyne's physical appearance. Curiously, each item about her ugly physique was defended.

Soon our chart was full. I asked the kids why it was so hard to fill the chart paper. They explained to me that Madalyne was a good friend, she liked to be read to, she smiles all the time, and she is nice. One by one came the exact responses I had desired: descriptions of Madalyne's personality and character that made her so lovable.

In closing the lesson, I explained that in life, there are many people that may look odd or different. There are many people who have various beliefs and ways of life. I instructed the children to remember Madalyne when they meet these people. Think about how ugly Madalyne was on the outside, and how wonderful she is on the inside.

Madalyne was invited back into the room, and we proceeded with our day. Madalyne was more popular than ever. There was no fear of peer pressure or teasing that often follows an oddball student. The rest of the school unfortunately did not know Madalyne. They did not know how sweet she was and what a wonderful friend she was.

The students in my class would have to endure a lot of teasing, laughing, hurtful comments about Madalyne. She was ugly, funny-looking, dirty, poor. But my students were very strong, and they stood up to the big kids who laughed and pointed. My kids would hug Madalyne tighter to their chest. Some even plugged her ears as rude comments were thrown our direction.

You see, Madalyne was not only a very special student with a lot of needs, she was a doll. A doll that I had specially made for a lesson on "don't judge a book by its cover." This lesson grew and bloomed into an incredible five months. I learned about how children think and act. The students learned about vicious bullies.

We all learned about what love really is. For the love we had for Madalyne was so strong, it inspired us all. Madalyne was definitely the most popular girl in the class.

This is to pass on some of that love. This is the story of Madalyne, the most popular girl in the class.

Thus, the time had come for some lessons that could not be learned from a book. These lessons were on life, friends, honesty, trust, and right versus wrong.

The institution we call "school" is what it is because we made it that way. If it is irrelevant, as Marshall McLuhan says; if it shields children from reality, as Norbert Weiner says; if it educates for obsolescence, as John Gardner says; if it does not develop intelligence, as Jerome Bruner says; if it is based on fear, as John Holt says; if it avoids the promotion of significant learnings, as Carl Rogers says; if it induces alienation, as Paul Goodman says; if it punishes creativity and independence, as Edgar Friedenberg says; if, in short, it is not doing what needs to be done, it can be changed; it must be changed.
—Neil Postman and Charles Weingartner,
Teaching as a Subversive Activity. Dell *(Delta).1969.*

and 30's, each very different from the others, all fully engaged in living their lives according to their own choices and beliefs. We are proud to claim them as "our own." My youngest son Mark, below, reflects, among other things, the disorder and occasional violence of our first two years in Albany's South End ghetto.

MY SCHOOL YEARS
by Mark Leue

My first memories of kindergarten at PS 16, the huge brick building across the street from my family's house on North Allen street in Albany are of "nap" time.

Our young woman (goes without saying) teacher, probably exhausted herself, would put on some suitably insipid music, roll out the mats as far as possible from each other, and spend the next fifteen minutes hovering over us. As she patrolled the room keeping a sharp lookout for potential "brush fires," I can remember trying to keep perfectly still, tense and almost rigid with the fear that she would find me less than completely immobile, trying even to control my breath so as to please her.

First grade was quite a shock to the tender young ones who passed muster in that first round of behavior shaping. Thirty desks in a rigid, rectangular, face-to-the-blackboard arrangement, symbolized the no-nonsense sadism that our ruler, the currently politically appallingly named (although not without poetic resonance) Miss Dyke embodied. In her 70s, and well hardened by many years of battle with imps of our age, she dominated the classroom with an iron will and a quick hand that could quickly twist your ear while pulling you from your seat on the march to the principal's office for some real or imagined breach of the public dignity.

Halfway through the year we had a heavenly reprieve in the form of a beautiful young woman substitute teacher, Miss Riffleberger. Imagine our joy when we learned that her position had been made permanent due to the death of Miss Dyke.

Second and third grade kind of blend together, although in different schools. A move closer to my father's work at the State University necessitated a change to PS 27.

In the summer before my fourth grade began we moved to a village on the Thames River not far from Oxford, the famous English "City of Spires" where my father would be spending the year on his first (and only) sabbatical leave from the philosophy department at Albany State.

The village school, St. Bartholomew's, was probably a typical "comprehensive" (kindergarten through tenth grade) school of the time. The majority of the kids were expected to get to tenth grade, pass their "O" levels and join the English working class. We studied several subjects which I found novel and sometimes at odds with my previous background. Penmanship was perhaps the most exotic item of curriculum. My efforts with a real dip pen (no fountains pens allowed until mastery was proven) consisted mostly of trying to keep the blots to a minimum. Some of the children, however, had been studying Italics for several years and could write in the beautiful way that seems to have died out in this country early in the twentieth century. What I remember chiefly, however, about Eynsham was playing. Schoolyard recess, players' field (the town fields on the edge of town near the river), the locks on the Thames, the alleys and warrens that twisted their way between the ancient stone houses and pubs, but most of all a nearly magical walled-in couple of acres called "Temples Garden."

I suppose it must really have belonged to a man named Temple once, and there was some evidence that it had in the distant past been a formal garden. (I can remember that along one of its encircling eight-foot-high stone walls there were some old espaliered pear trees). [*Ed. note: Actually, I was told by the owner of the village "curiosity shop "that it was originally the site of a Roman temple.*] But it seemed a jungle paradise of vines, elderberries and small watercourses winding through ruined artifacts of many generations of settlement and cultivation. In such paradises fantasy games of many varieties and seemingly limitless duration were lived by small English kids in shorts or skirts.

As a "Yank" my vocabulary and accent were different but we had no problem speaking the universal language of imagination. Yes, I'm sure many of our games followed the same sort of unwritten rules of the games back in my neighborhood in Albany. War, Explorers, or even organized games like Tag, "Conkers", or British Bull Dog were tried-and-true favorites— after all even "Doctor" has its rules and roles. But there was a feeling of timelessness (maybe influenced by the fact that it was still light in the summer till 10:00) that I haven't forgotten. The children had their own culture and the games seemed to have their roots in a past as old as the landscape we inhabited.

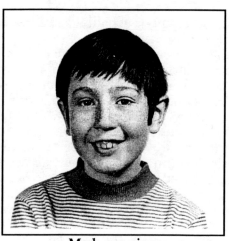

Mark, age nine

Somewhere during the year I began to become aware of and identify with the counter culture. The years were 1968 and 1969 and I don't know if it came as a subliminal message coded into the lyrics of my 16-year-old sister's Beatle records, or my fairly politically radical parents' views, but before our journey back over the Atlantic was complete I knew I wanted to stop having my hair cut.

After spending the summer driving around on the continent in a Volkswagen bug, we returned to the U.S. Never before or since have I experienced such a strange form of culture shock. Somehow my comfortable home and friendly neighbors had become transformed into suspicious bigots in an alien terrain. To make matters worse, several weeks before we returned, neighborhood kids had vandalized our house in a malicious and crude way. I was at an age of burgeoning self-realization and began to see how my family's "differentness" had always been there.

This self-awareness must have broadcast the kind of message a bleeding animal will to certain species of shark. At school I was immediately dubbed with the nickname of "Girl." Between the general prison-guard-like tactics of my teachers and the bloodthirstiness of my classmates, by November I was done with the fifth grade. I was simply *not going to go* any more, period.

Thus began what later would be called "The Free School." It started with my mother's agreement to homeschool me. In truth, she took little convincing. I think she had been "champing at the bit" for some time and had had correspondence with, and a visit to, A.S. Neill and the "Summerhill" school in England the year before. I, however, had never heard of home-schooling, or "free schools" and the only private schools I had ever heard of were run by discipline-minded nuns. You can imagine my surprise and gratitude at being granted clemency from my sentence.

This lasted at least several days, until my first math lesson from my mother. After a few weeks of mutual head-butting, she began to look for other kids, to change the energy as much as anything else, I surmise.

In my mother's true style, within a few months we were a group of four and the initial round of politics had been settled with the State Board of Education. We were a "school," of sorts.

It was a good first year. I remember mostly the big events; going to Washington for the moratorium to end the Vietnam War, spending the first Earth Day picking up bag after bag of trash alongside a road; the "Be In" at the University.

We started the next year with about six teachers and twenty kids. I guess it was an outgrowth of my mother's in-volvement with the Civil Rights and Black Power movements that influenced her decision to have the school move to the inner city. That, and the fact that the rent was cheap on Albany's Franklin Street.

Much of the experience for me was about an uptown boy learning about downtown life. Lining up with the other neigh-borhood kids for a salty sour pickle given out free by the "pickle man", Mr. Richmond. Smashing out tunnels in the brick walls of abandoned tenements to explore them. Hearing the stories about the Green Street bordellos in their heyday.

I think it must have been the year that some of us did an investigation of the bigger river polluters, seeing what the Tobin meat packing company dumped into Patroon Creek. Photographing the open sewers complete with turds and toilet paper dumping directly into the Hudson at the end of Troy's streets. Visiting the sloop "Clearwater."

Sex, drugs, and rock and roll were also becoming major in-terests. I spent hours in a school closet with a 15-year-old girl kissing and doing diffuse petting. Hours jumping up and down on a mattress listening to "In a Gada Da Vida" by Iron Butterfly. To be truthful I don't remember getting high at school.

Mark singing with his kids (four years ago)

and working in his shop (recently)

Group dynamics at the school ranged the whole gamut. We spent a lot of time working out our differences in "Council Meetings." I can remember some pretty violent incidents. A kid breaking a 2 by 4 over a teacher's back stands out in my mind. The most self-indulgent destructiveness came when either the teachers or the students or both decided to go "on strike" over some incident and the kids were allowed to completely trash the school. Bookcases were toppled, plates smashed and the shit generally hit the fan.

In retrospect, I think that part of the adults' willingness to let this happen may have been the knowledge that as part of the city's "Urban Renewal" program the whole block was being taken by eminent domain. Maybe this was the only way the adults could act out their anger towards the city's policy of what could be more aptly termed "Urban Removal." I don't think that this justifies it having been allowed to happen. Even then, I could stand back and say to myself, "Wow, so this is what a war is like." For the more destructive kids I wonder what the lesson really was. The school was out of the building within a few weeks and many of these kids were gone the next year.

Out of the ashes the school reformed itself and through hard work, good luck, and my mother's inheritance money acquired a rundown, ex-parochial school turned war veterans' post in the heart of the old Italian (now black) neighborhood not far from Franklin Street.

I had one more exciting, chaotic year at the school, and then a year back at the public junior high school. It was long enough to confirm that it wasn't where I wanted to be. By the end of the year a friend and I were putting up posters for kids interested in starting an alternative secondary school. How that came into being and where it went are another story.

So how has all this affected how I parent and educate my own children twenty-three years later?

Our kids are homeschooled and predominantly decide how to spend their time. They are also given a lot of structure and some very firm limits. I guess we want them to have the best of both worlds. They shouldn't have to attend a school where they are wasting a large portion of their time. "School is fine as long as it doesn't interfere with your education," to quote someone whose name I don't remember.

I think kids thrive best when given clear boundaries. A basic rhythm and structure to their lives is also very important for them. I certainly would have benefited from more structure at certain times in my childhood.

One of the most important values I want my kids to gain is the ability to make choices based on what they believe in. It's often touted as a fact that kids are tremendous conformists and enforcers of dominant cultural values. I believe that to be a lie. If we don't repress them at home and at school and keep them drugged with TV, they are quite capable of deciding for themselves what is right and wrong. It is people who have this ability that our society needs more than anything else.

LIFE DURING AND AFTER THE FREE SCHOOL
by Kaylana Mittleman

I don't exactly remember the beginning of my thirteen years at the Free School. That may have something to do with the fact that I was only seven months old. My mother is a teacher, and she brought me with her. So, the first few years don't really hold that big a place in my memory. The years following definitely do, though.

I remember a feeling of comfort, family and love. I learned to talk about my feelings, listen to others' feelings, and accept people for who they are. I learned to be open and honest with myself and everyone around me.

As far as schoolwork went, very little of the things we did were structured (in the "sitting at a desk and listening to the teacher for forty minutes" sense). Almost everything we studied was hands-on learning, whether it be all student-teacher interaction or going someplace to learn about something. My final year at school—I was in eighth grade—was a very relaxed year. I didn't do much schoolwork. I just kind of "hung out." When I think about it, maybe that was what I needed before the "big" transition. That transition was going from the Free School's forty students ranging from grades pre-K to eighth grade, to Albany High School's (AHS) 2400 students with only grades nine through twelve.

It would be a small understatement to say that I was scared to death to start AHS. But I did, and was utterly surprised to find that I was fine. In fact, I was better than fine. I made plenty of friends, did great in my classes, and even made honor roll for the whole year. Even though I had thought that the education I received at the Free School would not have prepared me for AHS's "real school" situation, I did great.

My first two and a half years at AHS (Albany High School) were fine. But after a few months into my junior year, the structure and the total unfeeling of the students started to get to me. Everything was just so impersonal, and I started to hate it. I just up and left the second day of my senior year. And after a three month struggle with myself and my parents, I went back, and found the strength to endure it and graduate. I feel like I got that strength from being in the Free School. After graduating, I took a year off, to take a break from all the structure. I am now in college and doing all right.

I visit the Free School frequently. I feel like I am a whole person with a whole lot of inner strength because of my years at the Free School. I've got a large family and support network inside the Free School and the community. The people have helped me many times since I graduated from the Free School almost six years ago. I feel that I am very lucky to have attended the Free School. Everything I learned there will be very valuable throughout the course of my life, and I am very thankful.

Kaylana during her Free School days

Kaylana now with Meighan

MEIGHAN'S FREE SCHOOL
by Meighan Carivan

I used to be so nervous about going to school that I had nauseous stomach aches every morning. The thought of school filled me with dread and I was always trying to avoid having to go. I did fairly well, but I had no real interest in learning. It was this negative outlook on education that The Free School changed for me.

I attended The Free School at two different times in my life. And although I was there for a considerable amount of time as a young child, it was the time that I spent there in junior high that had the most impact on me.

When I returned for junior high, for the first year and a half or so, I did a lot of academics. But as time went on and I got used to the general freeness of the environment, I began to do less and less. Since the teachers believe in trying to encourage students to do work instead of forcing them, when there came a point when I was resisting all the time, they decided to leave me alone to see what would happen. It was in doing this that taught me the value of education.

Despite the fact that I was not doing what many people would consider responsible, productive things, according to me, I was. I was completely satisfied doing whatever I suddenly had the desire for. And if I had an interest in something, no matter how strange or unimportant it seemed to my teachers, I was allowed to pursue it. Not only that, but I was supported in my efforts. I was never put down or called stupid or lazy and I never once had what I was doing belittled or discarded.

By finally being given the space that I needed, I was able to develop an interest in things and make a connection with taking the interests of my life and cultivating them into my education.

Today I am a full-time student studying music (singing) at a local community college, as well as teaching part time at the school. It has taken me this long to realize what I could have been studying before this year, but because I had to learn how to learn I am just coming to it now. I am beginning something completely new, and it is scary for me but I have been able to come to it because of what I have been taught about how to get what I want out of life. I have to be honest with myself about what I really want and not talk myself out of it because of fear. I need to always leave my options open and never limit myself. If I choose to view everything as available to me instead of letting my insecurities and inhibitions dictate what is possible, the world is mine. I believe that I owe this to The Free School for starting me on a path that has led me to where I am now.

My music is the love of my life and I can't imagine wanting to do anything else. Although it is hard to imagine my life any other way, I know that I might never have let myself follow my dreams if it weren't for taking that first step back in junior high.

"THE BEST THINGS IN LIFE ARE *FREE* "
by John Lester

First of all I would like to tell U a little about myself (John-boy). It was in 1973 and I was a young boy about nine years old at the time of my enrollment at **the Free school.** I am what some of U call *half bree, creo, redbone, high yellow, malloto* or whatever stereotypical name that some people may use to describe a person of two or more different ethnic backgrounds.

We (my family) and the school lived in a very diverse community, meaning that there was a lot of different cultures and types of backgrounds. A lot of people thought that we were kind of weird because we didn't do things in the traditional manner. But as we all know the traditional way hasn't been very successful.

It is now twenty-three years later and I am a young man that has been through it all.

The Free School way of teaching is looked on to be unorthodox but their methods work—trust me, I know; I experienced it!! At **the Free School** I learned everything from A-Z. There I learned so much in such a short period of time that if I wrote down everything I learned, there wouldn't been enough room for my fellow students and friends to tell their stories.

The Free School taught me the necessary tools to maintain a very healthy. happy and—most of all—a strong will to succeed in life. Don't get me wrong. My parents had a lot to do with it too. Two things that are most important in a young person's life are his family and his education.

John Boy on his birthday (those are Chris' hands)

John as he is now

The family is a major part of a young person's life because they are the ones that must encourage love, peace, togetherness, education, and also how to be independent.

The School's job is to mold all of the significant characteristics in a young person so they may carry out a happy and flourishing life. I feel when a young person is a high school graduate he or she should be able to maintain their own existence.

By this I mean having all of the necessary tools to get through life. If they need help they still will have their parents and teachers to fall back on for advice, and support, but don't let them hang around until they're twenty-five and unemployed. Let them get out there and learn about life because the only way to learn properly is to experience.

Without both the family and the School putting 200% of their effort into bringing our children of today up right, then our adults of tomorrow look pretty sad.

"Life is like riding a bike; put your child on it and give them a little push. When they fall, be right there to pick them

up. Sooner or later they'll get the hang of it and U won't have to be there all the time."

The Free School put me on that bike and I learned how to ride. This is why I call my writings "The Best Things In Life Are Free"—because **the Free School** is one of the best and most important things that ever happened in my life.

P.S. the proper way of spelling U is you.

"AN EDUCATION FOR LIFE"
by Audry Camacho

I was five years old when I became a Free School student. Surprisingly, I remember those early years quite vividly and with mixed feelings. I looked forward to the daily exercises and especially enjoyed the morning meetings. It was at a morning meeting that I learned my loose teeth had large earnings potential. Students who lost a tooth would bring it to the meeting and the teachers would pay handsomely to have a look—as much as a dollar sometimes. My little brother Kaleb tried to sneak our cat's tooth in with his own one time. Unfortunately, the pointy eye tooth was suspected immediately and he wasn't able to collect on it.

Audry, cartoonist

My fondest memories are of the jungle gym, worm-digging expeditions in the back yard and the haunted house which was set up in the basement every Halloween. The annual talent show was the birthplace of my fleeting show biz career—for some reason my guitar rendition of "Jesus Loves Me" never again found an audience as enthusiastic as my Free School classmates and teachers.

While the Free School always put "fun" high on the list of priorities, they were never shy about teaching some difficult lessons. In my five-year existence on the planet, I had learned early on that offending classmates could easily be dealt with by "telling on them." The first time I ran to tattle on someone at the Free School, I was stunned to hear my teacher say, "Fight your own battles, Audry!"

Children naturally want to learn and the Free School gave us the freedom to learn at our own pace. Beyond academics, we were encouraged to share our talents and our feelings. The Free School gave me the tools to build a career, but more importantly to build relationships with people.

"FAR OUT"
by Kaleb Camacho

Why do they call it the "Free School" if you have to pay money to go there? This is a question I remember asking my mother as a child. Little did I know that nothing in life was free, and that the word free had more than one meaning.

When I look back at the Free School with a little bit older, and hopefully wiser, outlook I can see that the Free School means something different for everyone. When I walk by the Free School I always envision a building infested with hippies and wall-to-wall flower children freeing their minds. Being a student of both public schools and the Free School I can honestly say they made learning easy and fun. I can't recall begging for homework in public school.

This school went further than vocabulary words and decimals. They took the time to hold each student mentally, physically and spiritually. One of the key motivators for strengthening students was the school's leader, Mary Leue. As a child I believed she had powers, but they did not include spells that could turn me into a frog. Instead Mary Leue was able to help

Kaleb gymnast

me overcome my biggest fear at that time: her. I remember being forced to sit under a cafeteria table without food. I was not to be given food until I returned one of the many "ugly faces" that Mary Leue had given me. Faces so hideous, by the way, each one made me cry. Bored with crying and embarrassment I finally got mad enough to make an ugly face back. Mary Leue saw I was weak and took the time to make me strong.

The Free School definitely has a radical approach to teaching. They've added to my character, and over the years have helped build so many characters that they will probably write a book. I can describe the Free School in two words—

FAR OUT!!!

Brother Kaleb and sister Audry on the porch of their new house

THE TURNING POINT IN MY LIFE
by Ethan Manning

After four years in public school I was about to give up on learning. I felt lost there. I felt I wasn't learning anything, that I couldn't learn anything. Every day I would come home angry and frustrated, feeling like I was stupid.

I started going to the Free School in grade five.

What words can you use to describe something so new, so different, it changes your life forever? The first thing I noticed at the Free School was that everyone wanted to be there. Everyone, the students and the teachers, were happy to be there. People listened to me. When someone talked to me it was with respect, I began to feel like I really was someone, that what I thought and felt mattered. And I started learning.

For the first time I wasn't told to "know stuff." For the first time school was fun, what we did was fun, learning new things was fun. Looking back on those years, I sometimes wonder who really was teaching who. When our teachers asked us questions I sometimes thought "I know that, I'll teach it to them." Sometimes you think of school as where you're pushed along by never-ending demands. Do this, learn that. At the Free School no one pushed. Instead it was like you were carried along on a wave of encouragement and enthusiasm. Along the way we learned to respect ourselves and each other, we learned to work together and on our own, how to speak up for ourselves and how to listen to others.

Ethan, a recent picture

Next fall I am going to college. It is too soon to be more specific but my general direction is towards a career in the environment, forestry, or wildlife management. Somewhere inside me there always was a love of the outdoors. At the Free School this was somehow noticed, encouraged, developed and brought out in me. I became involved with the Seneca Indian reservation. From the people on the reservation I learned many things about the environment which I had never known. I also was introduced to Ward Stone, a well known environmental pathologist who helped me stay interested by letting me do volunteer work at the Department of Environmental Conservation. These people opened my eyes to things I'd only dreamed existed for other people.

At the Free School you feel you are among equals.

They know things you don't but they let you know that in time you'll learn. They talk to you like you're an equal but still let you be a kid and respect you for that. It's a wonderful feeling.

People are always going on about the love of learning. What I experienced at the Free School was learning to love. I have not been the same and I will never forget what they brought to my life.

Richard Prystowsky homeschools his kids and he also teaches in the School of Humanities and Languages at Irvine Valley College in California. This is the most thoughtful article we've read on the subject of homeschooling, viewed (as it must be!) from a fully human— including a truly personal—point of view! Richard is raising the issues we've not seen addressed anywhere else—not that that means it hasn't been done! We'd love to see more of this kind.

"AM I *REALLY* QUALIFIED TO TEACH MY CHILDREN?"
Some Thoughts on This Common and Provocative Question
by Richard Prystowsky

There are many kinds of seeds in us, both good and bad. Some were planted during our lifetime, and some were transmitted by our parents, our ancestors, and our society.... Every time we practice mindful living, we plant healthy seeds and strengthen the healthy seeds already in us. Healthy seeds function similarly to antibodies.... If we plant wholesome, healing, refreshing seeds, they will take care of the negative seeds, even without our asking them. To succeed, we need to cultivate a good reserve of refreshing seeds.
—Thich Nhat Hanh, Peace Is Every Step

The kids are all learning, all the time. Life is their greatest teacher. The B.A.s and M.A.s and Ph.D.s on the staff are minor actors.
—Daniel Greenberg, Free At Last

> *In this essay, I would like to address some of the "psychological" and "spiritual" concerns raised by this question, couching this discussion within the context of some crucial links between parent-child teaching and holistic family living.*

Would that homeschooling parents had a dollar for each time that they asked themselves or have been asked by others why they think that they are qualified to teach their own. The question is certainly an intriguing one, and, for many homeschooling parents, a pressing one. In this essay, I would like to address some of the "psychological" and "spiritual" concerns raised by this question, couching this discussion within the context of some crucial links between parent-child teaching and holistic family living. I will be leaving aside concerns such as one's knowledge of the subject matter, one's ability to find important data, and so on; clearly, these latter concerns are important, but they are beyond the purview of the present paper.

My intention here is to help parents—especially those new to and those thinking about homeschooling—who are struggling with the questions of whether or not they really are both capable of teaching and qualified to teach their own and whether or not they are (or would be) acting responsibly by homeschooling their children. To this end, I offer a discussion of the following personal traits, which, in my more than thirteen years of college teaching, I have come to see as being essential for anyone to possess who desires to be a good teacher, that person's profound knowledge of her subject matter or in-depth training in teaching notwithstanding (N.B.: one's being "certified" to teach is not synonymous with one's being "qualified" to teach). My greatest mentors possessed these traits, although, to the best of my knowledge, none had taken a single course in educational theory or methods. If you yourself have or are striving to have all of these traits (the following list is not meant to be exhaustive), then you are probably fit to teach your own. On the other hand, if you lack and have no interest in attaining them, then perhaps you ought not teach either your own or anyone else's children.

1. The willingness to engage in child-led/student-led learning.

Like many homeschooling parents, I've discovered that *meaningful* learning can occur only if the learner *actively* wants to learn, gives her consent to learn from a particular teacher (unless she wants to be self-taught), and initiates the learning process. In other words, the desire to learn comes from within and not from outside of the learner. Moreover, as the output of mass public education demonstrates, one can even do great harm to a learner by trying to make her learn against her will.[1]

---

1. For some excellent discussions of this issue, see Daniel Greenberg's *Free At Last: The Sudbury Valley School* (Framingham, MA: Sudbury Valley School Press, 1987), pp. 15-18 and passim,

Unless you are willing to let your child lead the way—fully or partly—to her own learning, you might find yourself engaged in a home version of the worst sort of organized schooling, in which teachers force-feed students information that the latter understandably resist learning. In my college classes, I try to help students see that, although I can try to provide an atmosphere in which they can take some intellectual risks, I cannot learn for them. Only they can learn for themselves.

Before moving on, I should add that, both in the classroom and at home, I have often found that my best teaching moments occur when, learning along with my students or children, I discover meaning and uncover knowledge *in the process of teaching.* Additionally, I feel that one of my goals as a teacher/parent is to help guide my students/children so that they can teach themselves. Secure self-directed learners know when they don't know something, and they know enough to ask for help when they need or want it. In this regard, my six-year-old son, for example, acts no differently from my self-directed students. Last year, for instance, he virtually taught himself to write. When he needed help, he asked for it; when he didn't need help, he simply wrote, sometimes laboriously, sometimes not—as is the case with most (if not all) *professional* writers. As Daniel Greenberg and John Taylor Gatto (among others) have suggested, to teach successfully, one must have or cultivate the ability first to recognize a learner's desire to learn something and then to seize the opportunity to help him learn what he wants or needs to learn.[2] Thus, if I don't know how to assist my students or children when they ask me for help, I feel that I am duty-bound as their teacher to

---

and Herbert Kohl's *I Won't Learn from You! The Role of Assent in Learning* (Minneapolis: Milkweed Editions, 1991).

2. In a November 1967 *Redbook* article entitled "How Teachers Make Children Hate Reading," John Holt—still a public school educator at the time that he wrote this particular piece—analyzes the differences between what I'm calling child-led learning and what I'm calling force-fed learning. His article is reprinted in *The Norton Reader: An Anthology of Expository Prose,* ed. by Arthur M. Eastman, et al. (New York: W. W. Norton & Company, Inc., 1984), pp. 224–232.

try to help them discover how they can receive good assistance elsewhere.

2. Real, genuine humility and compassion.

I often try to teach my students that they will have achieved much in the way of good critical thinking if they come to realize about themselves what all great thinkers come to realize about *themselves*: to wit, that they have learned enough to know how little they really know. Concerning the present topic, we can say with certainty that someone who lacks genuine humility cannot be satisfactorily compassionate towards others, because she doesn't yet have the inner strength and security to be satisfactorily compassionate towards herself. Such a person, then, is not likely to be a very good teacher—a fact to which anyone can attest who has endured even a day in the classroom of a teacher who lacked compassion for others. In any event, a truly humble, compassionate teacher is often wise enough to lead her students to discover for themselves what they need to know and secure enough to validate those of their insights that are authentic, meaningful and moral in the highest sense of the word—even if (perhaps especially if) these insights are quite different from her own. Such a teacher gives her students a precious gift when she shows them she is strong enough to be humble and honest concerning what she knows and doesn't know.

Since most of my students have suffered humiliation during their schooling and other training in "socialization," they often have trouble distinguishing humility from self-loathing; in the worst cases, they act in the manner of seriously wounded animals—defensive, protective, and, in the main, wary of showing themselves vulnerable in any way to anyone. Neither I nor anyone else can teach such persons why they should be or how they can be humble; only they can teach themselves these lessons. However, I can and do try to help a number of my students discover their own paths to humility and compassion by helping them see how they themselves might begin healing those damaged parts of their inner selves that they now guard at all costs, those parts of their inner being, if you will, the damage to which the best "alternative" teaching efforts might have helped to prevent.

3. The inner security to teach others freely.

Although I don't consider myself a very secure person, I do feel very strongly that, when my students have reached the point at which they are humble enough and courageous enough to begin drawing out from within themselves their own deepest truths, I have outlived my usefulness as their teacher. To extrapolate, I would suggest that, whenever we teach, we should always try to do so freely, so that we can remain lovingly detached from our students' learning obligations, which are always personal. All teachers need to keep in mind that there is a world of difference between our *wanting* to help persons learn for *their* own sake and our *needing* to teach them for *our* own sake (of course, these two conditions need not be mutually exclusive). If the latter is the case, we might be either projecting onto those who learn from us our own insecurities or making them the vehicles by means of which we carry out our own political or social agendas. Using our students/children to fill the narcissistic voids and heal the narcissistic wounds in our own lives could eventually prove quite harmful to both them and us[3]

One final matter here: I have found that neither my own children nor my college students need me to tell them what is best for them or what they should know; in fact, they often resent (and rightfully so) my occasional efforts to own their responsibility to make meaningful choices in and for their own lives, especially when I am interfering with their choices to learn or not learn. Often, both my children and a number of my students seem to sense that such moves on my part represent controlling, co-dependent behavior, and they healthily resist these moves. They want to make their own decisions and be responsible for their own mistakes. For my part, I need to recognize when I am hindering learners from reaching rather than helping them to reach their own educational goals. I, too, need to own and learn from my mistakes.

4. The willingness to learn, often from those whom we teach.

If there is anything that is obvious in great teachers, it is their willingness to learn, often from their own students. Simply put, one cannot be a good teacher if one has lost the desire to learn, and any teacher unwilling to learn from his students is a teacher whose best days are past. If you have no desire to learn or no willingness to learn along with those whom you teach, or if

---

3. For a detailed discussion concerning these kinds of matters, see Alice Miller's *The Drama of the Gifted Child: The Search for the True Self*, trans. by Ruth Ward (New York: Basic Books, Inc., 1981).

you don't feel that those who study with you can teach you any-thing of real value, then you probably ought not to be teaching *anyone*.

5. Patience.

In the quick-fix, fast-food, narcotizing culture in which we live, patience is a rare commodity. But it is an essential ingredi-ent to good teaching. Since each child learns in her own way and at her own pace, we need to be patient enough to see how our children engage in their own ever-developing and sometimes changing learning processes so that we can help them be active, confident learners. We need to give ourselves permission to al-low them to learn differently from the ways in which we learn and from the ways in which other children (including *our* other children) seem to be learning. We need to accept as a perfectly normal state of affairs, for example, the fact that one of our children might want to read at age four but that another might not want to read even at age eight. In short, we need to be pa-tient with ourselves and our children as we all struggle to live individually and mutually meaningful lives. Oh, the possible dif-ferences in all of our lives had most of our own teachers under-stood this need for patience in *themselves*!

When you teach your children at home, you are doing far more than "homeschooling" them;[4] exercising maximum control

---

4. For a trenchant critique of the word "homeschooling," see David Guterson's *Family Matters: Why Homeschooling Makes Sense* (New York: Harcourt Brace Jovanovich, Publishers, 1992), p. 5ff.

Concerning some of the most important issues and controversies having to do with homeschooling in general, Guterson's book is possibly the best text on the market. However, despite the author's many good insights (his ideas on "socialization" are particularly cogent), like all books, Guterson's is not without its share of interpretive troubles. For example, in his controversial chapter "Schools and Families: A Proposal," in which he argues for a range of what one might term "ideal school programs," Guterson never even mentions the Sudbury Valley School. More generally, Guterson's often facile use of data leaves one with the impression that the author sometimes has only a superficial understanding of the matters that he discusses (consider, for example, Guterson's interesting but far too truncated discussion of philosophy [p. 118ff.]).

over your family's right to do what is in its own best moral interests, you are swimming against a tide of enormously destructive and powerful mediocrity and mainstreaming in your attempts to help your children live meaningful lives as whole, independent beings. You are trying to keep your children from suffering the fate of many of our nation's schooled children, who have been conditioned to be actively uninterested in and sometimes openly hostile to meaningful, shared, participatory communal living, and who, as passive, obedient learners, have little interest in themselves, in the meaning and value of their existence, or in the value of their communities. I have seen many such learners in my college classes. Often lacking good social skills, good study habits, a healthy dose of adult responsibility, and, most conspicuously, the self-motivation and self-reliance recognizable in a confident learner, they are frequently uninterested in and even hostile to learning, especially to learning new or controversial material, even if such material can help them live more meaningful and compassionate lives. More significantly, many of the students in this group who are trying to recondition themselves into becoming active, mature learners have trouble trusting themselves; not a few often seem to believe that their professors, and not they themselves, possess the answers to *their* most important questions.

If I have noticed any common denominator among those of my students who seem disinterested in their own pursuits, in their own learning agendas, sometimes even in their own and others' lives, it is that these kinds of students seem distanced from themselves. This state of being is common among persons who have been conditioned to be passive and whose psyches need to protect them from their being too emotionally harmed. For such students, "know thyself" is as foreign a concept as is the idea that they are responsible for their own learning, for their own *lives.* Self-knowledge and self-respect seem almost anathema to them, cruel reminiscences and temptations of vaguely desirable, ideal personal states of being that, to them, in their present existential dilemma, seem utterly unattainable.

These and other textual problems notwithstanding, Guterson's book is, in my view, mandatory reading for anyone seriously interested in understanding much of the sum and substance of homeschooling.

No, I don't mean to imply that, by homeschooling your children, you necessarily will insure that they will be self-reliant, mature adults with an unrelenting zest for learning. And I especially am not implying that you ought to be homeschooling your children *now* primarily to help insure their "success" in the *future*. Rather, I simply want to clarify what I see as being centrally at stake here: that you have both the right and the obligation to advocate for your child's needs, to do what's best for your child, even though the culture at large often makes it difficult, and even though you might occasionally have doubts or questions about your educational theories and practices or your aptitude as a teacher (all good-faith teachers have such doubts).

Remember that mass-organized schooling (public or private) sets up learning situations that are convenient for textbook publishers, teachers, administrators, and members of school boards, and for parents unluckily caught in the anti-family, anti-child trap that our culture has laid for us all. But holistic family living demands that the parent-teacher respond to the learning needs of her or his child by setting up learning situations that meet those needs. Few persons (if anyone) outside of your family will care as much as you care to meet your child's needs. You know the difference between being with your child and leaving him/her with even a warm, loving, devoted caretaker. And your *child* knows the difference, too. With this understanding in mind, think of those children who—as perhaps you once did—at the end of the school year or school cycle, feel utterly relieved finally to have the time to do the things they find meaningful in their lives, who can now spend more than a few fleeting moments with the persons who matter most to them. How sad that we have placed our nation's children in this bind. But how promising that, as homeschooling parents, we can avoid being a party to such madness.

Linda Dobson, Home Education Magazine's *News Watch columnist, writes that she is still learning at home along with her three children. We say she is also a super, feisty, involved person, and any of us would love to have been one of her kids, way up there in the Adirondacks! Here's a sample of her earthy good sense.*

EDUCATION TRUTHS
by Linda Dobson

Presidential candidate Bill Clinton told the National Education Association, "You'll be my partners. I won't forget who brought me to the White House." Is it because he understood his new partners' agenda *so well* that he chose a private school learning experience for daughter Chelsea? Certainly, here was a clue to the condition of public schools that the nation's education consumers should have heeded. But, alas, no alarm bells went off.

In June, two astute *Forbes'* reporters presented chilling evidence of the National Education Association's abuse of its monopoly and political and financial manipulation of the American education system. I could forgive a 2.1 million member union for possibly violating American constitutional principles as they spend $16 million each year on PACs if it was improving our education climate. After all, our public school teachers willingly contribute the money from their salaries. However, the *Forbes* report clearly indicates *the rise of the NEA is directly linked with a simultaneous 30-year decline in American education and corresponding staggering increase of its cost.* This clue, which should have fallen like a sledge hammer on parents' heads, hasn't awakened anyone, either.

What would you think of a dentist whose assistants leave town to get a tooth pulled? Or a restaurateur whose kids would rather pay for a Big Mac than choke down a free burger at Dad's place? Or 22% of NEA teachers (*twice* the national average) who send their own kids to private school? I think they all know something the consumer-at-large doesn't.

I think these teachers realize that the foundation of American public schools rests on myths about education that just aren't true today, if, in fact, they ever were. Good ol' William Torrey Harris (US Commissioner of Education at the tum of the century) was greatly responsible for turning schools into institutions—gray, drab, bureaucratic places that effectively separate youngsters from the real world, real people, and real work, continually perpetuating his mistaken notions about the purpose Or education. Through attempts to teach all children the same thing at the same time in the same way, Harris' goal is reached: "Substantial education, which, scientifically defined, is the subsumption of the individual." Our schools create the robots whom Harris described as "careful to walk in prescribed paths, careful to follow the prescribed custom."

Attempts at reforming current educational practices merely perpetuate something that should have died, or at least evolved, long ago. It probably would have, too, had education not turned into the huge, and, therefore, powerful business it is today. How much money do we have to feed these hungry giants before somebody who could really change things (Are you reading, Bill? Hillary?) listens to the increasing numbers of parents finding different ways that work? That work well. Less expensively. Joyfully.

The largest—and happiest—part of my job as News Watch columnist for *Home Education Magazine* is studying the growing mountain of national media coverage this education alternative generates. Yes, you're right—it doesn't work for everyone. But it *can* work for a lot more families once they understand. Once they examine their own educations to discover real selves buried under layers of programming, they can see the true meaning of learning. Beyond worksheets, tests and grades. Beyond the institution of school.

This study, and the subsequent exercise of educational freedom available at the home/family level, has brought forth some basic education truths our leaders would be wise to consider carefully. You've probably already heard some of these truths in other contexts. No matter, they are as valid for learning as anything else.

We can learn (better) when we follow our unique interests. A nationalized curriculum won't help schools any more than a local or state curriculum. When was the last time you saw a six-year old child interested in doing the same thing as 25 other six-year olds, for six hours at a stretch, outside of a classroom? If individual curiosity and imagination don't get time in the sun, how will they ever blossom? There's a definite correlation between our insistence on lining kids up in rows and giving each a precisely measured dose of whatever it is we deem important, relegating diverse and personally meaningful studies to oblivion, and our lack of scientists and mathematicians.

There are many paths to the mountain's peak. Those making money from the status quo will never share this truth with you. But the path American education took to fulfill the needs of the Industrial Revolution is not the only path. Indeed, this path is suitable to covered wagon travel, while alternative educators daily discover paths along which the Concorde could fly. Bypass the tangled clutter of bureaucracy, overgrown weeds of complacency, and the fallen, rotten logs of empiricism, and you'll be surprised how smooth—and enjoyable—the journey becomes.

If you do what you've always done, you'll get what you've always gotten. There's not a single, successful enterprise on earth today still doing business with methods unchanged since the early 1900's. If our graduates can't cut the mustard in 1990's business, their antiquated education is to blame.

The real world offers quantity and quality of learning experiences superior to institutionalized education. Yes, folks, I'm saying we can learn without being taught, without a certified expert controlling each step until knowledge, chopped and diced into measurable portions, becomes an education void of dignity and value. Maybe those bells ringing at 45-minute intervals all day contribute to shortened attention spans and the inability to attach significance to the learning experience.

Learning is a lifelong, joyous process. The person who emerges from the typical public school education understanding this truth is a rare bird, to be sure. Why do we insist on shoving school down our children's throats, focusing on an economic victory as a final reward for their suffering? In our rapidly changing world, can we continue turning kids off from the very learning that makes life fulfilling and happy as well as productive? 3500 teens drop out of school each day.

Our accepted methods never let them experience the joy and wonder inherent in the journey.

In *Advice to Youth*, published seventy years ago, Mark Twain said, "The history of the race, and each individual's experience, are thick with evidence that a truth is not hard to kill and that a lie told well is immortal." Say it isn't so, Mark. For our children's sake, say it isn't so.

Some years ago I (Mary) saw a program on television entitled "Son Rise," a dramatization of the real life story of the bringing-back from autism of their son and third child, Raun Kahlil, by a step-by-loving-step process carried through by Samahria and "Bears"(Barry) Kaufman, working against all medical advice. Being so moved by this account despite my "doubting Thomas" training at the Children's Hospital in Boston, which had taught me that infantile autism was incurable, I needed to discover for myself whether this apparent miracle was actually real—and so I began a process, initially with Bears, then later as an early participant at the newly-established Option Institute, both in order to learn the inwardness of the "Option Process," whereby a person is led from the ambivalent self-negating which is so characteristic of most members of our western culture to a sense of wholeness as a "child of God"—and to see with my own eyes the astounding work with autistic children being carried on at the Institute. And, incidentally, to meet, chat and laugh with this extraordinarily friendly and clearly "with it" young man who had once been so totally inside his own world, so oblivious to this one!

Barry Neil Kaufman and his wife Samahria, plus a dedicated staff, still devote their lives conducting the Option Institute and Fellowship in Sheffield, Massachusetts, which has become a center for several programs dedicated to the healing through total love and acceptance of wounded souls of all ages. Bears is the author of several books including Son Rise, A Miracle to Believe In, Happiness Is a Choice, *and a new book entitled:* Son Rise: The Miracle Continues, *from which this article was excerpted.*

I hear (from an old friend who works with families of institutionalized children with various disabilities) that the "word" among professionals who take care of autistic children that the news about Bears and Samahria is getting out—and the response from these professionals is that "the child wasn't really autistic, so no wonder!" I'm remembering the number of women who were burned at the stake for several centuries as witches because of fixed beliefs. No wonder the earth, let alone the human race, is in so much trouble! Why don't they just come and find out for themselves? Ah, well, some day ...

SON-RISE: THE MIRACLE CONTINUES
by Barry Neil Kaufman

> *The miraculous story of my son's healing journey from infantile autism to fullness of life. Raun was placed in a category reserved for all these seen as hopeless, unreachable, a tragedy. For us the question: could we kiss the ground that others had cursed?*

His little hands hold the plate delicately as his eyes survey its smooth perimeter. His mouth curls in delight. He is setting the stage. This is his moment, as was the last and each before. This is the beginning of his entry into the solitude that has become his world. Slowly, with a masterful hand, he places the edge of the plate on the floor, sets his body in a comfortable and balanced position, and snaps his wrist with great expertise. The plate begins to spin with dazzling perfection. It revolves on itself as if set into motion by some exacting machine. And it was.

This is not an isolated act, not a mere aspect of some childhood fantasy. It is a conscious and delicately skilled activity performed by a very little boy for a very great and expectant audience, himself.

As the plate moves swiftly, spinning hypnotically on its edge, the little boy bends over it and stares squarely into its motion. Homage to himself, to the plate. For a moment, the boy's body betrays a just perceptible motion similar to the plate's. For a moment, the little boy and his spinning creation become one. His eyes sparkle. He swoons in the playland that is himself. Alive. Alive.

> *If Raun was to get help, if this little autistic boy could be reached and brought into our world, it would have to be done by us and us alone.*

Before this time, this very moment, we had always been in awe of Raun, our notably special child. We sometimes referred to him as "brainblessed." He had always seemed to be riding the high of his own happiness. Highly evolved. Seldom did he cry or utter tones of discomfort. In almost every way, his contentment and solitude seemed to suggest a profound inner peace. He was a seventeen-month-old Buddha contemplating another dimension.

A little boy set adrift on the circulation of his own system. Encapsulated behind an invisible but seemingly impenetrable wall. Soon he would be labeled. A tragedy. Unreachable. Bizarre. Statistically, he would fall into a category reserved for all those we see as hopeless, unapproachable, irreversible. For us, the question: Could we kiss the ground that others had cursed?

Autism. Infantile autism. A subcategory of childhood schizophrenia. The most irreversible category of the profoundly disturbed and psychotic. Could the word destroy the dream, forever limiting the horizons of my son, and damn him to a deviant and sealed corner of our lives?

Just a hypothesis; yet it seemed correct. As I continued to observe my son, my recall sharpened. Suddenly, I could see the words lifting off a page in an abnormal psychology text my professor used in graduate school. I remembered a fellow student giving a short report on autism, saying that all the literature and evidence suggested these children were irretrievable and that most spent their lives locked up in state institutions. But now, I was not considering a statistic in a book or a sarcastic remark about a dysfunctional child. My God, this was my son. A human being.

We scheduled examinations. Several physicians and neuropsychologists identified Raun as classically and profoundly autistic as well as functionally retarded in his abilities. One test yielded a below-30 I.Q. score. Professionals marveled at our ability to detect autistic symptoms in a child so young. And yet, we found the bizarre and unusual behavior so pronounced that we could see no way not to acknowledge that something had gone terribly wrong.

One clinician shook his head sadly as he viewed Raun spinning happily around and around in dizzying circles. He muttered, "How terrible." I responded by saying that we never wanted to look at our son, or any child for that matter, and think or see "terrible." We were not in a state of denial. Our son looked as if he had just been dropped here from another planet. However, we wanted to see his uniqueness, his singularity, even his wonder, yes, even his wonder. The clinician now looked at us rather sadly and tried to convince us of the unfortunate prognosis for this condition. His associate suggested that we were lucky to have two normal children. In effect, he said, we should focus our attention on them and consider eventual institutionalization for our son. Never, ever, did we want to see our child through their eyes. My wife, Samahria, and I kept telling each other, it's just their judgments and their beliefs. No one can tell the future, not even these specialists.

We decided to be hopeful even if others called such a perspective unrealistic. Without hope we had no reason to go on.

After the evaluations, we were left with ample diagnoses and test scores, but no help. All our efforts left us with exactly what we already knew. We no longer wanted more confirmations. We felt we had to intervene, now. Each day we could see him slipping from us withdrawing more and more becoming more encapsulated.

We knew that now it would be up to us and to him. Perhaps it had always been that way. All the diagnoses and analyses might have statistical meaning to a number-hungry society, but they had none to a little boy with staring eyes. If Raun was to get help, if this little autistic boy could be reached and brought into our world, it would have to be done by us and us alone, now, while he was young, now, while we were wanting, now, while he was still happy in his infant playland.

We had little to work with but our own deep desire to reach Raun and to help him reach out to us. The professionals offered no real hope or help, but in our love for our son and his beauty we found a determination to persist. All alone, Samahria and I. Holding it together. What did we know about our son? Definitely distant and encapsulated, but gentle, soft, and beautiful. Raun was a flower, not a weed; an adventure, not a burden. What others portrayed as an affliction, we began to hold as a gift. We never felt obsessed, just dedicated and committed. Samahria and I held hands together late one night as we watched Raun sleep in his crib. We glanced at each other. We knew. We had decided. We would intervene and try to reach for our son, no matter what it took!

We had formulated a three-pronged program. We had already begun to demonstrate the attitude of approval and acceptance that would underlie every approach, every attempted contact, and every movement we made toward our son.

Raun Kahlil. A little man occupying the edge of the universe.

> *Raun was a flower, not a weed; an adventure, not a burden. What others portrayed as an affliction, we began to hold as a gift.*

Second, we would offer him a motivational therapeutic experience. Show Raun the beautiful and exciting world that welcomed him! Show him that it would be worth his extra effort to depart from his ritualized arena. We knew that our son would have to stretch himself beyond any present limits; he would have to climb the highest mountains just to accomplish what other children do with ease. Only the most motivated person would attempt such a journey.

The third phase would involve developing a teaching program for him that simplified every activity and every event into small and digestible parts. We would help him dissect his external environment into comprehensible portions so that he could build new pathways and construct new roads where old ones might have been damaged or broken.

We chose to make contact in an environment free of distractions. Samahria and I decided the optimum room for this was the bathroom, where we could limit interference from audio and visual bombardment.

Those first days marked the beginning of a very intimate human experiment. Samahria sat quietly with Raun for hours. Together, but separate. Raun stared at his shoes; then moved to his hands and finally fixated on the lights in the ceiling. Samahria watched, then joined his movements, searching for a meaning, hoping for some ever-so-minute indication that Raun was aware of her and interested in her presence. His alert eyes seemed like mirrors that reflected instead of absorbing or sending information.

Finally, Raun shifted his eyes. He dropped his gaze to some vague spot in space directly in front of him. Then he began to rock back and forth rhythmically. An eerie humming sound echoed from his throat, two notes timed to match each forward and backward movement. Samahria rocked with him now and sang in harmony with his song. Then, she concentrated on the same empty space, finally locating a spot on the wall and focusing on it. As she leaned forward, the spot became larger. As she rocked backward, the spot became smaller. She moved to Raun's rhythm, feeling her body and Raun's arcing through the

Raun and Samahria, absorbed in their private world

air in the same way. Raun lost himself in the motion.

Samahria's participation in Raun's movements was neither passive nor peripheral. Her genuine involvement and her sincere enthusiasm for these activities allowed her to share his world and, she hoped, communicate her love and approval. Samahria stayed fully active, but gentle; fully alive, but peaceful.

The hours became days. Most of the time Raun behaved as if he did not know that Samahria was there. And yet she knew, somewhere deep inside, that he knew she was there, that his awareness of her increased each time they came together.

On the eleventh day, after spinning with him for over two full hours, Samahria noted a single, casual, sideward glance at her. She acknowledged and softly cheered his action. That night, we celebrated that first self-initiated look from our son as if it had been a gift from heaven.

We continued our program of sensory enrichment and stimulation with Raun. We expanded the time frame, working with him every waking hour (about twelve hours each day). Every morning, Samahria entered the bathroom, giving our son continual input and exposure to gentle, loving, yet energetic and playful human interaction. In the evenings, before our nightly analysis of each day's process, I would sit alone with one or both of our daughters on the stairs that faced the closed bathroom door. We heard soft talk, laughter, clapping, singing, and silence. We had brought the best of the world into that tiny little room and made of it an amazing human laboratory. On weekends, I joined with my son. Our program ran seven days a week. Rather than draining our vitality, it dramatically energized our spirits.

One evening, nine weeks into our program, we sat with Raun in our bedroom and watched him walk around and play with our shoes. Suddenly, passing in front of the mirror, he became captivated by an image he saw there. Although he had certainly passed by the mirror many times, tonight something notably different happened. He stopped, startled by his own image. For the first time, he appeared mesmerized by a commanding form, the full length reflection of himself.

He surveyed his image cautiously. He moved back and forth, left to right. He walked directly to the mirror and touched his reflection nose to nose. His eyes beamed like electric lights. He moved out of the path of the mirror, then slowly looked back into it. As he did, he met his own face, saw his own eyes. He moved directly forward again, touched his belly to the belly of the child in the mirror, then tipped his head to the mirror as the twin facing him duplicated his movement with absolute precision. Suddenly, he emitted a wild, unfamiliar sound, a cry of incredible excitement and joy. He began to grunt and laugh with elation. Raun Kahlil had discovered himself. I turned to Samahria, amazed and dazzled. Tears streamed down her face. I felt wetness under my own eyes and realized that I, too, was crying. The first day of creation, a new dimension. Raun had found himself, and it was a joyful experience.

Each unfolding week ushered in new accomplishments, new breakthroughs. Yet I kept reviewing an area I knew to be critically important to Raun's ability to think and ultimately talk. Each evening, for weeks, I put him through the same test, hoping in this way to help him accomplish the near impossible. I would greet him in the kitchen and show him a cookie. When he put his hands up for it, I would slowly move it away while encouraging him to follow it with his eyes. Then I would make a great show of putting the cookie behind a piece of paper. He would lose track of it once it disappeared from sight and then stand there confused. He still could not keep an object in his memory when it was out of view. He still had a limited ability, at best, to solidify images in his mind for future reference. Developing and perfecting this area was critical; it would serve as a foundation on which he could build language.

We began the eleventh week in the program. As I came through the side door after a day at work, I bumped right into Raun, who had been standing by the table. He peered up at me very casually, brought his right hand up from his side as if to take the oath of office, and then moved his fingers up and down against his palm. My God, he was waving hello!

Dumbfounded, I waved back. He watched me for several seconds and then looked away. What a simple and profound hello, the best I had ever had! Three months before, if I had walked through the door and thrown a hand grenade, Raun would never so much as flinch or look up at me. Now this little man greeted me with a sweet and understandable gesture. My number was coming in. We were both the winners.

There was still enough time for Raun and me to play our favorite game before Samahria put him to bed. I took a cookie off the counter and showed it to him. I put it on the center of the floor, calling his attention to it. Then, as he watched, I ever so slowly placed a newspaper over it, hiding it from his view. He paused, staring at the paper for almost a minute. Then, with very little overt expression of interest, he walked over to the paper and sat beside it. He studied the photographs on the front page. His glance moved slowly across the newspaper and lingered at the edges. Samahria and I looked at each other, waiting silently. We had seen him do this before, each night, without ever going further.

But then, with a careful movement of his hands, Raun pushed the paper aside, sliding it off to the right until he had uncovered the cookie. Without ceremony, he picked it up and ate it. A random accident? We could only guess. We held our breath, reviewing the event excitedly. Try again. Take the chance I took another cookie and showed it clearly to Raun. I put it on the floor in another part of the room and slowly placed another piece of newspaper over it. From the corner of my eyes, I noted his primal intensity like an animal poised to pounce. My neck tightened and a flutter of energy ran through the upper part of my torso. As soon as I stepped out of the way, he followed swiftly in my tracks, lifted the newspaper, and quickly plunged the cookie into his mouth.

Amazing! He seemed filled with a new sense of authority, a new confidence. Had it really happened? Did this mean that he could hold images now in his memory and use them?

I grabbed a handful of cookies. I put one under the base of a light chair in full view. He followed, quickly lifted the chair, and took the cookie. I put another on the counter out of sight. He again followed, lifted his hand, and felt around the top of the counter, his little fingers walking around the formica until finding their mark. He grabbed the cookie and rewarded himself. I placed a cookie on top of the chair. Another under the pillow of the couch. Another inside my clenched fist, which he soon assaulted and forced open. Determination. He found every cookie. We applauded and cheered him. We were drenched in our exuberance. And he was too.

Although we both realized what this new milestone could mean, we encouraged each other not to form any expectations. Allow Raun to develop his own capabilities at his own rate, we agreed. We trusted that when he wanted to and could participate and learn more, he would.

The periods between those times when he appeared remote, aloof, and self-stimulating became noticeably more productive. He became increasingly willing to interact. In the park one day, he approached several children playing in the sandbox. When they offered him a shovel, he scooted away. But then,

from a distance, he watched them closely. Perhaps, for the first time, those random, unpredictable events around him had begun to make sense. Several minutes later, Raun turned and looked directly at one little boy standing near the swings. He smiled at the child and then, with no apparent warning, walked right up to him and hugged him, placing his cheek against the little boy's face. The youngster became frightened and started to cry. Oursonbacked off immediately, confused and concerned. He mimicked his little friend, scrunching up his face as if he too were sad. After several minutes, when the other child stopped sobbing, Raun moved cautiously toward him again and stroked his arm. His new friend eyed Raun curiously, then smiled. With this act of communion, this sharing of affection, a very delicate and often- times frail human being had made his mark.

This day, the sun began to rise in Raun's eyes.

We continued our intensive program with Raun for another three years, working twelve hours a day, seven days a week, until he showed no trace of his autistic condition. By age five, this once-withdrawn, mute, under-30 I.Q. child was demonstrating a near-genius I.Q.

> *Now twenty, Raun thrives in his second year of college with biomedical ethics as his major area of study. Next year, he becomes an exchange student at a university in Sweden.*

Now twenty, Raun thrives in his second year of college. He has a girlfriend, participates in his university's intercollegiate debating team, joined a coed fraternity, became politically active (working in the last presidential election), and chose biomedical ethics as his major area of study. Out of eight hundred applicants from undergraduate and graduate schools throughout the country, Raun was among fifty selected to design and teach courses for inner city junior high students in a special summer program. Next year, he becomes an exchange student at a university in Sweden, where he will continue his education and pursue his interests by studying Sweden's health care system.

What began with one special child in a bathroom as a unique experiment has blossomed into a method of working with children from all over the world who face special challenges. Most important, this attitudinal and educational approach, which is profoundly accepting and respectful of each child's dignity, has facilitated deepseated and lasting change in the hundreds of children and their families who have sought assistance at our learning center the Option Institute.

I don't remember asking God and the universe for a profoundly neurologically disabled child. Sure, both Samahria and I wanted the best for ourselves and our family. What we didn't know in the first moments of realizing that our son was different is that God and the universe had given us the best: we only had to discover it. And the discovery was not so much a revelation as a creation. We had to teach ourselves how to see differently and be far more open and loving than ever before. I used to think we were so alone, our family and our son. I used to think that no one really cared or wanted to understand. Perhaps, for a time, that might have been true. But now, as I watch the courage and magnificence of other parents using an attitude of love and acceptance to help their children, I am profoundly moved. Their commitment to change themselves for the love of a child speaks to a deep place inside. No one can ever guarantee whether someone you love will change or be healed, but embracing that person with respect and happiness can only be a gift, a gift for the giver and a gift for the receiver.

I don't know what's around the corner. I don't know what unanticipated challenges tomorrow will bring. But I do feel blessed to realize that I can continue to teach myself to be openhearted and to search for the lesson of love in every moment.

Following their miraculous success in working with their son Raun, the Kaufmans established the Son-Rise Program at the Option Institute. This program is designed to help parents of special children. Here is one of the many success stories.

JULIE'S STORY
told by her father John

Julie was having ferocious temper tantrums where she'd knock everything off the countertops and table. She'd eventually drop to the floor in hysterics; once in a while she'd even bite her arms and hands. It would last until we practically had to sit on her to stop her from hurting herself. As Julie drifted more and more into her own world, life became unbearable: the constant and fierce temper tantrums, the loud, endless crying and screaming, the destruction of our household possessions and the physical damage she did to herself.

One day while I was at work, Laura called up, hysterical. She said, "You've got to come home immediately." So I came home, and I saw that the house was in a shambles. Tommy's face was all scratched up and bleeding. Tina, our oldest, was crying and Julie was on the porch with a devilish look on her face. She had done it all! We lived on pins and needles. We became prisoners in our own home.

We both started to get really frightened. Julie was still very young, and we could barely manage her physically. What would we do in a few years when she was larger and more powerful?

Before I came to The Option Institute, my feeling was, "Oh, she's an autistic child. She's a special child. She has to be worked with in a very special way that only the experts know. Only these teachers and Special Ed personnel know. They have multiple master's degrees and so forth. I'm just an accountant. I don't know about these things."

The most wonderful thing that happened to me when I was at the Institute was seeing how easy it was to do what needed to be done for Julie. It was quite a departure for me, changing from a serious, methodical person into a childish, crazy joker, in order to be with my daughter.

I found that I totally had to change my conception of how to be with Julie. She was the teacher now. All I had to do was motivate her and connect with her. That was my guiding thought throughout the four years we did the Son-Rise Program with her. "I don't have to sit and teach her anything. All I have to do is be with her. If she just loves to be with me, she'll want to do things with me."

My wife and I both learned how to be more accepting of ourselves and each other. And what we learned about Julie has proved to be enormously successful with our other three children as well.

I used to get up in the morning at six and be at work at seven and by nine have a splitting headache. Now I get up at six, work with Julie till ten, go to work on Cloud Nine, and smile at all the people who have headaches there. I just say, "Hey, I am having a wonderful time!"

The last four years have been the most magical years of our lives. Earlier this year, I was alone in the kitchen one morning making my breakfast. Suddenly I heard footsteps and a little

voice saying "Daddy! Daddy! I am so excited. Today is the day of my dance recital." Julie walked into the room with a radiant smile on her face. She looked me straight in the eye, held my neck, and hugged me tightly.

"Daddy, it's going to be the real thing today," she said. "Are you going to be there with Mommy?" she asked.

"Of course, darling," I replied, "I wouldn't miss it for the world."

"I am not shy, Daddy, I know all my steps, and I'm going to be a good dancer like Mommy and Tina," said Julie.

With that, Julie ran upstairs. I walked down the stairs and sat down on the chair in Julie's playroom. I was filled with an overwhelming gratefulness to God. He had blessed us with a precious and wonderful gift, our Julie. And not only did we discover her, but we also discovered ourselves. And in the process, we achieved great joy, tranquility, and inner happiness in our lives. What more could we ask for?

For more information about programs at the Option Institute, write 2080 South Under Mountain Road, Sheffield, MA 02157 or call (413) 229-2100.

Pat Montgomery, noted author and lecturer, is the founder and director of Clonlara School and Clonlara School Home Based Education Program. and a bear for the legal defense of endangered schools and homeschoolers! She offers us two articles pertinent to homeschoolers.

HAIL TO THE VICTORS:
HOME EDUCATORS OF MICHIGAN
by Pat Montgomery

Seven years have gone by since Clonlara School filed suit against the Michigan Board of Education (MBOE) and the Michigan Department of Education (DOE) because of their hostility towards home schoolers. In September 1986, the MBOE rubberstamped a set of regulations (called "Procedures") designed to eliminate home schooling. All the while, these same state school officials were encouraging local school officials to be "proactive in court", a euphemism for "call 'em criminals, toss 'em in jail, and throw away the key."

The "Procedures" included such requirements as these:

a) Home schools would have to use state certified teachers inside the home for only a full 180 days per year and 900 hours of instruction.
b) Parents would be expected to complete a form, the SM-4325, annually assuring officials that a state certified teacher would instruct the students for 180 days per year.
c) Parents were to submit, under SM-4325: 1) name and age of each student in the home school; 2) the name and certificate number of the teacher, and 3) that the teacher instructs the students in English, reading, math, social studies, science, civics and government.
d) Parents who did not comply with the procedures, according to SM-4325, would be subject to truancy or other criminal charges without due process under the law.

Clonlara attacked these ploys from several directions, asserting that:

1. The MBOE/DOE acted illegally in approving the procedures because the document attempted to regulate and legislate home schooling. Neither the MBOE nor the DOE have the right to create laws; that belongs to the state legislature. The "Procedures" therefore were only the interpretations of state school officials and, as such, they did not have the weight of the law and could be ignored by home educators.
2. Parents' due process was being denied, and before any action could be taken against home schoolers, an administrative hearing must be held.
3. There was no basis in law for the 180 day per year requirement.

Judge Thomas Brown in Circuit Court agreed with Clonlara's assertions. He added, on his own, the ruling that only core subjects (reading, writing, math) should be of interest to the state. He deleted science and social studies from the required list. He stated that parents could use the services of a state certified teacher anywhere from two hours a year up to 899 hours a year, parents' choice. This use could be by telephone calls or video tapes or audio tapes or at a picnic or a church or wherever.

The MBOE/DOE appealed.

The Michigan Court of Appeals affirmed what Judge Brown ruled and added, on their own, that there is no law that requires face-to-face contact between any student and a state certified teacher.

On May 25,1993, the Michigan Supreme Court handed down the final ruling. Clonlara won on all of its assertions. (The Court went to great lengths to define what the MBOE/DOE can and cannot do by way of interpreting state school laws. It reversed one of Clonlara's original assertions that the MBOE/DOE should have gone through the legislature for approval before publishing the "Procedures". But the end result—that "Procedures" are NOT law—remains as Clonlara claimed.)

The Supreme Court ruled that the "Procedures" are not rules; they are interpretive statements that do not have the force of law.

The Supreme Court ruled that the MBOE/DOE must hold an administrative hearing if it differs with what occurs in the home school. At such a hearing, the DOE must use only the nonpublic school law (never its own interpretation) as the basis for drawing conclusions and making decisions.

The Supreme Court ruled that the 180 days of instruction per year requirement is not valid.

The Supreme Court ruled that "all hours of instruction in home schools must be conducted by certified or certifiable teachers." Certifiable means that the person holds a bachelor's degree and could, thereby, qualify for a state-issued teaching permit.

On the face of it, this looks as restrictive as the "Procedures" themselves threatened to be. It is not. The Court has muzzled the MBOE/DOE and forced them to obey the nonpublic school law as it is written: home schools (because they are ranked as nonpublic schools) must use state certifed or certifiable teachers for all of the instruction. THERE ARE NO NUMBER OF HOURS PER YEAR OR DAYS PER YEAR SPECIFIED IN THE LAW.

What this amounts to is that if the MBOE/DOE questions the operations of any home school, they cannot employ their old tactics of dragging people into court. They must hold an administrative hearing first and only use the law as the basis for any conclusions.

An administrative hearing is a process. The parents must be informed by mail of an alleged deficiency in the home school. S/He has fifteen days in which to respond. A hearing is setwithin another specific amount of time. The Superintendent of Public Instruction or his designee conducts the hearing. If a remedial plan is indicated, the parent has, again, a reasonable and specified amount of time in which to make modifications. It is only after this appropriately drawn-out process that any action can be taken. In all of its years as a bureaucratic entity, the DOE has never held an administrative hearing.

Now, as if this weren't victory enough, the Michigan Supreme Court simultaneously ruled on two additional cases. Both involved parents who had refused to send their children to institutional schools. Both were found guilty. Both appealed.

Mark and Chris DeJonge from the Grand Rapids area taught their children at home without using a state certified teacher at all because of their religious beliefs. The Court of Appeals upheld their conviction, ruling that the teacher certification requirement was then least restrictive means "to meet the state's interest. The Michigan Supreme Court (May

1993) disagreed; it overturned the DeJonges' conviction, ruling that the teacher certification requirement is a violation of the First Amendment which protects from government interference in the exercise of religion, and that the use of a state certified teacher is not the least restrictive means.

John and Sandra Bennett of Canton, Michigan, were found guilty of failure to send their children to Plymouth/ Canton Schools in 1985; they educated four of their children at home. They were enrolled in Clonlara's Home Based Education Program and used a state certified teacher twice a week, on an average. This wasn't enough time, the school officials claimed; the Bennetts were to be fined $50.00 per child.

The Bennetts appealed, asserting that they had a fundamental right under the Fourteenth Amendment to direct the education of their children, and that they had been denied due process under the law because they were prosecuted without first having had an administrative hearing to determine whether or not they were in compliance with the nonpublic school act.

The Michigan Supreme Court ruled for the Bennetts on the one hand: their conviction was vacated because, as administrators of a nonpublic (home) school, the Bennetts were entitled to an administrative hearing before they could be prosecuted. On the other hand, the Court made a distinction between First Amendment rights and Fourteenth Amendment rights, the latter are not violated by the requirement to use a state certified teacher, the Court said.

So, Michigan parents who home school for religious reasons do not have to use a state certified teacher. Others do, for all of the instruction, but the law does not state how much instruction is required. Perhaps Judge Brown's solution is the best: anywhere from 2 to 899 hours per year.

Michigan has always been a great place to home school. The growls and fierce barking by the MBOE/DOE frightened some who bothered to take note of their howling, biting, and salivating. The erstwhile pit bulls have effectively been banned with these recent Court rulings.

We have fought a good fight and have prevailed. We are in the company of families—the Bennetts and DeJonges—who have done the same. We were assisted in the struggle by a long-time civil rights lawyer, Kurt Berggren; by the National Association for the Legal Support of Alternative Schools (NALSAS) and its luminary, Ed Nagel; and by numerous Michigan Christian home schoolers. We will continue to be vigilant on behalf of Michigan home educators and home educators the world over. We will continue to work so that each and every parent and student is empowered to control his/her own life. Oooohhhhh, what a feeling!!!

Pat, co-founder of the National Coalition of Alternative Community Schools (see pp. vi to viii in volume I of Challenging the Giant *for a history of her efforts) and a strong leader of that organization, has lectured many times to Japanese parents and teachers, the first American alternative school educator to do so. She has a strong following there, as here!*

HOME EDUCATION IN JAPAN
by Pat Montgomery

Tokyo Shure is a school for "school refusers" located in Tokyo, Japan. It was founded ten years ago by Keiko Okuchi, a parent and a former public schoolteacher. The ties between Tokyo Shure and Clonlara are long-lived and solid, from the founding of the school to the exchange visits between Clonlara campus school students/ staff and Tokyo Shure students staff to the wedding of Nat Needle, Dean of Clonlara campus high school and Mihoko Wakabayashi, teacher at Tokyo Shure, to the "Home School Symposium" held by Tokyo Shure. I was one of the keynote speakers at this event.

First, a definition is in order. A school refuser is just that: a student who refuses to attend school. This is a phenomenon that is virtually nonexistent in the United States, but it is a major problem in Japan. I saw a ten story hospital in Tokyo entirely devoted to treating kids of all ages—four through eighteen years—whose illness springs only from their refusal to go to school. They are definitely ill with very real phobias, depression, suicidal tendencies, etc. They feel ostracized from their families, relatives, neighbors, the society at large. The pressures rampant in the educational system in Japan are more than these children can tolerate; more even, than the painful alienation that refusing to go to school can bring. The number of elementary age school refusers has more than doubled in the past five years; for older students the number has more than tripled.

I was very touched by the answer Keiko Okuchi gave to an assembly of parents, staff, and students when asked how she came to start Tokyo Shure. (I tell you this, not in a shy way!) "When Pat Montgomery was in Japan in 1984, I attended a seminar on alternative schools that she gave. I was a public school teacher at the time. I knew that changes were desperately needed in the public schools, but I was also very concerned about school refusers and I felt drawn to create a place where they could feel accepted and not be estranged from their families and friends. Pat pointed out that many others in that seminar had expressed concerns about public schools and were intent upon reforming them. You, Keiko, are the only one who feels drawn to help refusers. You have two choices: stay in the public schools and try to make a difference, or follow your urgings to create a school."

Keiko *san* made her choice; today Tokyo Shure has a full enrollment of 100 students on one campus, and 30 students (so far) on its newly-established second campus elsewhere in Tokyo.

Last spring, thirteen Clonlara students and two staff members, Nat Needle and Barb Maling, traveled to Japan and spent two weeks visiting Tokyo Shure and touring the country. They stayed at the home of Tokyo Shure students. Then, the Tokyo Shure students and staff accompanied Clonlara's group to the United States. They attended the NCACS Conference in Virginia, toured parts of the country, and stayed at the homes of Clonlara families while in Ann Arbor. Tokyo Shure had applied for and received a grant from the Japan Foundation to pay (in part) for the trips.

Nat Needle [*see Nat's letter and article on holistic education starting on pages* 155-169] met Mihoko Wakabayashi some years prior to the Spring '94 trip exchange; by that time, they were pledged to one another, and they got married in the Buddhist Temple in Ann Arbor last August. Several guests commented about the symbolic "wedding" of Clonlara and Tokyo Shure that also occurred.

Konomi Shinohara Corbin, Japanese translator and interpreter at Clonlara, accompanied me to the Tokyo Shure Home School Symposium. Keiko *san* expected perhaps 300 people to attend that gathering, since home education is not widely known or understood as an alternative in Japan yet. Eight hundred eighty-nine (889) people filled the auditorium to capacity.

It was a day long event. Paul Bentley, Chair of "Education Otherwise," the national homeschool group of England, and I explained and described homeschooling practices in Britain and the U.S.

Panel members responded to our presentations. One was herself a school refuser as a Japanese child. Her father supported her in that choice, realizing that the school was stifling the life of his child. (Most Japanese parents do not support their child's choice because they, too, feel pressure from relatives, neighbors, the community, and society itself.) It became obvious by the questions and comments from the Symposium audience that homeschooling is a fast growing phenomenon; the word is spreading.

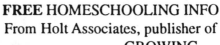

The following article by Pat Farenga is taken from Growing
Without Schooling *for Jan.-Feb., 1994. Pat is the president of
Holt Associates and also publisher of* GWS.

SCHOOLING + DIPLOMAS = JOBS?
by Pat Farenga

*Is it really true that more schooling will lead to a better job?
Do people with school credentials perform more skillfully than
people without them?*

The media have long pounded the drum about the need for
schooling. But the statement that bothers me most is the one that
keeps getting repeated year after year: the more schooling one
has, the better prepared one is for a well-paying job. Fortunately
there is a history of research on the connection between
employment and education, and by examining it, even briefly,
we can see that education's promoters are quite selective in what
studies they publicize. Let me cast aside for now the issue of
whether anyone can discern the future in such detail that they
can know what specific skills and knowledge our 10-year-olds
will need to know when they are 30. What I want to know is,
does possession of school credentials, particularly diplomas,
really mean people are better qualified for a job?

In 1971 various studies of the links between employment
and school credentials, plus original research on the subject,
were analyzed by Columbia University's Ivar Berg and
published as *Education and Jobs: The Great Training Robbery*
(Beacon Press, 1971). It would be hard to summarize this book
without going on for some time, so let me mention just a few
highlights. One of Berg's studies examined the educational
histories and job performance of air traffic controllers in the
FAA. He notes that when he studied FAA performance
evaluations, "College graduates were least likely to have received
honors; the most awards were earned by non-college graduates
without managerial training ... There is, in fact, more evidence to
support the proposition that educational credentials as such
have relatively little bearing on performance ... ."

In his concluding chapter Berg focuses on the educational
establishment:

"Education ... is the most important non-defense activity in the public sector as a field of government em-

ployment. Its growth has been accompanied by a dramatic change in the academic achievements of teachers—so dramatic that today [1971] as many as three-fourths of all jobs defined as requiring college degrees are teaching jobs. Not all teachers have such academic achievements, of course, but the figures are impressive.

"Meanwhile, the number of teachers increased by almost 50 per cent from 1950 to 1960, a rate of increase much higher than that sustained by the work force, which grew about 15 per cent in the same decade. One can conclude, accordingly, that the mounting demand for education feeds in no small part upon itself. "

Educators and politicians ignored Berg's analysis, especially his recommendation that government policies should allow for other ways, besides college, to enter professional careers. Ignorance may be bliss, but this is a very costly bliss, not only in dollars but in people's time spent in school when they could be pursuing more meaningful projects. For instance, a study entitled *Learning: In School and Out*, by Dr. Lauren Resnick of the University of Pittsburgh in 1987 concluded that the vast majority of skills taught in school are not transferable to the real world. "Growing evidence ... points to the possibility that very little can be transported directly from school to out-of-school use," writes Dr. Resnick. The FAA, industry, and educators have all made it more difficult for non-credentialed people to get jobs despite evidence that alternatives to school credentials not only work, but are more cost-effective than additional years of schooling. People now need college degrees for jobs, such as being an air traffic controller, that until recently were done just as well by people without such credentials.

The connections between diplomas and jobs are much more tenuous than we are led to believe, and yet much of our national school debate keeps coming back to defining what and when children should learn in order for them to be prepared for what President Clinton described in one of his Satellite Town Meetings as the "high-skill, high-wage jobs of today." Does a twelve-year long checklist of skills really help us prepare people for work? Where, precisely, are these "high skill, high-wage jobs of today?"

There is much evidence from alternative schools as well as homeschooling that there is no need to create and enforce a check-list of skills in order to prepare children for the world of work. Homeschoolers who follow little or no set curriculum, and who often receive no official credentials, continue to get into the worlds of work and college without special difficulty; we've been printing such stories for seventeen years now. The Sudbury Valley School, which has no set curriculum or grading system, has published the results of a study of its graduates and finds them all doing well either in college or in work *(Legacy of Trust: Life After the Sudbury Valley School Experience*, Sudbury Valley Press, 1992). *The Eight-year Study*, commissioned by the Carnegie Foundation in the late 1930s, proved that learner-directed, experimental schools using a wide array of alternative methods of learning prepared their students for college as well as, and in some cases better than, traditional high schools and prep schools. Non-traditional colleges, such as Marlboro, Bennington, and Goddard, had been in existence well before the 1960s popularized them. They have no grades and no preset courses of study, yet their graduates find work and take their place in society. Finally, we all know examples, and many teachers know this too, of children who couldn't do well in school, but who excelled outside of school. James Herndon, for example, wrote in *How to Survive in Your Native Land* about a student who couldn't solve simple math problems on a blackboard but who could keep score for large bowling tournaments. Yet professional educators choose to ignore such examples and insist, as the American Federation of Teachers has for years, that performance in school should be linked to eligibility for work, so if you fail math in high school, you can't become a carpenter as an adult, and so on. Despite the contrary evidence I've mentioned, and there is more, we are faced with national policies that insist that the best way for the equation of schooling + diplomas = jobs to be solved is for others to dictate what we should know and to sort out the winners and the losers as defined by the educational standards.

If only the real world would cooperate with this linear equation! But the real world is non-linear and it changes much faster than the world of school ever can. For instance, John Gatto has pointed out that most adults who now use computers have pretty much taught themselves how to use them at home, at work, and in banking, without formal schooling. Some of us may take a course on our own initiative to learn more about how to use computers, but this is not the same as having school and business officials decide that we must take a course in order to use our computers better. Nonetheless, we often hear that we need schools to "teach children how to use computers," as if this is the one and only time they will get to learn such skills and as if using computers is an incredibly complicated, specialized process that can only be taught to the young in classrooms.

So the drums beat on for more and more schooling for more and more jobs. "Without an educated workforce we can't grow this economy or remain competitive," the President told a Satellite Town Meeting audience. Of course, education is meant to be synonymous with schooling in such statements, and this isn't a perspective that is unique to President Clinton. This whole national goals and standards business started with the Bush administration, which proves that pedagogical hubris— defined by Ivan Illich as human beings doing what God cannot, "namely, manipulate others for their own salvation"—knows no political boundaries.

The most disturbing thing about the schooling + diplomas = jobs equation is the assumption that these "high skill, high wage jobs of today" really do exist in abundance. Certainly some new fields, such as biotechnology, might require specialized skills and knowledge, though I strongly doubt that school is the only place where people can learn these things. But we must remember that there will be, as there always is, a limited num-

> *Since there is no actual connection between diplomas and job competence, it is plain discrimination to fail to hire people due to their lack of schooling.*

ber of openings for these jobs. Like architects, English majors, and engineers in the '70s, our children may spend time and money getting diplomas for school-defined jobs, only to find that the market is glutted with graduates like themselves. In 1971 Berg warned of the social problems that will be created as more and more "unemployed college men" must face the music.

That was 1971. What about today? In the *New York Daily News (11/30/91)* a story with this headline ran in the Business section:

SCHOOLING IS OUT. '90S JOB FORECAST IS FOR LESS EDUCATION.

I quote from that article:

More than three-quarters of all jobs in New York State during the 1990s will require a high school education—or less—with most of the growth in the service sector," Samuel Ehrenhalt, regional commissioner of the U.S. Bureau of Labor Statistics, said yesterday.

Following this up, I went directly to the U.S. Department of Labor's own statistics (*Occupational Outlook Quarterly,* Spring 1992) and found that the service sector "is projected to add the largest number of jobs of any occupational group by 2005." The jobs highlighted for fastest growth in the service sector are correction officials, firefighters, guards, police, detectives and special agents, chefs, cooks, kitchen workers and "food and beverage service workers," salespersons, clerks, cashiers, receptionists and secretaries, nursing and home health aides, childcare workers, janitors, groundskeepers.

Add to this mix the fact that employment prospects for American youth are the worst in years, and one wonders where all these "high skill, high wage" jobs are. According to the U.S. Bureau of Labor Statistics, "While the nation's official unemployment rate is a nagging 7%, it is three times worse among 16-19 year olds. For young people ages 20-24, the rate is 50% higher than the national average."

Where you study appears to matter less than *what* you study. Economists Thomas Kane and Cecilia Rouse say that those graduating with a bachelor's degree from a four-year institution or an associate's degree from a community college do not earn significantly more than those with similar numbers of college credits but no degree. In other words, it is course work, rather than the credentials, which count in subsequent earnings. For homeschoolers, this means that it will in many cases be more important to document what you have done than to worry about getting a diploma. Further, since there is no actual connection between diplomas and job competence, it is plain discrimination to fail to hire people due to their lack of schooling.

As the job and schooling markets keep growing apart, as more unemployed or underemployed college graduates enter the workforce, homeschoolers are showing that completing years of schooling is not the only way to learn or, ultimately, the way to get a good job, and that the jobs school prepares students for may not be worth the social and personal costs.

Kate Kerman was for many years a houseparent, teacher, guidance counselor and head of the math department at The Meeting School, a small alternative Quaker boarding school in New Hampshire, as well as a mother of two daughters. Until recently, she also served as Chair of the National Coalition of Alternative Community Schools Board. I love the forthright honesty of her essays on teaching and parenting, and am eager to learn what she will take on next!

PUSH-HANDS AND PARENTING
by Kate Kerman

In one of my earliest T'ai Chi lessons, my teacher explained why he liked to teach not only the T'ai Chi form, but "push-hands," in which two people work to push against each other until one or the other loses balance. He told us that push-hands was a much greater teacher than simply working on a solo form, since the effort of the other person to throw you off balance gave you a great deal more information about those places in your body which hold stiffness and resistance rather than being able to relax and let the pressure from the other player slide by or even be used to throw her off balance. Biking home from that lesson, I had a flash of insight. To be a parent is to enter into a similar push-hands scenario. Our children and students are wonderful partners in teaching us our weak spots. Their instinct is infallible as they work vigorously to make sense of the world, to explore limits and boundaries. In their quest for growing up, they need to learn from both the strengths and weaknesses of the adults around them.

But this is not really an article about what children get out of their relationships with adults, but rather vice-versa. We all know that little children need adults in their lives, but it is easier to overlook the ways in which they are partners in our own journeys of self-discovery. Children make especially good partners for this self-discovery because they are so vigorous, so forgiving, so persistent. What weak spots have my children and students helped me examine? I think the greatest one has been my instinct to control what is going on around me. Although it ought to be impossible for a mother to maintain the illusion that she can control her child's behavior past the first few weeks, most of us seem to be remarkably blind to the fact that our children are shaping our behavior at least as much as we shape theirs. I continue to get caught out on this issue over and over again.

Take the idea that we can forbid our children to have certain experiences—junk food, television, war toys, Nintendo, horror movies—you name it, we as parents have tried to limit their experiences. I am not talking about what we allow into our environment or what we choose to purchase—I feel fine about having refused to buy war toys for my son, not having had a TV for much of our family life, choosing not to buy much sugary food. However, when I had to forbid sugar to my children, I ultimately realized that I had in effect told them that sugar was a really important commodity. Their desire for it increased and they were willing to be sneaky, manipulative and dishonest to get it. When I stopped forbidding it, their consumption of it was more open and accessible to discussion. They were able to choose to buy candy without the extra strangeness of being sneaky about it. And I found that ending my attitude that sugar is "bad" released me from silly self-guilt trips when I choose to eat it, which seems in general to have led to much less bingeing and to more honest enjoyment. Paying attention to my children's responses to my attempted control has in the long run brought me to a much saner place.

One thing I have learned along the way is that it is extremely helpful to notice when I am feeling uncomfortable and to look inside myself to find out why. Working with teenagers at The Meeting School on a twenty-four-hour-a-day basis is a grand way to learn about what makes me uncomfortable! And I have found out over and over again that it is fine to be uncomfortable, and to be honest about it. What isn't so effective is to be uncomfortable and to react in patterned and unconscious ways out of that discomfort. For instance, I often go on trips with nine to fourteen teenagers. At first, I would go into the grocery store with a bunch of people trailing me and making suggestions about what food to buy. This way lies insanity! I was often exhausted and annoyed when I got back in the van. At last I woke up to the fact that I was taking too much responsibility (control issues again) and that these people could work out their own system for buying food. Now I park in a store parking lot, hand out the allotted money, decree "don't buy sugary stuff and BRING BACK A RECEIPT" and take a nap. The food isn't always exactly what I would choose, but I am relaxed and the students have had to deal with all those interesting interpersonal and economic issues raised by group shopping expeditions.

I used to let myself be talked into driving students places just because I couldn't think of a reason why I shouldn't. This often made me feel resentful—a clear sign that I had once again ignored my own feelings in order to be a "good sport." Besides wanting control, one of my weak spots is the desire to be liked, to be friendly even if at my own expense. Gradually over the years I have learned to call a halt to wheedling or to those elaborate explanations of why a trip to the bowling alley is so essential to someone's mental health. I have discovered these ploys to have the effect of drowning out my own internal sense of what I can or cannot handle. I tell students, "don't give me a big song and dance, just tell me what you want and I'll see if I can help." Naturally, I have had to learn to do the same in return when presenting my needs, and to try to take "no" as gracefully as I wish they would.

I find more and more that if I can take the time to see why I am upset or concerned about a request for my time or attention, it opens up honest communication. There are times when I can be very spontaneous and hop in the car at a moment's notice, but at other times I need to think things through or flatly say no. What helps is to explain what's going on: "I'm feeling flustered because everything is so disorganized today and I just can't make last-minute changes of plans," "I need to do housecleaning and I can't go unless you guys help out first," or "I don't feel comfortable taking you to Amherst because you came back stoned the last time I did that." If I can state clearly what is going on for me, my response is more often taken gracefully or the supplicant can come up with a solution to my discomfort (such as doing dishes for me before we go.)

Being a parent or teacher is an opportunity to heal old wounds, to grow, to retain a sense of wonder *or* an opportunity to solidify, rigidify, act out of old hurts or throw power around to make up for the powerlessness of our own childhood. To accept the opportunity for healing and growth, we must welcome the information about our weaknesses in the push-hands dances of our relationships with children.

THE LANCASTER SYSTEM:
AN ALTERNATIVE TO PUBLIC SCHOOLS
by John Chodes

Public education has failed. It often produces illiterate, spiritless graduates who have neither the motivation nor the skills to find a good job or succeed. As a result, private sector schooling is growing by leaps and bounds. Unfortunately, these private schools are associated with small, localized efforts or élitism and high tuition.

There was however, a private enterprise system in the 19th century which taught millions of poor kids around the world for a few dollars a year. It was called "The Lancaster System". It encouraged children to develop personal initiative and responsibilities. Students worked at adult jobs within the schools and got paid for them. They learned to read and write in months instead of years.

The Lancaster System was also controversial and revolutionary because it caused considerable social upheaval by enabling the poor to break down traditional class and economic barriers with their new skills. The Lancaster idea may offer a clue to the way out of the mess we are in today.

Joseph Lancaster was born in the slums of London in 1778. As a young Quaker, he experienced the sting of religious discrimination. His family's faith barred him from attending the schools for the poor run by the Church of England. So his father taught him at home. Embittered by this painful memory, by age 18 he was instructing London urchins in his father's attic, for a penny a lesson.

He was soon deluged with hundreds of students. With so many pupils and limited resources, Lancaster had to devise radical methods to make ends meet. This is how the "monitorial" idea was born. It delegated to the students the responsibility for teaching and doing the paperwork. The better students taught the slower. When the slower developed, they became monitors. There was one teaching monitor for every ten students. There were other monitorial positions that involved many of the students and spread prestige and responsibilities around.

One monitor would assign new students to a class. Another would keep track of absences. When a student made progress, a monitor would promote him. Another made or molded pens. Another was in charge of distributing writing slates. A "monitor-general" was in charge of all the others.

This kind of student interaction—teaching and learning from their peers—eliminated boredom. Lancaster wrote: "A school, governed by such order, exhibits a scene of wonder to visitors, and happiness among the children, which baffles the power of description."

Under this system, there was little for the adult headmaster to do except organize, reward, punish and inspire. Lancaster's schools did not need a harsh master, for they were governed almost automatically. "The master should be a silent bystander because the system and not the master's vague or uncertain judgment will be in practice," Lancaster said. "In a common school, the authority of the master is personal and the rod is his scepter. His absence brings riot and confusion. In his absence his assistants will rarely be minded. Under my plan, the master leaves and business goes on as usual because the authority is not personal."

His method was unique, fast and effective. "I continually made experiments," Lancaster later recalled. "1,000 children could be taught in one schoolroom under the care of one master and a great proportion of them finish their education in 12 months. That education comprising the art of reading, writing and arithmetic." Beyond the three R's, his schools also emphasized geometry, algebra, trigonometry, religion and languages.

In seeking to motivate his students, Lancaster had stumbled on to a method that brought out their entrepreneurial spirit and taught them how to deal with money. This was no small matter, since all this took place in the early stages of the industrial revolution. Most of the students and their parents had rarely dealt directly with cash.

Lancaster awarded "Merit Badges" for various accomplishments. These were small paper tickets, much like Green Stamps in contemporary America. Like trading stamps, the merit badges were worth little individually but had considerable value when redeemed in bulk. They could purchase toys, children's books, pens, purses and clothing.

Merit badges were also used to borrow books from a library monitor. This job was a "concession." It was a bonanza for that monitor. Other students often bid to purchase the concession with their accumulated merit badges. Through this process they learned about the dynamics of buying and selling in a real marketplace.

Entrepreneurial themes dominated Lancaster's ideas. Adult teachers in Lancaster schools had part of their income created by class attendance. Thus a teacher became a salesman and promoter of the system to bring in more pupils. Anyone who could pay the few shillings a year was welcome, including girls. No other system at that time had accepted them on an equal basis with boys.

Lancaster's cost-cutting experiments brought the cost of education down to a fraction of what it cost competing church or private schools. For instance, students wrote on slate instead of paper. Paper was expensive, slate indestructible. To save money on books, one per subject per class was used.

Each page was separated, placed on a stand, then the class was called together, divided into groups which stood before the stand and studied that one page as a lesson. The groups would then rotate so that each one had access to all the lessons.

Lancaster even designed prefabricated buildings that could be assembled in days. This was truly mass-produced education. Soon the system was self-sustaining by charging as little as four shillings a year.

Joseph Lancaster was a zealot, which was both a source of strength and weakness. He believed his system would revolutionize society by eradicating illiteracy, therefore ending poverty. To propagate his ideas, he wrote a book, "The Lancasterian System of Education," and printed several thousand copies. He lectured all over the world, giving away copies to anyone who professed an interest in starting a school based on his plan.

During 1808 to 1810, in an era of slow carriages and slower boats, Lancaster made 16 missionary journeys, traveling 6,837 miles, delivering 141 lectures and establishing 95 schools for 25,000 children.

Lancaster was a great salesman but terrible at business. Although he earned huge lecture fees, he gave much of it away to sincere or not-so-sincere audience members who said they needed seed money to implement his plan. He also liked to live well, which was at odds with his pious Quaker background. Robert Dale Owen, the famed social reformer wrote that Lan-

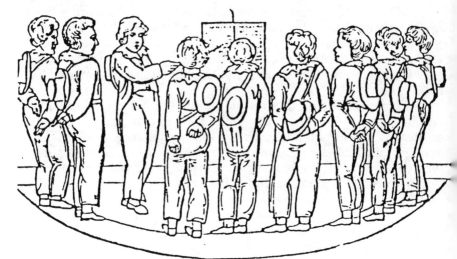

Picture shows a monitor teaching a group of his peers. They stand in a semi-circle about him. One page of a textbook is placed on a stand before them. When the students have completed studying that page, they move to another semi-circle where they study another page.

Students showing their writing slates to a monitor. Slates were used because they were indestructible, while paper was expensive.

caster was "a strange mixture of honest self-sacrificing zeal and imprudent self-indulgent ostentation." Later in his life this trait would come back to haunt him.

His major break toward national fame came when the aristocrat, Lord Somerville, attended a class and quickly became a backer in 1803. Somerville told others what he had seen and soon "foreign princes, ambassadors, peers, commoners, ladies of distinction, bishops and archbishops, Jews and Turks, all visited the schools with wonder-waiting eyes."

This ferment reached King George III, who granted an audience to Lancaster. "I have sent for you to give me an account of your system of education. You say one master teaches 500 children at the same time? How do you keep them in order, Lancaster?" the King asked. Lancaster described the monitorial system. The King was amazed. "I highly approve of your system, and it is my wish that every poor child in my dominions should be taught to read....I will do anything you wish to promote this object." King George promised 100 pounds annually, from his own funds, not the state's.

This modest patronage transformed a growing private business into a national institution. But in the end it proved fatal, since it aroused defenders of the Church of England to active opposition. To his critics, Lancaster was a dangerous radical intent on creating a social revolution. Teaching the "unwashed masses" to read and write and self-reliance made it possible for them to crack the traditional class barriers.

His most severe critic was the well-known writer, Sarah Trimmer. She warned that Lancaster's emphasis on merit, not class, might lead to the day when children "accustomed to consider themselves nobles of a school, may, in their future lives, from a conceit of their own trivial merits...aspire to be nobles of the land, and to take the place of the hereditary nobility."

Lancaster's opponents soon turned to championing a rival educational method, the "Madras" system of a Scottish clergyman, Andrew Bell. This system, while it relied on monitors, taught neither self-reliance or entrepreneurship. Bell had discovered his variation of the monitorial idea while on duty as an army chaplain in colonial Madras, India. He was in charge of an orphanage of Untouchable children. No adult would dare to teach these social outcasts. Bell, out of necessity, taught them to teach themselves.

But Bell's method reinforced all the negatives of the class barriers. "In Utopian schemes for the universal diffusion of gen-

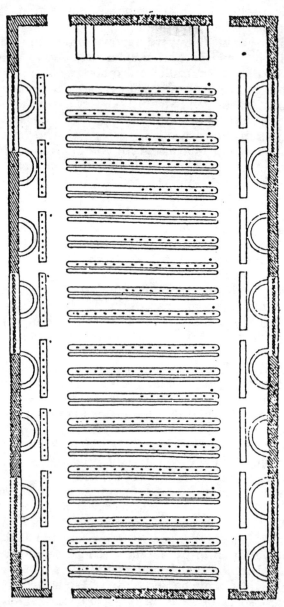

Ground plan of a Lancaster school, demonstrating how 1,000 students could be taught in one room at one time. Each dot represents a student. Some are seated at the long benches at the center, writing. The rest are divided into small groups along the semi-circles, reciting.

eral knowledge," Bell said, "there is a risk of elevating those who are doomed to the drudgery of daily labor above their station, and rendering them unhappy and discontented in their lot."

The Church of England, in promoting the Madras system to eliminate Lancaster's schools, used the same tactics that many modern retailers or fast-food chains use against one another. Wherever Lancaster opened a school, the church opened one of its own directly across the street. Backed by huge construction funds from Parliament, the tactic succeeded. Gradually the Church of England split Lancaster's market and, step-by-step, pirated all his students.

In 1805 the Lancaster System reached the United States. Eventually there would be more monitorial schools here than in England. Yet, for enthusiasts of private schooling, the story of Lancaster's rise and fall in America is more depressing than its demise across the ocean. Particularly in New York State, government involvement via subsidies marred the system almost from the beginning.

In 1805 the prominent philanthropists, Thomas Eddy and John Murray formed "The Society for Establishing a Free School in the City of New York." Its purpose was to educate poor children who were ineligible for instruction by the various church-sponsored schools. Benjamin Perkins, the group's Secretary, knew Lancaster and had seen his operation in England, and recommended it. Within a year the Free School Society (FSS) was incorporated and the first classes were held in Manhattan, with monitors as teachers.

One of the Lancaster system's most powerful American friends was DeWitt Clinton. He was one of the most important political figures of the era, being a ten-time mayor of New York City and also the governor of the state.

Clinton was an early member of the Free School Society. Upon his request, the New York State legislature granted the FSS a $4,000 subsidy to construct a building and another $1,000 for expenses. The money came from a tiny liquor and tavern tax, so the general public was not yet affected.

By 1818, three schools, teaching thousands of New York's poor, were in operation. DeWitt Clinton was now Governor. State-funded construction of five more schools was planned, which called for a wider tax. This one was imposed on real estate.

That same year Joseph Lancaster was invited to New York and Washington D.C. The mayor and DeWitt Clinton officially received him. He was treated like royalty when he visited the U.S. House of Representatives, which created a resolution honoring Lancaster as a "friend of learning and of man."

Soon New York State moved from subsidizing the Free School Society to managing it by legislating a general education tax which gave it the revenue to build new schools and to admit children of all economic levels. By the 1840's 98 schools taught 25,000 pupils annually under the Lancaster plan.

Then came the coup-de-grace for the FSS as a private system. As a closed corporation subsidized by the state, it came under fire. John Spencer, the Secretary of New York State, charged that the FSS had "acquired control of the system of public education; and the taxpayers, who contribute to this fund, have no voice in the selection of those who administer the system."

Spencer quickly extended the state's authority by creating the now-famous Board of Education to control the FSS. By 1852 it was completely absorbed by this bureaucracy, the cost of schooling quadrupled, taxes rose dramatically and the quality of education declined as the government now had a monopoly on education. Joseph Lancaster's great private system was dead but before it expired, 700,000 students in New York City had been taught by monitors.

Fortunately for Lancaster, he did not live to see its end. After coming to America he settled with his fellow Quakers in Philadelphia, but rumors about his profligate lifestyle and huge debts followed him from England, so that the pious Quakers shunned him. He was forced to wander from city to city, then Canada, and South America, briefly staying with friends before drifting on.

In October 1838, while in New York City to give a lecture, Joseph Lancaster was run over by a horse-drawn beer wagon, just a block away from one of his schools. He died. He was fifty-nine years old.

Shortly before his death he bitterly wrote: "Politicians have purposely interfered in what was originally a work of pure benevolence; and though they could neither corrupt or command the fountain, they have contaminated the stream."

Ron Miller, writer of the article below, is a historian of education and founding editor of Holistic Education Review. *He is deeply concerned about the quality of education and has written four books on the subject, the latest being* Educational Freedom in a Democratic Society. *He also produces an annotated catalog of books on education which he calls* Great Ideas in Education, *which you may order from him.*

THE TRANSCENDENTALISTS— HUMANISTIC EDUCATORS OF THE EARLY NINETEENTH CENTURY
by Ron Miller

Exactly one and half centuries ago, a humanistic approach was offered to the new American educational system. A small group of bright, young, rebellious scholars—the New England Transcendentalists— proposed a social and educational philosophy which was a clear alternative to the mainstream American ideology adopted by Horace Mann and his colleagues. The scope of the Transcendentalist vision, and the reasons for its failure, can be very instructive to educational reformers today.

"Transcendentalism" has meant many things—both to its participants and to historians. It was a religious, philosophical, and literary movement. It was also an archetypal rebellion of a young generation against its elders, of spiritual sensitivity against rising materialism and conformity, an all-encompassing critique of American society.

Of the ten or so most active Transcendentalists, those who applied the philosophy directly to the education of children were Alcott, Peabody, Thoreau and Ripley. But no account of their ideas is complete without including their mentor, the Rev. William Ellery Channing, and their leader, Ralph Waldo Emerson.

Channing:

William Ellery Channing (1780-1842) shed the harsh Calvinist theology and conservative politics of his upbringing to become the spiritual leader of the Unitarian movement. He emphasized the innate moral goodness of human nature, the wondrous depths of each person's "powers of intellect, of conscience, of love, of knowing God, of perceiving the beautiful..."

(Channing, 1900). Every individual, Channing preached, is intrinsically worthy, and must be free to develop his or her own inner resources. This trust in the latent capabilities of the human being is the essence of humanism. It led Channing to oppose social and theological limitations on the individual's opportunities for self-knowledge and self-expression. His views on education follow from this.

> We begin, perhaps, with ascribing a kind of omnipotence to education, and think that we can turn out a human mind, such as we wish it, almost as surely as a mechanic can turn out from his machinery a good piece of work. But...the human mind is more complex and delicate in nature, and especially more independent and self-active, than we had imagined. Free-will...belongs to the child as truly as to the man; and the child must be the chief agent in the production of his own virtue...It is well that no mind is put into the hands of another to be moulded at pleasure (W.H. Channing, 1880).

Essentially, Channing believed that the "object of education is not so much to give a certain amount of knowledge, as to awaken the faculties, and give the pupil the use of his own mind" (Channing, 1900).

Channing himself was known as "the great awakener"; his humanistic ideas, reinforced by his own sincere spirituality, inspired a generation of reformers. The Transcendentalists were especially thrilled, and though they took his theology a step too far for him (they concluded that knowledge of one's true self is sufficient for knowing God), their ideas and educational projects owe a great deal to his influence.

Emerson:

The leading theorist of the Transcendentalist movement was Ralph Waldo Emerson (1803-1882). His essays and lectures, especially "Nature" and "The American Scholar," announced the arrival of the rebellion in 1836-8. In "Self-Reliance" (1841), we find the most concise statement of Transcendentalism:

> The relations of the soul to the divine spirit are so pure, that it is profane to seek to interpose helps. (Emerson, 1965, p. 268)

Spiritual truth is revealed through a personal communion with Nature, not via social or religious authority.

> Truly speaking, it is not instruction, but provocation, that I can receive from another soul. What he announces, I must find true in me, or wholly reject. (Emerson, 1965, pp. 244-5)

Emerson argued that individual integrity and self-purification must be at the root of all social progress.

> ... the secret of Education lies in respecting the pupil. It is not for you to choose what he shall know, what he shall do. It is chosen and foreordained, and he only holds the key to his own secret by your tampering and thwarting and too much governing he may be hindered from his end (Emerson, 1965, p. 430)

Emerson was acidly critical of the abstract, bookish approach of most educators of his time; in "The American Scholar" he lamented that "meek young men grow up in libraries" instead of learning directly from life. After attending one of Mann's teacher's institutes, Emerson wrote:

> ... we are shut up in schools and college recitation rooms for ten or fifteen years and come out at last with a bellyfull of words and do not know a thing. We cannot use our hands, or our legs, or our eyes, or our arms.

For Emerson, education must be an active engagement of the soul with Nature.

Alcott:

More than anyone, A. Bronson Alcott (1799-1888) expressed this philosophy in educational practice. From 1823 to 1839, Alcott conducted schools in rural Connecticut, in Philadelphia and Boston. He was apparently a gifted teacher with a profound sensitivity to children. and early in his career he challenged prevailing pedagogical methods. In place of drab, uncomfortable classrooms he provided a cheerful environment with child-size desks, a library, slates, and real objects for children to handle and count. He taught through conversations and journal writing. He encouraged imagination, self-expression and self-discipline. He maintained order (reportedly very effectively) by cultivating children's responsibility for the classroom community. This was at a time when corporal punishment was *the* accepted method of ruling a class. Alcott rarely resorted to it.

He was one of the first educators (with Pestalozzi, whom he read) to recognize that children are naturally active and learn through movement. Intellectual and moral training must be integrated with physical education. Alcott wrote that "Genius is but the free and harmonious play of all the faculties of a human being" (Alcott, 1836). This holistic approach was radical in the 1820's; although a few educational pioneers approved of his methods, Alcott was mistrusted by the parents, who wanted their children drilled in "book larnin'"and disciplined the old-fashioned way. Many removed their children and opened competing schools.

Alcott was also a religious seeker with a mystical temperament. He was unsatisfied with orthodox churches and was naturally drawn to Transcendentalism. By 1834, inspired by extensive readings of Romanticism and Idealism, he had evolved a deeply spiritual philosophy of education, and, encouraged by Channing, he opened the Temple School in Boston. A fine summary of his approach is given by Cremin:

> The grand object of the curriculum was not learning in the traditional sense but rather self-knowledge—that understanding of the true idea of one's own being that permits one to use one's God-given endowments for the growth and perfection of one's spirit .(Cremin, 1980)

The purpose of life, to Alcott, was the cultivation of each person's spiritual essence. Children, as yet uncorrupted by "custom and convention," were open to direct inspiration if encouraged by the teacher. Alcott believed that Socrates and Jesus were the ideal teachers, for they sought to draw out the intellectual and moral qualities already latent in the human soul.

In 1835-36, Alcott reached the peak of his influence as an educator. Temple School, considered the best in the city, was attended by forty children from Boston's leading families. In 1835, Alcott's assistant, Elizabeth Peabody, published *Record of a School*, a diary of the daily proceedings, which was well-received. Emerson was excited by it and soon arranged to meet Alcott; their friendship lasted until Emerson's death.

But in 1836 and early 1837, Alcott published his two volumes of *Conversations With Children on the Gospels*, which revealed the fundamental radicalism of his approach and shocked his patrons. Essentially, Alcott was claiming that children's direct intuition of spiritual truth superseded the authority of churches and social custom. Immediately he was branded a threat to morality and social order. Newspapers ridiculed him. Even Channing expressed doubts (which embittered Alcott), and only the other Transcendentalists came to his defense.

THE CONVERSATIONS

MR. ALCOTT'S SCHOOL-ROOM
(Courtesy of the Concord Free Public Library)

Reprinted from Alcott's *Conversations With Children on the Gospels*, from a new edition by Alice O. Howell (See end of this article for more information)

Temple School closed in 1838; Alcott tried another school, but because he admitted a black student over the opposition of other parents, this school failed in 1839. He was left with five pupils; three of them were his own children. including 6 year-old Louisa May.

Bronson Alcott never taught school again. In 1847 he offered a lecture for Mann's teacher's institute, but Mann turned him down because his political views were "hostile to the state." After Transcendentalism died out as a radical movement, Alcott gained acceptance, and served with distinction as school superintendent of Concord, Mass. from 1859 to 1865. But the idealism of Temple School was never realized again in his lifetime.

Peabody:
Elizabeth Peabody (1804-1894) deserves further notice. She devoted most of her life to education, but unlike Alcott, was careful to bridge the gap between Transcendentalism and American society. After serving as Channing's secretary from 1825-1834 (while also conducting her own school), she joined Alcott and contributed to the success of Temple School. But she dissociated herself from *Conversations* and left the school. In the 1850's she advanced the teaching of American history in public schools, and from 1860 on was the leader of the kindergarten movement in the U.S.

Thoreau:
Henry David Thoreau (1817-1862), the self-sufficient naturalist and political essayist, was for a time a pioneering educator. In the winter of 1835-36, while a student at Harvard, he taught in Canton, Mass. and boarded with Orestes Brownson (1803-1876), the mercurial left-wing Transcendentalist who was then a Unitarian minister. I have been unable to determine the extent of Brownson's (or, for that matter, Channing's or Alcott's) influence on Thoreau's teaching approach. Thoreau was a Transcendentalist by nature (!) yet this letter to Brownson (seeking a teaching position after graduating college) contains ideas that very few Americans of the 1830's except for Channing and his protégés, would have had:

> I would make education a pleasant thing both to the teacher and scholar. This discipline, which we allow to be the end of life, should not be one thing in the schoolroom and another in the street. We should seek to be fellow students with the pupil, and we should learn of, as well as with him, if we would be most helpful to him....It hath not entered into the heart of man to conceive the full import of that word—freedom—not a paltry Republican freedom, with a posse comitatus at his heels to administer it in doses as to a sick child—but a freedom proportionate to the dignity of his nature.

Thoreau found a teaching job at home in Concord in the fall of 1837. He lasted two weeks. When a school committee member came by and found discipline too lax for his taste, he admonished Thoreau to apply corporal punishment. With characteristic sarcasm, Thoreau chose a few students at random, flogged them, and then resigned. He later began teaching four boys in his mother's boarding house, and in September 1838, took over the abandoned Concord Academy. His brother John joined him early in 1839, and for the next two years they ran a successful progressive school.

The Thoreaus were rigorous instructors, and prepared the older boys in traditional subjects (including Latin and Greek) for admission to college. Discipline was strictly maintained, although without punishment; each incoming student was asked whether he was committed to his studies, and if he became unruly, he was reminded of this pledge. But beyond the classroom routine, the school was noteworthy for the field trips which Henry led into the countryside and the shops of the town. He gave the students hands-on experience in surveying and other skills. And by all accounts, the relationship between teachers and students was unusually intimate for its day, marked by mutual respect and affection. The school only closed, in April, 1841, because of John's failing health. Although Henry tutored occasionally, his heart was no longer in teaching, and in 1845 he went to live at Walden Pond.

In his writings, however, Thoreau returned to education from time to time. He consistently stressed that true learning arises from one's direct experience of Nature.

> If I wished a boy to know something about the arts and sciences. ... I would not pursue the common course, which is merely to send him into the neighborhood of some professor, where anything is professed and practiced but the art of life. (Thoreau, 1950)

Brook Farm:

Finally, consider the school at the Transcendentalist-inspired commune, Brook Farm. George Ripley (1802-1880) the founder and head teacher, was himself a brilliant scholar who doubted the value of purely intellectual education. He wrote to Emerson in 184() that the goals of Brook Farm included forming "a more natural union between intellectual and manual labor than now exists; to combine the thinker and the worker, as far as possible, in the same individual" (Rose, 1981, p. 133). The Brook Farm school did combine rigorous college preparation with opportunities to work in the community. There were field trips, music and dancing, and visits by the stimulating Transcendentalist celebrities. The faculty was skilled and beloved; the relationship between teachers and students was close, and discipline was relaxed.

The school was the most successful part of the enterprise, even attracting students from outside. But it is significant that the school did not survive outside the protective atmosphere of the commune. Brook Farm lasted from 1841 to 1847, and its failure coincided with the decline of Transcendentalism as a social movement.

Conclusion:

The Transcendentalists were humanistic educators because they believed that the purpose of education was to unfold the potential human qualities of every child. Schooling must not be confined to intellectual drill or training for employment or citizenship. But this has always been a minority view. A pure Transcendentalist pedagogy—theorized by Emerson and Thoreau but practiced fully only by Alcott—was too anarchistic for accepted political and religious beliefs, too egalitarian for a patriarchic society that condoned slavery and was forcing Indians off their lands, and too "romantic" for the new urban/entrepreneurial/materialist identity of the emerging nation. In 1846 Transcendentalist idealism was shocked by the U.S. invasion of Mexico, and in 1850 by the Fugitive Slave Law.

American values have not changed much. Instead of Mexico we are bullying Central America. Conservative religious and social attitudes continue to limit educational progress; in some states even corporal punishment is making a comeback. The lesson for humanistic educators is this: although we believe passionately, like Alcott, that the unseen depths of the child's soul contain miraculous treasures, most of the public is not interested in them. Peabody, Thoreau, and Ripley were successful because they accommodated the demands of society; and it was Horace Mann, a middle class lawyer and politician, who captured support for public schooling, because he claimed that it was the best way to preserve social order and traditional values.

So each of us must decide how to confront the American educational climate. We can fight the establishment and suffer Alcott's fate, or withdraw into "new age" enclaves like Brook Farm. or, like Peabody, we can moderate our more radical ideas and possibly, though there are no guarantees, contribute to a slow, gradual humanization of society.

REFERENCES

Alcott, A. Bronson "The Doctrine and Discipline of Human Culture" Boston: 1836.

Channing, William Ellery *Works.* Boston: American Unitarian Association 1900.

Channing, William Henry *Life of William Ellery Channing, D.D.* Boston: American Unitarian Association 1880.

Cremin, Lawrence A. *American Education—The National Experience,* NY: Harper & Row 1980.

Emerson, Ralph Waldo *Selected Writings* (ed. Wm. H. Gilman) NY: Signet/New American Library 1965.

Rose, Anne C. *Transcendentalism as a Social Movement* 1830-1850 New Haven: Yale. 1981.

Thoreau, Henry David *Walden and other Writings* (ed. B. Atkinson) NY: Modern Library 1950.

The book from which the picture of Temple School was taken is called by Mrs. Howell:

HOW LIKE AN ANGEL CAME I DOWN
Conversations with Children on the Gospels
by Bronson Alcott
Introduced and edited by Alice O. Howell
Lindisfarne Press, Hudson, NY, 1991. pb $16.95

—a book all of us who work with children ought to read carefully and "visit" often.

—Robert Coles

Here is one of these priceless, quiet books that we hold up and declare, "Every parent, every teacher, every lawmaker, should know this work!"

—Joseph Chilton Pearce

You may order Ron Miller's catalog by writing The Resource Center for Redesigning Education, PO Box 298, Brandon, VT 05733 or call 1-800-639-4122.

This is my favorite section of Challenging. *I love it because there is so much variety in these writings, and because it sometimes seems to me that kids who are willing to write and to let you publish their writings are making an investment in their own lives, in their future. I hope you like them too!*

STUDENT WRITINGS

"We are a group of homeschooled students who attend a supplemental program called The Kalepaedeia House [near Ithaca, New York]. We are all very concerned about the earth and its creatures. "

SAVE THE ATMOSPHERE
by Timmy Maragni

The atmosphere has been in danger for about a century. Damaging gases have been released into the air. There is a hole in the ozone. And there is a lot more carbon dioxide in the atmosphere than one hundred years ago. If this crisis is not forestalled, the earth will become so hot that the poles will melt a little and the oceans will rise. I say that the atmosphere must be saved.

The atmosphere surrounds the earth and protects it from extreme temperature changes. People take this for granted because it's so far away. The ozone is a layer of special oxygen that protects the earth from the heat of the sun. But the ozone has been disturbed by man-made chlorofluorocarbons (CFCs). CFCs destroy ozone molecules. Because of this, there is a hole in the ozone over Antarctica. There is a lot more carbon dioxide in the air than there was one hundred years ago. This is caused by the cutting and burning of tropical rainforests. Trees in these forests absorb carbon dioxide the same way that we breathe oxygen. Carbon dioxide is also produced by the burning of more wood, coal, gasoline and oil. Carbon dioxide is a greenhouse gas. Greenhouse gases keep the earth from being too cold. Because all this carbon dioxide is in the air, the earth is starting to warm up. This warm-up is called the Greenhouse effect. If the earth warms up a little more, some ice will melt off the poles, and the oceans will rise. Cities like New York, Los Angeles,

Tokyo, London and Boston will be submerged. This disaster must be stopped.

If you want to help stop this disaster, you could plant some trees to absorb carbon dioxide. You could also send money to an organization helping to plant trees, or save the rainforest. This will help reduce carbon dioxide. Don't buy aerosols. Aerosols contain CFCs. Don't do much unnecessary driving. Unnecessary driving is, for example, driving a half a mile to go to the store, or see a friend. Instead, you could ride a bicycle or take the bus. Not doing any unnecessary driving will help reduce carbon dioxide by cutting down on burning gasoline. If you don't have any land to plant trees on, you could help plant trees at a nature center or in a city park. If you can only spare two dollars to send to an organization and think it won't be worth it, remember that every cent helps. People don't usually want to stop something like driving to the store instead of walking, or riding a bus. However, everyone is going to have to start worrying about other problems than not driving everywhere. They will have to start thinking about the crisis the earth is in.

—Timmy Maragni, age 12, Newfield, N.Y.

DAMAGE
by Sara Schultz

Do you care about the animals? Thousands of them are dying because of oil spills around the world. Birds such as the puffin, guillemot and razorbill are nearly at risk from all of the water pollution. Let's explain to the people that we care about our animals and maybe they will help us help them.

First let me tell you how oil spills occur. Lots of tankers are having accidents and they spill tons and tons of oil. In 1987 3.5 million tons of oil were spilled in the oceans around the world. Do you know about the Exxon spill in Alaska? This was an immense super tanker which was accidentally steered into the rocks. It spilled 232,000 barrels of oil into the Prince William sound, which is a location chock full of rich wildlife. The second most common way the oil gets into the water is that when the crew on the tankers clean the oil rooms they spill a lot of the oil.

Oil spills kill thousands of animals. Water with oil in it is calm. When birds land they get oily and sticky. The birds try to get the oil off their feathers with their beaks and it gets in their mouths and they die in a few days. Therefore, don't you think we need to help?

If you would like to help save the animals, here are some suggestions you could try. You could clean a little bit of water where there has been an oil spill. Even if we clean just a little bit, every effort will help the dying and helpless creatures of the sea. While you are there you can draw pictures, make movies, and start forming a group to save the animals. You could ask people who are on the tankers to be much more careful. It is amazing that every oil tanker is not double-hulled. There would be many fewer oil spills. Also, ships that have sailors from some other countries might not be as great at maneuvering a ship as other sailors because they are not trained as well. If there is a good captain there are fewer chances of oil spilling. If we could accomplish this there would be many fewer oil spills and many fewer animals dying.

Any objections to my suggestions? You might not have a place near you where there has been an oil spill. Then you can donate some money to an organization where they will purchase tools to clean the ocean and buy black tunnels that they will place on top of the ocean to stop the oil from going on to the shore. Even if you donate a little bit every bit will help. If you would like to learn more about oil spills read stores and find videos about them.

How much more beautiful the sea would be if we humans would be a lot more careful and stop being so careless. Most all oil damage is caused by humans' carelessness. Oil spills are destroying coast lines, giving birds terrible diseases, and killing all the marine life. Therefore, if you do something to help the creatures of the sea, even if it is just a little bit, it will help those animals live longer and better lives.

—Sara Schultz, age 10, Ithaca, N.Y.

SAVE THE RAINFOREST
by May Brinn-Beers

A long time ago there were very few people on earth, but now there are so many people that we are cutting down many many trees for lumber. Many of the trees that we cut down are from the rainforests. This destroys many animals' homes. And with no rainforests, not only the animals can't survive, but the people can't survive. I think we should all try to help save the rainforests because they are the most beautiful and wild ecosystem in the world. And they are very rare and they grow in very few places.

These rainforests mainly grow in the Guinea-Congo region of Africa and the Malay Archipelago. People travel all over the world just to collect plants and some kinds of foods from the rainforest. Many plants that grow in the rainforests are used for medicine. Without those plants we will have to lose many more lives than we already have. Also people are clearing out spaces to put their houses in and, as if that is not too much already, they are clearing out a wide space around their house for their yard. Furthermore, cutting down trees causes the climate to change, and all the moisture that was gathered by the trees will flow down the river which causes floods. Also, another very big problem is people are raising cattle to sell at markets for money and they burn the rainforest for cattle fields.

Many people chop down trees just for money. You can help save the rainforest by buying nuts and fruit that are from these forests. This way people obtain the money they need without having to cut down trees. Another way to save the rainforest is to buy a part of it from an organization who sells it. Then the organization will take good care of it. And if you need to buy wood, then make sure to buy it from people who grow fields of trees especially for lumber, and not from the rainforest. I'm sure you can think of some more ways to save the rainforest. But if you can't, try to do one of these.

But suppose you said "There are so many trees in the rainforest it would not hurt if I just cut down a few trees." Yes, that is true, if you just cut down a few trees, that would not hurt. But there are so many loggers in the world that 11 million acres are cut down each year, so we need as many people as we can get to stop cutting down trees. But if you then said "Fruits and nuts from the rainforest are very expensive and I can't afford to buy them." They are expensive but you could just buy "Rainforest Crunch" or rainforest crunch ice cream which is not as expensive as fruits and nuts. Or you could get together with a group and have each person contribute a little bit and buy a part of the rainforest. All ways to save the rainforest are important. If we don't get them done the trees will be gone—and we cannot survive without the trees.

The rainforest is the most beautiful and the wettest land in the world, so we all need to do our very best to save it and do at least one of the possibilities that I have mentioned to save the rainforest.

—May Brinn-Beers, age 10, Ithaca, N.Y.

LEMURS IN PERIL
by Lauren Cahoon

What species has a long striped tail, teeth that never stop growing, and can run on its hind legs!? The answer is the lemur, an inquisitive creature that only exists on the Island of Madagascar. There used to be forty species, but many of their species are extinct and the ones that are living may be in the same serious danger. Their forests are being cleared away for farmland and they are going extinct. We should save the lemurs, for they are one of the most special of Mother Nature's creatures.

Many people don't know that the lemur is special. In fact, the lemurs used to live in peace in their lovely forests—that is, until humans came. Soon the lemurs' main enemy was man. No wonder! They turned beautiful forests into parking lots and malls. Many villagers slaughtered the harmless aye-aye for supposedly bringing bad luck. People even eat lemurs! Also, Madagascar is a poor country where the average human lives to only forty...So the government is more concerned about establishing schools and hospitals than saving lemurs. Another heartbreaking fact is that people are clearing the jungle for farmland. But the people who are poor need land and cannot find any but the rainforest. The soil is poor so the barren ground is left while man clears away the rest of the lemurs' paradise. The reason for this conflict is that both the lemurs and natives want the forest; sadly, the lemurs, who are the ones who truly need it, are losing.

In order to help the lemurs, you can educate the children by bringing in an experienced person to teach about them. When they know more about lemurs they will want to help them. Also, raising funds by perhaps selling cookies or getting groups to donate money to the lemurs will help the lemurs' rainforest from getting cut. Instead of cutting down the forests we could find products that need the jungle. For example, a small periwinkle flower that cures a certain kind of cancer was found in the Madagascar rainforest. If we find more products like this people will want to save the forest, rather than slice it.

It would be splendid if you could find a way to save the lemurs. But if your schools can't get an experienced person or informative books in the library, write a letter to your congressmen for an address that has to do with saving lemurs. If you think raising funds is too difficult, go to your nearest nature center and ask about some other fund raisers that you could participate in. If you find all the suggestions above too difficult for you, just try writing an essay or a letter to the Madagascar government. If you care for the lemurs please do one of these things.

Unfortunately, not many people are undertaking these projects. A very disturbing thing is that the existing laws to save lemurs are hard to enforce. Many villagers do not understand about the lemurs' need to survive. Also, many people think the only animals needing help are the California condor, the grizzly bear and the moose. I am not saying that these animals shouldn't be saved. But what people should realize is there are many other species needing help too, like the delta sprelt fish and the large-eared bat and of course, lemurs. The lemur is such a wonderful animal and we've been cutting down their forests for years. Isn't it about time we do them a favor?

—Lauren Cahoon, age 12, Dryden, N.Y.

SAVE THE WHALES
by Isaac Furbush-Bayer

Whales are the largest animals on earth and occupy all the seas on it. They are very intelligent animals. But most whales are endangered, like the Blue and the Humpback. There was a law passed in 1986 banning the hunting and killing of whales, but people still do. An estimated 11,000 whales have been killed since then. This is a terrible slaughter and must be discontinued. People need to maintain working together very diligently to help keep hunters and pollution out of the water.

Whales are not safe despite the laws protecting them. They are still hunted in the name of scientific research. But whalers don't study them; they kill them and sell them for money. Whales are also hunted by poachers. Fishermen deplete their food. The Yellow Fin tuna fishermen have killed six million dolphins since the 1960's. Also other fishermen's nets kill 3,000 harbor porpoises each year. Greenpeace has inflatable boats that they drive in between the harpoon and the whales, but this does little when they're not there. Pollution is another problem. Noise can also interfere with the echolocation that whales use. In the 1860's steamships and an explosive harpoon gun were invented. This made it easier to hunt whales, which depletes them even further. All these problems make it a grim prospect for the whales.

There are many ways to help the whales. Some of them are to educate children. You could take them to an aquarium or bring in an experienced person to talk about whales and show a movie or slides. Another way to help is to write letters to the President urging him to help, or, take a group of people on a whale watching ship or donate money to either Greenpeace, National Wildlife Federation, or the Whale Adoption Program. There are many other ways to help. We should do them all very earnestly.

If you are not a teacher or do not have a nature center near you, then you could go to a library and get a book about whales or rent a movie. Even if you don't have a lot of money just a little bit would help. Educate yourself so you are not immune to factory ships or harpoons that explode inside the whale. Even just buying tuna fish caught in nets that don't hurt dolphins would help. If this is not done then the whales may become extinct.

Many countries have banned whale killing, but the slaughter goes on. You must help the whales now—don't wait. Just imagine, the most beautiful animals on earth are being killed like pigs. Possibly a whale has just been killed right now. Just think—the largest animal in the world! Let's not let extinction happen...remember, it means forever.

—Isaac Furbush-Bayer, age 14 Newfield, New York

HELP SAVE THE EUROPEAN WOLF
by Rebecca Furbush-Bayer

The European Wolf is a dangerous animal. These wolves usually hunt in packs and often kill and eat prey ten times more immense than themselves. Unfortunately, these wolves are in danger of extinction because they are being trapped and hunted. If we don't attempt to do something about it, then that will be another fantastic animal that we didn't succeed in saving. People should stop hunting them and start helping them.

But ever since people have had farm animals, the farmers have needed to protect them from wolves. Therefore, many wolves have been killed when trying to capture farm animals. One of the problems is that a dog and a wolf will mate occasionally, and so in the towns people can't tell the difference between dogs and wolves, and so the "dogs" will wander freely through the streets. Another problem is that people don't like these wolves. For instance, if a wolf is looking in their garbage, people don't like this because they don't like the idea of a wolf snooping around at night. The last wolf in Scotland died in 1743. The wolves in Ireland survived until 1770. Some people in European countries see no reason for not killing them for the sport of it, and will pay a great deal to do so. In other words, these wolves are very endangered and are in need of diligent help.

The reason these wolves are having such a hard time and need much assistance is that they have a bad reputation in storybooks and fairy tales, like the big bad wolf in "The Three

Little Pigs". To save these wolves we must think of something to convince people to help. One idea you could use would be to cut and paste pictures of these wolves and make a magazine, newsletter or an elaborate exhibit about them to encourage people that they should be saved. Another thing that could be done would be to go to a nature center and get the people there to bring out a wolf and show everyone how beautiful and intelligent these animals are. Or take them to the zoo to show them wolves. This is a very big problem and all people need to be convinced that the wolves should live. When you are trying to convince people, ... you can say "Get out a movie or some books about them." Or ...you could say that they should perhaps copy information about the wolves and give it out to friends. Also ... say, "They are a very important part of the food chain and should be saved." As you can see, there is no winning argument against saving these wolves. It is true that European wolves are dangerous carnivores and are very hard to protect. Most people agree that it should be done. But unfortunately shepherds and people with livestock don't always follow these rules. But even though not all people do, we must try our best to do what we can. Thus, the fate of these wolves is in our hands. We have the choice whether to let them just slip away, or to try to save them.

—Rebecca Furbush-Bayer, age 11
Newfield, N.Y.

SAVE THE WHOOPING CRANE
by Darius Lind

The Whooping Crane, standing nearly five feet tall, with its blood-red head and snow-white body, is one of the most graceful and beautiful members of the stork family. Sadly enough, it is severely endangered. The Whooping Crane's summer range used to extend all the way down to Illinois; now its range only reaches as far south as mid-Canada. Over-hunting and loss of habitat have made the Whooping Crane's numbers go down. Luckily, their population is increasing due to the help of concerned people. I think the Whooping Crane has every right—as much as we do—to live a full and natural life.

The difficulties that have made life hard for the Whooping Crane are the loss of swamps, bogs, and marshes in which they raise their young. Another reason for their decline in population was that hunters were killing them for sport, because they have a brilliant white body that makes an easy target. Another reason for the plummet of the Whooping Crane's population is that the Crane only hatches one out of the two eggs it lays. All three of these problems made the population drop down to twenty individuals.

To bring the population back up to normal, two different ideas have been used so far. The first approach was to take one of the two eggs the Whooping Crane lays and place the egg into a Sandhill Crane's nest. The Sandhill Crane would then hatch and raise the egg. Another idea people tried was to take one of the eggs and raise the chick themselves with a hand puppet that looked like an adult Whooping Crane. This made it possible for humans to raise and release the chicks. These two ideas were a great success. Since 1940 their population has slowly and happily increased from fifteen or twenty to two hundred individuals.

To help the Whooping Crane's numbers increase even more, people could better educate the children of the next generation about the environment and various different animals such as the Whooping Crane. This may teach them to have more respect for nature. Doing this might change the way people treat the animals like the Whooping Crane that live in ecosystems near them. People could also help the Whooping Crane by giving money to the organizations who help them. But people may be hesitant to give money to the Whooping Crane. For instance, people might say "If the Whooping Crane becomes severely endangered, or extinct, it would not have an immediate effect on us." But in the long run a slow chain reaction would increase or decrease the population of animals and plants, which would have an effect on us. These are reasons not to let the Whooping Crane perish. Thanks to all the help that the Whooping Crane has received, this wonderful stock may not perish. But the loss of their habitat still looms like a dark cloud in the distance. If the Whooping Crane becomes extinct it will be a terrible loss of one of Mother Nature's most beautiful and graceful birds.

—Darius Lind, Age 12
Brooktondale, New York

SAVING THIS SPECIAL HAWAIIAN BIRD
by Zachary Lind

An endangered wildfowl that looks somewhat like a Canadian goose lands on the volcanic island. This is a Nene goose (pronounced nay-nay). Scientists say Nene geese may be relatives of the Canadian geese. They say the Nenes most likely got off track and stayed in Hawaii. The Nene geese were almost put to extinction in 1949 because of loss of habitat and over-hunting. But they were saved by a group in England. Like all beings in this world the Nenes have a right to live, so we should preserve them as if they are our own family.

In 1949 there were fewer than thirty Nene geese in the world. The reasons they were nearing extinction was that Hawaiians killed them, then European settlers came to Hawaii and brought livestock. Then livestock destroyed the Nenes' habitat. What also made the Nenes' numbers go down was that people introduced mongooses to kill rats, but they also hunted Nenes and helped decrease the numbers of Nenes. The Nenes were living well for a long time but Europeans came and sent them flying toward extinction.

The Nene geese were saved by the Wildfowl Trust (WT) in Slimbridge, England. This is how they were saved: The people at WT started a breeding program (and it was successful). In twenty years there were one thousand Nenes in captivity. Two hundred lived in the wild. Now there are about 750 in the wild. You could help the Nenes by supporting breeding programs. In 1957 the Nenes became the Hawaiian state bird and this made people think more about Nenes. Another way of helping Nenes would be to tell people what happened to the Nenes and how it happened. People could study and learn about Nenes in their natural habitat and find out more about what might help the Nenes. If everyone tries to help the Nenes come back it will be good, and it will restore the Hawaiian ecosystem. That would be great.

If you are not able to support a breeding program for Nenes, then you could write a letter to someone to help the Nenes. If you can't easily get an address for a Nene breeding program. then write to the nearest nature center, or, if you're very desperate write to your congress-person to get an address for a Nene breeding program. Then you could try to help the Nenes in some way, shape or form.

for a Nene breeding program. Then you could try to help the Nenes in some way, shape or form.

As you can hopefully see, the Nenes badly needed help and they got help from people who cared for the Nenes and really wanted them on the planet, but the Nenes still need protection. Since this strong-legged bird was successfully brought back from being close to extinction, the other animals will not die out because of the Nenes' not being in the food chain. That's what might happen if the Nenes are not living in Hawaii any more. How would you feel if you were a Nene? You would want to be saved, right? Of course, right. So let's help the Nene geese.

—Zachary Lind, age 12
Brooktondale, N.Y.

You may write these kids or their mentor Elisabeth Furbush-Bayer care of Kalepaedeia House, 215 Miller Rd., Newfield, NY 14867.

The Free School:
Mary's History of Religions Class:

Here follows a group of essays written by the editor's little 1994 history of religions class, ages nine through twelve. Teaching this particular subject was their idea, not initially mine, which may be part of the reason it worked so well for us all! I include the essays as a kind of "curriculum aid" for others wondering if all this self-choosing of study material really works. wanting to get a look inside a free school, taken from the students' point of view (but also, let's face it, because I'm so delighted with their enthusiasm for our subject!)

Elisha Mittleman

In the History of Religion class what was important to me was that Jews were not the only people who had to hide their religion. The Christians had to also. In one of the stories the Christians had to practice in deep holes called catacombs because they might get killed if they were found. I guess it was important to me because I am Jewish and I thought Jews were the only people who had to do things like that because lots of

people thought they were different. But I still don't think it's right that anyone should have to be treated that way.

I think it was important that we all learned about all of the religions not just one or two. Some of the religions I never even heard of before like some Indian religions. I had heard of the Catholic religion but I didn't know much about it. It was exciting learning about new religions and what people did to practice their faith.

I liked the Greek myths that said a lot about the gods and goddesses. It was neat to learn about the sky gods and goddesses, and the underground gods and goddesses. Some of the gods changed their names to some of the names of the planets, like Pluto, Neptune and Jupiter.

There was one myth that I really liked. It was about this one god who wanted a goddess to be his wife and he had to kill this really big dragon in order to get her. He had to bring back some blood of the dragon to prove that he killed it. But he was afraid that he would still not be given her hand even if he did the deed. He went for help to another goddess who said to take out the dragon's teeth and plant them in the ground. They would turn into warriors and he could fight for her. I liked that he went to a woman for help because usually men think that they don't need women for help.

I liked drawing while Mary read to us. Usually my drawing related to what we talked about in class that day or to the reading. It helped me to understand the story more to look at the picture and to remember what it was about. I liked to hear what other people thought about what we were talking about. It was nice to be able to ask any question we needed to when we thought of it. Mary is the best History teacher I ever had.

Eve Minehan

I liked History of Religion class because it's fun learning about other religions, even the religions I thought I knew about like Judaism and Christianity. What I really like are the Greek myths because they are usually about love, gods and goddesses, warriors, blood, temptation or death. My favorite myth is the one where the hero went to kill a monster and he promised his father that if he himself were killed the ship would come back with black sails and if he killed the monster then it would come back with white sails. But when he killed the monster he was so happy that he got drunk and forgot to change the sails from black to white. When his father saw the black sails he was so sad that he jumped off a cliff. This story makes me feel sad because he was so careless that somebody he loved ended up dying.

We also talked about Jesus Christ and how he was supposedly killed because people were scared. He was helping people but I believe that when Jesus was on the cross he did not really die. I believe that someone gave him something to knock him out and make him faint and then when he was in the cave the angels came down and opened the stone. They said it was time for him to go from the earth and let the people figure out what just happened. None of us know what really happened to this day.

In the class I liked the way everyone could just talk about things openly and everyone could express his or her opinions. The only trouble I had with the class was that sometimes it was long. However, Mary would let us bring up our notebooks and draw while she talked. I really like Mary as a teacher because she is very wise and knows a lot about everything. She has been all over the world and seen many of the places that she talks about in class like India and Greece and lots of other great places. Her experience helped me to understand more in the class.

Gabrielle Becker

In our class we learn about things we want to know about. I found out that there are a lot of things to learn about that I didn't even know existed before. We drew runes. I asked about my Uncle Andy. He has cancer. Mary talked to me about that. It got us talking about death and things like that. We talked and we talked about Jesus. There are a lot of different theories; did Jesus really die? I think he's still alive but maybe he doesn't look the same or maybe he's in a different country. I think that there are people who have lived so many lives that they're done and they want to come down and help us with our lives and that Jesus was one of those people. Maybe even Mary or Jun *san* [a Japanese Buddhist nun who has been building a peace pagoda nearby which our children have helped with] are one of those people because they help the world in their own way just like Jesus did. Sai Baba is definitely one of those people. He lives in India. I hope to meet somebody like that when I travel. Mary has gone lots of places. She tells us stories of what it was like in those places or the people she's met.

Sometimes we draw and listen to Greek stories from the big book that Ted brought in. I never knew there were so many gods and goddesses. We learn about important things, too, like hunger in Africa, peace or pollution. There are so many things that we learned about that I can never remember them all. Mary shows us things from her books. There is one story she told us that sticks in my head. Mary was in a small town called Delphi. She saw olive trees. There were olives on the ground and people were just stepping on them. Mary likes olives so she picked up the juiciest ones and took them home. She soaked them in salt water and olive oil and they were the best olives she had ever tasted.

One of my favorite topics was Egypt. They had a really neat way of writing and ways of doing things. I think they were really sophisticated. They had mummies and their ways of building the pyramids and the sphinxes were really unique.

I like learning directly from a person rather than out of a book. You get more of what it was like because Mary explains with gestures and her voice and expressions and not just with words. I liked the freedom of it. If one person was not interested in the topic for that day then he was free to go and do something else just for that one class. That way no one felt pressured and then we wanted to come back.

Joe Mastantuono

An interesting group of individuals enter my spirit domain (the library of the Free School) of learning every firstday (but sometimes Thursday). They come and discuss the history and religion of humankind. The elder, who was referred to as Mary Leue, taught the humanlings much about humankind's mistakes, such as the Salem witch trials. I was extremely touched when the elder mentioned the library of Alexandria (one of my Elders) and referred to the destruction in scorn. I am manifesting myself in one of the humanlings' written essays which might enter my domain.

I believed I knew much but I was proved wrong. I had no knowledge of ancient China and scientific explanations for Jesus' rise from the grave. I also enjoyed the lulling myths of the ancient Greeks' religion. I particularly enjoyed the stories of the elder's travels all over the old land.

The elder's wealth of knowledge on ancient religions was impressive. I had never heard of religion of the great mother, which was a matriarchal society in what is now England and France. The religion of Crete worshipped bulls and dolphins. The palace of the king of Crete, Knossos, had running water and skylights, and this was impressive to me.

I felt honored to know that the tribes of the Americas worshipped spirits like myself.

I extremely enjoyed knowing the elder, Mary Leue, who taught with an openness that was unheard of compared to other history classes.

Lilian Mercogliano

I like history of religion with Mary. She is a great teacher and teaches a great class. The reason I wanted to do history of religion class was because it sounded fun to learn about religions from all around the world. I wanted to know about other people's culture and about their gods and how they worship them. I really only knew about a couple of religions and I even learned some stuff about the Christian religion that I didn't know.

My favorite part in class is when we talk about the Greek religion and all the Greek gods and goddesses. I especially like when Mary reads from the big yellow book of Greek myths. My favorite god is Zeus and my favorite goddess is Athena. The reason I like Athena is because she is the goddess of war but she is also always very fair and wise, and knows which side is right and when she should help with that side. My favorite myth is the one about the underground labyrinth where there was a Minotaur who had to always be fed humans or he would destroy the whole castle which was built above the labyrinth. Once, when the King of the castle needed to find new people to feed to the Minotaur, he told one of his enemies if they didn't give him 6 women and 6 men, they would declare war on them. One of the young men named Theseus who lived in the city of the enemy said he would go and try to kill the Minotaur. Even though the father, who was the king of the enemies, didn't want him to go, he finally agreed to let Theseus go. When Theseus got there with all the other people who were to be fed to the Minotaur, one of the daughters of the King of the castle took pity on Theseus and gave him a ball of string. She told him that when he was led to the labyrinth to tie one end of the ball of string to the gate. Then she said to follow the snore of the Minotaur until he found the Minotaur. So, that night he did what she told him to do. When he found the Minotaur, he pulled out his knife which he had been carrying with him and he stabbed the Minotaur and killed him. The way he got home is a long other story.

It's so fun to hear the different stories about different gods and goddesses and people. I think the Greek religion is neat because there are so many gods and goddesses, not just one. What I think is neat about it is that you can worship different gods or goddesses for different things and you do not have to only worship a male god, but you can also worship a female goddess.

Another thing I like about class is when Mary tells us stories about the places she has been in the world. They are really neat stories and I like the way she tells them. I remember especially a story that Mary told that I liked a lot about England and the three different places of the life cycle. One was for fertility called the Avebury Circle where the single men and the single women would come down the hill and dance. Then they would spend the night together. The second place was called Silbury Hill which people believed stood for the womb of a pregnant woman with an eye on top. The third place Mary said was kind of like catacombs because they were underground and a place where people were buried. I thought those places sounded special and spiritual because Mary said that when she went into the circle of stones, which was the first place, she felt something strange happen inside of her and it stopped when she stepped out.

Sometimes we just talk about theories and reality like did Jesus really die on the cross, or is God real? Everyone has a different opinion. I think that Mary is neat because she has been around for seventy years so she can tell you what it was like when she was a kid and answer a lot of questions, too. It has been a lot of fun for me learning about religions that I have never even heard of or things I did not even know about some of the religions. I hope I can do the class again next year.

Ted Becker

I think that the history of religion is almost like a story of creation and there are lots of different theories. I think that everyone should learn history because it helps to form your own point of view of what you believe in and what you don't. I also learned that people that tried to bring peace, like Jesus, were used as signs of war. For example, in history class I learned that one night a man had a dream that if he brought a banner of the cross to a war he would win the war. I think that that wasn't good because Jesus stood for peace.

Personally, I think Greek history is the most entertaining because it always makes sense in the end of how things that happen now came to be. And you don't have to ask as many questions about it. And it's a lot like a big science fiction fantasy book. Greek religion also shows that good doesn't always win.

I believe that when you die you go up to heaven and a god or goddess tells you everything they know and then they make you forget everything except one thing that they told you. And I think that Jesus and all the other great people have died and came back so many times that they learned everything. And once you know everything, you have one chance to come back to earth and teach. And then, you go to heaven and you are one of the teachers.

History is very confusing because it takes a long while before you can understand and there are still some things that no one can understand. For instance, why there are so many wars that in some countries the average age to live was thirty!

And the Christians had to pray underground because if they were found they would be killed because they were not allowed to pray to their own god.

In Greek religion there are many gods, unlike Judaism where there is only one. I believe that there are many gods. It seems that it would be very fun to be a Greek god because in one war all the gods started coming down and taking sides and switching sides. If I were a god I could live forever and do magical things. I would have lots of power over what happens on earth. If I could be any god I think I would be Zeus because he can change shape.

I really enjoyed being able to sit and talk for two hours about religion. I think my teacher is very good because she has gone to a lot of places. She learned about lots of religions and came back and told us about them. I liked being able to pick what we learned about and seeing the pictures from the history books. This was a very good class.

THE UNDERTOW
by Amelia Rose Brommer, age 14
(Arthur Morgan School Student)

Teo walks stiffly across the dilapidated playing field. Her stomach aches from the three punches she just received from Nathaniel, a clean-cut brat with a snotty nose and warts on his knees. She ignores the stuffy teacher walking next to her trying in vain to make her come back to school. Why don't they understand that she won't, that it's the last straw? Why don't they understand her? She stops, turns slowly around, and stares at him with big, sad, hazel eyes, giving him a look that means, "Go away. Crawl back to your small office with no windows." He is now saying something, but it's too late. Teo has slipped into her peaceful world and Josh is already waiting for her.

When she emerges from her world, she's sitting on her bed next to her foster mother, Jeannie, who is patting her hand and whispering soft, stupid, mothering things like, 'It's all right honey, you' re OK, now wake up." Teo lifts her face to look at Jeannie. She looks a little sad and Teo wonders what she's thinking of.

Jeannie seems to sense this silent question and answers, "You're moving, Teo. We can't keep you. Miss Cringe called and said you are moving to New York to live with a nice family, the Robinsons."

Teo for some reason isn't surprised. She's lived with Jeannie longer than she' s lived with any of the other families, and besides, she doesn't like Dallas anyway. It is too hot. She looks at Jeannie again and notices that she's talking to her.

"You' re leaving tomorrow, so start packing and I will make some cookies for your flight to New York. Did I tell you it' s New York City? Won' t that be fun?"

And with that she disappears into the kitchen. Teo doesn't really like Jeannie. She talks to her as if she doesn't understand, but she does, so that's Jeannie's problem. Teo walks half-heartedly across the floor to her closet to get her suitcase, the one she' s had for years.

Ever since she can remember, she's lived with different people like a stray dog. She was abandoned when she was about one. An old man found her and took her to live with Miss Cringe until arrangements could be made for her to start her life as a foster child. Life. Life. ... Teo ponders over the word for awhile and then laughs as she remembers that she has no life, and that's why her parents threw her away, gave her up, left her to find a life of her own because it sure as hell wasn't going to come to her, and they didn't want the responsibility of a girl with no life. Not a lot of people want responsibility for her. In fact, no one does, and the only place she feels at home is in her world.

Her world is a place where everyone and everything accepts people and things the way they are and don't try to change them. It is a place that accepts slightly, or maybe very, dreamy kids who have nowhere to turn to except a place that comes from their heads.

Teo doesn't think this place is made up by her; she knows it's real and she will go there even if it takes all she's got—even if it kills her. Teo sits still, thinking about the word "kill". To be killed is to die, and to die you must have a life, and she doesn't have a life, so does that mean she's invincible? Maybe. ... maybe not. Who knows? Maybe her world does, or Josh.

Josh is Teo's only friend. He lives in her world. He's tall and nice, but most important, he understands her. He means everything to her, and without him she knows she would be lost.

Teo stands and looks from her neatly packed suitcase to her old mirror. The paint is peeling on the frame, and its roughness casts shadows on her thin reflection. She looks at herself, studies every detail—her big, sad, hazel eyes, her slightly turned-up nose, her doll-like lips, her soft cheeks, her funny ears, her beauty mark above her left eye, and her short, auburn hair framing her face like the peeling paint frames the mirror.

Teo sighs and flops on her bed. When she wakes up she'll go to live in New York. She won't make any promises this move. It hurts too much when she breaks them.

When Teo awakens she's still fully dressed in her dark brown sweat shorts and forest green t-shirt. She doesn't bother to brush her hair and goes straight into the kitchen. Jeannie is standing over the stove scrambling eggs. She senses Teo's presence (even though Teo doesn't make a sound) and turns to face her. Jeannie doesn't look sad, but Teo isn't surprised. "She's probably happy I'm going to be out of the house," Teo thinks sourly. Teo doesn't eat much breakfast. She doesn't usually eat much at all, just enough to keep from fainting.

The morning moved by slowly without much talking and it was almost 1:00 p.m. when Miss Cringe came to pick her up.

Teo knew Miss Cringe's face well; it had been in and out of her life since the old man had brought Teo to her. Deeply creased with wrinkles and depression, it was not a happy face, and not exactly a welcome face to Teo. It meant moving, leaving and having to start a new life somewhere else—well, not exactly a life, for she had none, but a new something.

The good-bye to Jeannie wasn't spectacular. Teo didn't cry because she never does, and Jeannie cried a little, but Teo was sure she had been chopping onion so that didn't count.

When they reached the airport it was almost 2:00, so they had to run wildly to catch the plane. Miss Cringe didn't usually accompany Teo on plane rides, but since it was to New York City (a very dangerous place in Miss Cringe's opinion), and since Teo knew nothing about where she was going, Miss Cringe decided "it would be best."

The plane stunk, the food was horrible, and all the stewardesses had fake smiles. Other than that, the flight was fine. Miss Cringe explained to Teo that she would be living in the suburbs of New York with Miss Robinson and her 14-year-old boy, Joey. It didn't sound too bad, but Teo was a little mad that there was a child because they always made jokes about her and teased her. Also, she wasn't so thrilled about living in suburbia la la land. Kids like Nathaniel lived there; they were always stuck up, in Teo's mind.

Miss Robinson and Joey were waiting for them when they arrived in New York. They looked clean and surprisingly nice. Somehow Joey looked very nice. Teo had never had this feeling before in her life. She actually thought someone was nice, or looked it. She was so happy that she smiled. It was the first time Miss Cringe had ever seen Teo smile and it lightened her spirits incredibly.

On the ride "home," Teo said nothing. She just looked at Joey. He was about 5'10", sort of thin, and had sandy-blonde hair and green eyes. She almost laughed at him for he reminded her of a big puppy, always tripping over things. He seemed withdrawn from the world, like herself, but he talked and laughed—things Teo didn't often do. With this feeling of happiness and understanding came another feeling that wasn't so welcome. This was shyness, and with shyness came embarrassment.

Teo liked living with the Robinsons more than anyone she had lived with before. Miss Robinson didn't talk much, but it was different than the talkless people before her. They were intimidated by her strange ways and ignored her, but since Miss Robinson had Joey, she was used to silence and it was a much more natural feeling. She spent long, leisurely days being silent and talking to Josh in her world.

It was one of these days when she had her first talk with Joey. She was on the verandah sipping lemonade and watching the snooty neighbors playing croquet. She was in the middle of thinking how dumb grown-ups were, and that they were just big kids with bigger egos, when she heard his voice and he said, "Hi," but it sounded like a choir of angels, and it surprised Teo so much she spilled her lemonade all over her, and this made her face flush red with her new enemy, embarrassment.

After that short, embarrassing talk came longer and not so shy ones. At first Teo was hesitant, for she had never trusted anyone before, and learning to trust Joey was very hard at first, but soon it came easily, especially after she learned that he had a world that was the same as her own.

She found this out one day when they were taking a walk together around a big playing field. They had stopped to watch some small children playing baseball. It was a pretty bad game. All the coaches were yelling and some of the kids had begun to cry. Teo was beginning to lose interest when Joey said it, said the words that would make them become friends, break all of the barriers and let Teo trust someone. The words were "dumb humans". It might sound dull to you, but it meant everything to Teo. They were the most lovely words, for they were not only spoken with power, but they were spoken in the secret tongue of her world.

With this recognition of speech came a recognition of looks. She had thought before that Joey resembled Josh, but now she knew. She knew Joey *was* Josh. How could she have been so stupid not to notice before? But she was so happy that Josh had finally come for her that she laughed. It was the first time she had ever laughed on earth. It sounded strange and foreign, but it felt good, and it took the chains that bound her to depression off for awhile, long enough for her to lift her downcast face and get a wonderful look into Josh's beautiful clear-green eyes.

That look meant more than any words that they could speak. In that look came the knowledge that Josh had come to take Teo home to their world, the world that was untouched by humans and their material things, untouched by conflict and anger. In a way their world was too good. Before, Teo knew she didn't have enough strength to reach it, but with the help of Josh she could do it. With him she could face everything.

There was a change at the Robinson's after that day. The house was often filled with laughter and shouts of children that had been freed from solitude. Even though Teo talked and laughed with Josh, she still wouldn't speak much with anyone else. When Josh was gone she would step back into her old sad self.

It was now the end of July. Soon Teo and Josh would have to go back to school, something they both strongly disliked. Josh didn't like it because too many people made him more clumsy and nervous. For Teo it wasn't so much all the people (even though they didn't help). It was that she had a fierce temper and would get into bad fist fights with kids who challenged her strange ways. She was quite strong for her weight and age, but still she didn't always win. She often got bad cuts and bruises, but one thing she would never do was cry. There was something in her pride that wouldn't allow it.

She didn't like fights and she didn't like school, so that made Josh and her start planning for the runaway sooner. They knew they couldn't face school again. They had to go to their world for real now, not just in their heads—that didn't work well anymore. They both wanted to actually feel the long, silky grass and let the cool breezes of their paradise kiss their sad faces and go deep into their minds, lifting their depression and giving them happiness, and maybe if they were lucky enough, a life.

And Amelia Brommer sent us a second story, which follows:

BEYOND MY SANDY TOES
by Amelia Rose Brommer

"Can you tell me where he's gone?" she had asked, her eyes shining full of hope. I searched her face for an answer. I found none. My palms began to drip, sticky with sweat, and my red ball I was holding slipped from my grasp. Was I supposed to know what she was talking about? I looked deeper and harder into her eyes. Was I going deaf? Had she said something before that I had missed? .

Her eyes, so filled with unanswered questions, now changed to confused anger. She pushed me backwards. As I fell I saw her dart away, back to the dark outline of the woods where she had come from.

What did she want? This and many other questions danced and tumbled through my head that night. Who was she looking for? Who's "he?" Is "he" me? No... it can' t be me. I've never seen her before... or wait... Is she that face, that face that has watched me for so long? Is she that one who' s always with me but never there? Or maybe is she a messenger for the one I've been eternally bound to, the one my mother used to talk of, the one who is my equal and partner?

My head swims with unanswered questions. I sink into my bed. I let its warm quilted arms comfort my sore bones and hot face. I let its flannel fingers wipe away my tears. My fevered body now cools and I sleep.

"Tom ... Tom, wake up.... Thomas, get out of bed!" I was rudely awakened the next morning by Evelyn, a skinny, freckly, laughing-eyed brat who was unfortunately my baby sister. She managed to pull and shove until—"Thud!" —I landed sprawled on the ground. It only took one bluffing glance to send her running from the room.

"Mom!" she screamed, halfway between a laugh and a frightened squeak. "Tommy' s up!" This was not unusual and, like most mornings, I started my day mean and sleepy-eyed.

For the next week I could think of nothing but that girl, and the same old questions rolled helplessly and unanswered around in my weakening mind. It was like a disease thinking of her. I became withdrawn and moody. I snapped at people constantly and more than once sent Evelyn crying to our mom.

Gradually I forgot about the girl, thinking I would never see her again, so you can imagine my surprise to see her nine years later. I was now sixteen and I had come home from military school for the summer. My family and I were at the beach.

Even so many years later I still was not the same old Tom. It seemed to me that those many years ago on that fateful day when I had dropped my sweaty red ball, I had also dropped a part of myself, the part that makes you happy and nice. I had never found my ball, so did that also mean that I would never find my happiness? All I know is I lost my ball, my happiness, and the girl.

I was now standing, throwing my ham sandwich piece by piece into the darkening green-gray sea. The last sliver of the sun was slipping and shimmering deeper and deeper, farther and farther into the swirling depths of the sea. I felt as though my sanity would dive in after it, or that I might shatter into 3,004 pieces like my ham sandwich that now floated just beyond my sandy toes.

The sun was beckoning to me to follow him, and I would have if something had not bumped my restless foot. I stooped over, trying to make out the round red object.

"Oh!" I gasped. Could it be, maybe be? Was it my long lost ball...? Yes!

I tried to pick it up but it was covered in a seven-year-old's sweat and slipped from my grasp down and away to the hissing foam of the sea. I made a motion towards it but stopped, for a slender shape now appeared in the corner of my eye, and all of a sudden there she was, moving fast and steady towards me. I stood up and patiently waited for her.

"Can you tell me where he's gone?" she asked, her eyes shining once again full of hope. I smiled and held out a shaking hand. She smiled, but once again she pushed her long, bony fingers against my chest, pushing me breathless to the hard sand. But before I could feel the all too familiar pain, her bony hand was held out to me and instinctively I took it. With surprising strength she lifted me up and twirled me around and around. As our hands slipped from each other's grasp, I was afraid that I would fall to the sand so hard I would die. But when our fingers kissed their last good-bye and all my frightened hand felt was air, I did not fall. Instead I flew up and up into the appearing stars. I was now whole, but forever lost to the world.

The story , written by Gabrielle Bennett Becker, first appeared in the Wilbur Street Gazette and Weekly Post Dispatch. *Our thanks to its editor, Larry Becker, (who also happens to be Gaby's father) for permission to reprint Gaby's story. Gaby was thirteen years old when this was written.*

THE BRAVE COWS
by Gabrielle Becker

There once was a cow named Nicky who had two baby calves. She lived in Trantow by the butter factory. She made butter milk. But at present, she had her own stable for herself and her calves.

When-she was thinking one day, she remembered what Jan (her friend cow) had said about Teena and Bobby (her two baby calves) being brought to a hamburger farm in Green Island. Was it really true about her children being made into a two ninety-nine hamburger and fries?

She also was thinking about the broken board in the fence in the old grazing field. Maybe, just maybe, she could take them away and be free. Free from everything. But what was she thinking? It was ridiculous. Even if she wanted to, it would be too hard to get out unnoticed. Oh, much too hard with Bobby and Teena and all.

But when she thought of them being a hamburger, she couldn't bear it any more. She reared her back legs into the air (which was only 1 or 2 inches) stomping and blowing air out of her nose. After she calmed down, she thought out her plan. She thought maybe in the morning, when the guys take her out to the new field, she could wander into the old one when no one was paying any attention (no one ever paid attention, so it was easy).

Now the hard part was getting the loose board off. She pushed and pulled until it fell. First, Nicky went through. Then Teena and Bobby followed right behind. They walked for maybe a half an hour. Then they stopped for an hour when the sun was too hot. It was very different than Nicky thought it would be. No nice green grass and all these bugs. Ooow, but look. She saw a nice bog with clean water. That's where they stayed for a while. They started up again in the morning.

Meanwhile, there was a family about 100 miles away. A very poor family. Too poor to have bagels on Friday or even have their own beds. Everyone shared a bed of hay. But no one complained because they all knew that Father was doing the best he could to make money and Mama was stretching the money as far as she could. They all were saving for a cow. "One day," Mama would say, "One day we will have a cow and we can make cakes and bread and butter. And cow's milk has the most sweet taste," she told them.

There were five children in the family: three boys and two girls. Their names were Jessica the baby and little Loren. Then there were Ben and Joseph and Derrick, the oldest of all. He was fifteen already. He had a job making hats to sell in the city where Derrick and Daddy go every year. "It is so fun when they go," said Joseph, "Because Daddy always brings presents back for us. Remember the time he got us red pencils. It was so fun."

That night little Loren wished on a star. She said, "Please God. Will you bring us a cow. Because Mama says she will bake a cake with cow's milk. If we get a cow, you can have a piece of Mama's cake, I promise. Amen."

Also that night, Nicky prayed on a star because she didn't know about wishing. She said, "0, God will you give me a home. Please, for me and my babies. They aren't tough enough for the wild. Ahbulls."

In the morning, it poured forever. Bobby and Teena had mud up to their tummies and Nicky had mud on her legs. They ate grubs and bushes for breakfast. Teena said it didn't taste good and Bobby agreed. The rain stopped around 3 p.m. and it grew very cold compared to what Nicky and Bobby and Teena were used to. They took about a half an hour to find some dry place to be and to dry off and get warm. They went on like that for a week and now you could see their ribs.

One day when it was especially cold. Bobby slipped on a rock because it was raining. He sprained his hoof and slowed everyone down. Nicky was getting wired because she had not seen any sign of civilization since they left the factory. Was there anything else? Was the factory the only place where humans lived? she asked herself.

Teena would say over and over, "Mama. Mama, I know there are other humans. Jan told me. Jan told me. She did. She did. I know because Jan told me. Jan told me there were other people. Other people, Jan said there were. She did."

Nicky would have killed Jan if they were back at the milk factory. Every day Bobby's foot got more and more infected. More painful too. Bobby would wail the most loud and sad sound.

They had been away 18 days now when they saw a small house with kids running around. Teena started to run toward the house. When the kids spotted her, they started to yell and scream with joy. "Oh Mama and Daddy," Joseph yelled, "We have got our cows."

That night Loren took her piece of cake and put it outside for God to have. It was gone in the morning. She was so happy she didn't know Nicky ate the cake.

The End

And here is a recent poem by Gaby, followed by two by her brother Ted:

BEAUTY HELD

Once I heard a crystal laugh
Saw a sleeping child.
Danced across a flowered field.
Gazed up at a beauty held sky.
Strolled in a flowing stream.
Fell face first in a mountain of
leaves. Lit the Hanukkah candles.
Believed in a magic man
with a big belly and a red
suit. Fell asleep, arms wrapped
around my feline and dreamt of
a beauty held sky.

—by Gabrielle Bennett Becker, age 14

AND SOMETIMES

I am sitting next to my
dog and cat and writing
this poem. I love my dog and cat.
My dad gets mad at my
cat sometimes 'cause he pees
on the work telephone
sometimes.
And my mom is reading
Anne of Green
Gables to my sister
Gaby. She's nice.
My dog is biting
his fleas. It makes
a disgusting slurpy
sound and my dad is writing the Wilbur
Street Gazette. Well
I'm tired, so I guess
I'll go to bed.

—Ted Becker, eight years old

And Ted wrote the following poem at Auschwitz, on an Interfaith pilgrimage made by the whole Becker family (parents Ellen and Larry with Ted and Gaby) plus another community member and myself, at the end of November, 1994.

THE SOUL OF THE HOLOCAUST

I am dead, but still alive.
I can speak, but you can't hear.
I can't be trapped, but I can die.
You can see me, but you can't touch me.
I am living inside of you. If you go, I go too.
If you can tell them, I can live.
If you don't I will die inside of you.
Please remember. Please tell them.

—Ted Becker, ten years old.

Free School scene shot by Connie Frisbee-Houde

More Free School scenes taken by Connie F-H

And here are some stories by Ian Leue, who will tell you how old he was when he wrote them.

Human
catcher
by Ian

To my friend Tony
who alwys asked
what was rong

Once upon a time there was a fisherman that lived near a lake. One day

he was fishing when he saw a bill in the water. He reached out and picked it up.

Ouch! His hand stuck fast. He fell in the water. He saw the bill on a fishing pole. There was a big fish.

They put him on a table. He tried not to look scared. but really he was scared. Suddenly he looked up. (that

was a big mistacke.)
There was a big
back mouth. He jumped
up swam out of the
water stumbled to shore
ran home and never
fished again.

Human catchers uncle

written by Ian

Illustrated by Caleb Ward

for Ambjörn

Once upon a
time about the
same time as Human
catcher, the sort-of
fisher man went
frogging at his lake

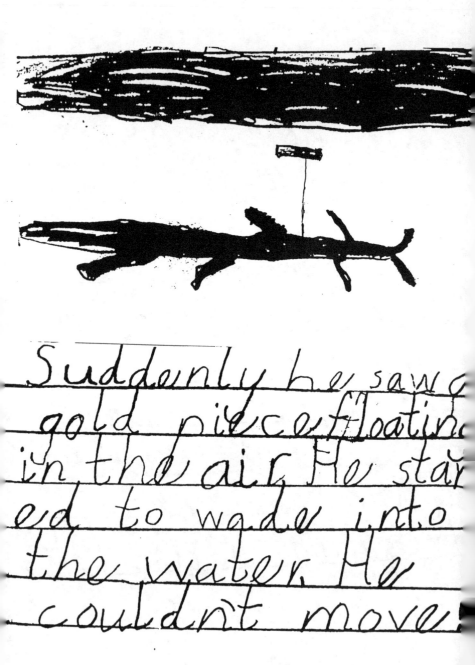

Suddenly he saw a
gold piece floating
in the air. He star
ed to wade into
the water. He
couldn't move.

He looked down
at a bullfrog
ranging onto
his leg. Then
the bullfrog let
go and leapd

at the fisherman
leg. It bent and
the frog dragged
him away. The next
thing he realized he
was in a cave. It look
ed like the fishe

ave. The same things appen and he never froged again.

Ian and Free School gang

Ian is 7.
He is in 1st
grade, he
says you
should read
Human
catcher
first.

I do hope readers won't think my editorial inclusion of lots of my grandson Ian's writing comes out of familial pride, even if it does! There's also a point to be made. Encouraging kids to do their own writing allowing them to feel supported when necessary as with lined paper as above or, in the case of the stories below, dictation to his mom, allows the "creative vent" Sylvia Ashton-Warner understood so well to erupt. By the time he came to write "Jacob's Rescue," (see below) Ian had taught himself to type! Kids who know their parents trust them to steam ahead on their own when they are ready, drop the pilot as quickly as they can.

THE BLIND MOUSE
by Ian Leue, age eight

CHAPTER I
CLEANING IT UP

The whole thing never would have happened if it wasn't for that blind mouse. You see, one day I was walking home from school with my best friend, Peter, when he said to me. "Hey George, why weren't you at the baseball game yesterday?"

"Groceries," I said. "Groceries, groceries, and more groceries."

Peter laughed, "You really do hate going grocery shopping, don't you."

"Are you out of your mind? No one could like grocery shopping."

"Are you kidding? It's one of the happiest times for me in the whole day."

"Why's that?" I said.

"Because you can find great things to gross out your little sister," he said.

"Really?" I said.

"Yup." he said.

Then we were at his house. "Want to come in and play a game of checkers?" he said. '

'Nah," I said. "I have to go home and see if mom will let us go to the grocery store."

"All right," he chuckled.

When I got home my mom stared at me. Go down to your room and clean up." She ordered. (My room is in the basement.)

"But mo-"

"No buts, just go clean up your room".

I hate it when I have to clean up my room. That's probably because it's so messy. When I'm done I usually just hope no one's going to open the closet. (I put all my stuff in there.)

I went down to my room and started to clean it up. As I looked to my right, I spotted a little mouse. "Aaagh!" 1 screamed, for I was afraid of mice. I backed into the corner keeping an eye on the mouse. As I looked a little closer at him, I noticed he was wearing black glasses and carrying a small stick! This was a little frightening; I had never seen a blind mouse in my life! As I continued to back up I bumped into my closet door and was shocked to feel it starting to move inward!

This was scary because my closet door opens *outward* and not inward. I felt like I was nowhere, then suddenly I was in this little house and in front of me was an old man dressed all in blue. Dark blue, with a dark blue hat that had moons and stars all over it.

CHAPTER 2
WORKING IT OUT

"Greetings," said the old man. '

'Hello," I said. "Who are you? Where are we?"

"I am a magician," said the magician, for that is what he was, "and we are in Magicland. I have been expecting you; what took you so long?"

"What do you mean?" I asked.

"I mean," explained the magician, "you have come here to help me resolve my dilemma."

"What's your dilemma?" I asked.

He bowed down low to whisper in my ear and then he told me. "Grossing out my little sister "

Oh", I giggled feeling a little surprised. "I'll do just that," I said, still giggling, "but how do I get back?"

"Not so quickly,' said the magician. "I didn't tell you how to do it, did l?"

"Oh, you didn't, did you,".

"No. I didn't, did 1, " said the magician.

"Well, why don't you just do it and get it over with!"

Then he told me. "Sweets, sweets," he whispered, "Sweets will gross out my little sister and anyone else in Magicland."

Then I got back to the point I had started with at the beginning,

"So how do I get back."

"Easy," said the magician. " Just step backwards," then he added, "in time.

I stepped backwards and was suddenly in my room. The blind mouse was nowhere to be seen and another surprising thing was that all the toys and everything else were on my shelves where they were supposed to be. This surprised me, but what surprised me more was when I leaned back on my closed door it didn't go anywhere. But when I opened it the way it usually went it opened right up and instead of Magicland being on the other side it was just my plain, old everyday closet.

I went back upstairs expecting my mom to ask me what had taken me so long, but she just looked at me and said, "George, you're not done with your room; no one could do it in such a time."

Then I realized what the magician meant about backwards in time; the time I had spent there wasn't any time in my time.

The next day, probably by luck, we went to the grocery store. I remembered that the magician had whispered how to gross out his little sister. By pleading I got my mom to get me a bunch of gumdrops. My sister looked a little weird when I got them, as if saying, "Why did you get those?"

When I got home I put the gumdrops in a safe place in my room, then I went to get Peter. I told him about all of it on the way home, everything from the blind mouse to the gumdrops. Peter and I went back into my room. I got the gumdrops and we both sat down with our backs to the closet door (facing the opposite wall) and pushed. At first nothing happened. Then suddenly the blind mouse appeared. Peter looked a little blank, obviously only half-believing the story. Then we leaned back again, the blind mouse still in sight. and the door started creaking inward. We were in the shop again.

"I'm glad to see you brought your friend," the magician said.

I introduced Peter to the magician and then gave the magician the gumdrops. "Good," he said only half looking at the gumdrops and making a disgusted face. He put them away on one of his shelves.

"Come over here," he said, nodding his head towards a door. He opened the door and led us in.

"What are you going to do," asked Peter.

"I'm going to teach you some magic," said the magician.

For a second I looked out with wonder at the room. At the walls there were bookshelves with books stacked on them and some piles of books on the floor. In the middle of the room was a circle of chairs. In the middle of the circle of chairs was a big round table. On the table were some more books. Around the chairs there was an assortment of: a magic wand, more books. some rolled up parchments, a big mug containing something that smelled, and a big black pot with a big spoon in it. Around the pile of stuff were more books. The magician led us to the book shelves on the left and picked up a book that said "Beginning magic" on the cover. He picked up another book that was exactly the same and handed one to each of us.

"Read," he said. Then he backed us up to the spot where we had come in and suddenly we were in my room again.

CHAPTER 3
BEGINNING MAGIC

Peter went home and I opened up my copy of the book. I couldn't find the author. but decided to read it anyway. When I opened it up I was surprised to see that all the first page were some pictures of towns. one of them being my town. I looked at the top left of the page, where the title usually is, and it said, "The Entrances and Exits of Magicland." Then I realized what it was. Why there was a picture of my town was, my closet was a way in and out of Magicland. I turned to the next page and there the title was: "How to Gross People Out (on earth)." This especially attracted my attention. I started reacting hastily. Let's see. There's "How to make pizza appear on your head"; no, that wouldn't do it. Ah, hah! This was the ticket. "How to make your hair turn into worms ."

Under the title was a chant. I said it and quick as a wink my hair was worms.

"This should gross her out". I said to myself.

I found my sister in her room

"Hi", I said.

"Ahhhhhhhh!!!!!" she replied. (Afterwards she said that I was the grossest human on earth.)

I decided not to keep my hair worms and turned them back into regular hair by saying another chant.

The next week we went grocery shopping again. I got my mom to get me lemon drops. I decided I would probably have to start buying the candy out of my own allowance. When I got back home I went to the closet and leaned back. Nothing happened. The blind mouse appeared. I leaned back again and I was in Magicland.

"So," said the magician, making another·disgusting face. "I am glad to see you like to get a variety of candy." He led me into the room again. This time I noticed the corner of the room which I hadn't seen last time. I was shocked. It was the only place in the whole room that didn't have books in it!

CHAPTER 4
LESSONS

He brought me to the corner I happened to be looking at. 'This," he said, "Is where you will have your magic lessons."

"Neat," I said. "When will it start?"

"It starts now," the magician said. " I will teach you invisibility, one of the simplest things of magic."

We both sat down in the corner.

"Everything with magic is much easier if you've been in Magicland and luckily you have," he said. "It'll also make it much easier if you've had a little magician dust on you. You haven't yet, but it's very easy."

And with this he pulled off his hat and held it upside down so it looked like a blue ice cream cone. He put his fingers in, took out a pinch of green dust and sprinkled it on me.

I shivered, it felt as if someone was tickling me (I am very ticklish}.

"As I said before." the magician said, "This will make magic much, much easier for you."

"Now the lesson really starts."

The whole thing was great. First he taught me how to make myself invisible, then how to make other people invisible, then he taught me how to make things invisible, and at the very end of the lesson he sprinkled a little more dust on me, but this time from his pocket.

"This will make you still have the magic when you're in human land."

He led me back to the starting room.

"By the way, my sister is really starting to get grossed out. Thanks," I said, and was in my room again.

The next few weeks we didn't go grocery shopping because the last time we went was a major big shop. When we finally grocery shopped I almost forgot about the magician until we got to the part of the grocery store where the candy was.

I decided to get him a packet of Hershey kisses. My mom asked me why I was getting all this candy. "Oh," I said. "I'll pay you all of the money back with my allowance. Promise, Ma!"

When I got back to my room the blind mouse was there and waiting. This time when I went through the backwards closet, he came with me. When we got to the magician's shop the mouse ran to the magician and curled up on top of his ear. Then I understood it all. I couldn't get in unless the blind mouse was there because he knew the magician and was his helper. The magician sent him out to get me every time he wanted me to come in. That's why he always knew when I was going to be here. Why the blind mouse knew it was me was because he was trained to smell anyone the magician wanted him to.

"So," said the magician, "I see you've discovered who my little mouse is."

"Yes," I smiled.

He had also taught me at our magic lesson how to sense when someone was reading your mind. For some reason this time he smiled when he saw the candy. He opened the package and took a bite.

"Mmmmm," he said. "Good. Listen, can I make you a deal? You just always get me theeese..."

He stared at the package with a discouraged look.

"Hershey kisses," I prompted him.

"Hershey kisses," he repeated. "What's in here that wasn't in any of the others? I tried them all just to make sure they weren't good!"

"Chocolate!" I said.

"I like it!" he said. "I like chocolate!"

"I'll be sure to get it every time we go grocery shopping."

"You know what?" he said, "I like chocolate even more than grossing out my sister. I think I'll stop grossing her out."

"I think you're right!" I said, "and I like magic more than grossing my sister out. I think I'll stop grossing her out too!!!!!!!!!!"

AFTERWARD

In the days that followed I gave the magician chocolate every time I went grocery shopping. And you know what? My sister actually started to like me!

TIME MACHINE
by Ian Leue, age nine

Chapter 1
Tomorrow

That was it. I, John Flixton, just had to make a time machine. The rest of my friends didn't believe in them and neither did my parents. I repeat, 'that was it.' I was going to do it that evening before my mom had finished supper and while my dad was all caught up in the newspaper.

Later that evening I went down to the basement to make the time machine. I had all the materials that I had gathered during the day; wires, old tin cans, a few broken clocks, and everything else I thought I'd need. Now it came to the hard part. I believed a time machine could be made, but the question was "how?"

First I decided to make a frame. I took some big old pieces of metal (rusty) and with the help of some of the heavy things that were down in the basement bent them into the shape of a tall sled with a back. Then I added the back of an old over-stuffed chair, on the back of what was going to be the time machine, to lean back on when I was on my trip. Then in front of where my legs would be I added some solid pieces of metal. The top one had what could be used as a steering rod. Then I added the handlebars of an old bicycle. I put an old clock in front of the bottom of the handlebars.

It would be ready for tomorrow. The reason I say tomorrow was because supper would be done before I had gone halfway to yesterday and my mom would be suspicious if she had to call me up for dinner and I didn't come.

The next day I woke up early and went down to the basement. There, as I knew, lay what I hoped was a time machine. I climbed in and set the hands on the clock (the glass had been taken out long ago for some other purpose) to 2 minutes. In that way I hoped it would work so that it would mean two days.

I pushed down on the handlebars and leaned back on the seat and hoped. Suddenly there was a whizzing around me and I leaned back even more. The whizzing stopped. I was in front of my house. I got out of the time machine and walked in the door. My mom was coming down the stairs as if she had just wakened up. Then I realized she had.

"Hi," I said. She didn't answer. "Yo, Mom," I said. She didn't even look at me. After trying every way I knew of saying Hello, I realized she couldn't see me. I walked up the stairs and into my room just to see me lying in bed asleep. The clock read the exact time it had when I had left for the day after tomorrow. This was fun.

I stayed around until the other me went outside to play at our apple tree in the front yard. I climbed with him (using the exact same route he did only a heart beat later). I climbed back down with him also, this time a heart beat before him.

I got back in my time machine and set the clock for 0 hours and 20 minutes. I was hoping this would bring me back exactly two days.

I leaned back and hoped. There was the whizzing again. It stopped and I was back in the basement. I tiptoed upstairs, slumped myself in my bed, slowly got myself out again, yawned a loud yawn, stayed in my room for a few minutes as if I was getting myself dressed, and went downstairs.

I lazed around on the couch a little while looking at the patterns on it—every cushion is different. My mom came downstairs and made breakfast. I ate it gladly. It was my favorite: porridge with lots of strawberries. I went outside to play. I played around for a little while and then decided to climb the apple tree a few times (every day went like this).

The next day I got up, got myself dressed and went downstairs. There my mom was making breakfast. After breakfast I went outside and climbed my apple tree, knowing that I was right under me. Then I climbed down still knowing that I was right under me. I couldn't see me or feel me, but I knew I was there because day before yesterday I had traveled to today. It was kind of like a radar. I knew everything I was going to do, but I *had* to do it.

That night before supper I went down to the basement to my time machine. I leaned back, set the clock for 1 minute and leaned back further and hoped. Like always there was the whizzing. Then suddenly I was under the dining room table. Mom was getting ready to make supper. I got out from under the table. This was the test to see if I could communicate with people in the future. I poked mom.

"Hey, mom," I said. To my amazement she said "Yeah," thinking I was the current me, although really I was I don't know where. "Can I go outside?" I said.

"No," she said, "it's almost dinner time. Go to your room and clean up."

This was a problem. I supposed I should just clean it up and amaze myself of tomorrow. I went up to my room and cleaned up. Suddenly the other me walked in. Luckily he couldn't see me, I suppose this is because I hadn't touched him yet. I put my hand on his shoulder and said, "Hi".

He stared at me in disbelief and said, "What ... the ... heck??"

"Hey don't get stiff, " I said, "I was just using the time machine. It's probably in the basement , but it's also under the dining room table."

"I don't get it," he said,"

"OK, I was going in the time machine yesterday. I set the clock for tomorrow. Then I sent myself to right now. I poked mom just to see if she could see me, and as soon as I touched her she could see me."

"What the..." he said.

"Listen, I just cleaned up your room—my room—and I think you should thank me for it."

"Thanks." He said. "Now could you please go to yesterday? Mom just sent me up here to clean up my room...again."

I climbed under the dining room table and brought myself back to my own time. The next day, just as I expected, I met the other me in my room. Of course, I was scared even though I expected it. You know one thing? When you're traveling in time it can sure get very complicated. For one thing, I had only seen myself right way around in photographs. Otherwise I just saw myself in the mirror and then I saw a backwards image.

Chapter 2
Kentick

The next few days went on like this, then I wondered if I could go up in time and then back to my time then why couldn't I go back into the past? I went to the time machine and set the clock so that I would go back 999,999 years. I hoped this would work and that before I was born I wouldn't just disappear and wait until I was born again (and have a twin).

There was the whizzing and suddenly I was on this weird planet only as big as our house with craters all over it. I got out of the time machine and walked to the other side of the planet. This, I thought, is probably what the earth was before the earth. I noticed that I could breathe and was glad that there was air. Suddenly I heard some noises. I walked just to the place that I couldn't see from any other place I had been on the planet and there it was—an alien city.

Now when I say city, I don't mean like New York City. All I mean is it was busy and had a million houses and, when I say houses I don't mean the kind of house you live in or the kind a kid in New York City lives in, if you don't live in New York City. I mean there were kind of these egg things rolling around on the ground. Each one was just about the size of a room. Now, all of these egg things that were rolling around had labels on them. A couple of them passed me that said "kitchen". One of them passed me that said "Ixcklar's Room", one of them said "living room" and so on. Then it happened. One of the egg shaped things bonked into me. Not that it hurt or anything, I went right through it. Now before it bonked me, I happened to see that it said "Kentick's Room". Inside there was the exact furniture you would have in your room, except it was all floating around in the air. As soon as I stepped in one of the chairs swept past me and I was on top of it, meaning I was sitting in it, but I'm getting ahead of myself. In the room I saw a boy, he looked just about the same as you or me (that is if you are a boy) except he had bright green skin and his clothes looked like they were made out of paint. He looked almost as startled as I felt but he kept pretty calm, compared to how I felt.

"Uhhhh, hello?" he said.

"Uhhhh, hello," I said.

"Uhhhh, I'm Kentick," he said.

"Uhhhh, I'm John," I said.

"Why do you look so weird?" he questioned.

Then I remembered that not only did he look odd to me, but I looked odd to him.

"Uhhh, can I ask a question first?" I asked.

"Shoot."

"All right, here goes. What year is it?"

" 5300 after Flank".

"Who's Flank?"

"Everyone knows who Flank is," he said in a matter of fact voice. "I'll tell you the story."

Chapter 3
Flank

"Well," he started. Flank was born in a cog labin ... "

"What's a cog labin?" I had to ask.

"Well," he replied, "A labin is what we're in right now."

"You mean a dwelling?"

"Yeah, that's right. And cog is a color. Well, a material. Like what color did this labin look like when you first came in?"

"Brown."

"Right, except it wasn't, it was cog. So anyway, Flank was born in a cog labin in the middle of the woods in the D'laskan Aesert."

"What kind of woods was it", I asked.

"Actually, it wasn't really a woods," he replied, "I just described it that way so you would understand it. It was a wine poods."

It was right about then that I noticed that a lot of things he said were backwards. For instance: A "cog Labin" is what Abraham Lincoln was born in, a log cabin. And the D'laskan Aesert is the Alaskan Desert. And, a "wine poods" is a Pine woods. Now that takes a lot of thinking over. So I decided to cool it even though we hadn't even started talking about who Flank actually was. So I said to Kentick, "Can I go home and think this over a bit?"

"Sure" he said, "I'll direct this labin to where I picked you up."

I hopped down from the chair onto the rug, which immediately went sailing into the sky, so I had to jump down to the actual floor itself and walked out. Meaning, walked out through the wall. There I was, standing right next to my time machine. I got in, set it to go back home and hoped. The whizzing which I had learned was usual came all around me and suddenly I was back home about three minutes before I left. (I noticed that I always came back just a bit earlier, probably because it takes a few minutes to go to and fro, if you know what I mean.)

I went upstairs and tucked myself to bed. My mom thought I had gone to sleep hours ago. Well, for me hours ago. Now that I think on it, I wasn't supposed to go to sleep for another 3 minutes. But anyway, the next day I woke up early and went to Kentick's time. I stood there until I saw Kentick's room coming around, then stepped in.

"Hi, Kentick" I said.

"Hi," he said. "Hey I have a friend over, you might want to meet him. His name is Findem."

"Hi, Findem," I said.

"Hi," he said.

"Hey, Findem," said Kentick, "I'm in the middle of telling John ... "

"How do you know my name?" I interrupted

"I just do," he replied. "... I was just telling John," he repeated, "about Flank."

"Cool!" he said, "Where are you?"

" We just said about how Flank was born in a Cog Labin in the middle of the D'laskan Aesert in the middle of a Wine Poods."

It turned out Findem was the best story teller on elanet parth (planet earth) and this is my version of his story: When Flank was nrob (born backwards) the first thing his father said when he saw him was "What an ugly baby boy." Well, for Flank things went down from there and when he was a teenager he aan rway from home.

So Flank stole a space ship and flew (Findem said that in his time they spelt it flu) to mlanet pars and landed. Soon a person walked by and Flank asked "How do you do?" and the person answered "Iay on'tday nderstanduay ouyay. "Oh," said Flank and walked away. Now Flank understood he would have to learn this language if he was going to live there so he walked till he saw another being.

Flank was a pretty smart guy so when someone said to him "Oodgay ayday s'ntiay itay." he wrote it down on a piece of paper. After a while Flank realized the first letter was put at the end then you added ay.

• • • •

After ten years of living on mlanet pars Flank got arrested for being a elanet parthian along with 20 other elanet parthians, which was half of the population. He got himself and 15 of those people out of jail. After that Flank started doing things for elanet parth left and right and that is why it is 5300 after *Flank*. But wait, don't go, there's more! Flank didn't die!! He disappeared one day and nobody has found him!!!

Chapter 4
Mlanet pars

When Findem was done telling his story, me and Kentik and I applauded.

"If Findem disappeared, why hasn't anybody looked for him?" I asked.

"Well......." Kentik replied, "that's one weakness with our brains. Once it has been about 100 years we only think of something as a story."

"You mean no one has looked for him?"

"Well...."

"You mean, if you looked you might be able to find him!?"

"It's not our fault......"

"If 5300 years ago you had spaceships, you must be very advanced, so we could fly there in about a second!"

"My father does have a spaceship,"he replied.

"What are we waiting for, then? Let's go!"

"I guess so!" he answered a little more convinced, "Let's go!

The spaceships—they had must have been enormous—I don't know, because Kentick's father had a space raft, which meant it was the size of five football fields and only went at the speed of sound, not light.

At one point Ian planned a sequel to this sage, but I suspect he has gone on to more serious things, such as this review:

JACOB'S RESCUE
by Malka Drucker and Michael Halperin

Reviewed by Ian Leue, age nine

This book is about the Holocaust. The Holocaust was a time from the late 1930's to mid 1940's, during World War II. Millions and millions of Jews were killed. They were killed because of the Nazis. The Nazis where a group of people who killed anybody who did not have blue eyes, blond hair and were tall. If somebody hid a Jew or another person not in the description above and the Nazis discovered them, the people and their hiders would be killed.

This story is about Jacob, his brother David, and their rescuers; Alex, and his wife Mela. Jacob was a Jew, and 8 years of age when he first went into hiding. Jacob also had a brother named Sholom who died shortly after coming into hiding with Jacob. David was the middle brother. Jacob and both his brothers hid with Alex and Mela Roslan, who were not Jews. They hid Jacob, David, and for a short time Sholom, out of kindness.

Jacob was a Polish Jew who escaped from the Warsaw Ghetto. The Ghetto was a place where Jews were forced to go to and where they got little food to eat. He escaped with his Aunt Hannah. She had arranged with the man that used to be their chauffeur to have some friends take care of Jacob. These friends were Alex and Mela. When Jacob first came to their house in the city, he would hide under their sink in a little trap door Alex made, when anyone except the family (Alex and Mela had two children) were around. Even when no one else was around, he was not allowed to go outside because he had curly black hair and brown eyes. Then they were able to buy a large apartment to make it easier. After this, Sholom moved in. Then Jacob hid in the bathroom closet. Sholom soon died of scarlet fever. After that they were forced to sell their large apartment and buy a one-room apartment, because they needed money to treat Jacob's scarlet fever. Then the last brother, David, moved in. One night the neighbor's house was bombed, so they moved to the country where Mela's brother lived.

Though many died, Jacob and David survived the war and are alive today, as are Alex and Mela. After the war Jacob and David heard from the Jewish Agency that their father had survived the concentration camps and was living in Israel and wanted them to move to him. Alex and Mela wanted to go too, but since they were not Jewish, the British would not allow them to go.

I think it is a wonderful book, but not something that one should start off learning about the Holocaust with, because it is very intense. The Holocaust was a terrible time and I think people should never forget it.

* * * * *

Here is a poem by Madeline Leue (who just happens to be Ian Leue's little sister).

WHERE ARE WITCHES

Where are the witches?
Under the mountains.
Under rocks and
   into fountains.
Witches fly very high on their brooms.
No one can see them in their rooms.

—*Madeline Leue, age four years old*

Twenty-six years of award-winning teaching have led John Gatto to some troubling conclusions about the public schools. A former seventh-grade teacher, Gatto has twice been named New York City Teacher of the Year and New York State Teacher of the Year. Praised by leaders as diverse as Ronald Reagan and Mario Cuomo, he's a political maverick whose views defy easy categorization.

Gatto lives on Manhattan's Upper West Side, where he grows garlic, plays chess, writes songs—and once won a Citizen of the Week Award for coming to the aid of a woman who had been robbed. His books include Dumbing Us Down: The Hidden Curriculum Of Compulsory Schooling; The Exhausted School, *and* The Empty Child *(a work in progress). We're including FOUR (count 'em) vintage Gatto pieces. How could we not?*

A MAP, A MIRROR, AND A WRISTWATCH
by John Taylor Gatto

Let me edge into this presentation by telling you something about the children I teach and about some of the changes I saw in the general character development of these kids in the 30 years I spent inside public school classrooms. By a series of accidents, certainly not through my own design, I came to spend about a third of my time with confident white children from prosperous families, about a third of my time with a very mixed group of kids who represented "problem children" of a fairly mild and manageable sort, and a third of my time with black, Puerto Rican, and Dominican children from Harlem and Spanish Harlem; so when I tell you in advance that the observations I'm going to make apply to all of these groups I have earned my opinion in long and arduous action as a front-line practitioner in the school wars our press coverage dimly reflects.

Who are the children I taught? If you spent a short time with them under carefully controlled conditions, as perhaps a visiting businessman or politician might, you would see children who seemed to meet traditional specifications of the genus: alert, intelligent, active, funny, emotional beings who through judicious application of adult attention and some occasional resort to tricks and tricky machines can be brought to listen, to question, to analyze, to record, and to respond in a heartening fashion.

It would be an error, however, to fashion a long-range teaching strategy of these quick impressions—yes, my kids look and act as kids have always done, but all of my children are marked deeply by their experience in a secret underworld of the industrial society in decay—the government compulsion school. Schools, too, look as they did prior to 1960, but they are not the same at all. For a whole host of complicated reasons schools have been converted into behavioral training laboratories, where intellectual development—the enlightened historical justification for *schooling* children at all—has been abandoned in favor of other forms of training. So in an era of great technical progress my students have been invisibly disfigured by historical placement in a time without moral logic; in a time without an ethical source in God, in natural law, or in other forms of traditional authority, this destines many of them, rich and poor, for meaningless lives of unrooted activity. Only the State, jealous of its final claim to total loyalty, speaks regularly through its rules and laws about proper behavior, and because the voice of the State is, by turns, too rigid, or too pragmatic (conditional/situational ethics), or too dishonest (playing favorites/promising what it cannot deliver), children listen less and less. Nor should they do any differently; their disobedience is an inborn defense: they are trying to save their sanity or their souls, though few would have the language to put it that way.

The children I teach are victims of a very specific human delusion, one which once affected only kings and priests, though now it infects big bureaucrats, public and private, and schoolteachers alike. I refer to the fantastic notion that something called "mass man" actually exists, that human intellectual talent is for the most part a function of economics and social class, and that these conditions can be scientifically managed by a huge, intricately articulated bureaucracy which itself is cantilevered with other huge bureaucracies. This is the ultimate statement of scientific materialism on human life since in this view human nature is the result of random environmental factors; if the randomness is removed a good result will be almost automatic. Thus, it is thought, the training of the young, the corporate world of economics, the political world of power, breeding, death, war, amusement, health, and other basic aspects of individual and social life should be centrally controlled and regulated because all men and women are the same at the core, need the same things, and are as malleable as plastic.

This peculiar illusion that people are a mass, based on fear, greed, the need to have security, the need to justify special privileges, and other dark sources in the human psyche, leads inevitably to a form of social organization which bleeds significance from individual lives by removing decisions of consequence from the individual. Without personal significance people go insane, many become outlaws. This is the world of modern bureaucratic society which can only exist in a stable form through the relentless, nearly comprehensive social and psychological training provided by mass schooling. It is easy to pierce the veil of fiction that schooling has anything much to do with reading, writing, or arithmetic. The frightening fact that particular myth is still perpetuated is ample testimony to how unwilling we have been to face a horrifying truth. Schools work exactly as they were designed to work; they produce incomplete and tractable human beings, exactly as they were designed to do. To a scientific morality such a scheme has much to recommend it. It makes management of mass-man seem necessary—and real.

Scientific management is an idea older than Plato. Its theory is found in cabalistic lore attributed to Solomon and in records of pyramid builders before him; but in 20th century schooling the thing derives from certain schemes of the American efficiency engineer, Frederick Taylor, who at the beginning of the present century was the driving force behind the imposition of mechanical ideals on every conceivable plane of human affairs including sexual love (think of sex manuals with their diagrams and recommended sequences), ways in which human energy could be regulated and utilized according to standards of machine productivity. Behind Taylor, of course, were the dreams of cosmic social engineers, intimations that a long-awaited planetary society was at hand, and that because of the troubling defects of "mass man" it could only be run as a beehive world, or a hospital planet, or a prison state. Such had John Calvin's dark outlook on human nature which had once provided the spine of New England life transformed itself in the public and private plans of those groups which thought of themselves as "progressive". Hell was no longer the destination of most of us after death, Life and Death themselves were only epiphenomena, organizing and regulating society and nature were the only remaining things of meaning in a machine world. Re-forming the past.

We won't have time here for a clinic in philosophy, but I'll ask you to examine the implications of some of this, if human beings are cleverly disguised mechanisms then where can the notion of "liberty" apply? Liberty and the theological notion of free will are joined irrevocably in a close relationship. You can say, "I don't have time for this lofty stuff," but your own actions will make a liar out of you.

People are free. Or they are bound, determined by forces out of their own control. The society you allow stems from the decision which. So I want you to think of this: if people are not mechanisms (let's say that for the sake of argument) then what is the net effect of treating them so? Adam Smith doesn't talk about this in *Wealth of Nations* but he does have something to say about it in *The Theory of Moral Sentiments*. If you treat people like machines the moral effect on them and yourself is lousy.

Or think of this: how can you "educate" a machine at all? Even in a loose usage of that verb, a machine is only improved from outside the mechanism or circuitry. But in a human sense people have a very limited ability to be improved by the attention of others from the outside; most of the job, according to every major thinker who ever turned attention to this, has to be privately accomplished in the private interior of each individual consciousness. You can't teach courage or perseverance, wisdom or piety. Such things can be learned, it's clear, but taught, no. Yet people only begin to be educated when they tackle such goals—indeed, they are hardly completely human until that moment.

Individual development has to be fought for privately in a free market of plentiful choices, no one can do it for you. Too much interference early on cripples our natural progress toward independence and produces its opposite, dependence. We all recognize the bad effect a too indulgent parent has, we should begin to see the same force at work in a too indulgent school. This formula has been clearly understood by the powerful of this planet for thousands of years; even a cursory inspection of the development of their own young shows plenty of early exposure to unmonitored experience, risk-taking, independence, high performance standards, and many other characteristics which receive only lip service in government schooling, even suburban government schooling. Elite education, where the kid does hard work and does it without interference, is one likely cause for the amazing continuity of certain families throughout history. Yet élite education can be provided at less cost than factory school training. Some irony there. Until roughly the same time of the Jackson presidency in the 19th century rich and poor alike could get this same sort of education in a variety of different ways, but from Horace Mann's time until today those possibilities have been deliberately—I feel tempted to say "scientifically"—closed down for all but the economic elites and a few very determined parents from all the other classes. Why has that happened do you suppose?

In spite of a long-standing knowledge how human education is done right, the model Frederick Taylor, high priest of scientific management, sought to impose was a machine model, a model whose results are highly predictable, one which eliminates risks by setting its sights very low. Although in a limited sense this procedure successfully increases material output when the target is cheap, standardized, mass-produced merchandise, it only manages this productivity by crippling the self-governing spirit. So there's a big price to pay. Whether you decide to pay it or not depends a lot upon your regard for your fellow human beings; perhaps it depends on your idea of God, who knows?

A few years back one of the schools at Harvard issued some advice to its students on planning a career in the new international economy it believed was arriving. It warned sharply that academic classes and professional credentials would be devalued when measured against real world training. Ten qualities were offered as essential to successfully adapt to what Harvard believed was a rapidly changing world of work.

See how many of these you think are regularly taught in the schools of your city, including its "gifted and talented" classes:

1) The ability to define problems without a guide.

2) The ability to ask hard questions which challenge prevailing assumptions.

3) The ability to work in teams without guidance.

4) The ability to work absolutely alone.

5) The ability to persuade others that your course is the right course.

6) The ability to debate issues and techniques in public.

7) The ability to reorganize information into new patterns.

8) The ability to discard irrelevant data and find what you need from the masses of information.

9) The ability to think dialectically.

10) The ability to think inductively, deductively, and heuristically.

You might be able to come up with a better list than Harvard did without surrendering any of these fundamental ideas, and yet from where I sit—and I sat around schools for nearly 30 years—I know we don't teach any of these things as a matter of school policy. And for good reason, schools as we know them couldn't function at all if we did. Try to imagine a school where children challenged prevailing assumptions or worked alone without guidance. How about a school where children defined their own problems? If you want your kid to learn what Harvard says is necessary you'll have to arrange it outside school time in between the dentist and MTV. If you are poor you'd better forget it altogether. None of the schools I ever worked for were able to provide any important parts of this vital curriculum for children. All the schools I worked for taught nonsense up front and under the table they taught young people how to be dumb, how to be slavish, how to be frightened, and how to be dependent.

Things weren't always this way in the United States, indeed for the first 250 years of our history schooling here was wildly entrepreneurial; before we had forced schooling on the government model we had abundant schooling of many different types and the result by any historical measure were quite spectacular. Tom Paine's *Common Sense*, the philosophical basis for the American Revolution, sold 600,000 copies to a population of two and a half million colonists (about 75 percent of them African slaves or indentured servants!), James Fenimore Cooper's novels, rich with periodic sentences and dense with allusions, sold five million copies in the first two decades of the 19th century in a population of about eighteen million; Scott's novels matched that sale as did Noah Webster's monumental Speller. All this happened long before compulsion schooling was more than a gleam in the eye of certain interested parties in the early Federal period.

Pierre duPont de Nemours, who had a monopoly on gunpowder sales for the War of 1812 said in a book he wrote in that year, *National Education in the United States*, that "less than four in every thousand cannot read and do numbers" with great facility, and the habit of Bible reading at the breakfast table had led to such skill in argumentation among the young that he predicted the new nation would soon hold a comer on the world's supply of lawyers. Tocqueville's classic *Democracy in America*, whose first volume appeared in 1835, confirmed duPont's conclusions, and a book written a few years later by another French aristocrat, Michael Chevalier, said in astonishment that the American farmer had such a mind that he entered the fields in the morning with the plow in one hand and Descartes in the other!

Literacy in language and number was, from the beginning, highly valued in the New World, far beyond practical need. It was as if the promise that each mind could soar to unprecedented achievement beyond the limit of class-bound European practice inspired the commonality to take what its natural gifts offered. In this new scheme schooling was everywhere considered important, but nowhere was it considered very important. The principle that the educated man, like Benjamin Franklin, is largely self-taught was the real dynamic honored, and though the decision to proceed in this fashion was probably an accident of time and place in the last New World on the planet rather than any determination of scientific pedagogy, by some unlucky happenstance it is exactly the brilliant spring of development twentieth century institutional schooling has broken.

Lesson XXVII, "The Self-Taught Mathematician", used at one-room schools in the northeast in the year 1833 (20 years before the first compulsion school law) for children who would today be fourth to sixth graders is a revealing window into the attitudes toward learning present fifty years after we became a nation. It is the story of Edmund Stone, a self-educated Scottish mathematician born at the beginning of the 18th century. His father was gardener to the Duke of Argyle. One day when the Duke was walking in his garden he observed a Latin copy of Newton's *Principia* lying on the grass and thinking it had been brought from his own library sought to carry it back to its place. Stone, a boy of eighteen, rushed forward to claim the book for his own.

"Yours?" said the Duke. "Do you then understand Geometry, Latin, and Newton?"

"I know a little of them," replied the young man.

The Duke, surprised, entered into a conversation with the young man who had not the slightest acquaintance with schooling and was astonished at the force, the accuracy, and the candor of his answers.

"But how," said the Duke, "came you by the knowledge of these things?"

Stone replied, "A servant taught me to read when I was eight. Does one need to know anything more than the twenty-six letters in order to learn everything else that one wishes?"

"I first learned to read. The masons were then at work upon your house. I approached them one day and observed that the architect used a rule and compasses, and that he made calculations. I inquired what might be the meaning and use of these things. I was informed there was a science called arithmetic. So I purchased a book of arithmetic and I learned it. I was told there was another science called geometry; I got the necessary books and I learned geometry. By reading I learned that there were good books in these two sciences in Latin. I bought a dictionary and I learned Latin. I understood also that there were good books in French. I bought a dictionary and I learned French."

"And this, my Lord, is what I have done; it seems to me that we may learn everything when we know the twenty-six letters of the alphabet."

Stone went to London at the age of twenty-three and published his first work, *A Treatise on Mathematical Instruments*. Two years later he was chosen a Fellow of the Royal Society. And such was the lesson conveyed to five and ten-year-olds in Boston in 1833, if you knew how to read well you could learn anything you chose by yourself. Let me stick my schoolteacher's nose in here for a moment to say that this is obviously the same lesson I learned at my mother's knee in Monongahela a hundred years after "The Self-Taught Mathematician" was taught in Boston and two hundred years after Stone himself had learned it. I knew how to read well before I was five, thanks to my mother, and never had much difficulty learning anything I chose to learn after that. It was only after the coming of an enormous, multi-layered, densely articulated form of government schooling, a form imposed on the total population at the beginning of the twentieth century, not with the intention of enhancing *literacy* but of controlling and shaping *behavior*, that Stone's lesson was pushed into the background or in places discarded entirely. Learn to read well and you can teach yourself everything.

I want to show you just how far modern schooling is a radical deviation from the past by taking you back to George Washington's boyhood as the middle of the eighteenth century approached. If you watch carefully as the images unfold you'll catch a glimpse of just what the average kid is capable of if an opportunity is extended to develop fully, and you will even see a little of what simple, inexpensive schooling can do when stripped of administrative ranks, expert hierarchies, specialized materials, and psychological counselors. It will be a revelation so pay close attention!

George Washington was no genius as all his friends would hasten to agree; John Adams, his contemporary, called him "too illiterate, unlearned, unread for his station and reputation,"; Jefferson, his fellow Virginian, declared he liked to spend his time "chiefly in action, reading little." As a teenager Washington loved two things, dancing and horseback riding, and he studied both formally with a passion not supplied by schoolteachers.

These studies paid off for Washington because the grace they communicated to all his actions allowed him to physically dominate any gathering. Think of Michael Jordan the basketball player of whom it has been said he plays so well it's exactly as if the other players aren't even playing the same game. Well, that was Washington thanks to his twin obsessions. Listen to his friend George Mercer describe him as a young man:

> He is straight as an Indian, measuring six feet, two inches in his stockings and weighing 175 pounds....His frame is padded with well-developed muscles, indicating great strength.

Wouldn't everyone wish this for their own son? Washington got there by spending a great deal of time doing things that government schools ignore and would hardly teach.

Washington was no intellectual giant his friends agreed, but because of the unusual position he holds in American mythology it might be useful to see what subjects his average mind studied as a boy, the better to understand just what it is we have accomplished by 20th century state schooling. First we should note that although Washington didn't attend school until he was 11 (the same age, incidentally, that Woodrow Wilson learned to read) he had no trouble learning reading, writing, and arithmetic on his own. None at all, nor did any of his contemporaries who cared to learn such things have much difficulty whether they were rich or poor. Indeed in most places in the colonies or the early republic you couldn't go to school at all until you had first become literate. Few wanted to waste their time teaching what was so easy to learn. There is an enormous amount of evidence that colonial America was comprehensively literate wherever literacy was valued; children became literate because they wanted to be and because they were expected to be because it isn't hard to do.

But back to George at eleven on his way to school for the first time. What did he begin to study there? How about geometry, trigonometry, and surveying? Is that what your own average-minded eleven-year-old studies in sixth grade? Why not do you suppose? Or perhaps you think it was only a dumbed-down version of those things that Washington got, some kid's game. Well, maybe, but how do you account for this? Two thousand days after Washington first picked up a surveyor's transit in school at the age of eleven he assumed the office of official surveyor of Culpepper County, Virginia, a wonderful way to make a living in early America. Not only was the job highly paid but the frontier surveyor could pick out and keep the best land for himself.

For the next three years Washington earned in modern purchasing power about $100,000 a year. Perhaps his social connections helped this fatherless boy to get the position, but in a frontier society anyone would be crazy to give a boy serious work unless he could actually do it. I mean, what would the neighbors say? Almost at once Washington began speculating in land; by the time he was twenty-one he had leveraged his knowledge and capital into 2,500 acres of prime land in Frederick County, Virginia. Not a bad place then or now to own a few acres.

Washington had no father and as we know he was no genius, but learned geometry, trigonometry and surveying in school starting when he was eleven, and he was rich by his own effort at twenty-one. In school he studied frequently used legal forms including bills of exchange, tobacco receipts, bail bonds, servant indentures, wills, land conveyances, leases and patents. From these forms he was able to recreate the theory, philosophy and custom which had produced them. He had an average mind but by all accounts this steeping in grown-up reality hardly bored him. I had the same sort of experience with disruptive Harlem kids 250 years later. They stopped being hoodlums when I gave them real things to do. When did we lose the understanding that young people *yearn* for this kind of knowledge? Or was that yearning disregarded deliberately in order to create a different social reality?

On his own hook young Washington decided to scientifically study what might be called "gentlemanly deportment", how to be well regarded by the best people. Out of his journals I've taken his rule 56 to illustrate how he gathered his own character in hand, becoming his own father:

Rule 56

Associate yourself with men of good Quality if you Esteem your own reputation.

A sharp kid, that one, is it any wonder he became our first President?

Washington also studied geography and astronomy, gaining a knowledge thereby of the continents, the globe, and the heavens. In light of the putdowns of his reading you'll be interested to know that he read regularly the famous and elegant "Spectator" from London, which was sort of like the "New Yorker" before Tina Brown got her hooks on it. By the time he was 18 he had read all the writings of Henry Fielding, Tobias Smollett, and Daniel Defoe. But he read much more than the great English novelists, he read, too, Seneca's *Morals*, Julius Caesar's *Commentaries*, and the major writings of other Roman generals. What an amazing standard Adams and Jefferson must have had to consider Washington illiterate.

At 16 he began writing memos to himself about the design of his own clothing; years later he became his own architect for the magnificent estate of Mt. Vernon.

George Washington, as we now know, had an average mind in the eyes of the people who knew him best, yet he had no apparent difficulty studying the spots off technical manuals about agriculture and economics without a guide. The mysterious nature of money particularly interested him, he perceived that to the learned money was a much less valuable thing than wealth. Using his own research about such things, Washington was able to figure out that the talk of British bankers, politicians, and creditors about the importance of internationalism and global markets was a cunning way to drain his own resources into their pockets. He saw that the economics of tobacco farming (which had been forced on Virginia) made the tobacco farmer dependent on international factors, put his well-being out of his own control. So Washington, in his early 20s, began experimenting with domestic industry—where he could keep a close eye on things himself.

First he tried to grow hemp. That's called marijuana today, but presumably he was growing it for rope, not to smoke. He was 25. It didn't work. Next he tried to grow flax. He was 28. It didn't work. But because Washington had been educated to think for himself and not to wait for a teacher to tell him what to do he kept trying. At 31 he hit on wheat. That first year he sold 257 bushels. The third year 2,600 bushels. The seventh year 7,500 bushels. He built flour mills in various parts of Virginia and marketed his own brand of flour, think of it, "George Washington's Finest Home Grown Flour", accept no imported substitutes! While that business was maturing he turned his attention to building fishing boats. By 1772 his boats were pulling in 900,000 herring a year. George Washington was no genius, but partly because he got an education and wasn't compelled to waste all his youth in a government school scheme he did okay for himself.

There is no public school in the United States set up to allow a George Washington to happen; an Andrew Carnegie, from a poor family, who was well on his way to becoming rich at age 13 through a combination of hard work and intelligence, would be referred for psychological counseling; a Thomas Edison would find himself in Special Ed. No doubt about it.

Anyone who can read independently and runs a comparison with the present school product and what the American past *proved* kids can do will discover the magnitude of our government school institution's negative accomplishment.

In its movement toward programmatic society at the turn of the 20th century, scientific management found ways to break apart the natural sanctuaries of family, religion, tradition and place where a student might flee to escape his allotted mechanical destiny. It is one of the rich ironies of 20th century secular schooling that certain traditional religious groups like the Amish, the Mennonites, the Quakers, the Mormons, the orthodox Jews, The Jesuits and a few others found ways to aggressively preserve religious sources of private meaning—and became prosperous and significant citizens as a direct result. But many of the rest of us were flushed clean away from our roots. We were forcibly retrained to regard our own families, churches and neighbors as expendable, disposable, exchangeable—to think of them as conditional on good performance.

Now if historic families, those timeless families which continue to exist for centuries have one distinguishing characteristic that cannot be duplicated by temporary, rootless families, it is the property of conferring categorical significance on their members. Categorical significance means that you count *because you are*, because you exist, not because of something you can do, or whether you are successful, strong, or beautiful. Being categorical cannot survive grading or comparison. This point cannot be overemphasized because networks which only simulate family, like school, the army, the workplace, your bridge club, etc., just can't do it. Categorical significance is the opposite of conditional significance, that form of status operating in networks where the respect you receive is directly proportional to your performance. The Prodigal Son parable is the Western world's symbolic illustration and it helps to think of it if you want to measure whether this priceless quality is present or absent. Does your family love you in spite of anything? Do you love *them* in spite of anything? Reciprocity in a good family is almost beside the point.

Back to the children I teach. I have noticed no one *talks* to my kids though everyone commands their time. Because of seating arrangements in orderly rows, because of the solitary nature of television and computer operation, my children have very little ability to talk, even to each other. They have been socialized to speak only to children their own age, and then only at approved intervals. Partly as a result of this and partly from a confluence of othet reasons, I notice with increasing discomfort that children do not know who they are, where they are, or even what time it is.

Certainly I mean that metaphorically, but also I mean it literally: certain basic tools of self-knowledge like mirrors, maps, clocks, and so on are kept away from children—at least in any classroom you would care to visit in New York City. Other basic tools aren't around either, like hammers, chisels, saws, glue, telephones, calendars, typewriters, paper, pens, scissors, rulers. They just aren't there, at least not in accessible places. Schools are stripped bare of effective tools, not because of lack of money but because the autonomy that tools confer works against the collective socialization logic schools are about.

Tools constitute a curriculum of power. This seems something too fundamental to belabor. It is hard to make tool-competent people into a proletariat. Did you ever wonder why kids don't do the cooking and serving in a school, or the glazing, wiring, plumbing, roofing, and furniture repair? I've wondered about that often. At any rate a malaise follows the withdrawal of tools from common life. Of 62 functioning classrooms in my intermediate school there is a clock in exactly one of them. And it's been years since I saw a student wear a wristwatch. What could be going on? Something spooky I can tell you.

The clock, Lewis Mumford tells us, is the foremost machine of modern technics, not merely a means of keeping track of the hours but a way to synchronize the actions of diverse individuals. And the watch is the personalization of time, a major stimulus to the individuality we cherish as a salient aspect of Western civilization. The turning hands of a watch (not a digital obviously) are a measure of time used and time remaining, time spent and time wasted, time past and time to come. As such it is a key to personal achievement and productivity. The watch is a defense against panic in a time of turbulence such as we all surely agree our kids are living through at present.

Just as my children have no clocks or wristwatches, they are seldom in a classroom that offers a mirror in which to see themselves, to verify their inner states outwardly, to try on attitudes with. A reflecting surface is one important way we come to know ourselves. If classrooms have none, then television—in the mental room it creates—is worse. Television takes a very thin sample of human physical types and broadcasts this unrepresentative fragment endlessly. Most of the black people on television have white features, have you noticed? How do you suppose that happens? And most of the white kids who are featured in that vaguely precise way we call "ethnic" are hardly ever shown in television commercials or programming. In the mirror of American school and video-culture, most of us are invisible non-persons, white or black.

Maps and children are kept apart, too, so some of my 14-year-old children think it is 100,000 miles to California, some think it is 9,000,000 miles. I seldom have more than one kid a year who can come within a thousand miles of the reality. My kids don't know what a mile is, not really, although I think they could pass a test on it; in similar fashion they don't know what democracy is, or what money is, or what an economy is, or how to fix anything. They've heard of Mogadishu and Saddam Hussein but they couldn't tell you the name of the tree outside their window if their life depended on it. That's what so-called global thinking since 1910 has done to reality, it put a utopian spin on things. Some of them can do quadratic equations, but they can't sew a button on a shirt or fry an egg; they can bubble in answers with a number two pencil but they can't build a wall. Many of them have no idea that most of the men and women on earth believe in God, or how that might affect the way they live.

The whole dull liar's world that government schooling has created is a form of abstract witchcraft, mumbo jumbo leading nowhere like Mogadishu or Saddam Hussein. The truth is that my kids are unable to plot a future because they don't know where they are or who they are. How can you know who you are if you don't know your own family, and how can you know your own family if none of you are home together very often? Who arranged things this way, because surely they didn't just *happen*?

Nobody I ever taught had any idea how many people live in New York City or what significance such a fact might have, few know what the city abuts upon, how long ago the Revolution was fought there, or why or who the enemy was. *They have been deprived of the proper experience to care about such things.* This is the characteristic profile of a proletariat, it cares about very little except avoiding punishment and filling its belly. People aren't proles by nature but by training, a proletariat doesn't just *happen,* it is *made*.

The fact we are a revolutionary nation and what that did to our subsequent history good and bad has been carefully screened from the view of children, even from ones who can parrot words about Patrick Henry and Sam Adams; the magnificent Second Amendment to our Constitution with its vast trust in the common sense of the common people, and its vast mistrust of government has been perverted by the rhetoric of our academic leadership into an eccentric privilege of misfits and scoundrels. We have the right to bear arms mainly as protection against *our own* government going astray, only secondarily to protect our homes. The proof of that lies in looking at what the British colonists in America did with guns when the British government went astray—they pitched it out on its ears and became Americans. They couldn't have done that without personal firearms. The possibility such a situation might arise again is commemorated in the Second Amendment. But someone decided you weren't supposed to learn that so you don't. Can you imagine why?

In the ongoing condition of derangement among my kids caused by ignorance of basic facts like knowing where they are you'd think one specific remedy would be giant wall maps of the neighborhood, the city, the state, the nation, and the world; you would think these things would be permanent decorations in every classroom and every corridor of the school hive, but you would be mistaken. What maps there are will be found in "social studies" rooms, but most often not even there. Whose interest is served by kids not knowing basic stuff like this?

I could go on and on about other fundamental, inexpensive tools missing from my students' lives but the point of this progression has been to draw a radical conclusion:

SCHOOL IS A BARRIER TO EDUCATION

It is quite impossible to think this happened by accident, although I am prepared to grant that the original group of social engineers who set up the school machine is dead, and for the most part the peculiar motives they had in a very successful free market in American schooling have been forgotten. School perpetuates itself today in the ugly form it was given originally because it has become the most profitable business in the United States. We need to look no further than that for a conspiracy. Structural reform of schooling would disenfranchise an enormous number of comfortable people. Talk about change is permitted, but never more than minor tinkering follows.

Schools are barriers to the education of children. This is particularly true for children of poverty, but I believe the statement holds for all classes of the young. Schools are black holes. If they miss the decisive significance of a mirror, a map, and a wristwatch, you can be certain anything else of importance has been missed, too. Reform will only come about when there is an angry national debate about the real purpose of these warehouse institutions, a debate in which sham defenses like "teaching children to read" are finally thrown aside and reality faced square on. Schools do exactly what they were assigned to do in the first decade of the 20th century—they contain the poor. Having taught poor children for many years I don't think they need to be feared any more than rich kids, but I want to be certain to put the bell on the cat. Fear of the poor in the United States first crested with the election of Andrew Jackson in 1828, that's the event that started the real drive for government schools. Who knew *what* the poor were capable of in a revolutionary democracy, better to get them locked up where they could be watched. Fear of the poor crested a second time just before and just after the Civil War when waves of Catholic immigrants from Ireland and Italy poured into this country strong, resourceful, energetic, and child-loving—people with family ties who couldn't easily be pushed around. Trying to push them led to a series of violent national strikes, railroad strikes in Chicago and steel strikes in Pittsburgh. Remember when Andy Carnegie sent an army of Pinkertons to shoot the steel strikers at Homestead? The Pinkertons got shot instead. It was those strikes which finally nailed the children in the school coffin where they've rested for just about a century. What nobody figured on was the ambitious reach of civil service bureaucrats. They would not rest content as guardians of the poor *alone,* but would seek to wax fatter so the destiny of all children would be in their hands. Thus was the road to Outcomes-Based Education paved.

Who will fix this thing now it has become a central core of the American economy, the single largest hiring agent, the largest contractor? We can't count on much help from professional school reformers or from state education departments because the business is their bread and butter.

And yet, even without our experts we're going to have to find some way to sidestep official owners of the school monopoly and relieve the terrible stresses growing up absurd this way causes. The elasticity of our children is nearly exhausted. I've deliberately borrowed a term from the world of structural engineering because I think it applies. When building materials lose their elasticity they don't fail immediately but pass through a stage of plastic behavior, where the deformations don't return to true but take some dangerous and unpredictable course. Our children as a class have begun to display plastic behavior.

What else would you call our world's record teenage suicide rate, teenage murder rate, and our national all-encompassing addictions to violence, alcohol, drugs, commercial entertainments, the narcotic-like addiction we have to magical machines, and a long list of other aberrations. Each generation we have produced since the very recent invention of government compulsion-school seems to me less elastic, more plastic than the one before it.

There are many fine and inexpensive ways to inspire children to provide a first-class education for themselves, we all know a few of them. But whether it's going to be possible to get an education in the new schools of the year 2000 will depend on political decisions made by those who hold power in trust for all of us. Or perhaps I am wrong. Perhaps it will depend on defiant personal decisions of simple people, like the quiet revolution of homeschoolers taking place under our noses right now, which to me seems the most exciting social movement since the pioneers, a revolution in which our type of factory schooling is not contested at all, just treated as monumentally irrelevant, which it certainly is.

Give me a minute to be visionary. If we closed the government schools, divided half the tax money currently spent on these places among parents with kids to educate, and spent the other half on free libraries, on underwriting apprenticeships for every young person, and on subsidizing any group who wanted to open a school a current of fresh air would sweep away the past in a short time. If further we made provisions for a continuous public dialogue on the local level—so that people in the street began to count once again—if we strictly limited political terms of office in order to weaken the protective legislative net around businesses which profit from mass schooling, and if we launched a national program of family revival with all the energy we reserve for wars we would soon find the American school nightmare changing into a dream we could all be proud of.

That isn't going to happen, I know.

Very well. The next best thing then is to deconstruct mass schooling, minimizing the "school" aspect of the thing and maximizing the educational one. What that means in simple terms is trusting children, trusting parents, trusting families, trusting communities to be the main architects in the training of the young. It means reversing the familiar teacher/student equation so that toxic professionalism which sees teaching, wrongheadedly, as the key to learning can be relegated to the Prussian nightmare from whence it sprang. That's a formula for a priesthood, not for an education. Socrates in the *Apology* told us that if we professionalized teaching two bad results would occur: first, what is easy to learn would be made to appear difficult; and second, what can be learned quickly would be stretched out indefinitely to provide some security for the pedagogue. Is there anyone who doesn't recognize this is precisely what we have allowed to happen? Even this simpler goal of deconstructing institutional schooling will require enough courage to challenge deeply rooted assumptions such as the assumption that the poor are stupid, bestial, or criminal. And it will require a great amount of stamina because this school monster is alive and growing, and very, very strong.

Now let me give you some practical suggestions drawn from a lifetime teaching and thinking about schools. I've arranged them in no particular order. Even invoking a few of these safeguards would bring beneficial changes to a school or district. I have ten suggestions in all, and you will likely have some of your own to add as you hear mine.

1) Make Everybody Teach.

The ghastly proliferation of non-teaching jobs began when it was imposed on schools by local and state politicians and the new Germanic teacher colleges about the turn of the century. It is wasteful and demoralizing. There should be no such thing as a non-teaching principal, assistant principal, coordinator, specialist, or any other category of school employee who doesn't actually spend regular time on intellectual undertakings with groups of children.

2) Simplify the curriculum and make it intelligent.

The purpose which confinement schooling can be most productively turned to is the development of the intellect. Such development is valuable for everyone and my long experience with ghetto kids taught me they are as capable of this development as any. Every other purpose schooling has been turned to is better accomplished *outside* of school, with the time freed up by taking a sledgehammer to the current silliness and confusion; each child could have apprenticeships, internships, and independent study throughout the community in areas of their own deepest concern.

3) Let no school exceed a few hundred in size.

Time to shut the factory schools forever. They are hideously expensive to maintain, they degrade the children they encompass, they hurt the neighborhoods in which they stand, they present ready markets for every kind of commercial hanky-panky. If schools were miniaturized a lot of worthless businesses would go belly-up on the spot. Make schools small and make them independent and autonomous. Everyone knows that is the right way, but not everyone knows that it is the inexpensive way, too. And make these small schools local. Curtail busing, neighborhoods need their own children and vice versa.

And let us save ourselves a fortune although the construction industry will scream bloody murder. Let us recognize there is no proper shape for a school building, schools can be anywhere and look like anything. In a very short time desktop computers will allow libraries of information to be everywhere, too, and contact with the best minds in every pursuit. Then what will the excuse for schools become?

4) Sharply constrict the power and size of state Departments of Education and large-city centralized school boards, they are a paradise for grifters and grafters and even if they were not their long-range interventions are irrelevant at best and horribly damaging at worst—in addition to being expensive. Decentralize school down to the neighborhood school level. In that one bold move families would be given control over the professionals in their children's lives. Each school under this governance would have its own citizen managing board elected from among neighbors. And full autonomy in purchasing and curriculum decisions. That's not a new idea, that's the way we had it for hundreds of years during which this country schooled—and educated—quite well.

5) Get rid of standardized tests completely.

Measure accomplishment by performance, most often performance against a personal standard, not ranking against a class or larger entity. Standardized tests don't work. Is that news to anybody? What a scam! They correlate with nothing of human value, their very existence perverts curriculum into an advance preparation for the extravagant ritual administration of the tests. Is this a good thing? Why do you think that? If you don't then why do you put up with it? Would you hire a newspaper reporter on the basis of his test scores in journalism? Would you hire a hair stylist who had an "A" average in Beauty School? Wouldn't you ask for a demonstration? I hope so. The fact is nobody is crazy enough to hire anyone on the basis of grades and test scores for important work with one glaring exception —government jobs, and government licensing. The reason for that is that tests are poor predictors of the future *unless* the competition is rigged in advance by only allowing people who score well on tests to have jobs. That is the whole sorry story of the government licensing racket in this century.

6) End the teacher certification monopoly which is only kept alive by illicit agreement between teacher institutes and the state legislature.

It makes colleges rich, it supports an army of unnecessary occupational titles, and it deprives children and unlicensed but competent adults from having valuable educational connections with each other.

Once again, it's hard to break the *illusion* that certification is there to protect the children so let me help. Think of this: the legendary private schools of this nation, Exeter, Andover, St. Paul's, Groton, Culver Military, wouldn't dream of restricting themselves to certified teachers. Why should we? Let anyone who can demonstrate performance competency before a citizen board, a parent body, or a group of students then be licensed to teach.

7) Restore the primary experience base we have stolen from kids' lives.

Kids need to *do*, not sit in chairs. The school diet of confinement, test worship, bell addiction, and dependence on low-grade secondary experience in the form of semiliterate printed material cracks children away from their own innate understanding of how to learn and why. Let children engage in real tasks, not synthetic games and simulations. Field curriculum, critical thinking, apprenticeships, team projects, independent study, actual jobs, and other themes of primary experience must be restored to the life of the young.

8) Install permanent parent and community facilities in every school, in a prominent place near the front office. We need to create a tidal movement of real life in and out of the dead waters of school. Open these places on a daily basis to family and other community resource people and rig these rooms with appropriate equipment to allow parent partnerships with their own kids. Frequently release kids from classwork to work with their own parents, frequently substitute parents and other adults for professional staff in classrooms, too.

9) Understand clearly that total schooling is psychologically and procedurally unsound.

Give children some private time, some private space, some choice of subjects, methods, and even the company they keep. Does that sound like a college? It is meant to. Human beings, a group of which children are a part, do not do well under constant surveillance and tabulation. Keep from numbering, ranking, and labeling kids so the human being can't be seen under the weight of the numbers.

10) Teach children to think critically so they can challenge the hidden assumptions of the world around them including the assumptions of the school world.

This type of thinking power has always been at the center of the world's élite educational systems. Policy makers are taught to think, the rest of the mass is not or is only taught partially. We could end this age-old means of social control in several short generations. What a society would look like where education instead of schooling happened for everyone I have no more idea than you do, but it would restore the exhilarating flux in human affairs we had in the early Federal period of this nation's history under President Jackson—before the dead hand of state schooling closed the door on it. Well, I said ten suggestions, but here's one more, number eleven:

11) We have to get down to business and provide legitimate choices to people; schooling can indeed be compulsory but education requires volition, *anti- compulsion is essential to become educated*—there is no one right way to do it nor is there one right way to grow up successfully, either. That kind of thinking has had a century and abundant treasure to prove itself and what it has done is to prove itself a fraud.

The word "public" in our form of public education has not had real meaning for a long time; public schooling will make a comeback when we strip control from the Egyptian pyramid of dubious experts *and force our government to return full free market choice to the people.* This is the only curriculum of necessity we need to see imposed by compulsion on everyone, the return of decision-making power to individuals and families. I hope we won't have to use guns to bring this second American revolution about.

NINE ASSUMPTIONS OF SCHOOLING—and
Twenty-one Facts the Institution Would Rather
Not Discuss
by John Taylor Gatto

I'll start off bluntly by giving you some data I'd be shocked if you already know. A few simple facts, all verifiable, which by their existence call into question the whole shaky edifice of American government compulsion schooling from kindergarten through college and its questionable connection with the job market. The implications of this data are quite radical so I'm going to take pains to ground it in the most conservative society on earth, the mountain world of Switzerland. You all remember Switzerland: that's where people put their money when they really want it to be really safe.

The Swiss just like us believe that education is the key to their national success, but that's where our similarity ends. In 1990 about 60% of American secondary school graduates enrolled in college, but only 22% did in Switzerland; in America almost 100% of our kids go to high school or private equivalents, but only a little over a fifth of the Swiss kids do. And yet the Swiss per capita income is the highest of any nation in the world and the Swiss keep insisting that virtually everyone in their country is highly educated!

What on earth could be going on? Remember it's a sophisticated economy which produces the highest per-capita paycheck in the world we're talking about, high for the lightly-schooled as well as for the heavily schooled, higher than Japan's, Germany's or our own. No one goes to high school in Switzerland who doesn't also want to go to college, three-quarters of the young people enter apprenticeships before high school. It seems the Swiss don't make the mistake that schooling and education are synonyms.

If you are thinking silently at this point that apprenticeships as a substitute for classroom confinement isn't a very shocking idea and it has the drawback of locking kids away from later choice of white collar work, think again. I wasn't only talking about blue-collar apprenticeships—although the Swiss have those, too—but white-collar apprenticeships in abundance. Many of the top management of insurance companies, manufacturing companies, banks, etc. never saw the inside of a high school, let alone a college.

Is that possible? The highest per capita income in the world and every single citizen also trusted by government to own dangerous weapons. [I forgot to tell you that the largely unschooled Swiss (by our standards) also *demand* universal gun ownership.] Ownership. If it puzzles you what connection I might be drawing between great prosperity, freedom from forced schooling where it is clearly inappropriate, and a profound mutuality, you think about it.

Well, shocking is the word for it, isn't it? I mean here you are putting away your loot in a Swiss bank because it's safe over there and not so safe here and now I've told you the bank president may only have a sixth grade schooling. Just like Shakespeare did.

As long as we're playing "did you know?", did you know that in Sweden, a country legendary for its quality of life and a nation which beats American school performance in every academic category, a kid isn't *allowed* to start school before the age of 7? The hard-headed Swedes don't want to pay for the social pathologies attendant on ripping a child away from his home and mother and dumping him into a pen with strangers. Can you remember the last time you worried about a Swedish Volvo breaking down prematurely or a Swedish jet engine failing in the air? Did you know that the entire Swedish school sequence is only 9 years long, a net 25% time and tax savings over our own 12-year sequence?

Exactly in whose best interest do you think it is that the *New York Times* or every other element of journalism, for that matter, doesn't make information like this readily accessible? How can you think clearly about our own predicament if you don't have it?

Did you know that Hong Kong, a country with a population the size of Norway's, beats Japan in every scientific and mathematical category in which the two countries compete? Did you know that Hong Kong has a school year ten and one half weeks shorter than Japan's? How on earth do they manage that if longer school years translate into higher performance? Why haven't you heard about Hong Kong, do you suppose? You've heard enough about Japan, I'm sure.

But I'll bet you haven't heard this about Japan. I'll bet you haven't heard that in Japan a recess is held after every class period.

Or did you know that in Flemish Belgium with the shortest school year in the developed world that the kids regularly finish in the top three nations in the world in academic competition? Is it the water in Belgium or what? Because it can't be the passionate commitment to government forced schooling, which they don't seem to possess.

Did you know that three British Prime Ministers in this century including the current one didn't bother to go to college? I hope I've made the point. If you trust journalism or the professional educational establishment to provide you with data you need to think for yourself in the increasingly fantastic socialist world of compulsion schooling, you are certainly the kind of citizen who would trade his cow for a handful of colored beans.

Shortly into the 20th century American schooling decided to move away from intellectual development or skills training as the main justification for its existence and to enter the eerie world of social engineering, a world where "socializing" and "psychologizing" the classroom preempted attention and rewards. Professionaliza-tion of the administrative/teaching staff was an important preliminary mechanism to this end, serving as a sieve to remove troublesome interlopers and providing lucrative ladders to reward allies and camp followers.

Non-intellectual, non-skill schooling was supported by a strange and motley collection of fellow travelers: from unions, yes, but also from the ranks of legendary businessmen like Carnegie and Rockefeller, Ford and Astor; there were genuine ideologues like John Dewey, yes, but many academic opportunists as well like Nicholas Murray Butler of Columbia; prominent colleges like Johns Hopkins and U. Chicago took a large hand in the deconstruction of American academic schooling as well as a powerful core of private foundations and think tanks. Whether they did this out of conviction, for the advantage of private interests, or any hybrid of these reasons and more I'll leave for the moment to others for debate. What is certain is that the outcomes aimed for had little to do with why parents thought children were ordered into schools; such alien outcomes as socialization into creatures who would no longer feel easy with their own parents, or psychologization into dependable and dependent camp followers. Of what field general it wasn't clear except to say that whoever could win undisputed control of hiring and curriculum in a school district would have a clear hand in selecting and arranging the contents of children's minds.

In those early years of the 20th century a radical shift was well under way, transforming a society of farmers and craftspeople, fishermen and small entrepreneurs into the disciplined workforce of a corporate state, one in which ALL the work was being sucked into colossal governments, colossal institutions and colossal business enterprises—a society whose driving logic was comfort, security, predictability and consensus rather than independence, originality, risk-taking and uncompromising principle. In the gospels of social engineering this transformation was leading to a future utopia of welfare capitalism. With the problem of "production" solved, the attention of professional intellectuals and powerful men of wealth turned to controlling distribution so that a "rational" society, defined as a stable state without internal or external conflicts, could be managed for nations, regions and eventually the entire planet. In such a system, if you behave, you get a share of the divvy and if you don't, your share is correspondingly reduced. Keep in mind that a small farmer, a carpenter, a fisherman, seamstress or Indian fighter never gave undue attention to being well-behaved and you will begin to see how a centralized economy and centralized schooling box human behavior into a much narrowed container than what it normally would occupy and you will begin to see why intellectual development for all its theoretical desirability can never really be a serious goal for a society seeking comfort, security, predictability and consensus. Indeed, such a fate must be actively avoided.

Anyway, once this design was in place—and it was firmly in place by 1917—all that remained to reach the target was a continual series of experiments on public schoolchildren, some modest in scope, many breathtakingly radical like "IQ tests" or "kindergartens", and a full palette of intermediate colors like "multiculturalism", "rainbow" curricula and "universal self esteem". Each of these thrusts has a real behavioral purpose which is part of the larger utopia envisioned, yet each is capable of being rhetorically defended as the particular redress of some current "problem".

But the biggest obstacle to a planned society is parents. Parents have their own plans for their own kids; most often they love their kids, so their motivations are self-reinforcing, unlike those of schoolpeople who do it for a paycheck, and unless held in check even a few unhappy parents can disrupt the conduct of an educational experiment;

The second biggest obstacle to a planned society are religious sects, each of which maintains that God has a plan for all human beings, including children. And the third biggest obstacle is local values and ethnic cultures which also provide serious maps for growing up.

Each of these three is an external force bidding for the loyalty of children against the directions of the political State which owns the schools. One final obstacle—and a colossal one—is the individual nature of each particular child. John

Locke pulled a whopper when he maintained that children are blank slates waiting to be written upon. He should have asked a few mothers about that. The fact is that if you watch children closely in controlled conditions as I did for 30 years as a schoolteacher, you can hardly fail to conclude that each kid has a private destiny he or she is pulling toward wordlessly, a destiny frequently put out of reach by schoolteachers, school executives or project officers from the Ford Foundation.

In a planned society individuality, cultural identity, a relationship with God or a close-knit family are all elements which must be suppressed if they cannot be totally extinguished. The Soviet Union was an object lesson in this utopian undertaking and the United States has been going down the same road, albeit with more hesitations, at least since the end of the first world war. To accomplish such a complex transformation of nature into mechanism the general public must be led to agree to certain apparently sensible assumptions. Such as the assumption, for instance, that a college degree is necessary for a high-status career—even though Swiss corporations and the British government are often run by managers without college training. The security of the school institution depends on many such assumptions, some which by adroit concealments worthy of a card sharp seem to link schooling and future responsibility, and some which serve to exalt the political State, diminish essential human institutions like the family or define human nature as mean, violent and brutish. I'd like to pass nine specimens drawn from these latter categories of assumption in front of your minds to allow each of you to gauge which ones you personally accept, and to what degree.

Nine Assumptions of Schooling

1. Social cohesion is not possible through other means than government schooling; school is the main defense against social chaos.

2. Children cannot learn to tolerate each other unless first socialized by government agents.

3. The only safe mentors of children are certified experts with government-approved conditioning; children must be protected from the uncertified, including parents.

4. Compelling children to violate family, cultural and religious norms does not interfere with the development of their intellects or characters.

5. In order to dilute parental influence, children must be disabused of the notion mother and father are sovereign in morality or intelligence.

6.   Families should be encouraged to expend concern on the general education of everyone but discouraged from being unduly concerned with their own children's education.

7.   The State has predominant responsibility for training, morals and beliefs. Children who escape state scrutiny will become immoral.

8.   Children from families with different beliefs, backgrounds and styles must be forced together even if those beliefs violently contradict one another. Robert Frost, the poet, was wrong when he maintained that "good fences make good neighbors."

9.   Coercion in the name of liberty is a valid use of state power.

These assumptions and a few others associated with them lead directly to the shape, style and exercise of school politics. And these primary assumptions generate secondary assumptions which fuel the largely phony school debate played out in American journalism, a debate where the most important questions like "What *is* the end that justifies these means?" are never asked. I once had dinner in Washington at the same table as Fred Hechinger, education editor of the *New York Times*. When I raised the possibility that the *Times* framed its coverage to *omit* inconvenient aspects of school questions (such as challenging the presumed connection between quantity of money spent and quality of education) Mr. Hechinger became very angry and contemptuously dismissed my contention; almost the same thing happened on a different occasion, also in Washington, when I had dinner at the Council for Basic Education at the same table with Albert Shanker of the AFT. With that history of failure in opening a dialogue with some of the powers and principalities of institutional education (and I could add Lamar Alexander, Bill Bennett, Joe Fernandez, Diane Ravitch, Checker Finn and many other luminaries who seemed to hear me with impatience) I've been driven to trying to catch the ear of the general public in meeting the assumptions schools rely upon with contradictory facts open to formal verification—or the informal variety grounded in common sense. What follows are 21 of these disturbing contradictions raised for your contemplation:

21 Facts About Schooling

1.   There is no relationship between the amount of money spent on schooling and "good" results as measured by parents of any culture. This seems to be because "education" is not a commodity to be purchased but an enlargement of insight, power,

understanding and self-control almost completely outside the cash economy. Education is almost overwhelmingly an internally generated effort. The five American states which usually spend least per capita on schooling are the five which usually have the best test results (although Iowa which is about 30th in spending sometimes creeps into the honored circle).

2. There is no compelling evidence to show a positive relationship between length of schooling and accomplishment. Many countries with short school years outperform those with long ones by a wide margin.

3. Most relationships between test scores and job performance are illegitimate, arranged in advance by only allowing those testing well access to the work. Would you hire a newspaper reporter because he had "A"s in English? Have you ever asked your surgeon what grade he got in meat-cutting? George F. Kennan, intellectual darling of the Washington élite some while ago—and the author of our "containment" policy against the Soviet Union—often found his math and science grades in secondary school below 60, and at Princeton he had many flunks, "D"s and "C"s. "Sometimes," he said, "it is the unadjusted student struggling to forge his own standards who develops within himself the thoughtfulness to comprehend." Dean Acheson, Harry Truman's Secretary of State, graduated from Groton with a 68 average. The headmaster wrote his mother, "He is...by no means a pleasant boy to teach." Einstein, we all know, was considered a high grade moron, as were Thomas Edison and Benjamin Franklin. Is there anybody out there who really believes that grades and test scores are the mark of the man? Then what exactly are they, pray tell? Q.E.D.

4. Training done on the job is invariably cheaper, quicker, and of much higher quality than training done in a school setting. If you wonder why that should be, you want to start, I think, by understanding that education and training are two different things, one largely residing in the development of good habits, the other in the development of vision and understanding, judgment and the like. Education is self-training; it calls into its calculations mountains of personal data and experience which are simply unobtainable by any school-teacher or higher pedagogue. That simple fact is why all the many beautifully precise rules on how to think produce such poor results.

5. In spite of relentless propaganda to the contrary, the American economy is tending strongly to require *less* knowledge and *less* intellectual ability of its employees, not more. Scientists and mathematicians currently exist in numbers far exceeding any global demand for them or any national demand—and that

condition should grow much worse over the next decade, thanks to the hype of pedagogues and politicians. Schools *can* be restructured to teach children to develop intellect, resourcefulness and independence, but that would lead, in short order, to structural changes in the old economy so profound it is not likely to be allowed to happen because the social effects are impossible to clearly foretell.

6. The habits, drills and routines of government schooling sharply reduce a person's chances of possessing initiative or creativity—furthermore the mechanism of why this is so has been well understood for centuries.

7. Teachers are paid as specialists but they almost never have any real world experience in their specialties;.indeed the low quality of their training has been a scandal for 80 years.

8. A substantial amount of testimony exists from highly regarded scientists like Richard Feynman, the recently deceased Nobel laureate, or Albert Einstein and many others that scientific discovery is negatively related to the procedures of school science classes.

9. According to research published by Christopher Jencks, the famous sociologist, and others as well, the quality of school which any student attends is a very bad predictor of later success, financial, social or emotional; on the other hand the quality of family life is a very good predictor. That would seem to indicate a national family policy directly spending on the home, not the school.

10. Children learn fastest and easiest when very young; general intelligence has probably developed as far as it will by the age of four. Children are quite capable of reading and enjoying difficult material by that age and also capable of performing all the mathematical operations skillfully and with pleasure. Whether kids should do these things or not is a matter of philosophy or cultural tradition, not a course dictated by any scientific knowledge about the advisability of the practice.

11. There is a direct relationship between heavy doses of teaching and detachment from reality with subsequent flights into fantasy. Many students so oppressed lose their links with past and present, present and future. And the bond with "now" is substantially weakened.

12. Unknown to the public virtually all famous remedial programs have failed. Programs like Title I/Chapter I survive by the goodwill of political allies, not by results.

13. There is no credible evidence that racial mixing has any positive effect on student performance, but a large body of suggestive data is emerging that the confinement of children from

sub-cultures with children of a dominant culture does harm to the weaker group.

14. Forced busing has accelerated the disintegration of minority neighborhoods without any visible academic benefit as trade-off.

15. There is no reason to believe that any existing educational technology can significantly improve intellectual performance; on the contrary, to the extent that machines establish the goals and work schedules, ask the questions and monitor the performances, the already catastrophic passivity and indifference created by forced confinement schooling only increases.

16. There is no body of knowledge inaccessible to a motivated elementary student. The sequences of development we use are hardly the product of "science" but instead are legacies of unstable men like Pestalozzi and Froebel, and the military government of 19th century Prussia from which we imported them.

17. Delinquent behavior is a direct reaction to the structure of schooling. It is much worse than the press has reported because all urban school districts conspire to suppress its prevalence. Teachers who insist on justice on behalf of pupils and parents are most frequently intimidated into silence. Or dismissed.

18. The rituals of schooling remove flexibility from the mind, that characteristic vital in adjusting to different situations. Schools strive for uniformity in a world increasingly less uniform.

19. Teacher-training courses are widely held in contempt by practicing teachers as well as by the general public because expensive research has consistently failed to provide guidance to best practice.

20. Schools create and maintain a caste system, separating children according to irrelevant parameters. Poor, working class, middle class and upper middle class kids are constantly made aware of alleged differences among themselves by the use of methods not called for by the task at hand.

21. Efforts to draw a child out of his culture or his social class has an immediate effect on his family relationships, friendships and the stability of his self-image.

Well, there you have them: nine assumptions and twenty-one assertions I think can be documented well enough to call facts. How are we all as a society going to get to a better place in schools than the one we've gotten to at the moment? The only way I can see after spending 35 years in and around the institution (53 if I count my own time as inmate) is to put full choice squarely back into the hands of parents, let the marketplace re-define schooling—a job the special interests are incapable of—and encourage the development of as many styles of schooling as there are human dreams. Let people, not bureaucrats, work out their own destinies. That's what made us a great country in the first place.

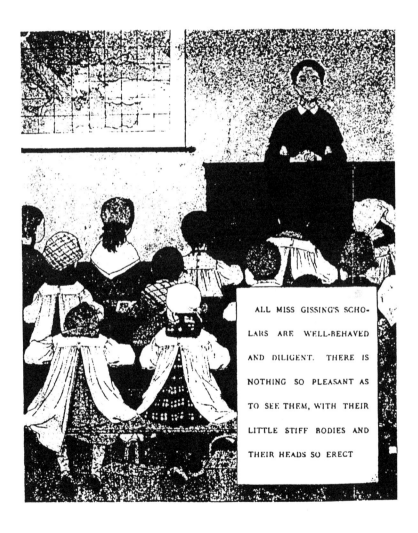

ALL MISS GISSING'S SCHO-LARS ARE WELL-BEHAVED AND DILIGENT. THERE IS NOTHING SO PLEASANT AS TO SEE THEM, WITH THEIR LITTLE STIFF BODIES AND THEIR HEADS SO ERECT

CONFEDERACY OF DUNCES:
THE TYRANNY OF COMPULSORY SCHOOLING
by John Taylor Gatto

Let me speak to you about dumbness because that is what schools teach best. Old-fashioned dumbness used to be simple ignorance: you didn't know something, but there were ways to find out if you wanted to. Government-controlled schooling didn't eliminate dumbness—in fact, we now know that people read more fluently before we had forced schooling—but dumbness was transformed.

Now dumb people aren't just ignorant; they're the victims of the non-thought of secondhand ideas. Dumb people are now well-informed about the opinions of *Time* magazine and CBS, *The New York Times* and the President; their job is to choose which pre-thought thoughts, which received opinions, they like best. The élite in this new empire of ignorance are those who know the most pre-thought thoughts.

Mass dumbness is vital to modern society. The dumb person is wonderfully flexible clay for psychological shaping by market research, government policymakers; public-opinion leaders, and any other interest group. The more pre-thought thoughts a person has memorized, the easier it is to predict what choices he or she will make. What dumb people cannot do is think for themselves or ever be alone for very long without feeling crazy. That is the whole point of national forced schooling; we aren't supposed to be able to think for ourselves because independent thinking gets in the way of "professional" thinking, which is believed to follow rules of scientific precision.

Modern scientific stupidity masquerades as intellectual knowledge—which it is not. Real knowledge has to be earned by hard and painful thinking; it can't be generated in group discussions or group therapies but only in lonely sessions with yourself. Real knowledge is earned only by ceaseless questioning of yourself and others, and by the labor of independent verification; you can't buy it from a government agent, a social worker, a psychologist, a licensed specialist, or a schoolteacher. There isn't a public school in this country set up to allow the discovery of real knowledge—not even the best ones—although here and there individual teachers, like guerrilla fighters, sabotage the system and work toward this ideal. But since schools are set up to classify people rather than to see them as unique, even the best schoolteachers are strictly limited in the amount of questioning they can tolerate.

The new dumbness—the non thought of received ideas—is much more dangerous than simple ignorance, because it's really about thought control. In school, a washing away of the innate power of individual mind takes place, a "cleansing" so comprehensive that original thinking becomes difficult. If you don't believe this development was part of the intentional design of schooling, you should read William Torrey Harris's *The Philosophy of Education*. Harris was the U.S. Commissioner of Education at the turn of the century and the man most influential in standardizing our schools. Listen to the man.

"Ninety-nine [students] out of a hundred," writes Harris, "are automata, careful to walk in prescribed paths, careful to follow the prescribed custom." This is not all accident, Harris explains, but the "result of substantial education, which, scientifically defined, is the subsumption of the individual."

Scientific education subsumes the individual until his or her behavior becomes robotic. Those are the thoughts of the most influential U.S. Commissioner of Education we've had so far.

The great theological scholar Dietrich Bonhoeffer raised this issue of the new dumbness in his brilliant analysis of Nazism, in which he sought to comprehend how the best-schooled nation in the world, Germany, could fall under its sway. He concluded that Nazism could be understood *only* as the psychological product of good schooling. The sheer weight of received ideas, pre-thought thoughts, was so overwhelming that individuals gave up trying to assess things for themselves. Why struggle- to invent a map of the world or of the human conscience when schools and media offer thousands of ready-made maps, pre-thought thoughts?

The new dumbness is particularly deadly to middle and upper-middle-class people, who have already been made shallow by the multiple requirements to conform. Too many people, uneasily convinced that they must know something because of a degree, diploma, or license, remain so convinced until a brutal divorce, alienation from their children, loss of employment, or periodic fits of meaninglessness manage to tip the precarious mental balance of their incomplete humanity, their stillborn adult lives.

Listen to William Harris again, the dark genius of American schooling, the man who gave you scientifically age-graded classrooms:

The great purposes of school can be realized *better* in dark, airless, ugly places than in beautiful halls. It is to master the physical self, to transcend the beauty of nature. School should develop the power to withdraw from the external world.

Harris thought, a hundred years ago, that *self-alienation was the key* to a successful society. Filling the young mind with the thoughts of others and surrounding it with ugliness—that was the passport to self-alienation. Who can say that he was wrong?

I want to give you a yardstick, a gold standard, by which to measure good schooling. The Shelter Institute in Bath, Maine will teach you how to build a three thousand square-foot, multi-level Cape Cod home in three weeks' time, whatever your age. If you stay another week, it will show you how to make your own posts and beams; you'll actually cut them out and set them up. You'll learn wiring, plumbing, insulation, the works. Twenty thousand people have learned how to build a house there for about the cost of one month's tuition in public school. (Call Patsy Hennon at 207/442-7938, and she'll get you started on building your own home.) For just about the same money you can walk down the street in Bath to the Apprentice Shop at the Maine Maritime Museum [*now in Rockport—ed.*] and sign on for a one-year course (no vacations, forty hours a week) in traditional wooden boat building. The whole tuition is eight hundred dollars, but there's a catch: they won't accept you as a student until you volunteer for two weeks, so they can get to know you and you can judge what it is you're getting into. Now you've invested thirteen months and fifteen hundred dollars and you have a house and a boat. What else would you like to know? How to grow food, make clothes, repair a car, build furniture, sing? Those of you with a historical imagination will recognize Thomas Jefferson's prayer for schooling—that it would teach useful knowledge. Some places do: the best schooling in the United States today is coming out of museums, libraries, and private institutes. If anyone wants to school your kids, hold them to the standard of the Shelter Institute and you'll do fine.

As long as we're questioning public schooling, we should question whether there really is an abstraction called "the public" at all, except in the ominous calculations of social engineers. As a boy from the banks of the Monongahela River in western Pennsylvania, I find the term insulting, a cartoon of social reality. If an institution that robs people of their right to self-determination can call itself "public", if being "public" means it can turn families into agents of the state, making parents spy on and harass their sons and daughters because a schoolteacher tells them to; if they can steal your home because you can't pay its "public" school taxes, and state courts can break up your family if you refuse to allow them to tell your children what to think—then the word *public* is a label for garbage and for people who allow themselves to be treated like slaves.

A few weeks is all the Shelter Institute asks for to give you a beautiful Cape Cod home; a few months is all Maine Maritime asks for to teach you boat-building and rope-making, lobstering and sail-making, fishing and naval architecture. We have too much schooling, not too little. Hong Kong, with its short school year, whips Japan in every scientific or mathematical competition. Israel, with its long school year, can't keep up with Flemish Belgium, which has the shortest school year in the world.

Somebody's been lying to you. Sweden, a rich, healthy, and beautiful country, with a spectacular reputation for quality in everything, won't *allow* children to enter school before they're seven years old. The total length of Swedish schooling is nine years, not twelve, after which the average Swede runs circles around the over-schooled American.

> How did I survive for nearly thirty years in a system for which I feel such disgust and loathing?...I did it by becoming an active saboteur, in small ways and large.

Why don't you know these things? To whose advantage is it that you don't? When students enroll in a Swedish school, the authorities ask three questions: (1) Why do you want to go to this school? (2) What do you want to gain from the experience? (3) What are you interested in? a whole life from the everyday world around you? No, you say, And they listen to the answers. Can you build a house or a boat? Can you grow food, make clothing, dig a well, sing a song (your own song, that is), make your own children happy, weave you can't? Then listen to me—you have no business with my kid.

In my own life, with my own children, I'm sorry I lacked the courage to say what Hester Prynne, the wearer of the scarlet letter, said to the Puritan elders when they tried to take away her daughter. Alone and friendless, dirt poor, ringed about by enemies, she said, *"Over my dead body."* A few weeks ago a young woman called me from Stroudsburg, Pennsylvania to tell me the state had just insisted she stop home-schooling her little girl, Chrissie. The state was going to force her to send Chrissie to school. She said she was going to fight, first with the law, although she didn't know where the money would come from, and then by any means she had. If I had to bet on this young, single mother or the State of Pennsylvania to win, I'd bet on the lady because what I was really hearing her say was, "Over my dead body." I wish I'd been able to say that when the state came to take my own children. I didn't. But if I'm born again I promise you that's what I will say.

A few days ago I got a call from a newspaper that wanted some advice for parents about how to launch their children into school. All the reporter wanted was a sound byte from a former New York State Teacher of the Year. What I said was this:

> Don't cooperate with your children's school unless the school has come to you in person to work out a meeting of the minds—on your turf, not theirs. Only a desperado would blindly trust his children to a collection of untested strangers and hope for the best. Parents and school personnel are just plain natural adversaries. One group is trying to make a living; the other is trying to make a work of art called a family. If you allow yourself to be co-opted by flattery, seduced with worthless pay-offs such as special classes or programs, intimidated by Alice in Wonderland titles and degrees, you will become the enemy within, the extension of state schooling into your own home. Shame on you if you allow that. Your job is to educate, the schoolteacher's is to school; you work for love, the teacher for money. The interests are radically different, one an individual thing, the other a collective. You can make your own son or daughter one of a kind if you have the time and *will* to do so; school can only make them part of a hive, a herd, or an anthill.

How did I survive for nearly thirty years in a system for which I feel such disgust and loathing? I want to make a confession in the hope it will suggest strategy to other teachers: I did it by becoming an active saboteur, in small ways and large. What I did resolutely was to teach kids what I'm saying here—that schooling is bad business unless it teaches you how to build a boat or a house; that giving strangers intimate information about yourself is certainly to their advantage, but seldom to your own.

On a daily basis I consciously practiced sabotage, breaking laws regularly, forcing the fixed times and spaces of schooling to become elastic, falsifying records so the rigid curricula of those places could be what individual children needed. I threw sand in the gears by encouraging new teachers to think dialectically so they wouldn't fit into the pyramid of administration. I exploited the weakness of the school's punitive mechanism, *which depends on fear to be effective*, by challenging it visibly, showing I did not fear it, setting administrators against each other to prevent the juggernaut from crushing me. When that didn't work I recruited community forces to challenge the school—businessmen, politicians, parents, and journalists—so I would be given a wide berth. Once, under heavy assault, I asked my wife to run for school board. She got elected, fired the superintendent, and then punished his cronies in a host of imaginative ways.

But what I am *most* proud of is this: *I undermined the confidence of the young in the school institution and replaced it with confidence in their own minds and hearts.* I thumbed my nose at William Torrey Harris and gave to my children (although I was well into manhood before I shook off the effects of my own schooling) what had been given to me by the green river Monongahela and the steel city of Pittsburgh: love of family, friends, culture, and neighborhood, and a cup overflowing with self-respect. I taught my kids how to cheat destiny so successfully that they created a record of astonishing success that deserves a book someday. Some of my kids left school to go up the Amazon and live with Indian tribes to study on their own the effects of government dam-building on traditional family life; some went to Nicaragua and joined combat teams to study the amazing hold of poverty on the lives of common people in that land; some made award-winning movies; some became comedians; some succeeded at love, some failed. All learned to argue with Fate in the form of social engineering.

I hope you saw the news story a while back about a national milk price-rigging scheme in schools from Florida to Utah. Fifty-six arrests have already been made in a caper that's existed most of this century. Schools pay more for milk than any other bulk buyer. Does that surprise you? Ask your own school administrator what unit price he pays for school milk and he'll look at you like your marbles are gone. How should he know, why should he *care*? An assistant principal once said to me, "It's not *your* money. What are you getting excited about?"

What if I told you that he was the second best school administrator I met in thirty years? He was. That's the standard we've established. The waste in schools is staggering. People are hired and titles created for jobs nobody needs. There's waste in services, waste in precious time spent moving herds of children back and forth through corridors at the sound of a horn. In my experience, poor schools waste much more than rich schools, and rich schools waste more than you could believe.

The only public aspect of these places is that they function as a jobs project, although large numbers of these jobs are set aside as political patronage. Public schools can't understand how the average private school can make profit on a per-seat cost less than half the "free" public charge; they can't understand how the average religious school makes do on even less. Homeschooling is the biggest puzzle of all. A principal once said to me, "Those people must be *sick* to spend so much time with children and not get paid for it!"

Consider the fantasy of teacher certification. Teachers are licensed and paid as though they are specialists, but they rarely are. For example, a science teacher is almost never actually a scientist—a man or woman who thinks about the secrets of nature as a private passion and pursues this interest on personal time. How many science classes in this country actually make any serious attempt to discover anything or to add to human knowledge? They are orderly ways of killing time, nothing more.

Kids are set to memorizing science vocabulary, repeating well-worn procedures certain to work, chanting formulas exactly as they have been indoctrinated to chant commercials from TV. The science teacher is a publicist for political truths set down in state-approved science textbooks.

Anyone who thinks school science is the inevitable precursor of real science is very innocent, indeed; of a piece, I think, with those poor, intelligent souls who, aware that television destroys the power to think by providing pre-seen sights, pre-thought thoughts, and unwholesome fantasies, still believe somehow that PBS television must be an exception to the rule.

If you would like to know how scientists are *really* made, pick up a wonderful book called *Discovering*, published in 1989 by Harvard University Press. In it you'll learn from a prominent scientist himself that not one major scientific discovery of this century, including exotica like superconductivity, came from an academic laboratory; or a corporate or government laboratory, or a school laboratory. You could have guessed the last, but I surprised you with the others, didn't I? All came from garages, attics, and basements; all were managed with cheap, simple equipment and eccentric, personalized procedures of investigation. School is a perfect place to turn science into a religion, but it's the wrong place to learn science, for sure.

> Harris thought, a hundred years ago, that self-alienation was the key to a successful society. Who can say that he was wrong?

The specialists in English, math, social studies, and the rest of the rainbow of progressive subjects are only marginally more competent, if at all. If three million teachers were actually the specialists their licenses claim, they would be a major voice in national life and policy-making; if we are honest, we must wonder how it is possible for an army so large to be so *silent*, of such little consequence, in spite of the new hokum being retailed about "school-based management." Don't misunderstand me: teachers are frequently good people, intelligent people, talented people who work very hard. But regardless of how bright they are, how gracefully they "schoolteach," or how well they control children's behavior (which is, after all, what they are hired to do; if they can't do that, they are fired, but if they can, little else really matters), the net result of their efforts and our expense is surely very little or even nothing indeed, often it leaves children worse off in terms of mental development and character formation than they were *before* being "taught." Schools that seem to be successful almost always are made to appear so by selective enrollment of self-motivated children.

The best way into the strange world of compulsory schooling is through books. I always knew real books and schoolbooks were different, but I didn't become conscious of the particulars until I got weary one day of New York City's brainless English curriculum and decided to teach *Moby Dick* to mainstream eighth-grade English classes. I discovered that the White Whale is too big for the forty-five-minute bell breaks of a junior high school. I couldn't make it "fit." But the editors of the school edition of *Moby Dick* had provided a package of prefabricated questions and nearly a hundred interpretations of their own. Every chapter began and ended with a barrage of these interventions. I came to see that the school edition wasn't a real book at all but a disguised indoctrination. The book had been rendered teacher-proof and student-proof.

This jigsaw fragmentation, designed to make the job site safe from its employees, is usually credited to Frederick Taylor's work of sinister genius, *Scientific Management*, written at the turn of this century. But that is wrong. The system was really devised before the American Revolution, in eighteenth-century Prussia, by Frederick the Great, and honed to perfection in early nineteenth-century Prussia after its humiliating defeat by Napoleon in 1806. A new system of schooling was the instrument out of which Prussian vengeance was shaped, a system that reduced human beings during their malleable years to reliable machine parts, human machinery dependent upon the state for its mission and purpose. When Blucher's Death's Head Hussars destroyed Napoleon at Waterloo, the value of Prussian schooling was confined.

By 1819, Prussian philosophy had given the world its first laboratory of compulsory schooling. That same year Mary Shelley wrote *Frankenstein*, the story of a German intellectual who fabricated a monster out of the parts of dead bodies: compulsory schooling was the monster she had in mind, emblemized in the lurching destruction caused by a homeless, synthetic creature seeking its maker, a creature with the infinite inner pain that ambiguous family brings.

In the nineteenth century, ties between Prussia and the United States were exceedingly close, a fact unknown these days because it became embarrassing to us during the World Wars and so was removed from history books. American scholarship during the nineteenth century was almost exclusively German at its highest levels, another fact conveniently absent from popular history. From 1814 to 1900, more than fifty thousand young men from prominent American families made the pilgrimage to Prussia and other parts of Germany to study under its new system of higher education based on research instead of "teaching." Ten thousand brought back Ph.D.'s to a then-uncredentialed United States, preempting most of the available intellectual and technical work.

Prussian education was the national obsession among American political leaders, industrialists, clergy, and university people. In 1845, the Prussian emperor was even asked to adjudicate the boundary between Canada and the United States! Virtually every founding father of American compulsory schooling went to Prussia to study its clockwork schoolrooms firsthand. Horace Mann's *Seventh Report To The Boston School Committee of 1844* was substantially devoted to glowing praise of Prussian accomplishments and how they should become our own. Victor Cousin's book on Prussian schooling was the talk of our country about the same time. When, only a quarter-century later, Prussia crushed France in a brief war and performed the miracle of unifying Germany, it seemed clear that the way to unify our immigrant classes—which we so desperately sought to do—was through Prussian schooling.

By 1905, Prussian trained Americans, or Americans like John Dewey who apprenticed at Prussian-trained hands, were in command of every one of our new institutions of scientific teacher training: Columbia Teacher's College, the University of Chicago, Johns Hopkins, the University of Wisconsin, Stanford. The domination of Prussian vision, and the general domination of German philosophy and pedagogy, was a fait accompli among the leadership of American schooling.

You should care about this for the compelling reason that German practices were used here to justify removal of intellectual material from the curriculum; it may explain why your own children cannot think. That was the Prussian way—to train only a leadership cadre to think.

Of all the men whose vision excited the architects of the new Prussianized American school machine, the most exciting were a German philosopher named Hegel and a German doctor named Wilhelm Wundt. In Wundt's laboratory the techniques of psychophysics (what today we might call "experimental psychology") were refined. Thanks to his work, it took only a little imagination to see an awesome new world emerging—for Wundt had demonstrated convincingly to his American students that people were only complex machines!

Man a machine? The implications were exhilarating, promising liberation from the ancient shackles of tradition, culture, morality, and religion. Adjustment became the watchword of schools and social welfare offices. G. Stanley Hall, one of Wundt's personal protégés (who as a professor at Johns Hopkins had inoculated his star pupil, John Dewey, with the German virus), now joined with Thorndike, his German-trained colleague at Columbia Teacher's College, to beat the drum for national standardized testing. Hall sponsored and promoted an American tour for the Austrian doctor Sigmund Freud so that Freud might popularize his theory that parents and family were the cause of virtually all maladjustment—all the more reason to remove their little machines to the safety of schools.

In the minds of disciples of German educational thought, scientific education was primarily a way of forcing people to fit. With such a "technical" goal in mind, the future course of American schooling was determined, and with massive financial support from the foundations—especially those of the Rockefeller and Carnegie families—new scientific colleges to share teachers were established. In Prussia these were aptly called "teacher seminaries," but here secular religionists were more discreet: a priesthood of trained professionals would guard the new school-church and write its. canonical text into state law. Thus the Torah of twentieth century compulsory schooling was in its Ark by 1895, one third of the way through the reign of William Torrey Harris as U.S. Commissioner of Education.

Teacher training in Prussia was founded on three premises, which the United States subsequently borrowed. The first of these is that the state is sovereign, the only true parent of children. Its corollary is that *biological parents are the enemies of their offspring.* When Germany's Froebel invented Kindergarten, it was not a garden for children he had in mind but a garden *of* children, in which state-appointed teachers were the gardeners of the children. Kindergarten is meant to protect children from their own mothers.

The second premise of Prussian schooling is that intellectual training *is not the purpose of state schooling*—obedience and subordination are. In fact, intellectual training will invariably subvert obedience unless it is rigidly controlled and doled out as a reward for obedience. If the will could be broken all else would follow. Keep in mind that will-breaking was the central logic of child-rearing among our own Puritan colonists, and you will see the natural affinity that exists between Prussian seeds and Puritan soil—from which agriculture our compulsory schooling law springs. The best-known device to break the will of the young, practiced for centuries among English and German upper classes, was the separation of parent and child at an early age. Here now was an institution backed by the police power of the state to guarantee that separation. But it was not enough to compel obedience by intimidation. *The child must be brought to love its synthetic parent.* When George Orwell's protagonist in 1984 realizes that he loves Big Brother after betraying his lover to the state, we have a dramatic embodiment of the sexual destination of Prussian-type schooling; it creates a willingness to sell out your own family, friends, culture, and religion for your new lover, the state. Twelve years of arbitrary punishment and reward in the confinement of a classroom is ample time to condition any child to believe that he who wields red pen-power is the true parent, and they who control the buzzers must be gods.

The third premise of Prussian training is that *the schoolroom and the workplace shall be dumbed down into simplified fragments that anyone, however dumb, can memorize and operate.* This solves the historical dilemma of leadership: a disobedient work force could be replaced quickly, without damage to production, if the workers required only habit, not mind, to function properly. This strategy paid off recently during the national strike of air traffic controllers, when the entire force of these supposed "experts" was replaced overnight by management personnel and hastily trained fill-ins. There was no increase in accidents across the system! If anyone can do any particular job there's no reason to pay them very much except to guarantee employee loyalty and dependency—a form of love which bad parents often extort from their young in the same way.

In the training ground of the classroom, everything is reduced to bits under close management control. This allows progress to be quantified into precise rankings to track students throughout their careers—the great irony being that it's not intellectual growth that grades and reports really measure, but obedience to authority. That's why regular disclosures about the lack of correlation between standardized test scores and performance do not end the use of these surveillance mechanisms. What they actually measure is the tractability of the student, and this they do quite accurately. Is it of value to know who is docile and who may not be? You tell me.

Finally, if workers or students have little or no idea how their own part fits into the whole, if they are unable to make decisions, grow food, build a home or boat, or even entertain themselves, then political and economic stability will reign because only a carefully screened and seasoned leadership will know how things work. Uninitiated citizens will not even know what questions should be asked, let alone where the answers might be found. This is sophisticated pedagogy indeed, if far from what mother and father expect when they send Junior to school. This is what the religious Right is talking about when it claims that schooling is a secular religion. If you can think independently of pre-thought thoughts and received wisdom, you must certainly arrive at the same conclusion, whatever your private theology. Schooling is our official state religion; in no way is it a neutral vehicle for learning.

The sheer craziness of what we do to our children should have been sufficient cause to stop it once the lunacy was manifest in increased social pathology, but a crucial development forestalled corrective action: schooling became the biggest business of all. Suddenly there were jobs, titles, careers, prestige, and contracts to protect. As a country we've never had the luxury of a political or a religious or a cultural consensus. As a synthetic state, we've had only economic consensus: unity is achieved by making everyone want to get rich, or making them envy those who are.

Once a splendid economic machine like schooling was rolling, only a madman would try to stop it or to climb off its golden ascent. True, its jobs didn't seem to pay much (although its contractors *did* and *do* make fortunes), but upon closer inspection they paid more than most. And the security for the obedient was matchless because the institution provided the best insurance that a disturbing social mobility (characteristic of a frontier society) could finally be checked. Horace Mann, Henry Barnard, William Harris, Edward Thorndike, William James, John Dewey, Stanley Hall, Charles Judd, Ellwood Cubberly, James Russell—all the great schoolmen of American history—made endless promises to industrialists and old-line American families of prominence that if the new Prussian scheme were given support, prospects of a revolution here would vanish. (What a great irony that in a revolutionary nation the most effective motivator of leadership was the guarantee that another one could be prevented!)

Schools would be the insurance policy for a new industrial order which, as an unfortunate by-product of its operations, would destroy the American family, the small farmer, the landscape, the air, the water, the religious base of community life, the time-honored covenant that Americans could rise and fall by their own efforts. This industrial order would destroy democracy itself, and the promise held out to common men and women that if they were ever backed into a corner by their leaders, they might change things overnight at the ballot box.

I hope you can see now that this Prussian theory of workplaces and schools isn't just some historical oddity, but is necessary to explain customary textbook structure and classroom procedures, which fly in the face of how people actually learn. It explains the inordinate interest the foundations of Rockefeller and Carnegie took in shaping early compulsory schooling around a standardized factory model, and it sheds light on many mysterious aspects of modem American culture: for instance, why, in a democracy, can't citizens be *automatically* registered at birth to vote, once and for all?

Compulsory schooling has been, from the beginning, a scheme of indoctrination into the new concept of mass man, an important part of which was the creation of a proletariat. According to Auguste Comte (surely the godfather of scientific schooling), you could create a useful proletariat class by breaking connections between children and their families, their communities, their God, and themselves. Remember William Harris's belief that self-alienation was the key to successful schooling! Of course it is. These connections have to be broken to create a dependable citizenry because, if left alive, the loyalties they foster are unpredictable and unmanageable. People who maintain such relationships often say, "Over my dead body." How can states operate that way?

Think of government schooling as a vast behavior clinic designed to create a harmless proletariat, the most important part of which is a professional proletariat of lawyers, doctors, engineers, managers, government people, and schoolteachers. This professional proletariat, more homeless than the poor and the sub-poor, is held hostage by its addiction to luxury and security, and by its fear that the licensing monopoly might be changed by any change in governance. The main service it renders—advice—is contaminated by self interest. We are all dying from it, the professional proletariat faster than anyone. It is their children who commit literal suicide with such regularity, not the children of the poor. ...

Printing questions at the end of chapters is a deliberate way of dumbing down a text to make it teacher-proof. We've done it so long that nobody examines the premises under the practice or sees the permanent reduction in mental sovereignty it causes. Just as science teachers were never supposed to be actual scientists, literature teachers weren't supposed to be original thinkers who brought original questions to the text.

> Well-schooled people, like schoolbooks, are very much alike. Propagandists have known for a century that people are easier to lead than ignorant people.

In 1926, Bertrand Russell said casually that the United States was the first nation in human history to deliberately deny its children the tools of critical thinking; actually Prussia was first, we were second. The school edition of *Moby Dick* asked all the right questions, so I had to throw it away. Real books don't do that. They let readers actively participate with their own questions. Books that show you the best questions to ask aren't just stupid, they hurt the intellect under the guise of helping it, just as standardized tests do.

Well-schooled people, like schoolbooks, are very much alike. Propagandists have known for a century that school-educated people are easier to lead than ignorant people—as Dietrich Bonhoeffer confirmed in his studies of Nazism.

It's very useful for some people that our form of schooling tells children what to think about, how to think about it, and when to think about it. It's very useful to some groups that children are trained to be dependent on experts, to react to titles instead of judging the real men and women who hide behind the titles. It isn't very healthy for families and neighborhoods, cultures and religions. But then school was never about those things anyway: that's why we don't have them around anymore. You can thank government schooling for that.

I think it would be fair to say that the overwhelming majority of people who make schools work today are unaware *why* they fail to give us successful human beings, no matter how much money is spent or how much good will is expended on reform efforts. This explains the inevitable temptation to find villains and to cast blame—on bad teaching, bad parents, bad children, or penurious taxpayers.

The thought that school may be a brilliantly conceived social engine that works *exactly* as it was designed to work and produces *exactly* the human products it was designed to produce establishes a different relation to the usual demonologies. Seeing school as a triumph of human ingenuity, as a glorious success, forces us to consider whether we *want* this kind of success, and if not, to envision something of value in its place. And it forces us to challenge whether there is a "we," a national consensus sufficient to justify looking for one right way rather than dozens or even hundreds of right ways. I don't think there is.

Museums and institutes of useful knowledge travel a different road than schools. Consider the difference between librarians and schoolteachers. Librarians are custodians of real books and real readers; schoolteachers are custodians of schoolbooks and indentured readers. Somewhere in the difference is the Rosetta Stone that reveals how education is one thing, schooling another.

Begin with the setting and social arrangement of a library. The ones I've visited all over the country invariably are comfortable and quiet, places where you can read rather than just pretend to read. How important this silence is. Schools are never silent.

People of all ages work side by side in libraries, not just a pack of age-segregated kids. For some reason, libraries do not segregate by age nor do they presume to segregate readers by questionable tests of reading ability. Just as the people who decoded the secrets of farming or of the forests and oceans were not segregated by age or test scores, the library seems to have intuited that common human judgment is adequate to most learning decisions.

The librarian doesn't tell me what to read, doesn't tell me the sequence of reading I have to follow, doesn't grade my reading. Librarians act as if they trust their customers. The librarian lets me ask my own questions and helps me when I need help, not when the library decides I need it. If I feel like reading in the same place all day long, that seems to be OK with the library. It doesn't tell me to stop reading at regular intervals by ringing a bell in my ear. The library keeps its nose out of my home, too. It doesn't send letters to my mother reporting on my library behavior; it doesn't make recommendations or issue orders on how I should use my time spent outside of the library.

The library doesn't have a tracking system. Everyone is mixed together there, and no private files exist detailing my past victories and defeats as a patron. If the books I want are available, I get them by requesting them—even if that deprives some more gifted reader, who comes a minute later. The library doesn't presume to determine which of us is more qualified to read that book; it doesn't play favorites. It is a very class-blind, talent-blind place, appropriately reflecting our historic political ideals in a way that puts schools to shame.

The public library isn't into public humiliation the way schools seem to be. It never posts ranked lists of good and bad readers for all to see. Presumably it considers good reading its own reward, not requiring additional accolades, and it has resisted the temptation to hold up good reading as a moral goad to bad readers. One of the strangest differences between libraries and schools, in New York City at least, is that you almost never see a kid behaving badly in a library or waving a gun there—even though bad kids have exactly the same access to libraries as good kids do. Bad kids seem to respect libraries, a curious phenomenon which may well be an unconscious response to the automatic respect libraries bestow blindly on everyone. Even people who don't like to read like libraries from time to time; in fact, they are such generally wonderful places I wonder why we haven't made them compulsory—and all alike, of course, too.

Here's another angle to consider: the library never makes predictions about my general future based on my past reading habits, nor does it hint that my days will be happier if I read Shakespeare rather than Barbara Cartland. The library tolerates eccentric reading habits because it realizes that free men and women are often very eccentric.

And finally, the library has real books, not schoolbooks. Its volumes are not written by collective pens or picked by politically correct screening committees. Real books conform only to the private curriculum of each writer, not to the invisible curriculum of some German collective agenda. The one exception to this is children's books—but no sensible child ever reads those things, so the damage from them is minimal.

Real books are deeply subversive of collectivization. They are the best known way to escape herd behavior, because they are vehicles transporting their reader into deep caverns of absolute solitude where nobody else can visit: No two people ever read the same great book. Real books disgust the totalitarian mind because they generate uncontrollable mental growth—and it cannot be monitored!

Television has entered the classroom because it is a collective mechanism and, as such, much superior to textbooks; similarly, slides, audio tapes, group games, and so on meet the need to collectivize, which is a central purpose of mass schooling. This is the famous "socialization" that schools do so well. Schoolbooks, on the other hand, are paper tools that reinforce school routines of close-order drill, public mythology, endless surveillance, global ranking, and constant intimidation.

That's what the questions at the end of chapters are designed to do, to bring you back to a reality in which you are subordinate. Nobody really expects you to answer those questions, not even the teacher; they work their harm solely by being there. That is their genius. Schoolbooks are a crowd-control device. Only the very innocent and well-schooled see any difference between good ones and bad ones; both kinds do the same work. In that respect they are much like television programming, the function of which, as a plug in narcotic, is infinitely more powerful than any trivial differences between good programs and bad.

Real books educate, schoolbooks school, and thus libraries and library policies are a major clue to the reform of American schooling. When you take the free will and solitude out of education it becomes schooling. You can't have it both ways.

[Reprinted from The Sun] *This is the text of a speech John Gatto delivered several years ago at the University of Texas in Austin. A friend from Texas sent it to me. Ed.*

And here's one more of John's passionate essays exploring the roots of our society's problem of ambivalent acceptance/rejection of real democracy. This is only the first half of it, and I hope John will forgive me for cutting it short, but I think what I have had space for gives the gist of his argument pretty well!

SOME THOUGHTS ON THE NATIONAL SOCIALIZATION OF CHILDREN
by John Taylor Gatto

American institutions were born in a revolt from the tyranny of a centralized government symbolized in the British monarchy and mercantilism.
> —E. Digby Baltzell, *The Philadelphia Gentleman*

In the past 75-100 years two ideas came insidiously into American political life in the shadow arena of public policy-making. One, the notion that common people thinking for themselves constitute a crisis of governance; the other, that local control of education must be stamped out and transferred through a series of progressively remoter masking layers to a small centralized élite of decision makers.

What élite would have the hubris[1] to want such control in a democracy? Or in a democratic republic! in which final choices are in the hands of an elected leadership, not a group of self-appointed ones?

Prior to 1850 such an élite—had it been felt necessary to convene one—would have been composed mostly of landed aristocracy and trading families; after 1890 it would have been a more professionalized leadership: university voices, foundation officials, mass media powers, members of key associations like NAM, CFR, FPA, CED, NAC, or BAC/BC/BR,[2] all representing various powerful interests. But as the twentieth century closes

---

1. Hubris: chutzpah, arrogance, swelled heads, megalomania, take your pick.

2. For purposes of this argument the names behind these initials are irrelevant with one possible exception: the Business Council (BAC) became the Business Council (BC) in the sixties and in the eighties the Business Roundtable (BR),a progression from humility to grandiosity in just a hundred years.

the managing élite is seen to be visibly arising out of the same élite which runs the global corporations, speaking directly and in person, not from behind a screen of agencies.

Whether I'm right, half-right, or mostly wrong about the constituents of the élite policy layer is less important than that we all agree that *any* élite perspective, welcoming little voices at the policy table of the greater society—or to be in control of the minds of young people—simply cannot be tolerated. Democracy as a form of governance contradicts the scientific intentions of a centrally managed society. Under what kind of worldview would you have a "mass" decide important issues it can know nothing about?[3]

The only debate currently being entertained about governance among those who have reason to think they matter is whether society should function as a mechanism on the behavioral psychology model or as an *organism* made up of interacting hierarchically arranged systems, on the humanistic model. In either case democracy is considered either anachronistic or a dangerous fantasy—take your pick.

Tracking the origin of these ideas is tricky because at first glance they seem to arise out of the great scientific socialisms, out of Marx or Bismarck, perhaps Italian fascism, perhaps Franklin Roosevelt and the American experiment in welfare capitalism inherited from John Ruskin and Fabian socialism under the Webbs. But by holding your head under the cold water faucet for awhile your head clears and without difficulty you see that the operating policies of gigantic international corporations can have no use at all for democracy either.

In an engineering sense, "the will of the people" just gets in the way of scientific decision-making. Not a good diagnosis for libertarians. Now this feeling was precisely the conclusion great titans of international capitalism reached at the turn of the century just passing. That's how we got welfare capitalism. Powerful industrialists and financiers like Andrew Carnegie, J. P. Morgan, John D. Rockefeller and the like agreed to allow an exchange of relative comfort and security for a free hand wheeling and dealing without too much interference from public opinion. Many people think it was a good bargain but a fair hunk of liberty had to be surrendered, and from that time to now the children were confined to scientifically managed schools and

3. Under the world-view that "a mass" does not exist, but is an illusion of the manufacturing mind.

were scientifically managed. It was enough to satisfy the élite leaders until about 1975. Since then they've wanted much more.

If we are to understand the well-orchestrated campaign underway to set national goals and standards, have national testing, national teaching licenses, curriculum, etc., we need to take a closer look at words like "democracy" and "liberty" and "the state, the family, the individual"—because if nationalization of schooling comes about, the definitions of all those things are going to change. We have near monopoly government schooling right now which has already twisted our historic notion of individual liberty; national pedagogy would make us a lot like Germany, which is, I think, its intended function; so it will be necessary in a while to talk about what that really means.

I'm aware that from a libertarian perspective the tyranny of mobs is seen as great a danger as the tyranny of states, but from where I stand, government is the worse threat because its incursions are written in laws, licensing, taxes, police powers and permanent bureaucracies—while mob passion is always a transient phenomenon. The brilliant dialectical balance struck in the U.S. was to allow the people's will free expression as a check on the power of government (this was dramatically illustrated in the street riots of the Vietnam period), and to allow government power to check the tendency of public opinion to interfere with individual rights. In the push/pull of democracy vs. that state, space for persona, family, and small group sovereignty is kept open.

A vigorous democracy is our guarantee of liberty, but thinking for an instant of liberty as a philosophical value you can see it isn't compatible with scientific management. Liberty is the right to follow your own star, to raise your children as you choose, whether the scientific managers of society like it or not. Liberty is that thing out of which independent personalities arise. No independent identity can survive too much close direction of its behavior by strangers; by loved ones and neighbors, sometimes, but by strangers, the non-poisonous dose is strictly limited. Liberty can be seen as an evolutionary principle because with hundreds of millions of people free to plan their own lives the chances of serendipity are much much greater than if only a few thousand, functioning as policy-makers, tell everyone else—and all the children—where to go and what to think.

It is the constant confrontation, the unwinnable war—between the collectivizing principle in government and the much different collectivizing principle in democracy which produces liberty for those who want it. In the stalemate of these forces, freedom escapes. Any serious government sabotage of democracy must be opposed with energy because it would threaten the dialectic which produces liberty.

Three sharp demonstrations of the power of democratic expression, the first in 1832, the second between 1885-1895 and the third from 1965-1973, determined what kind of public schools we got and set off the current drive to nationalize them. But ironically, school was *not* a response to democratic demand; just the opposite: it was the response of frightened and angered élites to democratic muscle flexings. I'll take them on one at a time.

1) The need to colonize the minds of common children first took root in Boston and Philadelphia in 1832 because the tremendous power Jacksonian democracy unleashed was frightening to Unitarian Boston; and when Jackson broke Biddle's National Bank, it became frightening to Quaker Philadelphia, too. A great many comfortable, complacent men woke up the day after, realizing the potential of the institution. They did not like what they saw.

An idea that had been around for centuries (since Plato in fact), government compulsion schools, seemed to some as if it might nip democracy's career in the bud. If young minds could be massed away from the sight of their parents and the working community, as Rousseau had advised in his book *Emile*, a cure for democracy was possible by instilling a kind of internal governor in children. This governor would direct them to listen closely to authorities other than mother or father or the local minister. Installed early enough this might check the potency of public opinion by the ancient Roman principle of divide and conquer. School would have other uses, of course, but keeping another Jackson out of office was a major motivation, or keeping him relatively powerless if a second Jackson did get in. Exactly one year after Jackson left office, the famous "Boston School Committee" which was fifteen years later to give our free country compulsion schooling, opened up shop under the direction of ambitious politician, Horace Mann,[4] and fifteen years later Massachusetts was our first state with compulsion schooling.

---

4. Mann was a son-in-law to the famous Peabody family, in the congregation of legendary Unitarian William Ellery Channing. A little later, Peabodies went partners with young J. P. Morgan, and after the Civil War became the main proseletizers for compulsion schooling in the South. Mann's sister-in-law, Elizabeth, was a principal mover in American education.

This first phase of schooling, from 1852 until the 1890's, was pretty much a dud. The school year was only 12-20 weeks long, the dynamic structure of one-room schooling was superb at teaching literacy in word and number, argumentation, public performance, etc. at low costs, and there was more than enough flex in the system for liberty to survive.

2) But in the same way as the democratic expression under Jackson motivated schoolmakers to get compulsion laws passed, the populist immigrant uprising of the 1880's and 1890's demonstrated to the managers of society that people were not being sufficiently controlled by short-term one room schooling, chautauquas, and the other ministries of the day. Careful plans were now laid for a new form of longer confinement schooling, one which could be tied to the economy. It would no longer be so easy to get a *job* or a license if you hadn't learned your lessons. This particular turn of the screw was originally Andrew Carnegie's idea. Just because you could argue a legal case like Lincoln, or build a fine building like Frank Lloyd Wright was no longer going to be sufficient. In the new system you would have to prove yourself to the state, on the state's terms. And no appeal from its decision.

And a huge, multi-tiered bureaucracy of management was set into place over school teachers in order to make the classroom teacher-proof; books were centrally approved and ordered—what once had been an individual decision; the community could no longer pick its own teachers, now the state licensed them. By 1930 schools had become teacher-proof, parent-proof, and thanks to a long school day and year, student-proof. This massive response to the democratic resistance to industrialization gave us the schools we had until about 1975.

3) Today we are faced with an even more radical centralization of state power hidden behind various proposals for the national socialization of schoolchildren, an initiative propelled by memories of a third populist revolt, one I'll talk about shortly. If it succeeds, we can expect the already stifling orthodoxy of government schooling, especially on the mostly bogus "gifted and talented" level, to become total. You can expect a lot of talk about "teaching the whole child" and "parents as teachers" and "multiculturalism" and "choice", but it will be bologna any way you slice it: the last two radical centralizations had their press agents, too.

In a national system the important goals, decisions, texts, methods, and personnel are displaced from local hands to invisible hands far away. Even in phase two schooling this happened to an extreme degree and the psychological effects of being "managed" are already all around us. Displaced decision-making tends to cause general apathy.

One striking example of this apathy directly resulted from the "great transformation" to a planned pedagogy/planned society at the beginning of the century and is still with us. Prior to 1880 about 80-88% of Americans eligible to vote voted; after 1930 about 25% of the eligible voters voted—a contingent over *twice* as large was now eligible in the later period because woman now had the franchise. But it did no good, the citizenry stopped voting and has remained dormant ever since. If my words puzzle you, remember that the percentage of vote tabulated is a ratio of *registered* voters, and as of 1992 only a bit more than half of the total pool bothered to register.

This political apathy is not an accident but has been designed into the system for reasons we discussed earlier; in a management science model, public participation in decision-making is not a desirable thing. If nationally socializing children increases their apathy—as I expect it to do—the future of democratic politics will not be a glorious one.

In 1893 Frederick Jackson Turner, the historian, offered a theory that a mere accident of geography had given us working democracy. That accident was the presence of a moving frontier. By 1890 the frontier was gone. Turner implied we might expect democracy to erode without its help. Whatever the truth of the alleged connection, democracy has steadily eroded ever since and the centralization of schooling constitutes one of the principal causes. By 1965 the situation was as John Dewey had predicted in 1900, the business of the country was decided by large associations working in concert for the most part, however nominally they disagreed. Virtually the entire national economy was tied with strings to schooling as Andrew Carnegie advocated. And by 1965 this intricately balanced, reciprocating social machine was involved in an undeclared war in southeast Asia. Effective democratic access to war-making decisions was impossible. Here was the world of the future envisioned in 1890; thanks to centralized schooling and other forms of central regulation scientific management prevailed.

Or so it seemed until the streets began to fill with nobodies shouting, unfathomable, "Hell no, I won't go!" and "Hey, hey, LBJ, How many kids did you kill today?" One presidency collapsed and another was grievously wounded; military loyalty, the bulwark of the republic was suddenly in question, and a disturbing number of front-line officers were shot to death from the rear by their own troops. "The people", that grand meaningless abstraction élites use to describe anyone outside the loop of decision-making, had come to the policy table uninvited.

Here was an event as significant as the first outbreak of popular democracy under Jackson in 1830, as significant as the great national strikes of the 1880's—soon after the war furor subsided in 1973, calls for a better, tighter system of national schooling began to be heard more often, from many different quarters. A campaign was being carefully orchestrated from the usual quarters: key foundation centers, the Business Roundtable, other important associations, the most important universities, and a powerful nucleus group in the mass media, to make a final end to local control, to more completely tie work to school training, performance, and behavior, and to nationalize the goals, procedures, assessments, and personnel of schooling once and for all. How could a nation founded only three lifetimes ago on the principle of a weak state and a strong society now have utterly reversed the founding formula? How have we gotten a huge and powerful state and an unhappy, disintegrating society in its place? I can ask the question but only partially answer it here, yet the part of the puzzle I have is a vital one: we are dealing with a crisis of democracy which has been provoked by the unacceptable power democracy represents to other centers of power. Government and governmental institutions like schools are used to order and regulate society rather than allowing the free market mechanisms of *un*-monitored reflection and choice to determine the social order and its regulations. What is happening is *profoundly* un-free, profoundly manipulative, and profoundly destructive to our traditions of liberty.

An entire intellectual class has been subtly seduced into believing the planet is imperiled by the individuality and free choices of common people and this class has been enlisted to propagandize for a final end to freedom. A representative piece of evidence is found on the last page of Karl Polyani's magnificent study of the political origins of our times [*The Great Transformation*]. As his book ends, Polyani addresses the need to destroy common liberty to save the planet. He says "we must be resigned to the reality of the end of our liberty as we are resigned to the reality of death". The end of liberty is a necessary evil, but by redefining freedom as "a collective thing" the loss of liberty will not hurt so much. This redefining of root concepts to manipulate attitudes is not, of course, uncommon in these end-of-days times—all of us are familiar with the relentless attempts to redefine the word "family", or the destruction of the children in Waco, Texas by our government in order to save them—but it is something to watch out for particularly in the language employed by the national socializers of schooling.

If my guess is correct, Polyani's redefinition of "liberty" requires first a massive assault of "democracy" because public will mobilized is strong enough to overturn the will of the state. And as I said at the beginning, the *impasse* between state power and public power is what creates liberty—for those who want it.

School is the most effective tool ever devised to prevent individual will from forming and public will from coalescing. But it only works if its texts and procedures, goals and human relations, can he determined from afar. Centralized management in its turn requires that outside influences of students like families be weakened, that student loyalties be suborned by continual references to school/job linkages and an onrushing future, and that the bulk of the student population be dumbed down. This conjures up the most sinister images of conspiracy, but it is *crucial* if you are to make use of these ideas to help yourself that you see the dumbing down as a simple management technique growing out of a philosophy of social order (and probably a theology of strict materialism). *If you think of the people who do this as bad guys, you are lost;* indeed it's useless to see them as real human beings. Better to see them as mere machines programmed to perform a function; you can break the machine, sabotage it, or try to avoid it, but it is a suicidal waste of time to try to negotiate with it.

Dumbing kids down is essential not only for management reasons but increasingly it will become a political necessity because the centralized economy will provide less and less work of real substance. Thinking people unemployed, dispossessed, or given busy work are political dynamite. What has been done to the African-American population since about 1955 is going to have to be done to others if the present economic course—where all work is sucked up into immense government agencies, immense institutions, and gigantic global corporations—is to continue to its logical conclusion. One way to look at the international trade treaties, the de-industrialization of America, and the ongoing attempts to give the United Nations a permanent military presence is to see it as part of a strategy to place the power to change things beyond the reach of democratic citizenries; one way to look at the dumbing down of government compulsion schools is to place the power to change things, or even to *assemble effectively*, beyond the power of individuals and families.

Two crazy ideas have been abroad for most of the twentieth century. One, dumbing children down so they are unable to use our democratic machinery and traditions to defend themselves against a managed society and find their way to a freer one; and two, eliminating local control of schooling goals and procedures can be muzzled and replaced by the hired voices of social managers. As the century ends, a sophisticated modification of this plan is going on. The global business strategy called "Management By Objectives" has appeared in pedagogical form as "Outcomes Based Education" in concert with a variety of "free-choice" plans which will nominally return control to localities. The *apparent* concession in "voucher", "tax credit" and "charter school" plans can be easily contraverted by imposing a template of state-mandated goals, requirements for testing and assessment, controls on who is eligible to teach, requirements to purchase supplies from approved lists, and other soft-core sanctions of this type. Under a system of centralized management such as I've just described, the efficiency of central management—however invisible and low-key the new system makes it—would be vastly improved. The *feeling* of freedom and dignity would remove a great deal of friction from the school machine, dissent would be made to appear brutish ingratitude (or worse, from the dissenter's point of view, a psychological impairment to be "adjusted"), and the costs of schooling would be certain to drop (because internal management of classrooms would replace expensive external, friction producing management).

The advantage to a philosophy of scientific social management of *dispersing* the present system is great enough that although the present system works fairly well (barring the occasional Vietnam rioting) I would expect to see versions of the newer, "freer" way thriving by 2005. But that advantage *only* exists if at least the degree of centralized direction existing today can be maintained. For that reason I can guarantee you that "choice" in whatever form will only come equipped with "goals, standards, assessments" and probably some extension of the licensing function.

The hopeful fact for a liberty-lover is that such a dispersed national system will be much easier to sabotage by local action than the present one is; the downside lies in the probability that individualized schools*will police themselves* even more rigidly and thoroughly than is presently possible in the adversarial system we have.

Make no mistake about it, both "choice" and "national schooling" of some type are coming because it is in the interest of the state to allow them soon (just as it is in state interests to appear at present to *resist* the pressures to liberalize the current system, to be properly deliberative about changing it, etc.)

Is there any visible evidence that such anti-democratic motives are loose among the managers of society? Is this merely the fantasy of an old schoolteacher? Let me mention a few things casually. Once you begin to see the rules of the game the evidence is abundant:

In January of 1995*Time* magazine ran a cover story ostensibly to protest the unwarranted reach talk show hosts have into the public mind. Under that surface argument a revealing subtext played which I can paraphrase as this. "Too much democracy is in the worst interests of our national goals: the world is too complex to allow common people to shape the decisions of management."

Using our provisional theory that democratic outbursts always provoke antithetical attempts to foreclose democracy, I didn't have to look far to determine what put the bee in *Time's* bonnet. It was the dramatic turnaround in the Fall, 1994, elections. Neither *Time* nor anyone who matters cared that one party's control replaced another's for at least two reasons:

1) Congress has lost most of its power in this century because it is too accessible to the democratic impulse. If you don't call giving up the constitutionally granted money power to the private banks of the Federal Reserve a loss of power, or giving up the war-making power in all but name real losses of real power, then you won't understand my reference. But in national decision-making our legislative branch has been crippled badly.

2). In important national matters like bombing Iraq or surrendering national sovereignty to trade treaties like GATT and NAFTA the U.S. is virtually a one-party state, political labels mean so little.

So how can I argue simultaneously that the elections didn't matter and that they did, too? Easy. What mattered was the shock sent through the world of spin-doctors that decisive public opinion can still be generated by voices outside the power-loop. In this case, whether it was the Christian Coalition or a national disgust at being managed matters less than that this was not supposed to be possible after an age of manufacturing consent. How can a properly dumbed down public slip its leash and sink its fangs into the trainer? Hence the *Time* cover story about the inadvisability of too much democracy—to take a sounding in troubled waters.

Now from this trivial example let me rush you to the big time. Twenty years ago an international policy élite called the

Trilateral Commission sponsored a book called *The Crisis of Democracy* published, I believe, in 1975 by New York University Press; it was widely read and discussed by policy-makers in this country and overseas. The book's thesis is that the world is suffering from a serious disease called "hyper-democracy", a sickness stemming from, you guessed it, too much political participation by common people.

International order, readers learned, was being threatened along with the progress of globalizing business. Common citizens, it seems, are *resisting* further surrender of their national identities and local allegiances. Well, how about that? Who the hell do they think they are?

The Trilateral prescription for this crisis of democracy consists of two sharp recommendations: 1) "a narrowing of the meaning of democracy;" 2) "a forceful assertion of élite control". We've already talked a bit about redefining key words like "liberty" and "democracy", but it might be useful to consider for a minute what a "forceful assertion of élite control" would look like. Historically, if we stick to this country and the past hundred years or so of attempts (mostly successful) to nationally socialize children, we might think of Andrew Carnegie's private army of Pinkertons firing from armed barges at the steel strikers of Homestead, Pennsylvania as one; the assault on the miners' tent camps in Ludlow, Colorado by private gunmen paid by John D. Rockefeller II as another[5], and perhaps the execution of strikers at Ford's River Rouge plant in the 1930's, also by hired gunmen, a third. But all of these will have meaning only for students of American history.

Fortunately, recent events are rich in illustrations of forceful assertion of élite control as well. We might think of the public extermination of Branch Davidians by fire in Waco, Texas, the execution of an unarmed woman, Mrs. Randy Weaver, and her unarmed 14-year old son by FBI snipers in Idaho several years ago, to teach her husband and his supporters a lesson, or the most forceful illustration of all: the spectacular immolation of 100,000 retreating Iraqi peasants by igniting a gasoline-

---

5. On April 20th, 1914 a private army representing the interests of John T. Rockefeller II charged through tent camps containing strikers against the Rockefeller-owned Colorado coal and iron mines in armored cars raking the tents with machine-gun fire, and burning one camp to the ground with coal oil. Nineteen men, women and children were killed. No one was ever prosecuted for the killings.

drenched sky above their heads—an event seen all over the world on television—as a model of forceful display.

But melodramatics aside, I hope the concern shown by *Time* and its anti-democracy story in 1995 and the Trilateral book, *Crisis Of Democracy* in 1975 are enough to convince you that certain well-placed voices have been saying, and are saying, that lesser folk should keep their silly opinions to themselves. With only a slight effort we can track that identical attitude back to Vilfredo Pareto's *The Mind and Society*, which was a "must read" among policy-makers during the second Franklin Roosevelt presidency. Pereto's scathing remarks on majority rule, equality, and the like are wonderful to read for their honesty. If Pareto is too esoteric an allusion, then we can find exactly the Trilateral position in Walter Lippman's influential book, *Public Opinion*, 1922, where Mr. Lippman suggests the public shouldn't have any opinions, or even back to Gaetano Mescal's brilliant study of 1896, *The Ruling Class: Elements of Political Science,* which is thought to be the very book which convinced Teddy Roosevelt he needed a secret police force answerable to himself—in other words, the book which caused Roosevelt to establish the FBI, in defiance of Congress, by executive order.

Bill Kaul lives, sometimes teaches, always works—and thinks his heretical thoughts in Waterflow, NM 87421. He cares about kids and about the state of our nation's mental, philosophical, spiritual health—and most particularly, our educational system, as you can tell from these articles.

SOME NOTES TOWARD A DISINTEGRATIVE EDUCATIONAL NON-SYSTEM
by Bill Kaul

Since the time of the pre-Socratic philosophers, it has been the onus of Western (Eurocentric) education to provide a system of education. Initially, this system was not geared toward educating the young or even the masses of people: it was geared to groom wealthy young men for a successful life of public service. This is our heritage.

As Eurocentric education passed through the times of Christian (Roman) domination, it became fully enmeshed in a system that was at once metaphysical and ecclesiatically hierarchical. That is to say, it was a system designed (in Augustine's terms) to educate the same class of wealthy (or handpicked) young men not only for service in the City of Man but also in the City of God (since one was a mirror for the other).

The medieval university system was a good example of this compound purpose: its divisions of Law, Theology, Medicine, and Arts, etc. were all bound within a system which had at its head deans, ranks of professors, ranks of degrees, administrative functionaries and so forth whose role was to insure the smooth boundary subsumption of Church and State within the training. These leaders held sway not only over "subject matter" but also the bodies and souls of their charges.

This system is still the basis for our university system today, and its neat hierarchies (with their metaphysical trappings and intentions) are still in place. (If you don't believe it, just attend the installation ceremonies for a new college president sometime. Gad! It's like being in Freiburg or Paris in 1250.)

Only later did education move into the truly public arena—this in the "democratic" era, that time when the buzzword was "freedom" and "rule by the people." *Which* people, of course, would be a matter the years would decide. At first—and during the many years prior to this era—it was far too dangerous to educate the masses of people; to do so would practically insure rebellion and blatant widespread questioning of accepted teaching.

Afterward (especially in America, it has been taught) the system of "free public education" was a sign of liberty: yet the structures of education did not change—the ruling classes still had sway over not only the curriculum but also over who counted as a "free person" in terms of eligibility for education. The academic hierarchies of medieval Europe were transferred and translated, but the flow of power and the notion of complete physical and mental control over those to be educated ("students," a peculiar class of human animal) were basically unaltered. (q.v. professor Beck's social histories of education)

Hence, "education" (as it was called) was assumed to be of that (Western/Eurocentric) nature *only* by the governmental bodies which regulated it—there was no other form of education, at least none which prepared its learners to be "acceptable, useful, and productive members of society."

To see that this is a peculiarly narrow—even tortured and contorted—view of both the structure and function of education doesn't take a great deal of vision. Surely education was (and is) always happening outside of these structures, surely mothers taught their young from the first suckling, surely brothers, sisters, aunts and uncles always taught: surely the very air, sights, and sounds around any growing, nominally perceptive human were alive with teaching, quivering with lessons. Surely all humans learn, it is, in Doug Robinson's words, a "explosively human activity." It cannot be stopped. It can only be channeled, and that channeling—as noted above—is nearly always for a political purpose. The political purpose of education is nearly always linked with the hoarding of power, and those in power determine what is to be an "education." Success is determined not in the degree to which a human is integrated with its environment—it is determined by the degree to which a human is twisted to fit a job description or set of outcomes (outcomes determined not from within the learner's own cultural/personal milieu but from within the hierarchy of the academy itself.) Social maladjustment—which may be a sign of health—is diagnosed as a "problem" and is remedied by a good dose of "education."

I will say it again: learning cannot be stopped: it can only be channeled into streams or paths: those streams or paths are always laid out to a purpose: that purpose is linked to the preservation of a social order, to keeping power in its place.

The streams or paths of Western (Eurocentric) education are rooted in their aristocratic and theocratic soils, so much so that most people who are schoolers or schooled never question those structures: alternate structures are practically unthinkable without hierarchy, without careful control of outcomes and procedures.

This is a farce.

If, indeed, learning is an explosively human activity, then it behooves those involved in it to set spark to the powder keg, to begin the process of disintegration, of destruction, so that alternate visions—even personal visions—of learning can begin to take place.

I am speaking here of family, tribe, gang, group, introspective, exploratory learning, of the reintegration of the loving and caring that should in a functional family or tribe (or nation?) be the system, insofar as there is a "system."

You may call it "family" or "tribal" values—but if so, I mean it in the sense of values generated from a synthesis of the members of that tribe, not as a governmental body, but as a family body. people caring for one another: that's the system.

The subject matter is the world around us, and the question is, how do we relate to it? The method is already there: it needs no training, until it is beaten out of us through fear and intimidation and odious unrealistic ranking, it is always there. Think of a child, exploring the world around them, asking questions. Think of that child being told to learn it at school, or being told some answer that shuts off all further inquiry: think of why elders have no time to explore the world with their children: the children are in school and the elders are laboring at a job. The system continues: the child is to become the new overworked, disembodied, unattached drone.

Perhaps it is only through the disorganization and disintegration of today's social reality that a new one (maybe an old one) can be born (or reborn)—perhaps (look around!) there need be no calls for this, perhaps it is already happening.

WELCOME TO SCHOOL, PRISON, COMPOUND, WHATEVER
by Bill Kaul

From the Santa Fe Reporter, March 2, 1995, Santa Fe, New Mexico

CAPITAL FLIGHT SONG: DON'T FENCE ME IN
by Anne Constable

At 7:20 am. a teen-age boy in a white T-shirt and blue jeans already is hanging out in the parking lot of Capital High School, behind a large clump of chamisa. Parents begin arriving to drop off their kids. The parking lot gradually is filling with the cars of students who drive themselves to school. A group of boys gathers around two pickup trucks parked in adjoining spaces in the aisle farthest from the school. One newly arrived group gets into a white sedan and drives off.

Shortly after 8 a.m., the bell rings. Nobody is in a hurry. Kids continue chatting with friends in the parking lot. Others lean from the second floor balcony, watching the scene below. At 9:10 am., after nearly two hours on campus, the boy in the white T-shirt—and some of his buddies who are sporting Harley Davidson T-shirts—slouch toward the school entrance.

At 9:30 am., girls in twos and threes begin to emerge from school, get into their cars and leave campus. Nobody stops them. There is no security guard in sight. A teacher walking down a hallway with a female student listens to her protests. "I'm so bored," the student says.

The parking lot, which was full earlier in the morning, has 20 empty spaces by 11 am. A red pickup with a double cab pulls in. Four young men slump in their seats listening to music on the radio and wait for a friend. It's lunchtime. Dozens of kids head for their cars. Six girls pile into a blue Buick; another five squeeze into a tan Jeep.

A steady stream of vehicles exits the lot and heads for Cerrillos Road. Eventually there are 145 empty spaces in the student parking lot. Many of them still are empty long after classes resume.

A typical high school scene? In some ways, yes. But at Capital High School (enrollment of 1,230), hundreds of students may be absent from one or more classes each day.

(Officials say the exact total is not available, although this information is scanned into student records.) The number reported missing for the entire day is much lower. Last week it ranged from a low of 40 to a high of 210. ·

"This is a 45-acre campus with 1,200 students," says Capital Principal Andrew Rendon. "The two security guards are responsible for the classrooms, restrooms and hallways. It's next to impossible to be sure everyone is in class."

Many aren't. The ditching problem at Capital is so severe that Rendon recently announced a crackdown. In the past there has been nothing to prevent students from leaving the campus at will. Now, two new gates have been installed. Beginning this week they will be locked, except at lunch and after school is dismissed. One is located across the outlet from the parking lot, another at the entrance. A security guard will be posted at the emergency exit to check the passes of students authorized to leave campus.

"On any given day, too many kids leave campus. The number is high, too high," Rendon admits. "We are hopeful that by using the gates, once they arrive, they will remain here." Rendon says he plans to compare attendance before and after the gates are operating. Ditching has long been a problem at Santa Fe High, where a new administration is trying to deal with it. But according to at least one school board official Capital till now has been in denial about the problem.

Sophomores Teresa and Julia (not their real names) question whether the new Capital gates will be effective. Teresa started cutting classes last year at Santa Fe High with her 18-year-old boyfriend. By April she had missed so much course work that she didn't bother attending the last month at school

Transferring to Capital didn't improve her school attendance. Her friends from Santa Fe High would drive over to pick her up for lunch. They stayed away the rest of the day. According to the school Teresa has been absent without an excuse 40 times since Jan. 1, a figure she doesn't dispute. "Ditching is so fun. It's an addiction," she says.

Earlier this month Teresa's parents were summoned to the school and warned that she would be suspended for the rest of the year if she continued to ditch. Teresa, who is taking a challenging course load that includes chemistry and algebra II, agreed to a contract stipulating that she would not be tardy, cut school or break other Capital rules.

"The past month I've been trying to get back into school," she says. "I can't afford to get dropped." Her friends at Santa Fe High, however, have quit altogether.

Julia, a pretty girl with long pale hair, was caught ditching recently. "I ditched a lot last year, too," she admits. "Students are not afraid of the authority figures at school. Nobody is taking this seriously."

Capital's policy on unexcused absences is strict—at least on paper. The first time a student is absent from class, the teacher is supposed to call the parent. After the second absence, the parents are warned that another infraction can lead to a one-day suspension. Recently the school has offered community service (cleaning the grounds) as an option to suspension after a student has been caught ditching three times. The policy clearly has not been enforced in every case.

The computerized notification system that Capital (and Santa Fe High) uses to inform parents of unexcused absences is seriously flawed. It is set up to dial a telephone number for the student's parents. Trouble is, many of the numbers and addresses on file are fictitious—deliberately so. In some cases the computer doesn't reach parents or the message left on home answering machines is erased before they can listen to it.

One parent discovered her child had 13 unexcused absences last month when a school official called up to check on information from another student that the girl had withdrawn from school. The mother was never notified of the absences. Furthermore, she says, "No one I have talked to has gotten one of these phone calls."

"We will do what we can to inform parents of these absences," Rendon says. But, he adds, while some parents complain when they are not notified that their kids are ditching, others complain when they are.

"We get irate parents who are demanding that we stop calling them, that the calls are a nuisance," he says.

The announcement that Capital is installing gates was greeted by a similar mix of parental reaction. Some, according to Rendon, argued that the open campus at least gave their kids the option to attend classes in which they were interested. But, he declares, "At this point we are willing to do what is in the best interest of the children." Some of the kids ditch because, they say, school is boring. Others are lured into the practice by friends, often older boys. Sometimes kids ditch to use drugs, according to students interviewed, but more often they cruise the malls, hang out in fast-food restaurants or in the empty houses of working parents. Some ditch because they are tired out from partying the night before.

"I have friends who go to parks and sleep in their cars during the day," says one student.

Students who get used to ditching find it's tough returning to the school routine. While some say they actually enjoy their classes, one grounded ditcher said, "I don't want a better schedule, because now I'm so used to messing around."

End of Newspaper Article

...A teacher walking down a hallway with a female student listens to her protests. "I'm so bored, " the student says.

1. The Obvious.

When the students become bored, it is necessary to infuse them with a new sense of enthusiasm, not about their lives, no—enthusiasm for school, a willingness to sit in a seat in a classroom for hours and hours, to listen, to learn and learn and learn, forever and ever, school without end, amen. So, at Capital High School and institutions like it all across the USA and elsewhere, there is a problem: boredom. Well, not boredom exactly, but student maladjustment to boredom. It seems that when students express boredom by *avoiding* it, this is called "ditching" or "skipping school" or "truancy." Now, how can these students learn to be good punctual uncomplaining cogs in a corporate wheel when they can't learn the basic lesson of school: sit still, memorize, do tasks, and learn to enjoy—or at least accommodate boredom. Be physically present and do what you're told: that is the lesson. Complaining of boredom? Running away to find more exciting things to do? Unacceptable behavior! What can be done?

..."On any given day, too many kids leave campus. The number is too high," Rendon admits. "We're hopeful that by using the gates, once they arrive, they'll remain here."

2. The Solution.

Fence 'em in! Gad, it's blindingly simple! If the students don't want to be in school, build a fence and see to it that they stay in school. If mental barriers to freedom don't work, then physical ones are the next thing to try. It's as old as the saying "get 'em by the gonads and their hearts and minds will follow." See, once they are locked up in school, their cars effectively impounded and unavailable as a means of escape, *then* real learning can take place. Of course, the teachers—poor fools!—will think they are teaching "subject matter," and will cluck sympathetically as students walk with them complaining of boredom, but *really* the teachers will be imparting the most important lesson of all: *learn to enjoy boredom. When you go out into the real world, you'll have to adjust to a boring job, boring routine, boring life. So get it now. Avoid trouble later.*

What we don't want, of course, are crowds of young people following their bliss, doing what they enjoy, what they are good at. Much better they should be drunk and wandering the streets to avoid "reality." Of course, with a gate to prevent automotive getaways, people might yet *walk off* campus. And also, we must remember, the gates are not necessary to keep all students in the school; it is only when the numbers of escapees becomes "too high" (according to Principal Rendon's figures): many students (the "model prisoners") never attempt escape. *They* already know the lesson that others are hopelessly putting off. You can't escape reality. There is no escape from America, from "making a living," from "being a productive citizen." These escapees are learning valuable lessons, however—lessons of escape and trickery that will serve them well in other institutions of learning: prison, hospital, etc.

...Students are not afraid of authority figures at this school.

3. But what of escapees?

Hey, if there's no fear of authority, how effective can gates and bars and bells and guards be? There will yet be escapees. People will walk off campus. (Not a leisurely stroll, but a USMC, close-to-the-ground-duck-behind-natural-cover escape.) People will meet up with getaway vehicles after leaving on foot, or crawling through land mines and barbed wire, or whatever. What can be done about that? Fences? Land mines, etc.? Well, maybe—and maybe even a little grant money could be found to finance it in this era of prison-building. Maybe the same industries that will eventually hire these drones and workers could come up with a little cash to help insure a compliant and uncomplaining work force. Or maybe it would be easier to simply to create a new institution altogether:

The Prison-school-factory.

Yes, a combination of prison and school, it would offer the ideal alternative to duplicating three institutions in our society: a school, prison, and job all in one! I mean, why build a prison with gates and bars to keep people in, when the people who will be in prison will be these same school-skippers in a few years anyway? Go ahead and put 'em in prison and teach 'em there! Teach 'em what? Verrrry simple: teach them to work in the industry that is included in the package. No more troubles about find jobs for dropouts and ex-cons: they can't drop out and they are never "ex" anything. They stay in this institution for their entire lives. Bored? No, they won't be bored—just supply plenty of drugs, TV, and gratuitous sex, and they'll be happy. I mean, after all, nobody ever said life has to have any *meaning.*

...Students who get used to ditching find it's tough returning to the school routine.

4. Routines.

Routines are after all the heart of the system. Break the routine and the system shudders and cracks, the cogs in it come under extreme pressure and begin to overheat. Not that I'm suggesting that anyone break routines, god forbid—no, my suggestion is as above: the prison-school-factory. Why, heck, if a whole bunch of humans started wandering around—or quietly sitting, as is their wont—and seeking their bliss, their purpose in life, industry would grind to a halt. Civilization would crumble. The economy would collapse. Japan and China would take over the number one spot. And no one in his or her right mind would ever suggest *that* would be a good thing. Would they?

BATTLE OF THE TITANS

I borrowed this phrase from an account sent to us by Emanuel Pariser of the Community School in Camden, Maine, from an account he wrote for ΣΚΟΛΕ of an alternative education conference he had attended in the summer of 1995, referring to a lively and sometimes acrimonious debate between John Gatto and Bob Barr, Dean of the Education School in Boise, Idaho (whom Em characterizes as a"true believer" in good education), over the issue of whether there are signs that our public school system may be getting better or whether it is actually getting worse for our children.

The discussion that follows has to do with a similar divergence of viewpoint, this time between John Gatto and Ron Miller, founding editor of Holistic Education Review. It feels to the editor that Miller's review of John's book Dumbing Us Down belongs here rather than in the REVIEWS section so that readers may follow the "argument" concerning school reform in a context that ties it into Dan Sullivan's analysis below of the differences between "libertarians" and "greens." Ron belongs in the "green"category, whereas John Gatto is passionately "libertarian" in temperament and background, despite his protest at being labeled. They need to speak for themselves, but first, here's the setting for this great debate:

GREENS AND LIBERTARIANS
The Yin and Yang of our Political Future
by Dan Sullivan

Dan Sullivan is a contributing editor of Green Revolution, *the* newsletter of the School of Living. *His article is reprinted from the Summer, 1994 issue. Dan's analysis of major political parties may seem only tangentially relevant to the issue of education, but it is our editorial belief that this marginality is only an appearance, and that the underlying reality of the fundamental differences Dan is writing about deeply divides proponents of educational reform as well as other political, environmental and social issues because of profound disagreements about reform stemming from governmental involvement versus grassroots initiatives.*

Opinions concerning the entire "school choice" issue, for example, are deeply split along this fault line (see below for a fascinating debate between Ron Miller and John Gatto, with echoes from the sidelines by Chris Mercogliano, and a review by Michael Traugot at the end of this volume, pages 489-91, of an article on school choice by the editors of Changing Schools). *It is our belief that the tenor of these disagreements among educators cannot be fully grasped without an understanding of the historical roots of these two groups.*

Over the past three decades, people have become dissatisfied with both major parties, and two new minor parties are showing promise of growth and success. They are the Libertarian Party and the Green Party. These are not the only new parties, but they are the only ones that promise to attract people from across the political spectrum. Most other small parties are either clearly to the left of the Democrats or to the right of the Republicans. Such parties would have a place in a system that accommodates multiple parties, but are doomed to failure in a two-party system.

The Libertarian Party is made up mostly of former conservatives who object to the Republican Party's penchant for militarism and its use of government to entrench powerful interests and shield them from market forces. The Green Party is made up mostly of former liberals who object to the Democratic Party's penchant for centralized bureaucracy and its frequent hypocritical disregard for natural systems of ecological balance, ranging from the human metabolism and the family unit to the ecology of the planet.

Both minor parties attempt to adhere to guidelines that are much clearer than those of either major party. Libertarians focus on rights of individuals to control their own lives, limited only by the prohibition against interference with the rights of others. These rights include their right to the fruits of their labor and the right to freely associate and form contracts. They advocate limiting government to protecting those basic rights.

Greens advocate ten key values (ecological wisdom, grass roots democracy, social justice, nonviolence, decentralization, community-based economics, post-patriarchal values, respect for diversity, personal and global responsibility, and sustainable future focus as a guide for government as well as for their own party organization.) These different guidelines underscore basic differences between the approaches of the two parties and their members. Libertarians tend to be logical and analytical. They are confident that their principles will create an ideal society, even though they have no consensus of what that society would be like. Greens, on the other hand, tend to be more intuitive and imaginative. They have clear images of what kind of society they want, but are fuzzy about the principles on which that society would be based.

Ironically, Libertarians tend to be more Utopian and uncompromising about their political positions, and are often unable to focus on politically winnable proposals to make the system more consistent with their overall goals. Greens on the other hand, embrace immediate proposals with ease, but are often unable to show how those proposals fit in to their ultimate goals.

The most difficult differences to reconcile, however, stem from baggage that members of each party have brought with them from their former political affiliations. Most Libertarians are overly hostile to government and cling to the fiction that virtually all private fortunes are legitimately earned. Most Greens are overly hostile to free enterprise and cling to the fiction that harmony and balance can be achieved through increased government intervention.

Republicans and Democrats will never reconcile these differences, for whatever philosophical underpinnings they have are overwhelmed by vested interests that dominate their internal political processes. These vested interests thrive on keeping the distorted hostilities alive and suppressing any philosophical perspectives that might lead to rational resolution of conflict.

But because minor parties have no real power, they are still primarily guided by values and principles. Committed to pursuing truth above power, they should be more willing to challenge prejudices and expose flaws in their current positions.

There is nothing mutually exclusive between the ten key values of the Greens and the principles of the Libertarians. By reconciling these values and principles, we can bring together people whose allegiance to truth is stronger than their biases. This could be of great value to both parties, partly because any new party that wants to break into a two-party system has to appeal to a broad spectrum of voters. But even more importantly, each party needs attributes the other has to offer. Libertarians need the intuitive awareness of the Greens to keep them from losing touch with people's real values, and Greens need the analytical prowess of the Libertarians to keep them from indulging in emotional self-deception. Libertarians can teach Greens about the spirit of enterprise and the wonders of economic freedom, and Greens can teach Libertarians about the spirit of compassion and the wonders of community cohesion.

Reconciliation is absolutely necessary. Even if one of the parties could rise to power, it could do great harm by implementing its current agenda in disregard for the perspective of the other Moreover, proposals that violate values and principles of one party often violate those of the other. If members of both groups come together to discuss each other's proposals, they are likely not only to find areas of agreement, but to find conflicts between each group's proposals and its own principles. If this happens, and the two parties work in concert, they stand a real chance of overtaking one of the major parties and drastically altering the political power structure.

Many third parties have had important impacts on American politics, but the last time a political party was dislodged was when the Republicans knocked the ailing Whig party out of contention over 130 years ago. It should be noted that the Republicans were a coalition of several minor parties with seemingly differing agendas, including the Abolitionist Party, the Free-Soil Party, the American (or Know Nothing) Party, disaffected northern Democrats, and most of the members of the dying Whig Party.

A similar coalition of parties has a much better chance of repeating this success today. Anyone who looks at current national platforms of Greens and Libertarians will conclude that bringing these groups together is no easy task. For example, the Libertarian platform states dogmatically that they "oppose any and all increases in the rate of taxation or categories of taxpayers, including the elimination of deductions, exemptions, or credits in the name of "fairness," "simplicity," or "neutrality to the free market." No tax can ever be fair, simple, or neutral to the "free market." On the other hand, the national platform of the Greens leaves one with the impression that they never met a tax they didn't like.

Yet the historical roots of the Greens and the Libertarians are quite similar. That is, early movements for alternative, intentional communities that live in harmony with nature greatly influenced, and were influenced by, anarcho-syndicalists who advanced principles now embraced by the Libertarian Party. This essay will attempt to show that the differences that have emerged are due less to stated principles and values of either group than to the baggage members have brought to each party from their liberal and conservative backgrounds.

On Conservatism and Liberalism

It is said that Libertarians have a conservative philosophy and Greens have a liberal philosophy. In reality, conservatism and liberalism are mere proclivities, and do not deserve to have the name "philosophy" attached to them. People who have more power than others are inclined to conserve it, and people who have less are inclined to liberate it. In Russia, as in feudal England, conservatives wanted more government control, as government was at the root of their power. Liberals wanted more private discretion.

In the United States today, where power has been vested in private institutions, conservatives want less government and liberals want more. What passes for conservative and liberal "philosophies" is merely a set of rationalizations that power-mongers hide behind.

Conservative support for traditional approaches and liberal support for new ways of doing things also follows from the desire for power. Traditional approaches have supported those now in power, and change threatens to disrupt their power. Changes are often embraced by conservatives once they prove unable to disrupt the underpinnings of power.

For Greens and Libertarians to rise above the power-based proclivities of liberalism and conservatism, they must focus on their roots and reconcile their positions with their philosophical underpinnings.

On the Roots of the Greens

In *The Green Alternative,* a popular book among American Greens, author Brian Tokar states that "the real origin of the Green movement is the great social and political upheavals that swept the United States and the entire Western world during the 1960's." As part of that upheaval, I remember the charge by elders that we acted as though "we had invented sex." Mr. Tokar acts as though we had invented Green values.

Actually, all the innovative and vital features of the Greens stem from an earlier Green movement. The influx of disaffected liberals to the movement since the sixties has actually imbued that movement with many features early Greens would find offensive.

This periodical, *[Green Revolution],* for example, has been published more or less regularly since 1943, calling for intentional communities based on holistic living, decentralism, sharing natural bounty, freedom of trade, government by consensus, privately-generated honest monetary systems and a host of other societal reforms. Yet the founder, Ralph Borsodi, wrote extensively about the evils of the state, and would clearly oppose most of the interventionist policies brought to the Green Party by disaffected liberals and socialists. The same can be said of more famous proponents of Green values, such as Emerson and Thoreau.

The Green movement grew slowly and steadily and quite apart from mainstream liberalism throughout the sixties and seventies. In the eighties, however, it became clear that the liberal ship, and even more clear that the socialist ship, was headed for the political rocks. The left had simply lost credibility, even among those who felt oppressed by the current system. Gradually at first, discouraged leftists discovered the Green movement provided a more credible platform for their positions.

Because of their excellent communications network, additional members of the left quickly discovered the Greens, embraced their values (at least superficially), joined their ranks and proceeded to drastically alter the Green agenda. For example, early Greens pushed for keeping economies more diverse and decentralized by promoting alternative, voluntary systems, and by criticizing lavish government expenditures on interstate highways, international airports, irrigation projects, and centralized bureaucracies that discriminated against small, independent entrepreneurs. Today the National Platform of the Green Party calls for "municipalization" of industry (that is, decentralized socialism), limits on foreign trade to save Ameri-can jobs (which they insist is not protectionism), and other devices to create artificial decentralization under the guiding hand of some benevolent central authority.

The influence of Greens who are fond of government intervention (referred to as Watermelons by more libertarian Greens) seems to be strongest at the national level and weakest within most Green local organizations. Despite the National Green Platform's resemblance to a new face on the old left, many people who are genuinely attracted to Green principles are either undermining or abandoning the left-dominated Green Party USA. Specifically, the principle of decentralism is being used to challenge the right of a national committee to dictate positions to local Greens. This is fortunate for those of us interested in a coalition of Greens and Libertarians, as reconciliation between the Green Left and libertarianism is clearly impossible.

On the Roots of the Libertarian Party

The Libertarian Party was born in 1970. Like the Green Party, it has philosophical roots that extend far back into history. It emerged, however, at a time when conservatism was in decline. Just as Greens attract liberals today and are strongly influenced by the liberal agenda, Libertarians attracted conservatives and were influenced by their agenda. However, as Libertarians are more analytically rigorous, there are fewer blatant inconsistencies between their positions and their principles.

Libertarian bias tends to show up more in prioritization of issues than in any particular issue. For example, Libertarians are far more prone to complain about the capital gains tax than about many other taxes, even though there is nothing uniquely un-libertarian about that particular tax.

Many Libertarians ignore classic libertarian writings and dwell on the works of Ayn Rand, Murray Rothbard and Ludwig von Mises. The classical libertarians get mere superficial attention. For example, few have read *Tragedy of the Commons*, but many quote the title. Specifically, they are unwilling to recognize that the ecological mishaps like those referred to in that work had been absent for centuries when almost all land was common. As with the tragedy of the reservations, commons were abused because so many people had to share access to so little land. All this was a result of government sanction, allowing vast tracts of commonly held land to be appropriated by individuals without proper compensation to those who were dispossessed of access to the earth. These facts are ignored because they cannot be reconciled with pseudo-libertarian conservatism.

Just as contemporary Greens have fondness for government and contempt for private property that their forebears did not share, Libertarians take an extreme position on private property and have hostility to all forms of government that their philosophical predecessors did not share.

Their refusal to acknowledge natural limits to private property and their insistence of unlimited protection of property by the state is their one great departure from their predecessors and their principles. For example, they dismiss the following statement by John Locke, known as the father of private property:

> God save the world in common to all (hu)mankind. Whenever, in any country, the proprietor ceases to be the improver, political economy has nothing to say in defense of landed property. When the "sacredness" of property is talked of, it should be remembered that any such sacredness does not belong in the same degree to landed property.

They similarly ignore Adam Smith's statement that:

> Ground rents [land values] are a species of revenue which the owner, in many cases, enjoys without any care or attention of (her) his own. Ground rents are, therefore, perhaps a species of revenue which can best bear to have a peculiar tax imposed upon them.

Private ownership of the earth and its resources is the one area where Libertarians depart from their own philosophy.

After all, their justification of property is in the right of individuals to the fruits of their labor. Because the earth is not a labor product, land value is not the fruit of its owner's labor. Indeed, all land titles are state-granted privileges, and Libertarians deny the right of the state to grant privileges. Even here, Libertarians are on solid ground when they argue that freedom could not survive in a society where land tenure depended on bureaucratic discretion. They are split, however, over devices like land value taxation that would, with a minimum of bureaucracy, put the landless in a more tenable position with respect to land monopolists. Just as liberals dominate the National Greens, conservatives dominate the Libertarian position on this issue, though many Libertarians, including Karl Hess, former editor of the Libertarian Times, do not share that conservative position.

Again, this is a key issue for reconciliation. The Green tradition cannot be reconciled with pseudo-libertarian claims that a subset of the people can claim unlimited title to the planet.

Compromise is too often a process whereby people on each side give up what they know to be right in order to gain a supposed advantage for their interest group. What I am proposing is that each side give up supposed advantages in order to harmonize with what is right. It takes an open mind and a great deal of courage, but the results can be magnificent.

* * * * *

And now, here's the great debate. It starts with a very fine review by Ron Miller of John Gatto's book:

Dumbing Us Down:
The Hidden Curriculum of Compulsory Schooling
by John Taylor Gatto
New Society Publishers
(4527 Springfield Ave.,
Philadelphia, PA 19143),1992;
104 pages, $9.95 paper.

Reviewed by Ron Miller

John Taylor Gatto's fiery speech to the New York legislature, upon being named the state teacher of the year, was reprinted in several publications and widely circulated among alternative and radical educators, making Gatto an immediate hero within the alternative education movement. That speech, along with four other essays, are brought together in *Dumbing Us Down*, a book that should further establish Gatto as the most visible contemporary critic of public schooling. Like Paul Goodman, John Holt, Herb Kohl, Jim Herndon, and Jonathan Kozol in the 1960s, Gatto is a morally sensitive and passionate teacher who is thoroughly disgusted by the spirit-crushing regimen of mass schooling, and unafraid to say so. Both Kohl and Kozol are still writing important books that present a progressive/radical critique of schools, but Gatto (like the late John Holt) gives voice to a growing populist rebellion against schooling as such. Whether this rebellion will support or counteract the holistic education movement is an open question, to which *Dumbing Us Down* may offer some clues.

One thing must be said up front: Gatto is a superb essayist. His writing is not academic or pedantic, but a model of harnessed passion. He builds his argument carefully and smoothly and then unleashes bold attacks that cut right to the core of many problems of modern education. He clearly has a solid understanding of the historical foundations of modern education, but generally makes his own personal interpretations rather than citing sources or scholars. Indeed, his essay "The Green Monongahela" is an intimate account of his own life and how he became a teacher. He tells a simple story from early in his career, of rescuing a young Hispanic girl from the stupid injustice of the system (she later went on to become an award-winning teacher herself), that captures the essence of his moral crusade against institutional schooling.

Gatto summarizes his argument in an introductory chapter:

> Was it possible I had been hired not to enlarge children's power, but to diminish it? That seemed crazy on the face of it, but slowly I began to realize that the bells and the confinement, the crazy sequences, the age-segregation, the lack of privacy, the constant surveillance, and all the rest of the national curriculum of schooling were designed exactly as if someone had set out to prevent children from learning how to think and act, to coax them into addiction and dependent behavior.(p. xii)

In his speech to the legislature, he makes this charge explicit, describing seven "lessons" that form the heart of the compulsory curriculum.

"These are the things you pay me to teach":

1. Confusion. "Everything I teach is out of context. I teach the un-relating of everything." (p. 2)

2. Class position. "That's the real lesson of any rigged competition like school. You come.to know your place."(p. 5)

3. Indifference. "Indeed, the lesson of bells is that no work is worth finishing, so why care too deeply about anything?" (p. 6)

4. Emotional dependency. "By stars and red checks, smiles and frowns, prizes, honors, and disgraces, I teach kids to surrender their will to the predestined chain of command." (p. 7)

5. Intellectual dependency. "Of the millions of things of value to study, I decide what few we have time for, or actually it is decided by my faceless employers.... Curiosity has no important place in my work, only conformity." (p. 8) Gatto says this is "the most important lesson, that we must wait for other people, better trained than ourselves, to make the meanings of our lives." (p. 8)

6. Provisional self-esteem. "The lesson of report cards, grades and tests is that children should not trust themselves or their parents but should rely on the evaluation of certified officials. People need to be told what they are worth." (p. 11)

7. One can't hide. Surveillance is an ancient imperative, espoused by certain influential thinkers [such as Plato, Augustine, Calvin, Bacon, and Hobbes]. All these childless men ... discovered the same thing: children must be closely watched if you want to keep a society under tight central control." (pp. 11-12)

And here is the crux of Gatto's critique: In the past 125 years, social engineers have sought to keep American life under tight central control. Compulsory schooling is a deliberate effort to establish intellectual, economic, and political conformity so that society can be managed efficiently by a technocratic elite. "School," claims Gatto, "is an artifice that makes....a pyramidal social order seem inevitable, although such a premise is a fundamental betrayal of the American Revolution" (p. 15). Along with the media—especially television, which Gatto criticizes harshly in another essay—schooling removes young people from any genuine experience of community, any genuine engagement with the world or immersion in lasting relationships. It robs them of solitude and privacy. Yet these experiences are what enable us to develop self-knowledge and to grow up "fully human," argues Gatto, and he asserts that our most troubling social pathologies, such as drug abuse and violence, are the natural re-action of human lives subjected to mechanical, abstract discipline.

Gatto insistently calls for a return to genuine family and community life by rejecting the social engineering of experts and institutions. In a particularly powerful passage, he rejects the notion that a "life-and-death international competition" threatens our national existence, as *A Nation at Risk* (National Commission on Excellence in Education, 1983) warned. Such a notion is "based on a definition of productivity and the good life" that is "alienated from common human reality." True meaning is genuinely found, Gatto writes,

> ....in families, in friends, in the passage of seasons, in nature, in simple ceremonies and rituals, in curiosity, generosity, compassion, and service to others, in a decent independence and privacy, in all the free and inexpensive things out of which real families, real friends, and real communities are built.... (pp. 16-17)

And these are the things we have lost in our hierarchically managed, global empire-building society.

In the essay "We Need Less School, Not More," Gatto draws a sharp distinction between true community (in which there is open communication and shared participation) and institutional networks (which value the individual only in terms of the institution's particular goals). A network cannot be a healthy substitute for family or community, Gatto argues; it is mechanical, impersonal, and overly rational. Schooling is a prime example of this:

> If, for instance, an A average is accounted the central purpose of adolescent life—the requirements for which take most of the time and attention of the aspirant—and the worth of the individual is reckoned by victory or defeat in this abstract pursuit, then a social machine has been constructed which, by attaching purpose and meaning to essentially meaningless and fantastic behavior, will certainly dehumanize students, alienate them from their own human nature, and break the natural connection between them and their parents, to whom they would otherwise look for significant affirmations."(p. 62)

This is a brilliant, radical critique of the nature of modern schooling. Gatto has certainly earned his heroic stature with his deeply insightful observations into the very essence of what public education has become. His writings deserve to be pondered seriously by holistic teachers and can contribute a great deal of insight and energy to our work.

[But now, having done "on the one hand," our Tevye has got to do "but on the other!" Carry on Ron!]

Nevertheless, there is a fundamental issue at stake here, which could end up sharply dividing the holistic education movement if we do not sensitively address it. Gatto, like John Holt and a great many homeschoolers, holds and defends a *libertarian* social philosophy; in the John Locke/Adam Smith tradition. Gatto argues that a common (social) good arises only out of the free interaction of individuals and intimate communities pursuing their own local good. Individuals and families are seen as the primary human reality, while social forces are generally treated as a distressing nuisance. (The term "social engineers" seems to include anyone who seriously addresses social issues.)

In the spirit of dialectical discourse (honest disagreement leading to a more inclusive synthesis), which Gatto admires and knows to be the heart of genuine education, I wish to oppose the libertarian position with one that is more socially conscious. I am especially sensitive to the nuances of this question, since I spent several of my intellectual formative years as an enthusiastic student of libertarian philosophy and political theory, and still have a great deal of sympathy for it. Gatto is justified in calling for a genuine community life—to replace the stultifying power of the state, huge corporations, self-serving experts and professionals, and all impersonal institutions. Like other libertarians and homeschool advocates, however, Gatto throws the baby out with the bathwater by categorically defining "school" as an impersonal network and virtually equating educators and activists with "social engineers."

The problem is illustrated vividly in the book's closing essay, "The Congregational Principle." Here Gatto lauds the Puritan settlers of Massachusetts Bay for organizing their churches and towns largely free of higher authority, thereby bringing about local solutions to social and political questions. He explicitly recognizes the parochialism inherent in such radical localism: He discusses the towns' practice of banishing people whose religious views or personal qualities were discomfiting to the community, and he even acknowledges that dissidents (such as Quakers) were publicly humiliated and whipped (a few were also executed). Gatto's main point in relating this story is to celebrate the fact that New Englanders eventually evolved to a more open, liberal worldview—without compulsory schooling or social engineering.

But Gatto's historical interpretation is flawed by his libertarian bias and is quite unconvincing: He asserts that the colonists enjoyed "nearly unconditional local choice" in a social "free market" (pp. 90-91)—a strange claim to make for a rigidly moralistic society with a single established church! Gatto claims that New England culture was transformed by "something mysterious inside the structure of Congregationalism." (p. 90) (read: Adam Smith's "invisible hand" that magically turns self-interest into common good). But this utterly ignores the distinctly social events that forced New Englanders to alter their parochial culture in the early decades of the nineteenth century—the nationalistic impulses released by the War of 1812 (which New Englanders had bitterly and futilely opposed); Irish Catholic immigration; enlightenment and romantic movements; the rise of science, industrialism, and urban centers; and the growing tensions between North and South over trade, tariffs, and slavery. More important, it doesn't bother Gatto in the least that the liberalization of New England culture took two hundred years and probably would have taken far longer had these crucial societal events not intervened.

Libertarian thinking is a much-needed antidote to the hierarchical, mechanical power that has been amassed by social institutions in the twentieth century. We surely do need to pull the plug on these monstrous organizations. But that is not all we need to do. We live in a society that is poisoned by inequality, racism, and grossly materialistic values. We live on a planet that is threatened with biocide within the next decade or two. We simply do not have two hundred years to wait for some "invisible hand" to lead individuals and families and self-satisfied little communities to begin addressing these tremendous issues! We must find a way to incorporate personal and communal independence into a social movement that recognizes our interdependence.

As I see it, this is exactly what holistic thinking attempts to do. Holistic educators are not "social engineers"—we reject the compulsion and fragmentation and alienation of public schooling as earnestly as Gatto—but we recognize that the modern crisis demands a concrete response grounded in certain moral, philosophical and spiritual principles. Holistic politics—

otherwise known as the Green movement—explicitly embraces decentralization and personal empowerment, but within the context of severe social and ecological problems that need to be addressed. In a society of blatant inequality, how will the "free market" provide quality educational opportunity for poor children? In a society driven by addicted consumerism, how will families, on their own, deal with environmental devastation, media brainwashing, or corporate control of resources and jobs? These are problems of a social dimension, not solely a personal one. Getting rid of compulsory regimentation in school is an important part of our task, but by no means is it a panacea that will restore our society to some golden age of free people and whole families. A holistic response—not an atomistic one—is required.

The point of contention is this: Is a school necessarily an "artifice," as Gatto calls it, an impersonal network, an agent of coercion and social engineering? Or is it an organic social creation that can serve a wide variety of moral purposes, from totalitarian indoctrination to complete human liberation, depending on the predominant values of the larger culture? I hold the latter view. Compulsory, authoritarian schooling is a symptom of our social and cultural sickness, not its cause. Genuine individuality and community are purged from schools for the same reason they are so difficult to find in families today: The larger society is driven by mechanistic, reductionistic, competitive values. But holistic educators—from Johann Pestalozzi to Rudolf Steiner to progressive and whole language educators—have argued that a school can be a nurturing community, a place where young people and their families might find respite from the oppressive forces of society. Radical educators—from John Dewey and George Counts to Herb Kohl and Paulo Freire—go further, and assert that school can be an active agent of social renewal and reconstruction by empowering young people to think critically and act cooperatively against the forces that oppress them.

The value of Gatto's position is to raise a crucial question: Can public schools—government-run schools—ever truly embrace a holistic or radical pedagogy that threatens the existence of the power structure itself? Steiner raised this question. So did Holt. So does legal scholar Stephen Arons (1983). My own respect for libertarian thinking leads me to take this as a very serious and fundamental question, which holistic and radical educators often overlook. I don't know the answer to it. Here is where the dialectic, the dialogue, between libertarians and holistic/radical social activists needs to begin.

REFERENCES

Arons, S. (1983). Compelling belief: the culture of American schooling. New York: McGraw-Hill.

National Commission on Excellence in Education. (1983) A nation at risk: The imperative for educational reform. Washington, DC: Author.

And here is John Gatto's reply. The battle is joined, and we're off and running!:

Dear Editor:

I thank Ron Miller for the generous words of praise in the review of my book *Dumbing Us Down: The Hidden Curriculum of Compulsory Schooling* and at the same time am sending along some brief comments, in the spirit of the dialectic, about the "fundamental issue" (Ron's characterization) he finds at stake in my perspective.

To begin, some amendments are necessary. Ron says I hold and defend a libertarian social philosophy. While I have an approximate idea what he means by that, I live in horror of any labels (including, to be frank, "holistic") that box people in. My own observation of reality is that classification systems should not be taken seriously—they interfere with clear thought and virtually prevent discovery when they go beyond casual convenience. Having said that, let me classify myself more accurately than Ron did: The social philosophy I hold is a hybrid of Scotch-Irish folkways, Italian *Presbyterian* iconoclasm, some aristocratic seasoning (we were Lords of the Straits of Messina in the 13th century), a certain amount of classical training, a year spent with the Jesuits, a spell as altar boy for a wonderful priest who drank sacramental wine and played baseball (the Catholic strain through my Irish/German grandmother), and three decades of constant experimentation as a junior high teacher of both the near-rich and the dirt poor.

Those are the external influences of substance; internally I've tried to push beyond the conditioned circuitry to discover the perimeter of my own singularity. Still finding things out at 57. Calling me a libertarian would eventually mislead you. On the other hand I *like* most libertarians I know of (Robert Ringer being one exception, Ayn Rand another), but I could say the same of most capital "C" conservatives, too.

In an understandable urge to establish the poles of dialectic, Ron accidentally sets me up as inhabiting a location I don't live in, and misstates some of my positions. I understand the realities of book reviewing and take no offense (in his position I would hardly have done as well) but in a contest of ideas it's crucial that all parties agree what ideas are actually being contested.

In his first assertion, that I argue common social good arises only out of free interaction of individuals and intimate communities, he's about 95% accurate but the premise is an exceedingly complicated one requiring years of Jesuitical reflection to comes to terms with. I expect argument, of course, but in its nature it isn't a *debating* point but a tool designed to help people challenge their own assumptions. Challenge, that is—not necessarily discard. In the coda of this assertion Ron makes—that I believe individuals and families are the primary human reality— he is only a bit better than half right. The largest omission is the importance of nature and location. I regard the fabric of the natural world, *unaltered,* as a central part of sanity. Not a minor part, not a dismissable part, not an exchangeable part, not an amenity, but one of the few primary *essences.* In my codebook people without places are incompletely human, to move frequently is to display derangement. That accounts for the essay, "The Green Monongahela." It's in my book to demonstrate the role of place as a teacher. I am who I am because of Monongahela. If my place had been Erie I would not be who I am. I won't belabor what must seem to most "well-schooled" Americans an eccentricity, but most of human history including the best part honored this very conservative idea and lived it. The tale of Jews in history is inexplicable unless it is seen in some important part as the story of a people deprived of their place; the tale of America and its strangely Procrustean institutions is another story from the same genre.

However, if Ron had said individuals, families, rocks, trees, water, air, places are the primary human reality, he'd have been nearly right. If he'd have added our mortality and relation to the mystery we call God, completely right. But in his leap to a guess that I think something he calls "social forces" are a "distressing nuisance," he falls far short of where I really am. It's my turn now to guess, and if I guess correctly what he means by *social forces*, then "nuisance" doesn't begin to describe the distaste I feel. Substitute "horrifying psycho-pathology" and we'll be closer to the truth.

People who mind other people's business, materially, in any arbitrary way are always bad news. It's the movers and shakers; I mean, the "great" names of history. It would be impossible for me, in a short compass, to explain adequately how damaging the Pasteurs, the Copernicuses, the Columbus's, the Newtons, the Horace Manns and all the rest of the Egyptian hierarchy have really been, but the mechanism is not hard to see— each of these men (and of course they are all men, mostly childless men) short circuits the human dialectic, arrogating to themselves a false and morally corrosive authority that *creates* the dependent human mass it then "illuminates." I would follow Paul Valéry's M. le Teste in throwing the mass of prominent men in the ocean. The brilliant, and as yet largely unseen, American homeschooling movement is brilliant *precisely because* it is leaderless, lacking canonical texts, experts, and laws. At the moment true leadership emerges—which I pray will not happen—it will be co-opted, and the movement regimented, routinized, drained of its life.

I despair in the short time I have with you of explaining adequately these contentions but let me go at least a part of the distance: Short of preserving your immediate world the only justification possible—moral justification, that is—for interfering in someone else's life is that *you* know more than the other fellow does and are "intervening" (that's the "helping profession" jargon, isn't it?) "for his own good."

I reject that view in the overwhelming percentage of cases, believing with cause that the mathematical bell curve in human intelligence is a bald lie, albeit an exceedingly profitable one. What is good or bad is either a religious question or a philosophical one and not easily addressed—never by creating a demonology that relegates any individual into a *mass* that is managed for its own good. It might shed some light on that last conclusion by confessing I was deeply depressed by Jonathan Kozol's contention that money would improve the schools of the poor. It would *not*,—any more than money has improved the schools of the middle class. What money has done is to dehumanize *most* of the lives it touches, not least those in the sinecures of academia; nor could it be expected to do better in the hands of any other group than the present government gang.

What Kozol accomplished is truly depressing—by transmuting his wonderful rage into a nasty, envious petulance, he has called attention away from his hardwon, and well-deserved, role as a biographer of human Justice. All synthetic mobilizations must similarly be exercises in pen and pencil abstraction, or cynical exercises in manipulation, or display a fatal gulf between fecund natural reality and the reductionism inherent in collectivizing it.

This is a subtle thing to consider: on one hand, the best way is hands off anything outside a local reach (the architects of "global community," who date back before Plato, are the single great manifestation of Evil in human affairs), but not minds-off. I think we have an absolute obligation to preach to each other, chide each other, praise and condemn each other, take hold of hands held out for help—in Vonnegut's words, if you are no use, you must be useless. I believe that, I taught that, and as a toll for associating with my classes through much of my teaching career, I demanded a full day's community service work each week. If kids freely chose to associate with me, the price of our association was community service (which I encouraged kids to self-design). I hope you can see the difference between this kind of compulsion and the kind that social engineers effect.

The immense danger which inevitably comes to pass when you set up social machinery compelling people to be "better" is that that machinery will be inherited by people whose "better" is your own "worse." Jefferson saw that, in imploring our original legislators to give us a weak central government. Were it not for the unholy and largely unexamined close relationships between Germany (especially the synthetic state of Prussia) and the colonial and federal leadership classes, we might have followed Jefferson's prescription. Certainly it was the overwhelming choice of the common people. But the curious company of Deists and Unitarians who pulled the national strings were too enchanted with Adam Weishaupt's vision, and too intoxicated with victory and prosperity; too vicariously identified with the lessons of Frederick the Great, Prussian compulsion schools, research universities, and ultimately the deadly world view of Wilhelm Wundt to allow the nascent urges of freedom and democracy to develop. By 1850 both were stone cold dead. We have only a memory of our stillborn democracy.

There is no way to avoid the passage of effective social machinery into dirty hands; that is what history teaches to anyone with eyes. The only way to avoid this, the best defense, is to strike down ambitious organization before it grows (Cassius was right) or once grown, to combat it through relentless sabotage. That is what I did on a daily basis as a government schoolteacher, I broke the machine, I threw sand in the gears, I falsified papers, spread dissension among new recruits so subtly it was undetectable, broke laws regularly, destroyed records, undermined the confidence of the young in the institution and replaced it with confidence in self, in friends, in family, in neighborhood. I taught kids how to cheat their destiny so successfully that they created an astonishing record of successes; it is this latter course of silent warfare that much of our country's population has unconsciously chosen. It explains why few things work very well here—least of all schools. Nothing that John Gardner or Ted Sizer or (so far) Chris Whittle has done will change that need to sabotage the web that is strangling us. They ask the wrong questions and in any case would be unwilling to accept their own large contribution to the persistence of schooling problems. All sane solutions would eliminate them!

The only acceptable way to make people "better," your own children or strangers, is by your own personal living example to make a better way. The only curricular arrangements worth arranging are those that help an individual, not a class: (1) to know himself, (2) to love responsibility, (3) to feel obligation as a joy, (4) to need very little in a material sense, (5) to express love, (6) to love truth, (7) to hate tyranny, (8) to gain useful knowledge, (9) to be involved in loving families at work, (10) to be involved in communities at work, and (11) to be humble in the face of the great mysteries, and to keep them constantly in mind because only from that wellhead does the meaning of life flow.

As a schoolteacher/saboteur I was able to help poor kids come to see such things just as easily as I was able to help prosperous ones; with a modest income I was able to finance all my classroom enterprises without assistance from foundations, universities, the business community, or the school administration—and so could anyone else so disposed.

Now to turn to a charge Ron makes honestly, but which, upon examination dissolves into smoke:

> Gatto throws the baby out with the bathwater by categorically defining "school" as an impersonal network and virtually equating educators and activists with social engineers.

There's a lot of slipperiness here. Does "educator" mean schoolteacher? Do the activists Ron refers to have an agenda to eventually gain control of our compulsion-schools? If both guesses are correct, then he is right, I do believe they are social engineers of the worst stripe. But perhaps he means something different.

How in Heaven's name can "school," in any of the varieties of definition possible for mass employment by a central government, NOT be an impersonal network? Can you school anything "personally?" I know you can fake it—most "good" schools do—but I find the really dangerous places to be the ones that preempt the family role, pretending to be families instead of networks; that's the horrible lesson I try to read in the chapter, "We

Need Less School, Not More." We're all dying of networks. Networks are not families. Pseudo-family schools confuse the rising gorge of their student prisoners for a long time (although never permanently; the disguise wears through). If you find my "prisoner" to be infamous rhetoric, then you will have to explain to me the social logic that allows you to use the police power of the state to command children's presence and respect, to pre-empt their daylight hours, to prescribe what they will think about, to judge them constantly and rank them.

It makes no sense to me to drain children from a living community and confine them with strangers for all of their natu-ral youth—from a human community perspective, that is. It seems to make great sense, of course, to minds that wallow in dreams of human life as an anthill or a beehive, the great world society crowd. And of course, too, though we seldom talk about it because the prospect leaves us dumbfounded, it makes great sense to those still-free, if mean-spirited, minds who benefit substantially from the docile, confused population that central planning leaves in its wake. That great, timeless families, who follow a different directive than the progressive one, have taken advantage of—indeed are imperfectly in charge of—the move-ment toward the nightmare of a global society seems to me not only beyond question, but the only conservative explanation of a crescendo of anomalies. For those who, reading these words, might be intrigued by this admission of madness, a little research into the utterly central role of family foundations in giving us the schools we have—a role curiously overlooked by school histo-ries, or dealt with *en passant*—will, I guarantee, reward the time spent with numerous marvels.

Back to business. Once you claim for your cause the sweeping power of compelling mass behavior, you have forfeited any claim at all to moral ground in my book. This is the rock on which all holistic ships founder, Rousseau's, Froebel's, Fichte,'s *et al.* You are practicing religion, then, and you are engaged in a holy war. I would imagine that nobody in 1992 is so naive not to recognize that the religion of our schools, since their inception, has been the Unitarian faith, but I am constantly disappointed. I may be misreading the conclusion of Ron's review: if you pub-licly disavow any right to assume control of the compulsion ma-chinery, Ron, including those exquisite controls Jacques Ellul dis-cusses in his wonderful book, *Propaganda,* I hope God smiles on your undertakings; but keep compulsion and it's hard for me not to regard cynically *any* justification which might be offered. Convincing me to accept your religion is legitimate and dialectical; forcing me to do so or tricking me into it is so vile that disdain or violence is the proper response.

There's much more at stake here than a little old-fashioned coercion—one-party systems are always corrupt; that is a fundamental truth of human nature. Eric Hoffer's *True Believer* was a turning point in my own life, however invested I seem to be here in my screed. In my view the only consensus ever valid is that consensus that arises slowly, painfully, naturally from millennial combats. Such consensus at its heart is a challenge to the premises of rationality. It cannot be hurried, cannot be hastened by Mind or Directives, by the Associations that John Dewey so loved. It contradicts the premises of the academic life as Francis Bacon conceived it, in service to the Central State. Such a belief calls for the destruction of Salomon's House as an unsurpassed agency of harm.

Again, if you regard this as airy rhetoric, look about you at the cities and the natural world that Salomon's House, the haunt of the social engineers, has given us. I don't need to recite the dreary catalogue; use your own eyes and ears. What got us into the mess won't get us out, in the immortal words of Nixon's "Checkers" speech.

Such consensus assumes a timeless wisdom that realizes a scale of historical process much vaster than the scale of human life. One of the instrumental advantages of a belief in Family, God and immortality is that it allows such a stepping back from the social arena that spans one's life. It's not hard for me to understand that Ron—or any other activist interested in collective action—wants to see substantial change in the span of his own years. But from my view, all such forced changes are doomed to cause harm, regardless of how beneficently they are conceived.

Such consensus at its heart is *sui generis*, exclusionary in the early part of the going, relatively local, slow spreading. The revolution that produced the Chinese peasantry or American native cultures is an example of the historical process in action at its finest—the human solutions in both cases are transcendentally brilliant, inspiring, funny, wonderful. Neither was fully worked out when they were destroyed by the demon of Western homelessness which sent European pirates and their slaves intervening in every laboratory of human life on the planet. That thousand-year destructive swath, currently managed by an academic service class, a secular priesthood, and protected by compulsion schooling, is what I write about in *Dumbing Us Down*, however indirectly. To dispossess the magical human possibilities underlying the appearance of Indians and Chinese, Queeg-Queeg and Dagoo, and replace these infinitely complex processes with a monochrome utopia is the act of a lunatic or a desperate man. All remote assignments of children's time and attention must, as I've said, be grounded in a vision of the good life, by its nature unprovable, by its nature religious at the core.

To the extent the Puritan vision was that of a world order, it was diseased and murderous, but genius implicit in the Congregational *mechanism*, by a wonderful irony (which unfortunately became *obvious* over time to Unitarians) is so relentlessly *local*, so unmistakably *personal*, it sabotaged the global vision of Calvinism right from the beginning. It is a fascinating paradox never examined to my knowledge by academic scholarship and it is the real point I explore in "The Congregational Principle" (first published in *Maine Scholar*).

It wasn't "something mysterious" inside the structure of Congregationalism in any sense like Adam Smith's "magic hand," to use Ron's phrase in the area where he goes farthest astray—it was one of the great fundamental discoveries of human social genius. What is mysterious is how it ever came into being—and sustained itself until the Unitarians destroyed it—right under the noses of the very social engineers who were giving New England its global economic mission. In Marx's felicitous locution, it illustrates strikingly the ignorant perfection of ordinary people, a perfection which is really the guiding inspiration of my teaching, my book, and my life. I learned the lesson from Monongahela, a town of ordinary people who perfected a community and the secret of meaning.

I was not "asserting" that colonists enjoyed nearly unconditional local choice. In point of fact that truth is built right into the structure of Congregationalism, which demands that no two communities be alike, that all be rigorously tuned to that single congregation. *Mirabile dictu,* I grow weak with the joy of merely *saying* it! You have choice because there are choices to have under a Congregational system—under a Unitarian system there are none. The confusion here arose, I would guess, because Ron misread individual choice where specifically I meant *local* choice. Choice by local consensus. However, it isn't too long a reach to argue that individual choice had to be there, too, because of the boundless dark woods, the many different states available, (each independent in its culture), and always, too, the frontier. The sarcastic among you will say, "Some choice if I have to move out!" but consider first that even that option isn't available today in the Theocracy of Unitarianism, and consider, too, that moving out is as just a choice as human affairs offers: would that we still had it. If the global people get their way we're not even going to be able to move abroad—every place will be here.

Then we will have arrived at the Utopia of social engineering, where everyone has to be "adjusted" to fit the pre-conceived model. Naturally a liberal interpretation will allow a 10% deviation either way from True North to accommodate human error economically.

For a wonderful example of human courage in just such a rigidly moralistic society as Ron characterizes New England to be, and what individual human courage can accomplish, see Hawthorne's *Scarlet Letter* where the elders plan to take little Pearl from her mother, the letter-bearer, and she—alone and friendless, poor and ignorant—says starkly, "... over my dead body!" So much for that batch of social engineers with the power of the state behind them.

My point is that *only* by trusting ordinary people thoroughly and *only* by emphasizing the individual, the family, the neighborhood, the local economy, can we slowly win through to a better life. All synthetic schemes radically distort the only *slightly* plastic material of humanity; all of them are impious, all rob the future in many ways, none *work* for very long—see official human history for evidence. All leave the world worse at their dissolution than before they found it. The Progressives are right, there *has* been a progression through recorded history, but it has been a progression *backwards*—just as Plato said it had been. We might mark the decline symbolically from the time the invisible labor engine was fabricated to build the Great Pyramid, an event strangely commemorated on the back of our dollar bill, though no one can produce an adequate explanation why. Disraeli knew, I think, but he spoke about it in riddles.

So what to do with the strong human impulse to meddle, tinker, dominate, improve, to not accept destiny? Well, my own answer is to do what you personally can, and suffer what you personally must. Accept the punishment of Prometheus if you want to play the part. And do I think you *should* play the part? Yes, of course, I've tried to, myself, all my adult life—but the other side of that dialectic is that I also believe brilliant and beautiful lives are possible everywhere, under any duress or deprivation, as long as you see clearly what really matters.

Now what scares me a little about Ron's conclusion is that he, toward the end, seems to be calling some sort of invisible army together for mass social engineering projects. He says, "we simply do not have 200 years to wait for some "invisible hand" to begin addressing these tremendous issues, "to lead" individuals and families and "self-satisfied" little communities, etc. OK, there seem to be two lines leading out from that one, that we act locally with like-minded people and try to convince the rest, and two, that we seize control of the apparatus and do it differently. I'd be with him on number one, and I'd cheer him on on number two if he led a *small guerilla band* in some boldly suicidal stroke. But change one master for another? Nope.

Ron asks how the free market would provide educational opportunity for poor children, and the answer is that that is the wrong question. Of course the "market" can't do anything but act as a field for action; its a necessary pre-condition for solutions but in and of itself, it's neutral. But government action is never neutral and cannot be—it must impose one or another religious view of the good life on everybody. And that is a pre-condition for bad things to happen, most often immediately, but also frequently when the second generation of zealots inherit the compulsion machinery and the police force. And even zealots are preferable to bureaucrats, who are the likeliest heirs.

This response has been a quick, spontaneous draft. I wish there were time to spend on creating a careful answer to some of the points Ron raises but there isn't, so this is the best I can do. I'd ask him and all your readers to carefully examine one huge unstated assumption that deeply disturbs me, namely, that government schools have ever merited the term "public," implying a service to the commonality. This is based on such specious reasoning, and such a peculiar definition of what the public is, that it won't bear scrutiny. These are not public schools we are talking about, they are government schools—as much different from public as flowers are from weeds.

Indeed, that there is a "public" at all except in the bizarre fantasy of utopians and Deweyists and positivists of all stripes is something that merits careful consideration before reflexively accepting its existence. As a western Pennsylvanian I find the term more than mildly insulting. A cartoon of reality. The forces that oppress the public, to borrow some of Ron's language, are the forces that rob it of its right of self-determination—without which people cannot be principals, but only agents (or "educators").

Anyway, the dishes aren't washed, the shirts aren't ironed, a colony of ants has taken up residence in my bedroom, and I've got to fly to Spokane tomorrow to tell people why I think a schooling, any flavor, can't be an education. Deconstruct these synthetic institutions: the machinery is a constant temptation to the worst people on the planet to scheme for its control. As I read history they always win in the long run. But ah, if we broke the machinery. . .?

Sign me,
John Taylor Gatto

I quote from a review of three years of Holistic Education Review *by Chris Mercogliano (acting as referee after the fact?) on the need for compromise and cooperation among educational reformers:*

Farenga's [Pat Farenga, from Holt Associates, one of Ron Miller's "libertarians"] call for unity, as it occurs between the issues of the *Review* where Miller and Gatto square off, is more than timely. The current crisis, whether or not one chooses to limit its scope to our educational system, is immense and growing exponentially. (I recently met with the head of the Albany, N.Y. School District's department which addresses children's special needs, and he informed me that nearly 15% of the local student population now fall within that category—with the number increasing daily—and his people are absolutely overwhelmed. He also told me that the severity of the nature of the needs is increasing as well. And Albany is a small city of under 100,000 people, where one ordinarily expects problems to remain on a manageable scale. The alarming reality is that this is no longer true in our school system.)

No one individual, or social movement, has a monopoly on the truth. The truth is that we each tend to hold a piece of the truth, and that it takes a diversity of approaches to solve any complex social problem. Firesign Theater taught us that, "We're all bozos on this bus," and it is critical, at this juncture, for all of the strong voices in the cry for a new direction in American education to resist the temptations of territoriality, professional jealousy and intellectual one-upsmanship. United we stand, divided we fall.

THE PLIGHT OF OUR CHILDREN

Claire Saffian is a contributing editor at Woman's Day *and has won many awards for her articles, Reprinted from* Woman's Day *for 5/28/91.*

WHAT IT'S *REALLY* LIKE TO BE BLACK
by Claire Saffian

"Toughen up, kid. That's the way it is!" Clara Villarosa said when kids called her daughter "nigger."

"This year it happened to me twice: A white stranger passed me on the street and hissed, 'Nigger! Nigger!'" Frances Ruffin

"He is not a *pimp.*"

In Boise, Idaho, Bertha Edwards is talking about her own son. A black mother, she's good at reading white minds.

In the autumn of 1990, her son Jim's car, a Mercedes Benz, was stolen. It was his dream car, bought secondhand with honest money earned as a local disc jockey. But Bertha knows what people say about black men and fancy cars, and she's quick to set the record straight. "And, no, he's not into drugs."

When the car was found, the windows were smashed, sand had been poured into the gas tank and more sand and rocks had ruined the engine. The thief signed his work with a one-word message, "Nigger," scratched into the side of the car.

In recent weeks, I've been talking with black women and men in cities and towns across the country. In the 1990s, they tell me, it still pinches if you try to walk a while in a black person's shoes.

In St. Louis, Missouri, Maisa Tisdale—Yale-educated—returns to her hotel after a business meeting. "I'm in my navy-blue suit, like any woman traveling on business," she says. "I'm not in Day-Glo Lycra. But a policeman follows me. "'Where do you think you're going?" he wants to know. Before I can get on the elevator, I have to show him my room key. I'm black, so he sees only two possibilities—thief or whore."

In Denver, Colorado, which may be the most integrated of America's large cities, Clara Villarosa taps her feet impatiently. "A few years ago, in some restaurants, the waiters were awfully slow to take my order. The food arrived a lot faster at white tables. The same thing happened at the supermarket deli counter. People came after I did, but they were taken ahead of me. And I hardly ever saw a white customer step aside and say, 'No, she was here first.' Now it's less overt, but it still exists."

In San Francisco, California, Gloria Williams is thrilled when her husband, a Navy lieutenant, is transferred to this romantic city with its reputation for tolerance. Then she spends two weeks trudging up and down the hilly streets, rental ads in hand. Every apartment she likes is "already taken" or "no longer on the market." Finally, she asks her husband, who is white, to take over. Quickly, he manages to rent one of the many places that was "unavailable" to Gloria.

Gloria shrugs. She knows there will always be white people who don't want to live or work next to blacks. "Or even sit next to us," says a black executive from Westport, Connecticut. In his three-piece suit, aboard the crowded commuter train to New York City, he can't help noticing that the seat next to him is always the last one that a white passenger will take. "And then only in desperation," he says wryly, "because it's a long trip."

The People Behind the Statistics

In human terms, these stories confirm what statistics from the U.S. Department of Justice's Community Relations Service (CRS) tell us—that racism is on the rise.

Reports and alerts of interracial conflicts rose 31 per cent between 1987 and 1989, the latest years for which CRS figures are available. Reports of community disorders, demonstrations and riots were up by 44 percent. Alerts of racial incidents or problems on college campuses almost tripled in that same period. Alleged "excessive use of force" by police in racial incidents has risen 39 per cent. Racism may even be changing its address: The CRS has been getting more reports from peaceful suburbs than teeming cities.

"We were making some progress," reports Earl Shinhoster, director of the NAACP regional office in Atlanta, "but now it's getting worse rather than better."

Behind the official numbers, there are acts that no one can count, the daily incidents that may not break the law but may break the heart.

Consider the simple act of shopping. In Champaign, Illinois, Donna Jackson, a minister's wife, goes to the mall with a special code of conduct. She makes sure she's well-dressed. She keeps her purse closed and her hands off the items, especially the small ones on display counters. Still, she's aware that she's being watched closely.

"Sometimes, if I'm with my children, we make a game of it. First one to spot the security guard wins an ice cream. But then there's something else. When I put my hand out for the change from that ice cream, does the clerk avoid my hand? Does she put the money on the counter? At times," Donna says, "racism can be hard to pin down. Not knowing can drive you crazy. If a clerk is rude to me, is she having a bad day? Or is it my skin?"

Consider catching a cab. "Even in the daytime, I can't get a taxi unless I'm in a suit and tie," says David Ruffin, a magazine editor in Washington, DC. "And even then, I'm sometimes asked to pay the fare in advance."

Consider trying to get ahead on the job. In Columbia, South Carolina, Jacquelyn Gladden feels racism as a weight, slowing her down in her career as a social worker. "If I have a plan for one of my clients, it's dismissed as nothing," she says. "If a white social worker proposes the same thing, it's a great idea." She sees her white colleagues gaining important information at professional meetings. "But I'm black, so I only get to go to meetings if no one else wants to go."

Consider getting a loan. Clara Villarosa owns the Hue-Man Experience, an African-American bookstore in Denver. Not long ago, she asked her bank for a $6,000 line of credit. "The savings and loans were lending millions of dollars to those good old boys, with no collateral at all. But I was a black woman, asking for a few thousand. I have a thriving business, but I needed three co-signers."

As blacks and whites think about these issues, they are "worlds apart," according to a 1989 poll for the NAACP Legal Defense and Educational Fund. Close to 70 percent of whites think that blacks now have all the equality they need at work, but two out of three blacks disagree. In similar numbers, whites and blacks disagree about how equal the opportunities are in education and housing.

Life and Death

Racism is more than a question of hurt feelings, inconveniences or lost opportunities—it can be a matter of life and death. Dr. Alvin Pouissant, the noted black psychiatrist and author, worries that the bigotry of "nice people"—the closed doors, the suspicious looks, the little snubs and slurs—explains why some blacks feel angry toward whites and retreat to their own groups.

In 1990 the CRS investigated the shooting of young Philip Pannell by a white policeman in suburban Teaneck, New Jersey. Philip was one of a group of black teenagers hanging out in a school playground. Was he shot because the officer, now indicted for manslaughter, thought Philip was reaching for a gun? Or was he shot because he was black?

Teaneck had long prided itself as a racially peaceful town. Yet black youngsters were often stopped and questioned by police as they walked to school. "What are you up to?" The youngsters never told anyone until the Justice Department investigated. Black grown-ups were stopped as well, sometimes as they were driving within half a block of their own homes. They too kept silent, accepting it as the price you paid for being black in a white world.

Suspicion and fear are the emotions of the day. Blacks make up only 12 percent of our population, but they account for 31 percent of our crime. If you're white, do you blame poverty and despair for at least part of that? Or do you think it's in the black genes? Do you clutch your purse a little tighter when a black man passes? Even if he's well-dressed? Do you quicken your step, thinking about the brutal gang rape of the Central Park jogger?

If you're black, do you tremble over other racially charged headlines—a white mob chasing a black man to his death in Howard Beach, New York; jackbooted "skinheads" choosing still another black man at random and clubbing him to death in Portland, Oregon?

In Fort Wayne, Indiana, Virginia Blackburn spends much of her day working on racism and sexism at the Women's Bureau. At night, she's just another black mother, staring into the night, dizzy with an anxiety that's virtually "unbearable" because her teenage son is late getting home.

Worry is an equal-opportunity occupation for all mothers, but this is different. Virginia's son is a young black male in sneakers, the modern-day bogeyman. "What if he's in the wrong place?" On any given day, one in four young black males is involved with the criminal-justice system—in jail, on probation or parole. "Will people see him as a threat?" Will a stranger understand that Clay belongs to the other group, the three in four who are good, law-abiding kids?

"Clay's not sure either," she says. "I can see his body tense up when a white male approaches. He's asked me whether I think his species can survive."

Suffer the Children

The hardest questions are about children. Clara Villarosa is still angry as she remembers the day when one of her daughters, now grown, came home crying because a white classmate had called her bad names like "nigger." While hugging and comforting her child, Clara gave her harsh words to live by.

"Toughen it up, Baby," she told the girl. "Because that's the way it is." Is Clara right? In the 1990s, is that how it still is?

"Recently, when his third-grade class was performing *The Wizard of Oz*, Donna Jackson's son, Patrick, had his heart set on playing the Wizard. The teacher told him heed be "better off as a Munchkin." On opening night, Donna couldn't help noticing that white children had all the lead roles—and black children were all "better as Munchkins."

To many blacks, racism is the fourth R. In Hartford, Connecticut, Elizabeth Sheff asks her son's teacher about the "D" on his report card. Earlier in the year, the white teacher had told her, "Don't worry," when her son wasn't doing well. Now she says, "Well, we didn't expect the children to do well."

Elizabeth is fighting back. She's become "the ringleader," as she calls herself—and "the troublemaker," as some white teachers call her—in a lawsuit to raise the quality of education in the city's schools to that of the surrounding, mostly white suburbs. "Black children don't get smarter just by sitting next to white children," she says. "But the teachers get a lot better."

Clay Blackburn's mother teaches him about black pride, but he goes to school in a neighborhood where the Klan has marched. When his class is told to write about presidential candidates, he wants to do his paper on Jesse Jackson—but his teacher isn't having any of that. Another day he's sent to the principal's office when he refuses to sing "Dixie" in a music class. "It's your heritage, " the teacher insists. "The teacher can't understand," says his mother, "that for my son, the heritage is slavery."

In Wilton, Connecticut, Janus Adams, founder and president of Harambee, a book club for African-American literature, says, "I've achieved something, but the schools still didn't expect my children to do well." Today, one of her daughters is at Spelman College, a traditionally black school in Atlanta, and the other is at mostly white Wesleyan in Middletown, Connecticut. "The daughter at the white school gets tons of mail from banks, offering her credit cards. The daughter at the black school has never heard of such a thing."

Says Adell Adams, president of the local NAACP in Columbia, South Carolina, "In school white kids get suspended, but black kids get expelled."

What If You Were Black?

We're at the Galaxy Diner, shiny with chrome, a mirror image of diners in a thousand other towns. This one is on Main Street in Bridgeport, Connecticut.

The diner is crowded with working-class and middle-income people having supper at 6. I share a leatherette booth with the Tisdale family—Loyse and her Ivy League-educated children, Preston and Maisa. They are the only blacks in the place.

"What if it were the other way around?" Preston asks. I look at the pleasant white faces around me, trying to imagine them with darker skins. "What if you were the only white person here?"

So there it is, obvious as the ketchup bottle, the fear on both sides of the table. In this clean and friendly place, is that how my new friends are feeling?

"If you're black, you live with stress," says Maisa, delicately beautiful, fiercely intelligent. "You have no security. If I get a job, maybe it's 'the black job,' with its own pay scale and job description. In one office I was told not to be so serious. 'Why don't you make us laugh,' they asked, 'like the black person who was here before?'

"Or maybe it's not the black job, so everyone is wondering what I'm doing there. I'm a Yale graduate, but in one office they wanted someone else to double check all my letters. Give me a break! A white woman with half my education is going to check my spelling?"

Preston, a lawyer, sums up the precarious life of a black male by quoting playwright Melvin Van Peebles. "If I stand, I'm loitering. If I walk, I'm prowling. If I run, I'm escaping." His mother, Loyse Tisdale, works as a travel agent. "Last week I was standing on line, waiting to cash my pay check. When it was my turn, the bank teller took one look and told me, 'Lady, the food stamps are at the other end.'" Loyse shakes her head. "White people," she says, "always know how to ruin your day."

Around the country, as I ask about racism, I keep remembering Frances Ruffin. In a way, this report is my apology to her.

Frances is a handsome woman, bright, ambitious, quietly stylish. A few years ago, when we worked together, she was one of several blacks on the editorial staff of a national magazine. We were colleagues, 9-to-5 chums in an office of liberals, with only a couple of people who pretended to be color blind.

Color blind? As a white woman, I could take my own skin for granted. Did Frances have to think twice about hers? I didn't ask, and Frances didn't walk around with a black chip on her shoulder. As she tells me now, she could forget about color for months at a time.

"And then something would happen." Frances remembers the day two co-workers came by her cubbyhole and told her that a purse had been stolen. Frances sat there, stiff and silent. "As they left, one asked me if I was sure I hadn't seen it."

Sorry, Frances. I never knew. As she tells me now, our little office was an ordinary place. "Nothing excruciating happened. Just a few insensitive individuals. The polite prejudice. The small things that can ruin your week."

She remembers another day, when an editor called out to her. "Frances, I've got something to show you. " The woman displayed a shopping trophy, a gorgeous pair of white silk pants. Frances admired them. Then the woman asked, "Frances, could you hem them for me?" What? Frances was never famous for her skills with a needle. "Some people look at you and see a stereotype," she sighs. "So they always know who the maid is. Or who the thief is."

Sorry, Frances. I never noticed. My friend no longer works for that magazine. She worries that the ugly old words, taboo in the glow of the civil rights era are being heard again. "This year, after all these years of living in New York, it happened to me twice: A white stranger passed me on the street and hissed, 'Nigger! Nigger!'" Frances is angry. "I'm a grown-up. I can handle it," she says, "But I'm also a mother." Her son, Timmy, is 8 now, cute, smart, a bit shy. "My heart stops when I think that someone might call Timmy a bad name."

Does growing up black have to mean growing up hurt? Why? One day, that may be Timmy's question. And how will Frances answer? How would you?

THE STREETS TAKE A SON
August 30, 1992 By Linda Yglesias
Daily News Staff Writer

CRAIG PRENTICE WAS ONE OF THOUSANDS GROWING UP AROUND DRUGS. DESPITE CARRYING A GUN, HE WASN'T INVINCIBLE.

STEPHEN PIERCE ran out on the street in his bedroom slippers. "Gunshots were blazing," he said.

He saw a body cradled beside a police car. The cops were trying to find a pulse. Blood was everywhere. It was his son with 14 bullet holes and more than 50 spent shell casings at his feet.

"I got to get him to the hospital," Pierce screamed.

A cop hugged him: "He doesn't need a hospital," he said.

Frances Pierce didn't know it was her son under the sheet. "I couldn't see his face, but then I saw his sneakers sticking out," she said. "I made them show me. His eyes and his mouth were wide open like he was shocked. I know he called out for me. "The first time he got arrested, when they had him handcuffed to a pole, I said, 'Don't you know you can die? He said, 'I can't die. It can't happen to me, Mommy.'"

On June 23, the Pierces' 11 year-old son, Craig Prentice became just another peachfuzzed wanna-be caught up in the city's burgeoning drug world, who found out that despite carrying a gun he wasn't invincible.

The bullet has become the leading cause of death for the city's teenagers, and so far this year 313 16-year-olds and under have been shot, at least 43 fatally.

And Craig Prentice (who used his mother's maiden name) was just one of thousands of neighborhood kids growing up around drugs, scratching for sneaker money and aspiring to be druglords. "He idolized drug dealers," his father said with anguish in his eyes.

Tried Everything

The Pierces used everything in the parental arsenal from heart-to-heart talks to public embarrassment to dissuade their son from making a life on the streets. Craig Prentice—who still played hide-and-seek with his sister, made funny faces and played silly pranks to get a laugh—was selling a little crack here and there for Nike sneaker money and Boss jeans. A week before Christmas, he was arrested for possession.

"I don't think Craig was one of the bad kids into doing wrong things," said Lt. Joel Pierson of the 46th Precinct. "He was a kid sucked into a young, violent-prone group that carried weapons, a loose-knit group of six or seven. He happened to go along with peer pressure. He got entangled. He was acting on behalf of an older drug dealer who was using the kids. Death was the result."

Craig Prentice, tall, gangly and baby-faced, a 3-pound preemie born June 2, 1976, died a little after midnight, June 23 in an ambush on Macombs Road and University Ave. on a South Bronx sidewalk near his home. He was hit with bullets from an AK-47 assault rifle and .45-caliber and .9-mm. automatics. He never had a chance to pull out the .25-caliber handgun he carried. By all the rules of cause and effect and parenting, he should not have even been hanging out on the streets.

Stephen Pierce, 36, director of office services for a midtown law firm, belonged to the Black Spades gang in the early 1970s. He had done a little purse-snatching and a little numbers, nothing more. In 1982, his own baby brother, Darryl, 22, was murdered and left in a plastic bag on 118th St. Pierce suspects it was a drug execution.

Gun Didn't Help Teen In Ambush

Pierce went arrow-straight and thought he was street smart enough to keep his son off the corners where he once had rumbled with chains and knives. In the end, he admits he wasn't. "He was a nobody trying to be somebody," said Pierce, sitting in his living room where baby pictures of Craig, his brother, Wesley, and his sister, Tiffany, fill the wall in his apartment. "He was a small fish in a big pond. He wanted to be recognized as a big potato. I did my best. I took him to see the Knicks and the Mets and the Yankees. I took him skating. I bought him a drum set. I'd sit him down and preach to him what the streets really are. But I couldn't snatch him back. The streets got my son."

"This is the truth about Craig," said Frances Pierce, who works the night shift at a White Castle hamburger restaurant. "Anything positive, he wanted no part of. All he lived for was sneakers and jeans. That was 'fly' (hip), bigtime, to him."

Drug dealers know that poor kids looking for status, be it money or power, is where the trail to death begins, said Lt. Tom

Kelly, an 11-year veteran who has worked narcotics in the city's roughest precincts.

"Kids don't just jump right into the business," he said. "They start out as a lookout, standing on the corner and whistling or yelling 'agua' ('Cool it'); that's their job."

Dealers know it's good to have younger lookouts and younger steerers. If they get arrested, they're not going to do any time. If they prove themselves reliable, capable of hanging out all day, they can move up to steerer.

Craig Prentice never made it that far. In his elementary and junior high school, Prentice's brother, Wesley, 18, brought home straight A's and "Most Valuable Player" trophies.

Ignored Advice

"I'd tell him again and again, 'Just be yourself. That's enough for me.' But he felt like he had to do the same thing Wesley did, straight A's, sports," Pierce said. "He did it in another way. By the time my son got to seventh grade, when he was barely 13, the streets were easing in."

At Community Junior High School 82, Prentice joined his friends for subway performances, dancing in the trains for change.

"They'd come back with $300, $400,' said Wesley.

In March 1990, he was arrested for receiving stolen property. His older buddies stuck him, the 15-year-old juvenile, with the VCR, TV and radio because they knew a kid wouldn't do jail time. In June 1991, the day before his junior high graduation, he was arrested while joy-riding in a stolen car. One of his older friends had taken the car and picked him up. A week before Christmas between his transfer from Lincoln Academy to John F. Kennedy High School, he was arrested for possessing three vials of crack.

"I saw the way he was going, I tried to warn him," said Wesley. "He'd started dealing crack whenever he wanted sneakers or Boss jeans."

"In March, he asked me for $70 to buy some sneakers," said Frances Pierce. "I wouldn't let him have it because he'd been cutting classes."

When the cops called her, she refused to get her son out of juvenile detention. "I told Craig, 'Three strikes, you're out. You think this is a joke.'"

She told a family court judge about the problems she was having with Craig and pleaded for help. He told her the law wouldn't let him hold her son for any length of time, but placed Craig for a week in a boys' group home.

"When I went to visit he was crying," she said. "He begged me to let him come home."

Prentice's parents said they tried everything they could to steer him away from temptation.

"Once I snatched him by the collar from these kids he was standing with and they followed me into my apartment building," said Pierce. "They didn't know I was his father. One looked like he was about to pull a gun. 'What you doing to my man?' he said. 'My man?' I said. 'My son, you mean.' He was getting a big reputation. Too many people, were beginning to know him for the wrong things."

In the past few months, four of Prentice's friends had been fatally shot. One, "Champ," died with a .357 bullet in his head, the victim of a long-running gang dispute.

The Pierces had heart-to-heart talks with their son. His mother took him several times to a doctor to have him tested for drugs.

"I knew by then he was running with a wolf pack—I don't care what they say about calling it that—I knew he was running with the wrong set of kids," said Stephen Pierce. "I'd search him randomly for weapons or drugs. I'd check his hands to see if he'd been smoking reefer."

Shortly before midnight on June 22, Pierce was watching the Arsenio Hall show. Prentice was being recruited in an ugly Jamaican-Dominican drug war. Frances Pierce had left for work around 5:30 p.m. that day feeling particularly cheerful. Her boss had told Prentice earlier that day he had a job at White Castle, and Prentice had seemed happy.

Gunned Down

According to investigators, the 25-year-old leader of a violent Jamaican posse, Christopher Livingston—who was later gunned down — was moving his drug dealers into the neighborhood, which was basically controlled by a Dominican drug gang. Livingston wasn't on the street, police said, but was the mastermind who convinced Prentice and his young friends to swagger down the street in a show of power.

"They were apparently having a dispute with some Dominicans who had control of a drug location," said Pierson of the 46th Precinct. "They were attempting to move in on somebody else's turf."

Based on police, family and street accounts, one of Prentice's acquaintances had mouthed off to a member of the Dominican drug gang. That night he was bragging about his bravado to a handful of the boys along Macombs Road, includ-

DRESSED TO DIE
by Linda Iglesias
Daily News Staff Writer

YOUR TEENAGER comes home with a $100 pair of Air Jordan sneakers, Boss jeans, a couple of silk shirts and a fancy bomber jacket. He has started hanging out with a slightly older crowd. He's cutting classes if he goes to school at all and he's staying out late. He won't tell you where he got his beeper. He's probably not doing drugs, though. Most likely, he's beginning in a trade where those who use the product aren't allowed to sell it.

You won't find a gun in his room. He stashes it in a mailbox, in the basement at his girlfriend's house or maybe in his locker at school. His customers won't be anyone you know. This is a business in which the clientele are kept at arm's length.

He has signed on with his hero, the local drug czar who doesn't have to recruit too hard. He already knows about your child, whether he's a mama's boy or a home boy, cold-blooded or cowardly. He knows when your child comes and goes. He knows where you live.

"These are poor kids," said Detective Cedric Wilkinson of the 70th Precinct, which covers Flatbush and Kensington in Brooklyn. "They see the quick, fast dollar. "It's not a hard business to learn. These local dealers know these kids. If the dealer's going to make an investment in a kid, give him some of his drugs, he'll know where the kid lives, his family. He'll know how to contact the kid."

It's all part of life and death in the inner city.

"We're out on the street at a heavy drug location, Stratford Ave in the middle of the block, 7 p.m. making sure the dealers weren't on the corner. It's still light outside," said Lt. Tom Kelly of the 43d Precinct. "This kid comes up, he couldn't have been more than 13 or 14, and says, 'Why are you bothering us? We're not doing anything. We're just selling drugs.' I said, 'That's all you're doing?' And then he said, 'Everybody's got to make a living.' "

ing Prentice. A little while later, some Dominicans drove up on the sidewalk and tried to run down some of Prentice's friends. One of Livingston's dealers decided he wanted to show the

Dominicans he wasn't afraid and got Prentice and his friends to walk down Macombs Road with him.

His father says Prentice didn't know he was going up against a Dominican drug gang. "My son wouldn't have been stupid enough to cross them," he said. "They've owned the block for years."

Shortly before midnight, as Prentice and his friends walked toward University Ave., somebody handed Prentice a .25-caliber pistol.

"One or two Dominicans came around the corner with an AK-47, a .9-mm. and a .45," Pierson said. "Without notice, the Dominicans opened fire. "

Pierce heard the gunshots as he watched television. He was afraid his wife would come home from work and wind up in the middle of whatever was going on. He put on his bedroom slippers and went outside to wait for her.

The bullets came from both sides, the Jamaicans and the Dominicans. After the first volley of shots hit him, Prentice played dead, eyewitnesses and neighbors said. After a while he figured it was all right to get up and run. He started yelling "Don't shoot," but was hit by more bullets.

Pierce got a foot away from his son's body, his head nestled in a cop's hands. "I went over to hug him," Pierce said. "All I could see was his blood running down the sidewalk."

Craig Prentice died in dark blue Boss jeans and white Nike sneakers. The little .25-caliber pistol was tucked under a blue hooded sweatshirt. A plastic crucifix hung around his neck.

FOR KIDS, DEATH IS A WAY OF LIFE

THEY ARE wet behind the ears in a drug civilization where "old" means 17. They live precariously short lives in a world where turf changes hands like clockwork in ambush executions.

ANDREW WHITTAKER saw the two men approaching. He knew they were drug dealers. They looked him over without saying a word, then walked away. It was around 1 a.m. July 19. Ten minutes later, they returned to the schoolyard in the St. Albans section of Queens and accused him of selling crack on their turf.

Whittaker, 16, was with some friends and didn't want these home boys showing him up. Maybe he should go home and get his gun and his bulletproof vest, he said.

One of the dealers pulled an automatic pistol and fired point-blank into his chest. Whittaker ran 30 yards before falling dead. The shooter stood over his body: "Where's your vest now?"

RICHARD PERDOMO was killed in a driveby shooting on 176th St. at Audubon Ave., his friends told cops. The lie quickly unraveled. He'd been hanging out with a bad crowd, would go missing for days and come home wearing new clothes. He always had money and he carried a beeper.

His mother, fearing he was selling crack, hired a cab to follow him. Her worst fears were confirmed. On June 29, in apartment 68, Perdomo was showing off his .9-mm. He handed the gun to Luis Deschamps who shot him in the chest, police said. Deschamps and another friend carried Perdomo to the street and took him by gypsy cab to Columbia Presbyterian Hospital. He was dead on arrival. Deschamps, 18, who has been charged with murder, claimed the gun discharged.

JASON LABOY's decomposing body lay in the hallway, his eyes, hands and feet bound with duct tape. A tenant in the apartment building had called police on July 16 to complain about loud music. Heroin, lactose, strainers, masks, cutting spoons, cutting cards and a scale were scattered around the small apartment at 2034 Benedict Ave. in the Parkchester section of the Bronx. Inside a box, hundreds of envelopes had recently been puffed open like mouths of fish, ready to be filled.

The 16-year-old's father, Eusuerio Rivera, 53, and his stepmother, Adrienne Jones, 28, lay dead nearby from head wounds. Before Jones was killed, she hid her 3-month-old daughter under a bed. Someone, police said, had ripped off the family business.

AMBROSE ROBERTS, 15, stood with his drug-dealing mentor, Darren Jones. At 8:30 p.m., July 8, members of a rival posse from a block and a half away walked into the courtyard at 654 Kingsboro Walk in Brooklyn. They were looking to expand their territory. They wanted to show Jones, 23, they weren't scared to walk down his street. The posse opened fire with a .38, a 9mm and a .380. Jones, who had six vials of crack in his pocket, was killed instantly. Roberts tried to run away and was fatally shot in the head.

KENDALL JOHNS0N and **HAROLD THORTON**, both 16—"Hippie" and "Fats" on the streets—were hawking crack on 132nd St. and Madison Ave. As they walked out of an abandoned building on the corner, two gunmen opened fire. Police said the dealer who ran the local crackhouse had hired the killers and provided a .38-caliber revolver and a .9-mm. automatic to do away with the two upstart dealers trying to take over his corner. They shot Thornton in the back and Johnson five times, close up, in the head.

—Linda Iglesias

Reprinted from THE DAILY NEWS *for Sunday, August 30, 1992.*

Kevin Powell is a freelance writer who lives in New York City. His article is reprinted from the August, 1994 issue of ESSENCE *magazine.*

TWO SCHOOLS
by Kevin Powell

Unequal state funding for education means unequal public schools and African American children are usually the losers. Kevin Powell discovered just how cruel the differences between public schools can be when he paid a visit to his predominantly Black alma mater and then dropped by a predominantly white suburban school. Here, two schools in the same state that are savagely unequal:

It is the first time I have visited Henry Snyder High School in Jersey City since graduating in 1984. As I approach the long, sandy-colored edifice that covers a two-block area, I notice that one of the iron gates is lying on the lawn and that several letters are missing from the school's name above the entrance. Litter and broken glass clutter the lawn. Not much has changed in eight years.

As I approach the office of Mrs. Lillian P. Williams, the teacher I am visiting, the bell rings, and black and brown bodies rush into the hall. The school is not well lit, and that, combined with its aging, broken lockers, missing or tattered window shades, and half-painted walls, gives the school that "prison vibe" that students in my graduating class used to talk about.

Nearly all of the 1,167 students who attend Snyder High School are African-American and Latino. School officials claim that only 17 percent of the youngsters who attend Snyder High drop out and that nearly half of those who graduate will attend two- or four-year colleges. But parents say that far more youngsters drop out and far fewer attend college than school officials are willing to admit. There are eight guidance counselors in the school, but only three of them are African-American. There are no Black male guidance counselors, but there are three Black male vice-principals.

As Mrs. Williams, a short, meticulously dressed woman who has taught English at Snyder High for the past 22 years, guides me through the familiar corridors, I notice plaster blotches dotting the walls and I am told that the school is in the process of being renovated. I stop at the boys' bathroom, but it is locked. I ask a student why, and he explains it's because "niggas be fuckin' them up, smokin' and shit."

In the classrooms, most of the students sit slumped at their desks, passing notes, talking, sleeping and ignoring the teachers. The library is virtually empty save for a library attendant and one lone student who sits at a long table reading a sports magazine while listening to a Walkman radio. There are two computers. Much of the reading material is old.

As I enter a science class, a teacher explains that "we don't have enough equipment and we need to update what we have. Some of this stuff has been here for 30 years or more." He points to an electrical socket sitting near a water faucet and explains that it's dangerous for a water faucet to be positioned so close to all electrical socket.

In the school auditorium, wooden boards cover the entrance door where glass once was. The piano sounds untuned, and the auditorium looks as if it hasn't been refurbished since I graduated. The seats are covered with graffiti.

In the gymnasium, nets are missing from several basketball rims and some backboards don't have rims at all. Volleyball nets, worn from several years of use, hang limply. In the school detention area, there are huge holes in the walls and graffiti cover the doors. Snyder High's swimming pool has been broken for more than a decade, and there is no practice field for any of the sports teams. In the school cafeteria, students play cards, argue and eat lunch. A square-dance mat has been placed in the center of the cafeteria although, according to several students, "There ain't never no parties at Snyder High."

Mrs. Williams has strong words for Snyder High and the public-school system that supports it. "My feeling is that the people downtown are grandstanding," she says. "They really don't know or care about these kids. There is no incentive to come to school. We've lost a lot of students to the streets, but nobody talks about them."

A Visit To Cherry Hill High School West:
As I walk through the first floor of Cherry Hill West, I can't help but notice how well lit, clean and modern it is. The school, located in Cherry Hill, New Jersey, is a spacious complex in a neighborhood filled with one-family homes and neatly manicured lawns. Since its erection in 1956, several structural additions have been made to the school. As a result, the wings of the building are lettered A through G.

There are 1,440 students at Cherry Hill West; the vast majority are white, but there are 89 African-Americans, 43

Latinos and 150 Asian students on the school roster. Of these students, 60 percent will attend four-year colleges, while another 20 percent will attend two-year colleges. According to the school's principal, the school employs five regular guidance counselors and two special counselors to handle things such as eating disorders, domestic violence, divorced families and drug and alcohol problems.

Among the amenities are a student-run school supermarket, an industrial-arts class that includes a computer-aided drafting program and a television station, which is equipped with the latest technology and has a 24-hour message board. Every Wednesday there are specially televised programs. The school also shares a huge practice field and a football stadium with Cherry Hill East, the district's other high school.

The library is the newest part of the school. It is a totally computerized facility featuring ProQuest, a program in which students can display virtually any news or magazine article and print it out. Each English class meets six times a week and students attend writing labs. In the labs students can place their essays into computers that will analyze them for grammatical mistakes.

"There's a lot offered to us here," observes Celia, a Cherry Hill senior. "No matter what you want to do with your life, Cherry Hill West has the courses and the extracurricular activities to help you. The teachers really care about us and go out of their way to prepare us for life."

HELPLESS RAGE/HOPELESS LOVE
by Bill Kaul

We live in scary times. People run to and fro, trying to find peace of mind, protection of property, freedom from want, approval, and who knows what else. Everybody's looking for something. Desiring something. Trying to fill the empty holes. Scary.

Like not being willing to teach—or even mention—contraception to a group of teen moms enrolled in an alternative school. Scary.

Like that feeling of oppression that comes over me when I am being told to suppress the truth, to not tell students how I really feel about something. Where lying and pretending to be other than what I am is the ticket to success. The more plastic you are, the more proper you are. Don't ask, don't tell. Scary.

I saw a child yesterday. He was in trouble. He was being made to face the wall for his infraction of the rules—his sin was talking, I believe. There's nothing profound here, I guess, but when I saw him, and he kind of glanced at me from under his arm when I patted him on the back quickly (so the teacher wouldn't notice and say that I was "undermining her authority")—the look on his face. I have been trying to capture that feeling his look gave me. I can't. Scary. Like the look of a little girl whose hand is slapped away by her father as they are crossing the street. She just wanted to hold his hand. The look on a little boy's face when he realizes I'm not going to hit him for spilling his milk. The look a stray dog gives you when it realizes you're going to feed him, not beat him. These looks do something to my guts. I don't know what to call it. I don't know what to call it, but I think it has something to do with love and compassion, something to do with the very heart of being a teacher or a learner.

And it seems to be missing in the hearts of many. An emptiness. Empty like the halls of a school during classes, at the sound of a bell, to be filled with screaming desire.

I'm afraid for us. I would prefer to be driven by love and compassion, but I live in a world driven by emptiness and fear. Mostly.

Sometimes, every so often, when I'm not worried about how I'm going to pay my bills, I just reach out to another and that thing happens. What is it? Electricity? Some sort of connection through the spiritual ether? I don't know, but it fills the emptiness like no drug, no applause, no success can ever do.

While we argue over dividing up money and success, land and honors, turf and profits, we overlook those resources most essential: love, hope, compassion, honesty. Totally renewable resources. "We belong to the earth; the earth does not belong to us." What if? What if we all lived as if that rather non-Christian sentiment was our world view? What would our society look like? If that axiom is true, and we ignore it, what is the cost to us as a species?

I'm just wondering now, no thesis, no particular argument, my revolutionary fervor is diminished by a real desire to connect with simple truths.

I met a man from Taos Pueblo, in Durango, Colorado. I was walking down the street, sort of carefree, taking in the bustle of New Age-Old Age, and he stumbled out of a bar. He looked at me and said, "Heyyyy, brother!" and I knew right away. "Hello to you," I said, and we ended up smoking cigarettes and eating crackers from my backpack, and he told me before we parted, "Stay close to Mother Earth, bro." Just like that. "Stay close to Mother Earth." And then, "I mean it, bro. Stay close. It's the only thing. I'm saying this for you." And then he wandered on, to "look for some yellowhairs, " he said.

Seemed like good advice.

I pass it on to you: Stay close to Mother Earth. Tell the children, too, and say I love you to them. This is the pedagogy of the oppressed: I want everything for you that I want for myself. And the methodology—? It is to ask: What do I want? What do you want? Is there a desire that, being quenched, would extinguish all other desire? Is it a thirst for God? A longing for Mother Earth? To know, as surely as you know your body, that you are loved?

What, indeed, do we want?

It's scary to look at government. What do we want?

It's scary to look at schools. What do we want?

Those glances from the children: my guts are twisted with fear, and love, and compassion.

Well, anyway, this is a bit different for me. I usually react with anger and in-your-face criticism to what I perceive as injustice and foolish pride.

Lately, though, I have been recognizing that the stool upon which I sit is no throne of judgment, that my intolerance is no better than anyone else's, and that humility and character building are sufficient exercises unto themselves. As a result I am once again a complex human being, and now, having exhausted the inner, I find that reaching out in love is the only way I can heal.

As a friend of mine once said, "True ambition is not what we thought it was. True ambition is the profound desire to live usefully and walk humbly under the grace of God."

Best wishes and heathen blessings,
Bill
Waterflow, NM

Here follow two articles by Dayle Bethel, professor and Dean of the Kyoto Learning Center of the International University in Kyoto. Dayle has long been a friend of alternative education, both in the United States and in Japan, and has sent a number of articles to both ΣΚΟΛΕ and the Journal of Family Life, *our sister journal.*

MODERN CULTURE AND THE PEER SOCIALIZATION MYTH
by Dayle Bethel

Myths, the stories and legends which grow up to explain "why" things are as they as they are an indispensable part of culture. Myths provide the justification or rationalization for a culture's core beliefs and practices. Myths are powerful. They play an important role in the shaping of individual character and have a major impact on a society as a whole. But myths, on the other hand, are but natural emergents from the assumptions and values which underlie them. Thus, myths can be beneficial or detrimental for individuals and for societies, depending on the nature of the assumptions and the quality of the values from which they spring.

While recognizing that there are many noble and constructive myths which sustain modern industrial societies, it will be my purpose here to consider a deeply rooted myth which is being called into question today by some scholars and social critics. The essence of the myth to which I refer goes something like this: "Healthy, normal development of children requires that they be 'socialized' by being placed with other children in play groups, nursery schools, kindergartens, and schools, and the earlier this 'socialization' begins the better."

This myth is powerful. In the United States and in Japan, two of the world's leading industrial societies, it is extremely rare to find persons who do not accept the myth of the need for early childhood socialization of children by other children. The members of these two societies, with but few exceptions, seem to be convinced that placing their child with other children as early as possible is the essential, appropriate, and "right" way to assure healthy social and emotional growth of a child.

This myth legitimates and justifies our practice of taking children away from their parents and placing them in school rooms for twelve or more years of their early lives. Modern societies are dominated by their schools, and it is taken for granted that spending the early years of life in school is the best if not the only way for a child to grow up.

There is, however, another point of view which merits being heard. Those who hold this viewpoint point out that, contrary to what our history books have led us to believe, schools, as we know them, did not develop to strengthen liberty and democracy. Rather, as Alvin Toffler notes, schools developed in modern industrial societies to ensure a constant supply of obedient workers needed by the industrial and business élites of those societies, thus enabling the members of those élites to make profits. Mass education first came into being for purely economic reasons. Mass public schooling machined generation after generation of young people into a pliable, regimented work force. ...Taken together, the nuclear family and the factory-style school formed part of a single integrated system for the preparation of young people for roles in industrial society. (*The Third Wave*. New York: Bantam, 1981, pp. 29-30).

Sydney Jourard, an American psychologist, notes also the economic basis of schooling in the United States:

> The ultimate source of our curricula, in my opinion, has been the demands of the business-military-industrial-complex leaders, who by one means or another (mostly money) ensure that those views are inculcated, those views and people are validated, and those skills indoctrinated which will perpetuate the status quo. And so we let a population which is not educated but one that is trained to do what it must do to keep the system running; a mystified population which believes that the highest purpose of man is to consume goods. (*The Transparent Self.* New York: D. Van Nostrand Company 1971, p. 113)

Dissatisfaction with schools. together with a growing understanding of the extent to which schools and education in modern societies have been influenced by economic factors, has led a small minority of persons to reject the popular view of the need for early socialization of growing children by other children in schools. And while we may not agree with them or their conclusions, the issue they are raising is an extremely important one which must, I believe, be confronted. Thus it may be wise for us to listen to what this growing minority of people in our midst are saying.

There are two aspects of the alternative view. First is a realization, based on a growing body of research findings, that little children are better socialized by parental example and sharing than by other little children. Small children who spend little of their time with their parents and most of their time with their peers tend to become peer-dependent, and in recent years this tendency has moved down to preschool.

According to the results of studies conducted by Raymond Moore of the Hewitt Research Foundation, such peer dependency brings loss of (1) self-worth, (2) optimism, (3) respect for parents, and (4) trust in peers. Moore concludes that, contrary to popular opinion, little children are not best socialized by other children because the more persons they have around them, the fewer meaningful contacts they have. Furthermore, he found that socialization is not neutral, but tends to be either positive or negative:

> Positive or altruistic and principled sociability is firmly linked with the family —with the quantity and quality of self-worth. This in turn is dependent largely on the track of values and experience provided by the family, at least until the child can reason consistently. In other words, the child who works and eats and plays and has his rest and is read to daily, more with his parents than with his Peers. senses that he is part of the family corporation— needed, wanted, depended upon. He is the one who has a sense of self-worth. (*The Tropical Homeschooler.* No. 5, May/June, 1993.)

Moore suggests that it would be best for children if they did not enter school until they are at least 8 or 10 years old. He has found that children who do wait until they are older to enter school usually become social leaders. They know where they are going. They tend to be independent in values and skills. They are able to avoid the dismal pitfalls and social cancer of peer dependency. And they tend to become productive, self-directed citizens .

Moore concludes that negative, me-first sociability in a child develops in most cases because peer group association has replaced meaningful parental contacts and responsibility experiences in the home during the first 8 to 12 years. The early peer influence generally brings an indifference to family values which defy parental correction. The child does not yet consistently understand the "why" of parental demands when her peers replace her parents as role models at too early an age. In other words, the overall effect, of school experience and the peer dependency it fosters is alienation of the child from the parents and the family.

We have already seen that the peer-dependent child becomes stripped of a sense of self-worth and attitudes of hope, respect and trust to which self-worth gives birth. What the parent does, then, in sending very young children off to school is akin to casting them adrift on the vast sea of life without a compass or necessary guidance. If this is a valid assessment of contemporary schooling and the youth culture it has created. it is little wonder that young people today tend to be confused.

This brings into focus a second reason that a few people are beginning to question the myth of early childhood socialization by peers. Peer socialization is not only damaging to individual personality growth, it is ultimately devastating for society in that it; creates an alienated, artificial culture composed of frightened, hurting, angry, and irresponsible youth.

The reality of modern youth culture has been noted—and deplored—by Joseph Gauld, an American educator. He writes that we have created

> .. a new and mindless youth culture that dominates youngsters today. In *Lord of the Flies* William Goulding portrays the brutal inadequacies of youngsters who were forced to cope with life without benefit of adult guidance. We see this alarming gang and clique mentality everywhere in America today: the drive-by shootings; the metal detectors in schools; the dominant themes of drugs, sex, and violence; and not just in disadvantaged areas. Students nationally would tell adults that their schools are "unsafe"—if adults were tuned to hear them.
>
> Underneath a protective bravado, students are unhappy and intimidated by their youth culture. But it has become so commanding, and adults so unaware. students cannot express their deeper concerns to parents and teachers, much less to themselves. (*The Hyde Foundation Newsletter*, Vol. 3, No. 1, July 1993.)

Gauld recognizes, as many critics of contemporary education do not, that any attempt to confront the problems of modern youth culture must look not only at the negative socializing effect of contemporary schools, but at the woeful lack of effective parenting in our societies as well. Thus, he calls parents to recognize the importance or being positive role models for their children and to educate themselves so they can carry out that role effectively.

One attempt to confront the problems posed by contemporary youth culture has led to the development of a homeschooling movement which is growing in the United States and is just beginning in Japan. Much more research is needed of this phenomenon, but some comparative studies of homeschooled children and children who had attended traditional schools have been conducted in recent years, and the results are eye-opening, to say the least. A study conducted at the University of Florida, for example, concluded that children who were taught at home by their parents had consistently fewer behavioral problems than children who had attended traditional schools. (*The Tropical Homeschooler* No. 5, May/June, 1993). This study found that homeschooled children tended to talk quietly, play well together in groups and take the initiative in inviting other children to join them. Traditionally schooled children tended to be more aggressive, loud, and competitive than home-schooled children of the same age. Other studies indicate that home-schooled children are proving capable of superior academic work as well. (Pat Montgomery, "Parents as Teachers: It Works," Clonlara School, Ann Arbor, Michigan, unpublished paper).

Gail Nagasako, a mother in Hawaii who is homeschooling, is convinced that homeschooling is better for her children than attending traditional schools. (*The Tropical Homeschooler* no. 5, May/June, 1993). Her ten-year old son Thumper has attended traditional schools as well as spending some years in homeschooling. In a revealing comment, Thumper makes an interesting comparison between his feelings when he shares in special social events with other homeschooled children and when he is with school children: "You know what I like about being around the homeschoolers? I can just be myself. I don't have to worry about 'being cool' like I do around the school kids."

Not everyone will agree that homeschooling is the answer to our educational problems or to the problems created by modern youth culture. Furthermore, most parents today would have to make major adjustments in their own lives, in their values, and in their priorities in order to serve as positive role models and learning guides for their children in homeschooling situations. On the other hand, the youth cultures we are creating are not going to go away. All indications are that youth cultures, to which policies prompted by the peer socialization myth have given birth, will increasingly draw children and young people into webs of fear, violence, and other forms of anti-social behavior. If nothing else, the comparisons between homeschooled children and traditionally schooled children which are now coming to light may cause us to rethink and reevaluate the peer socialization myth and give greater attention to the needs of children and youth.

Tsunesaburo Makiguchi, in his day, warned against separating children from their families, from nature, and from society as we have done. Makiguchi called his countrymen to build an industrial society and schools on foundation principles and values very different from those the people of the United States had chosen. If the Japanese who lived in that earlier day and since had heeded his call, Japan would likely be a better society today. As we prepare to enter a new century, we will do well to look more seriously at Makiguchi's alternative image of what makes a good society and at his efforts to realize such a society in Japan.

VISUAL MEDIA AND CHILDHOOD'S DEVELOPMENTAL NEEDS
by Dayle M. Bethel

An artificial youth culture which has emerged within some contemporary societies is one aspect of a larger problem of cultural values and assumptions which underlie those societies. Some of these values and assumptions are flawed and at variance with reality. As a result, some of the social structures and behavior patterns which are based on them are harmful for psychological health and social well being. Two of the key social structures of these societies in particular have contributed to the creation of a youth culture, mass compulsory schooling and the mass media. The role of schooling in the development of widespread peer dependency among children and youth has been considered in a previous article. It is my purpose here to examine the effects of visual media in creating some of the pathological conditions inherent in the youth culture.

It has been estimated that the average child in the United States will have been exposed to 20,000 hours of television by the age of 20. This estimate is probably conservative because in recent years even many preschoolers begin watching several hours of television per day at about age two. There are, to be sure, differences between Japan and the United States with respect to children's television viewing, of which the hours many Japanese children spend in study at jukus is one. But in spite of juku time, an average Japanese child interacts with some type of visual media many hours each day. One 13 year old girl, for example, confided that she routinely watches television and video programs in her room, rarely getting to bed before midnight, and she understood that some of her peers were staying up until one or two o'clock in the morning.

To television and VCRs we must now add computer games and, if some of the producers of visual hardware and software have there way, each child will soon have her own personal computer in school. What this means is that many children in the new "information age" will spend a large portion of their waking hours sitting in front of some form of visual media.

Some parents worry about the long range effects in their children's lives of so many hours sitting in front of a screen. (And now, with the advent of hand-held computer games, watching a screen need no longer be confined to sitting. A child can carry it with him wherever he goes). Many parents would like to act to make changes in the way their children's time is spent, but the obstacles which they confront are formidable. Most do not have the motivation or the patience to endure the hassles involved in separating their children from viewing. In most families, for instance, any attempt to remove the personal television sets that children watch alone in their rooms would create a major family crisis. When to these internal family factors is added the intense pressure exerted by the influence of peers who obtain every new media toy or gadget as soon as it comes on the market and who can make the screens in their homes available to a child faced with restrictions on viewing, even minimal control of children's time appears, to parents, to be next to impossible.

Some educational specialists, and some parents, too, feel that concerns about the effects of visual media on children have been exaggerated. Those who express this view point to the positive aspects of these media for learning, particularly their potential for stimulating imagination and creativity. This cannot be denied. Visual media do offer rich possibilities for life enhancement of both children and adults. Yet this implies a recognition of the use of such media within a context of limits and for clearly defined purposes. That this does not describe the present situation in regard to children and visual media is obvious. These media are now generally being used without regard for limits or for constructive purposes.

A considerable body of research, as well as practical experience, indicates that parental concerns about the amount of time their children are engaged with television and other visual media are justified. Some of the evidence which is accumulating, for example, suggests a possible relationship between the violence and pornographic material children are seeing on television and VCRs and the increasing violence and anti-social behavior committed by children and young people, such as that described in Seiji Fujii's *Boy's Town: The Concrete Murder*. Parents cannot help but be concerned about much of the content of commercial television and computer games which their children watch. But apart from issues of content, making children into passive "watchers" and program manipulators as opposed to "initiators" is an alarming perversion of childhood's developmental tasks.(Jane Healy, Holistic Education Review, Vol. 6, No. 2, p. 15) Robert MacNeil, one of America's prominent TV anchormen, has warned of the adverse effects on children of excessive television viewing. (The Presidents Leadership Forum, State University of New York, November 3, 1984) According to MacNeil, constant television viewing robs a child of one of his most precious gifts, the ability to concentrate and focus his attention. Television discourages and destroys the child's ability to concentrate. Why is the loss of this ability disturbing? It is because almost anything interesting and rewarding in life requires some concentrated, consistently applied effort; its absence in a child's experience is limiting and ultimately impoverishing. Television conditions a child to apply no effort. It provides instant gratification; it makes time pass without pain.

Have you ever wondered why young people today are so easily bored? I have had young mothers tell me that they dread days when their children are not in school. It drives them frantic trying to come up with ways to entertain their children and keep them from becoming bored, irritable, and getting into trouble. The average young person today becomes bored almost the instant he cannot find some ready-made activity to occupy his time. He must be constantly on the move, when there is no screen available, to avoid boredom. We have come to accept this as normal behavior for children and youth. In fact, it is not normal behavior.

Children who are fortunate enough to grow up within a context of the world of nature and a real, human-scale community are not easily bored. They develop as a normal dimension of their personalities what Rachel Carson calls a "sense of wonder." A child who is enabled to acquire a sense of awe and appreciation for the life-giving systems, natural and social, which sustain her life, develops deep inner resources: curiosity, resourcefulness, creativity, which endure throughout a lifetime. Such a child does not suffer from boredom, is not constantly seeking new thrills and distractions, and does not require constant supervision and entertainment.

This was one of Tsunesaburo Makiguchi's central teachings. He believed that a sense of vibrant aliveness, a sense of wonder and awe and appreciation toward life and nature was every child's birthright. He believed, further, that a child can attain the full potential of his humanness only through direct, active, personal communication with the natural world, and for Makiguchi this meant the child's immediate social world as well. To live as a human being, in his understanding, meant to love and understand and appreciate the earth. To live as a human being is to grow up feeling and experiencing the mysterious cycles and processes of nature and to sense that one is oneself an integral part of nature. It is through such interaction with the earth that the characteristics which we recognize as truly human are ignited and nurtured within us. The earth is the source of morality and ethical behavior in human experience. Thus, Makiguchi wrote upon one occasion:

> The natural world inspires us, fosters our wisdom, and family, friends, neighbors, and community groups nurture us in so many ways. This immediate, direct experience which we can have with the natural and social environments of our communities fosters compassion, good will, friendship, kindness, sincerity, and humble hearts.

—Jinsei Chirigaku, 1903

It is rare to find young people today who possess this sense of wonder, this spiritual aliveness, and the attitudes of love and responsibility toward nature and society which stem from it. These characteristics are lacking in the lives and personalities of a majority of modern youth. Why is this? What has happened? What have we done? What we have done is becoming increasingly clear. We have short-changed our children. We have cut them off from their roots. We have treated children like so many cut flowers which we pick and keep alive in a vase. We can keep the flowers alive for a while, but sooner or later they will die. Their roots are gone. There is no way for them to gain nourishment. They can no longer grow normally.

In much the same way we have in our society cut children off from the sources from which they can obtain spiritual and emotional nourishment. We have plucked them out of their natural and social communities and created an artificial, sterile world for them to inhabit during the most important, formative years of their lives. The process whereby this separate, artificial world was created in modern societies for children to inhabit is, of course, a complex and many-faceted one, including the rise of giant cities and the concurrent destruction of authentic community life. But, as noted above, one of the key social structures directly involved was the school. We began building this artificial world for children when we decided to place them in a school room and make them passive recipients of masses of fragmented, and to them meaningless, factual knowledge for six or more hours every day. We proceeded further in the creating of that sterile world our children inhabit when we gave them television and computers. Many hours of passively sitting before a television or computer game each day, in addition to their school experience, cuts them off completely from active participation in the systems upon which their lives depend for nourishment.

Makiguchi was horrified when he realized what the schools of his day were doing to children. It was that realization which led him to propose, among other things, a half-day school system. I wonder how he would feel if he were alive today.

Even as I am writing, a news report indicates that police are at a loss as to how to deal with hot rodders. Groups of concerned parents, PTAs, educators, government officials, meet throughout the country to consider and deplore the growing incidence of *ijime*, "concrete murders," youth suicides and, more recently, increasing drug use among young people. These conditions are the inevitable outcome of the kind of world we have consigned them to.

The problems for parents and children posed by visual media and the youth culture are difficult and complex, but they are not insoluable. One reason for hope is a realization that a very few of today's young people have managed to retain a sense of wonder and appreciation which they express in loving, responsible behavior toward nature and society. But they are exceptions; they are the fortunate ones who have had, in the midst of the negative influences of their culture, opportunities to glimpse a different world; or, as the poet has so meaningfully expressed it, they have listened to a different drummer. These young people, it turns out upon close acquaintance with them, have been able to find character models outside of their peer culture and the vapid, media-created models afforded by television and the popular and sports cultures. We can learn from such youth something about the sources of their wholeness.

Another cause for optimism is that some families and communities, both in Japan and in various other countries, are beginning to work together to better understand the problems affecting youth and to seek solutions. Some families, for example, have found creative solutions to the problem of television viewing. Reports of their efforts and the methods which have proven successful for them can help us in our own search for solutions and our efforts to create more nurturing environments for children and youth.

More on the Community School in Camden, Maine: .

INTIMACY, CONNECTEDNESS, AND EDUCATION
by Emanuel Pariser

This article is based on seventeen years of teaching, learning, and living with high school students who have left school before graduating. Our experience at The Community School, a small, residential alternative school, has suggested that these students' successful education is the result of a learning environment which provides an experience of intimacy and connectedness. By intimacy I mean a sense of emotional closeness between two or more people.

In his foreword to John Holt's seminal work *How Children Fail*, Allan Fromme writes:

> What does the child hear when he is called on? What does he feel? What does he think?....What does the teacher think and feel and do as he awaits the answer? ..Does his relationship with the child have the intimacy ideally necessary for intellectual growth or is it a dull contractual one which fosters non-learning as much as it does learning?.....

Teachers can be no more successful in their classrooms than they can be in their marriages without this quality of sensitivity. The reason for this is that there is as much *intellectual intimacy* in the teaching-learning relationship as there is *emotional intimacy* in the husband-wife relationship.[1]

Taking Fromme's point a little further I would add that *both* emotional and intellectual intimacy have been prerequisite learning conditions for our students, many of whom have experienced long histories of social and academic failure. The presence of these forms of intimacy in The Community School has led them to a sense of connectedness: with themselves with other people, and with the larger community.

---

1. John Holt, *How Children Fail*, (New York: Dell, 1964), p. 12.

In this article I will examine how a school can foster the necessary sense of intimacy and connectedness in its educational process, and what the ramifications are of making these elements primary ingredients of an educational approach. The students, programs and situations described below are all taken from experiences at The Community School; it is my hope that their explication will be useful to others in all forms of education.

The Need for Intimacy:
Many students need to experience closeness because there has not been enough of it in their lives. As they move from personal failure to academic and social failure, their intellectual abilities become neutralized or redirected towards finding a "way out" of their intolerable lives.

A social worker referred Tracy to The Community School six months after her second suicide attempt. She was 18 years old, had left school as a junior, was a heavy drinker, and had lived through a long series of depressingly self-destructive and abusive relationships.

She was disconnected from her family and out of touch with her own feelings. Her life was chaotic. She knew that finishing school and getting a high school diploma was "important". She was accepted at the school as a "long-shot," since in the past two years she had never lived in one place for more than a couple of months.

Students like Tracy are products of failed human relationships and failed institutional remedies. Their families did not provide them with the love they needed to develop as children; as teenagers these students find it terrifying to accept love when it is offered. Their lives alternate between seeking the intimacy which never materialized in their childhood, and fleeing from the pain of intimate relationships in the present.

These adolescents are vulnerable to addictions or depressions that shield them from the pain of this failed intimacy; they are constantly wounded by the uncaring atmosphere which greets them in school and other social institutions designed to "help" or "educate" them.

Our students' inability to trust adults is a mirror image of their distrust in themselves. Their rejection of "the system" and social norms, their sense of themselves as helpless, is the other side of the system's rejection of them as lazy, unmotivated, desocialized, hopeless students. This mutual rejection leads them further into isolation; into groups of other similarly wounded kids where they feel accepted and are left alone.

A high percentage of our applicants feel that "no one cared" about them in their high school; that they were "just a number;" that the authorities were glad to see them go. The Pink Floyd song, "We Don't Need No Education," eloquently expresses both sides of the equation: delivered in a menacing chant, the song portrays an educational system which treats the singer as "just another brick in the wall."[2] While the threatened violence of the singer's voice corroborates the system's perception of him as the archetypal "bad" student, the lyrics of the song convey the singer's view of education as an archetypally malevolent system.

Just as the social outcomes of failed intimacy are withdrawal, alienation, mutual rejection and stereotyping, the intellectual ramifications are fear of learning and an inability to think.

In *How Children Fail*, John Holt describes how children must sustain a certain amount of intellectual insecurity to think about a problem:

> Schools give every encouragement to producers, the kids whose idea is to get "right answers" by any and all means. In a system that runs on "right answers," they can hardly help it. And these schools are often very discouraging places for thinkers.
>
> Until recently it had not occurred to me that poor students thought differently about their work than good students: I assumed they thought the same way, only less skillfully. Now it begins to look as if the expectation of fear and failure may lead children to act and think in a special way, to adopt strategies different from those of more confident children.
>
> Emily is a good example. She is emotionally as well as intellectually incapable of checking her work, of comparing her ideas against reality...She makes me think of an animal fleeing danger—go like the wind, don't look back, remember where the danger was and stay away from it as far as you can.[3]

---

2. Roger Waters, "The Wall", (New York: Pink Floyd Music Publishers, 1979), "Another Brick in the Wall".

3. Holt, *How Children Fail*, p.48.

For people who have been traumatized by unpredictable, uncaring, disrupted home and school environments, the ability or desire to sit with intellectual uncertainty becomes infinitesimal. Too much in their lives is already insecure; they retreat from thinking because it is too painful.

The questions then become how best can we structure an educational environment so that it becomes "safe" to think, to feel, to be? How does one differentiate the learning environment significantly enough from past situations that students feel they have a chance; that learning need not be painful, oppressive or boring?

Structuring Intimacy in Education: Structural and Programmatic Elements:

Program Size: Size is the most obvious environmental condition necessary to produce the felt sense of intimacy. The school-community must be small enough to allow for formal and informal personal encounters between students and staff. One of the secrets of the Community School's longevity is that we've stayed small. The program works with a maximum of eight students a term; there are six faculty members, one of whom is present at all times. According to *High Schools As Communities: The Small School Reconsidered* by Gregory and Smith, schools of up to 250 students can also achieve a strong sense of interpersonal intimacy.[4]

Space: Students need to have a definite physical space which is *theirs*. It should be comfortable, inviting, and personal. When students enter the Community School they come in through the kitchen; they are interviewed in the living room. The furniture is worn but serviceable; the bookshelves, wall decorations and plants make the environment much more reminiscent of home than school.

Staff Structure: In most conventional schools little effort is spent on creating a sense of "collegiality" among faculty. Gary Whelage defines this term as "the key characteristic of a success-

---

4. Thomas B. Gregory, G.R. Smith, *High Schools as Communities: The Small School Reconsidered*, (Bloomington, IN: Phi Delta Kappa Ed. Fdation,'87), p. 59, 60, 74.

ful teacher culture.[5] He describes the importance of teamwork and participation in group activities, some of which are not work-focused. Developing a sense of collegiality will lead to a feeling of intimacy among faculty, and hopefully will allow staff to "model" productive, respectful relationships for the students.

Educators of high school students, especially troubled ones, must come to grips with their own interpersonal issues that are often mirrored by the students they have chosen to work with. If self-reflection, insight and openness are encouraged among staff, the roles of teacher and student as educators of each other take on a much more reciprocal nature. The possibility for meaningful educational encounters have been maximized.

To create and support a sense of intimacy among staff the School devotes 5 hours a week to a full faculty meeting. An outside consultant facilitates the meeting. Staff all "check in" on how they're feeling at the moment, and bring up compliments and resentments they wish to discuss with their colleagues. Program decisions are made as much as possible by consensus, and the faculty formally evaluates itself four times a year.

The connections between staff culture and student culture are subtle and powerful. When there is a significant turnover of staff one term, more students than usual are apt to drop out the next one. As in a family, the level of trust and intimacy experienced among the faculty has a direct impact on the development of trust between students and the School.

To be successful in the long run, programs need to structure ways for their staff to become close, to support and teach one another. Programs must pay as much attention to the needs of the faculty as they do to the needs of the students.

If schools do not build in mechanisms for taking care of the caregivers, faculty will burn out quickly, substantially reducing the program's effectiveness.

Attention: The Interview, The One-to-One, The Group

To teach successfully one must have the opportunity to pay attention to one's students. One must learn what *they* are experiencing, and how it feels to be who they are.

---

5. Gary Wehlage, "Effective Programs for the Marginal High School Student." *Fastback* #297. (Bloomington, IN: Phi Delta Kappa Ed. Foundation, 1983), p.45.

"Ninety percent of learning," to quote Garrison Keillor, "is paying attention." But (to quote Bob) both teacher and student must be paying attention.[6]

In 1962 Paul Goodman pointed out in *Compulsory Mis-education* that:

> Adolescents (in America) are spiritually abandoned. They are insulated by not being taken seriously. ...Disregarded by the adults, they have in turn excluded adult guidance...[7]

Have we managed to change this pattern of disregard in the last 30 years? The following descriptions illustrate the three primary modalities through which The Community School focuses attention on its students.

The Interview: An interview is a student's first contact with the School. The interviewer asks the applicant serious and challenging personal questions, listening carefully and supportively to the answers. The process can take from 1 1/2 to to 2 1/2 hours and includes time for the student or her parents to ask questions and air concerns about the program. The encounter as depicted below, is a cross between an interview and a counseling session:

Frank enters the room gingerly as if any false step would disturb something. His mother follows self-consciously, finding a place to sit as quickly as possible. They sit on opposite sides of the room.

When Frank explains how he heard about the School from a former student, his mother adds, "I'm just not sure what I'll do without him at home, but I'm so proud that he's trying to finish school." Her reddened eyes water over imperceptibly.

Frank deftly sidesteps the emotion-laden moment by asking the interviewer whether or not one can play the game Dungeons and Dragons at the School. His mother leaves the room to allow the actual interview to begin.

Bob, the staff interviewer, has a brusque style. He gruffly asks Frank the ninety questions which cover family, school,

---

6. Bob Dickens, Community School Newsletter #52, (Camden, Me: Community School Press, 1989), p. 1.

7. Paul Goodman, *Compulsory Mis-education*, (New York: Vintage Books, '62), p. 74.

work, and legal history. Frank is impressed by Bob's casual appearance; he wears a T-shirt and jeans, and has a lengthy white beard. Bob seems attentive and interested in Frank's responses, particularly those relating to substance abuse issues. He is not sure if Bob is suspicious, or if he really cares.

Questions about his family are the hardest to answer. Despite his loyalty, there is not much to be proud of. When asked to name one good quality of his—Frank replies: "I wouldn't take up much space."

Often the important bond formed between applicant and interviewer can last the entire term. The faculty interviewer "presents" the interview to the full staff after discussion with another staff member. Conditions for acceptance are based on the full staff's recommendations. The interviewer works with an applicant until s/he is finally in the program, on a waiting list, or not accepted. This process may take as long as 6 hours of individual and group staff time.

Student acceptance is determined by staff consensus. The interview is the beginning of a student's integration into the school-community; it is a process based upon careful listening and attention. For the process to work, staff must listen and attend to *each other* as well as they do to the applicant.

The One-to-One: The advisory relationship known as the "one-to-one" is the most powerful method of focusing attention and care on a student at the Community School. Each student meets regularly with one teacher who acts as their advisor, coach, advocate and friend for the entire term. In many instances it is the strength of this relationship that sustains the student while s/he meets the demands of the program.

The character of a one-to-one meeting is dependent on the relationship that can be forged between staff and student. A typical meeting will include: reviewing the student's preceding week; problem solving to resolve conflicts; planning for the group meeting if the student has issues s/he wishes to, or will be required to, address; discussing future goals and current concerns.

One-to-ones may be held while teacher and student sit in a quiet room, walk around the block, drive to work, climb a tree. They may take an hour, or be accomplished in three ten-minute sessions.

Regardless of the form these meetings take, their two primary purposes are to establish a trusting relationship between student and teacher, and to facilitate the student's progress through the program.

Although students who take advantage of the one-to-one process tell us how important it is to them, some students cannot use the one-to-one. Getting close to anyone is too painful and frightening. As one of our first students once said, "I'd rather have someone hit me over the head with a bat than care about men."[8] In these cases the teacher becomes more of a manager, facilitating the student's practical success in the program. Whether fully utilized or not, the one-to-one offers all students the possibility of carrying on a sustained relationship with one supportive and trustworthy adult.

The Group: The conscious use of group process is a third modality for structuring intimacy in education. Because adolescents have a tremendous drive to belong to groups of peers which accept them, their initial impetus to join a community of peers is naturally strong.

For students who have never felt that they fit or belonged anywhere the prospect of joining a group, however—especially one which includes adults—raises ambivalent feelings.

For these students, groups must be accessible, accepting, and respectful.

The Community School offers an array of differently structured groups for all students to participate in: cooperative learning experiences in which all students and tutors take part precede evening tutorials; physical education requirements are met by weekend camping trips which are a combination of family outings and challenging physical experiences; every Thursday evening the entire school-community meets in the living room to vote on issues of school governance and discuss conflicts and interpersonal upheavals; seminars focus on special issues such as sexuality and self esteem, substance abuse, and non-violent conflict resolution, and finally, since the School is residential, many unplanned interactions take place in a group.

In a paper written for a community college class, Steve Hayden, a former student, expressed the impact that his Community School experience had on him:

> I am a very lucky person to have a need for group support. When I first found out I had a necessity for this type of thing, I thought my life had come to a miserable

---

8. Community School Student to Emanuel in 1974 during a one-to-one session.

slump....Today I think back to the first group I attended. This was at an alternative high school. On Thursday nights we had group rap.

This may well have been my first structured family. Now I have five or six families I can put a face on, and thousands I haven't yet.[9]

The group format teaches not only content skills but helps students learn how to be contributing members of a community. It establishes a sense of comfortable connectedness.

Drawbacks of Providing Intimate Learning Environments:

To stress intimacy in an educational approach raises major issues for staff and student alike. Overwhelming feelings may be conjured up by living and learning in homelike environments, by trusting again, by being trusted and enfranchised. The following descriptions detail a few key problems that can arise in utilizing an intimacy centered

Often the most "successful" student experiences the greatest pain in an educational setting like The Community School. She comes to the School as Tracy did and allows herself to trust a bit more and feel safe. This process unleashes several dragons: first, she begins to get in touch with some of her previously suppressed and denied experiences; second, she notices all that has been missing in her previous relationships, both emotional and intellectual; and third, she must deal with the undeniable fact that her term at the School is time-limited—she must leave at the end regardless of how well she has done.

In a recent meeting of graduates, Jory, now a 28-year-old truck driver who had no family support when he was at the School, likened his experience of graduating to a plane ride. "...when I came to the end, there was no one there to meet me. I felt lost again."[10] Several years after she graduated Tracy commented to me, "I worked so hard just to stay in the program; to complete something for the first time in my life. Then after all these struggles, I was successful and you (the School) said I had

9. Steve Hayden, Community School Graduate, Community School Newsletter #52, (Camden, ME: Community School Press, 1989), p. 2.

10. Community School Student at former student group, 1990.

to go!"[11] Tracy's feelings of anger and loss are common among graduating students.

The School has begun to address this issue by creating a post-graduate program: Project Graduation and Beyond, which will support students once they leave by providing ongoing tutoring, referral, and group work.

In the context of post-graduate work, a focus on close relationships can be problematic because of the importance specific staff-student relationships attain. Students who had strong attachments to a specific staff member who is no longer teaching at the School have to come to grips with "change", and do not feel as trusting of unknown new staff. Dora, the School's co-founder, Bob, Agnes, and I might be the only familiar faces left.

There are enormous consequences if students and staff are unable to address the myriad personality and behavioral issues which arise in a residential group. It is not infrequent that a student will threaten to drop out of the program if "something isn't done" about a fellow student. The feeling is expressed as "either they go or I do."

If in a larger, more impersonal setting the force of one personality is diminished; in an intimate setting it is potentiated. How to put up with people one does not like is one of the most difficult lessons to learn at The Community School.

A problem arises as well for faculty. Interpersonal relations among staff form the hub of the School's relational community. These relationships can become convoluted and complicated as the work stirs up innumerable personal issues. Hours of self-reflective work are needed to restore a sense of clarity and common purpose. But this time is usually not available because of the pressing programmatic issues that take priority. The faculty must walk a tightrope, balancing the need to take care of its students with the need to attend to itself. Furthermore the staff must find a way to both support and supervise itself, so that feedback can be clearly distinguished as interpersonal or task-related.

Positive Effects of an Intimacy-Based Methodology:
The personal encounter: One of the most powerful consequences of generating a sense of closeness within at learning community is that staff and student can experience genuine per-

---

11.   Community School Student to Emanuel two years after graduation, 1987.

sonal encounters with each other. Such encounters are the unplanned, but vital curriculum of programs like the Community School. They involve two or more people within the community discussing or doing something which is of import to each without anyone feeling that their participation is compulsory.

In *De-Schooling Society*, Ivan Illich points out that:

> ...reliance on institutional process has replaced dependence on personal good will. The world has lost its humane dimension...The relational structures we need are those which will enable each person to define themselves by learning and contributing to the learning of others.[12]

Moments of unplanned learning form an aspect of the core curriculum at The Community School. In fact, Einstein's favorite definition of education was: "what we remember after we forget everything we learned in school."[13] For people such as our students who have defended themselves rigidly against formal education these unselfconscious learning encounters can be a re-entry into the realm of thinking and learning.

In ten days Sam will to graduate from The Community School. He and I go out for a coffee to talk about his plans for the future and to have a final meeting before he leaves. He is proud of the fact that he's been accepted at a technical school; he had never considered going beyond high school. The subject of his father's death comes up. It happened almost a year ago. Sam says he would have gone crazy if it hadn't been for his girl friend being there with him. He thinks she may be away at college when the anniversary of the death comes this year. He hopes he can "handle it" alone.

I ask him if he's thought about coming back to the School for a day or two near the anniversary; perhaps he could spend some time with his one-to-one. Sam is pleased at the suggestion. He'll talk about it with Buck, his one-to-one, when he gets back to school.

This momentary discussion has taught us both several things: that emotions can be tied to events which are tied to specific times of year; that one needn't tough it out alone even if

---

12.   Ivan Illich, *Deschooling Society*, (New York: Harper & Row, 1970), p. 111.

13.   Albert Einstein, *Out of My Later Years*, (N.Y., Philosophical Library, 1950), p. 71.

one is an American Male; that a sense of community can extend over a geographic distance; that taking care of ourselves properly involves feeling, thinking and communicating.

Academic Contagion: A learning environment which promotes closeness also increases the chances that one person's enthusiasm will rub off on someone else. One of the primary results of an intimacy-centered learning environment is that students have direct contact with adults—faculty, volunteers, community members—who have found joy and mastery in a specific field of knowledge. The hoped for effect is that the adult's joyful and knowledgeable interest will stimulate a resonance of similar interest in the student, or perhaps tap into a reserve of interest as yet unknown to the student.

Reg is a Passamaquoddy Indian from Zebayig—a reservation in Perry, Maine. Along with having a variety of behavioral issues, he has never managed to sustain an interest in school. His big frame and muscular body, his constant angry awareness that he is from an oppressed culture, make him an intimidating person to work with, at first.

In the course of his stay at the Community School Reg loosens up a bit. He has a reservoir of humor. Bob, a staff member who is an avid poetry enthusiast, and is committed to working with Native Americans, introduces him to Native American poetry as part of his literature curriculum. Reg likes what he reads. The rest of the staff joins in suggesting their favorite poems to Reg. He reads them. He begins to write his own. He continues to write poems through his most difficult moments at the School. I call him three months after he has completed his term—he still has several requirements to finish before he graduates. Is he still writing poetry? I ask. Every day, he answers. I ask him to send me some; I'd like to read them and perhaps put them in the School's newsletter. No, he says, I can read them when I come to visit.

Removal of Blocks: An educational environment which creates a sense of safety and care allows students to begin to trust others. They let down emotional and mental guards which so effectively protected them from their past educational abuse and neglect. Their "learning disabilities", diagnosed or not, have functioned as an armor to keep their own and other's expectations of themselves at as low a level as possible. Their conception of themselves as "stupid" blocks learning and results in "brittle" minds that are scared to risk thinking.

Joe arrives at the School from Houlton. He is 19 and designated a "slow learner". He has failed ninth grade three times and is firmly convinced that he is basically dumb. A few weeks into the term he chooses math as his first subject to cope with. Sitting down with his tutors to work, he struggles for the "right" answers and fails. He is embarrassed by his inability to grasp the material.

In the middle of a particularly difficult lesson he asks Dora, the Co-Director, to talk with him. They go into the office, shut the door, and Joe proceeds to explain that he just can't do it, he'll have to leave. He likes the School, but he just can't do the work. He never liked math. At this point Joe is shaking. Tears roll down his cheeks. He is 19 years old, a man capable of a good hard day's work in the potato houses, and the prospect of continuing on in the pain and confusion which math inspires in him seems unbearable.

Dora listens to him carefully. She tells him that it's normal for him to feel the way he does after having tried so hard for so long and failed. She adds that the School will work with him as long as he needs to on academics, there is no rush. A year later Joe gets his diploma, it has taken an extra six months, but, in the process he has re-learned to trust his own thinking abilities.

Perseverance: Students who begin to experience a connection to others in their learning environment become more persistent learners. They become less afraid of failure and more willing to take intellectual risks, to sit with unanswered questions, to work towards long-term goals. In a beautiful passage John Holt describes how we all are persistent learners at the beginning of our lives:

> A baby does not react to failure as an adult does or even a five year old because she has not yet been made to feel that failure is shame, disgrace, a crime. Unlike her elders she is not concerned with protecting herself against everything that is not easy and familiar; she reaches out to experience, she embraces life.[14]

Holt ascribes less importance than I would to the fact that the baby is carrying out her "experiments" within the context of a loving, attentive family which protects her from the "natural"

---

14. John Holt, *How Children Fail*, p. 89.

disasters which could befall her in the course of her explorations. When students feel that their acceptance as people is not contingent upon a particular academic success, they can relax; the energy they have used to defend themselves can be used to learn; they learn to persist despite their mistakes and setbacks.

In the light of the many little successes students experience regularly at the School, failure takes on a different complexion. It is not an annihilating experience. Students are honored more for their efforts than their ability to take tests. Students understand that the School will work with them as long as they need in order to graduate. Ultimately learning becomes a cooperative rather than a combative experience, more like the explorations of Holt's baby than the standardized mechanical experiences which make up the worst of conventional education.

Long Term Results in One Setting: What have been the educational and social outcomes for students at The Community School over the past 17 years? Approximately 70% graduate with a high school diploma from The Community School, another 5% to 7% will complete their education via the service, G.E.D., or adult education. Roughly 20% have gone on to some other form of education.

Perhaps the most unexpected result is that over 60% of our former students have remained in contact with the School. During the past year the program received more than 450 contacts from former students ranging from letters to phone call to visits. It often feels like our work has only commenced at matriculation.

It is my belief that any program which places the same high value on interpersonal and intellectual closeness could achieve similar or better short and long-term results. Larger programs could make effective use of older students, parents, and volunteers to bring down the staff:student ratio. Wherever faculties make long term commitments to these educational goals, students will take the risk of connecting and learning.

Conclusion: I have tried to make a case for what most of us in the world of education should find obvious: the opportunity for students and teachers to be close with one another intellectually and emotionally is a crucial aspect of any truly effective educational process. Why does this need to be reiterated? Because we get so wrapped up in our drive to find and use educational technologies which "work" and labels which help us sort out and define different student populations we forget that one of the fundamental pre-conditions for learning to take place is the experience of intimacy.

Neither computers, nor interactive videos, nor programmed textbooks can save us from this fact: if we don't provide the space and time for our children to meet, and think and learn together with their teachers as complete human beings, they will never connect to form the educational communities necessary for learning to occur. The system will continue to spew out disaffected, alienated, and disenfranchised people, people who have given up, people who are afraid to think and terrified to learn.

DESCHOOLING
OUR LIVES

EDITED BY MATT HERN
Foreword by Ivan Illich

Alan Bonsteel is a Family Practitioner from San Francisco, California and has been a leader in the educational choice movement for sixteen years.

SCHOOLS OF CHOICE AS COMMUNITIES
by Alan Bonsteel, M.D.

For those of us who would build a better world, who would lend a hand to the AIDS victim in the American inner city, who would think of the day laborer in the far-off Crossroads shantytown as our neighbor, who would treat this planet as one would treat one's mother, the central issue is community. Is our purpose serving our own private gratifications, or are we all in this together, sharing the larger purpose of service to the greater good? The struggle between belonging and alienation, between meaning and emptiness, between connectedness and drift, is the central drama of our lives.

Having been active in the freedom in schooling movement for sixteen years, and having visited schools of choice in eleven countries, I contend that choice in schooling is crucial to building communities.

The most important attribute of any school is that experience of community, that sense in the students of belonging and of the camaraderie of learning, that the teachers are there for them, that their families are involved and will be heard. There was a time when public schools were such community schools, and some still are, but for most of us the suspicion has set in that the shattered windows are not a sign of lack of custodians but of profound alienation, and that the racial and class segregation inherent in assigning students to a particular school based on geographical residence will not go away.

In my years of work in the field, I have visited literally hundreds of schools of choice. In the United States, that has meant either low-cost private school alternatives, or, in a few isolated instances, charter schools. In the other Western democracies—Europe, Canada, Australia, New Zealand, Israel and others—schools of choice generally mean independent or "free" schools subsidized by the government at a fixed percentage of per-pupil expenditures in public schools. What I have seen again and again are schools that are under *neighborhood* and *local* control; that are on a human scale with a human face, and that take to heart Schumacher's dictum that "small is beautiful;" that embrace genuine workplace democracy, with far more creativity and professional satisfaction on the part of the teachers, that recognize that each child is an individual, with his or her unique needs that must be met and unique gifts that need to be nurtured; and that, as Henry David Thoreau expressed it, "March to the beat of a different drummer."

In 1987 I spent a month studying Denmark's system of educational freedom of choice, established more than 140 years ago by the great educator N.F.S. Grundtvig and encompassing such diverse alternatives as Steiner and Montessori schools. I remember especially a "Folkhighschool" of fine arts I visited on the Jutland peninsula. Although I arrived virtually unannounced, the students were all busily at work, and the school was neat and clean. The teacher saw my astonishment and commented, "You know, Alan, it is a joy to teach in this school because the students have *chosen* to be here and they *value* what we have to offer." What I sensed in these students as I spoke with them was a passion for their art and an excitement and creativity that bonded them together in a true community that I could only envy.

I asked the teacher about discipline problems.

"Well," she said, "We have a hard time keeping some of them from smoking, because a few of our own teachers still smoke and I'd have to say it sets a bad example. And you know here in Denmark we have different cultural attitudes about sex than you do in the United States, so I imagine you might think of that as a discipline problem. We don't try to keep them from being sexually active, but we do teach responsibility and we have very explicit sex education classes. Most years we don't have any pregnancies, and our sexually transmitted disease rate is much lower than in American high schools. Serious discipline problems are truly unknown here. Even a mild reprimand is considered a severe embarrassment. Remember, the kids *want* to be here because this is family for them."

In 1988, I spent a month studying Holland's system of choice in education, a right enshrined in their constitution and a source of intense pride to the Dutch people. After I'd looked up the superintendent of the Protestant independent schools, I told him, "Look, everybody knows you have superb schools for ordinary Dutch people. Show me your schools for your kids who are different, who live in poverty, who have special needs."

After he'd thought for a while, he said, "All right, I'll send you to the school for the trailer people. But don't expect too much. These are our toughest kids with the most problems."

The "Trailer School" turned out to be on the outskirts of Rotterdam. A few hundred families lived a Gypsy lifestyle, returning from time to time to their home base, a dingy trailer court with rudimentary sanitation facilities. Lest one imagine that this was like a typical American mobile home park, these trailers were truly Lilliputian, so tiny that the average American would find them cramped even for a weekend trip, and towed by diminutive European-sized cars. The kids had every problem in the book, and would have given an American education bureaucrat plenty of excuses for failure: poverty, multi-ethnic backgrounds, Dutch as a second language, single-parent families, and worst of all, a lifestyle in which the kids would disappear with their parents for days or weeks and then reappear without explanation as to where they'd been.

And yet, I was once again blown away. The school was neat and tidy, and the kids were an inspiration. The fifth graders were already speaking English, and they courteously asked me why I had come all the way from the United States to visit their school.

After I'd toured the school, I met with the teachers.

"Our school is totally oriented toward working with the special problems of these transient kids," said one of the teachers. "We're always amazed at the way these families live—we're not even sure how some of them make a living. We think that when they go off wandering, they bring things back into the Netherlands they're not supposed to. All of the trailer people come here, and it's rare that we get anyone else."

"Could they go elsewhere if they wanted?" I asked.

"Of course. There are more spaces in the schools than there are students, so every school is trying to get more students to come. It's always in the back of our minds that they can leave any time they want. We always treat the parents courteously and with dignity, and listen carefully to their suggestions. And when we do that, we notice that they come around more often and take more interest in their children's education—at least when they're not off leading the Gypsy life!"

"There are five other schools within an easy walk that accept Dutch government scholarships," said another teacher. "But it's been two years since we've lost one of the trailer children to another school. This is *their* school—they understand that everything we do is for them. So they feel a sense of ownership."

Among the hundreds of schools of choice I have visited, for me a very special type of community is the school offering spiritually-based instruction, and the one I know best is the school of my own spiritual community, the Ananda village near Nevada City, California, where three hundred people live and work together in a meditation community. Although I don't live there

-451-

myself, I return every year for a retreat, and from time to time I cover the family practice clinic so that the docs there can take a vacation. And sometimes when I get discouraged with the cynical and corrupt world of politics, I return to visit my friends at the school and remind myself of why I have worked so long and so hard the last sixteen years for freedom in schooling.

At the Ananda school, the focus is on education for life rather than memorization, a philosophy that teaching responsibility and service and respect for others is more important than rote learning. And I see in the students a sense of community of the deepest and most intense kind, where they share the experience of life as an exciting journey, with an ever-expanding sense of oneness with the world, and where they strive to see everything that happens to them as having a purpose, however cleverly hidden at the time.

A friend of mine who teaches at the Ananda school told me a story that epitomizes what a school of this kind can offer.

"The local national forest has a program where school kids can spend a day planting trees," she said. "On the day we went out there, the forest rangers couldn't believe what they saw. Our kids were far more focused than any they'd ever had before. The rangers had their best men out there with automatic hole-drillers, and they still couldn't stay ahead of us! We finished early in the day after we'd run out of trees to plant."

"I'll never forget the look on the head ranger's face at the end of the day," she recounted. "He said, 'Those kids were planting trees like their lives depended on it, and then they were watering them out of their canteens. I even saw some of them stop to pray for the trees they'd planted. And you know, I think those little trees are going to grow real good.'"

For our lower-income minority groups in the United States, schools of choice have almost always been Catholic parochial schools, where the average yearly tuition nationwide is only $1457. There are a few exceptions like the Marcus Garvey school in Los Angeles, or Polly Williams' voucher plan in Milwaukee, or the public school choice plan in East Harlem. But schools of choice in the United States, unlike in the other Western democracies, have largely been limited to wealthier families. It is not surprising that the groups that have been most hurt by being restricted to low-quality, dangerous, alienating traditional public schools, Blacks and Hispanics, have been shown in poll after poll to be the strongest supporters of school choice.

The 1947 United Nations declaration of universal human rights establishes freedom in schooling as a fundamental right, but that doesn't mean much to a low-income family unable to pay private school tuition. The single parent who empties the wastebasket at night should have the same right to choose, the same right to quality education for his or her children, as the bigshot in the penthouse office.

The evidence that school choice produces higher academic results and lower dropout rates is overwhelming, but the issue goes far beyond simply a question of quality. There is a creativity, an energy, a vitality in schools of choice. There is a commitment that comes from having freely chosen. The right to choose carries with it a dignity, a sense of community, a shared purpose. Neighborhood schools of choice will bring us together.

Ernest and Elizabeth Morgan organized The Arthur Morgan School in Burnsville, NC, in 1962 on land donated by the Celo Community, a project of Ernest's father Arthur, who had also founded Antioch College in its present form. The school is still going strong (see pages 32-35 for a description of the school by Jeff Goldman)—as is Ernest Morgan himself! He is also a great believer in and proponent of his father's ideas and accomplishments, of which he writes from first-hand experience. See also an account by Ernest of its history in Challenging the Giant, *volume II pages 1-10.*

DIMENSIONS OF COMMUNITY,
The Seed Bed of Civilization
by Ernest Morgan
Reprinted from *Community Service News.*

Arthur Morgan held that it was in the face-to-face relationships of the small community that the best qualities of human culture tended to develop—honesty, good will and social responsibility. He commented that these qualities tend to erode in urban life, despite steady renewal there through the influx of people from the small communities.

I observed a dramatic illustration of this while serving as an administrator of Arab Relief in the Middle East, in 1950, where my work brought me into contact with the three types of Arab culture.

One of these was the culture of the nomadic people—the Bedouins. Though not without some special virtues, the Bedouins would steal the shirt off your back. A colleague of mine, visiting a Bedouin sheik, came out of the tent to find the wheels stolen off his Jeep. The sheik was outraged. "To steal from the Sheik's guest is like stealing from the Sheik himself. Dig those wheels out of the sand and put them back on the Jeep."— And they did.

The urban culture was similar, and the people were a mixed lot. Walking down the street in Cairo I was carrying a pen-light in the outside pocket of my jacket. My companion cautioned me: "Remove that light from your outer pocket and put it inside. Someone will brush against you and it will be gone."

The third Arab culture was that of the villagers, or Fellahin, as they are called. I had a crew of a dozen or so of them in my Food Distribution Center, and found them to be industrious, friendly—and completely honest! Similarly, whereas the Bedouin and town women felt it necessary to wear veils to shield their faces from the lustful gaze of strangers, the Fellahin women found no need for veils.

It would seem that the small community was, indeed, "the seedbed of civilization."

The Enhancement of Group Life

"Community" is not the monopoly of villages and communes. It can be developed to excellent advantage in many types of groups. Scott Peck places strong emphasis on this, and on procedures for bringing it about.

One of the most striking experiences of community in my career took place in the Middle East. I was a member of the team of 52 volunteers (a full deck!) who were brought together by the American Friends Service Committee to administer food, shelter and health care for the Arab refugees in the Gaza Strip.

We were a mixed bunch, from several countries, and varied ethnic backgrounds—African, Asian and European. Our religious affiliations were equally varied—Moslem, Catholic, Protestant and unchurched. Our responsibilities were tremendous. We were responsible for food, shelter and health care for 200,000 refugees living in very difficult conditions, but our group had a wonderful spirit of community and fellowship which enriched our lives. This was one of the most meaningful periods of my career.

This was not an accident; it had been planned that way. Each evening we had supper together in a big hall and after supper we sang songs from the International Songbook published by World Around Songs. Then members of the team were called upon to tell of their experiences. We shared our daily problems. An important unifying force was that we were all unpaid volunteers—we were there because we cared. Inevitably, the community spirit of the Gaza team impacted on our relationship with the Palestinian refugees, especially the 1400 of them who were employed to help carry on the necessary work.

The quality of community did not appear to be diminished by the substantial turnover which took place. This turnover happened because the project ran beyond its original time frame and many of the early volunteers were unable to stay. A striking testimony to the strength of the community feeling is the fact that at a reunion of the team members forty-two years later, more than sixty showed up!

Let me offer a totally different experience in group community. For years I ran a printing business. I wanted my staff to come together not as unrelated individuals but as a cohesive group who cared about one another and enjoyed their time together.

When I hired a new person I took him or her on a tour of the establishment, explaining how things worked and introducing the new person to all the people, as one might do with a new guest arriving at a party. Everyone was given a key to the plant and was free to come and go at all hours. Staff members were free to use the equipment to do printing for themselves or for non-profit institutions or projects with which they were concerned. For retired staff members we arranged regular part-time jobs so they could retain their fellowship and identify with the group.

The pursuit of community in the business has structural aspects, too. For forty-five years the staff have taken part in electing the Board of Directors. In recent decades, when my son came into the management, he instituted an Employee Stock Ownership Plan (ESOP) whereby the staff now own fifty-six percent of the stock—and the percentage is growing.

At one time our company had a visit from Henrik Infield, who was Executive Secretary of an organization devoted to community development. He was impressed with our outfit and urged that we do more things together, carrying on together as many of the activities of life as we could.

After reflecting on his advice I found myself in partial disagreement with him. I felt that each of us belonged to several communities; for example, the family, the neighborhood, the church, the bowling club, what have you. I wanted our group to be a good and happy community of people working together, but I didn't want it *competing* with other communities. Community should be a way of life—not an experience to be focussed on a single group.

One more reflection on "group community."

In the course of growing up I attended nine different schools. In one or two of these there was a sense of community. In the rest it was every man for himself. Years later, when my wife and I launched the Arthur Morgan School, community was central. Even more important than the curriculum is the habit of mutual affirmation which the school cultivates. It is from community and mutual affirmation that a sense of self-worth is derived, and there can be no more important function of education.

Human Uranium

A frequently overlooked dimension of community involves what Arthur Morgan characterized as "human uranium."

A cubic yard of granite, he said, contains enough uranium to blow up a mountain, but the particles are inert because they are separated from one another. Bring them together in a critical mass and you can blow up the mountain.

So it is with people who have active social concerns. Too often they are lost in the mass, and their concerns do not find effective expression. Bring them together in community and things begin to happen.

This time I cite my personal experience with Celo Community. Though diverse in religion and in educational background, and living in separate homes, Celo Community members enjoy active fellowship, and come together spontaneously to make things happen.

A group of them took the initiative in launching an innovative and highly successful food co-op. Today, I might add, eighty percent of the members of that co-op are from outside the Community. Similarly a group of community members launched "Cabin Fever University"—an arrangement whereby people share special knowledge and skills with their friends, with no money changing hands (except $1 for the catalog). As with the co-op store, people from outside the community flock to the "University." Craftspeople in Celo Community—potters, weavers and such—set up a cooperative retail shop on the highway, to sell their wares. They were joined promptly, and in force, by craftspeople from outside the community. Similarly, an ambitious project "The Rural Southern Voice for Peace", an organization concerned with peace and social issues, is based in the Community, as are other important projects. Here, indeed, is "human uranium" at work.

Collectives

An important but highly varied dimension of community consists of communes and other forms of collectives. Their number is growing and there is much diversity among them.

Twice in the early years of my business I set about to form a collective. In both cases I was dissuaded by the reluctance of my colleagues. This was probably just as well, since I didn't have an appropriate social base for a collective and didn't know what I was doing.

Later I had occasion to visit some successful collectives and observe their operation at first hand. One interesting project was the Sasa Kibbutz, in Israel. A group of Polish Boy Scouts years before had formed a strong group bond. After they had grown up and married they moved to Palestine (not yet Israel)

-457-

where they lived together communally as a "working kibbutz," holding such jobs as they were able to find. They studied farming and saved their money and after a time took over an area of salt swamp at the foot of Haifa Bay. The land was too salty for food crops but provided good hay and pasture, so they started a dairy. Areas too salty for hay or pasture they coverted into fish ponds for raising carp. The Kibbutz was prospering.

The children there seemed to enjoy a positive relationship with all the adults—not just their parents. When they grew up, children were encouraged to join the kibbutz, but before they could do so were required to go out into the world and make their way for a time. I was impressed with the Sasa Kibbutz.

I visited another interesting collective, the Bruderhof, at Rifton, New York. Originally founded in Germany (hence the name Brother House) it had shifted to Britain, then to Paraguay and finally to Rifton, N.Y. It has a "common purse" and common ownership of property, and operates some small businesses. Its unifying principle is "the Fatherhood of God and the Brotherhood of Man in Jesus Christ." It expects total commitment from its members and has strong leaders ("Servants of the Word").

The Hutterite Community in Canada long ago affiliated with the Bruderhof and more recently some successful branches have been established.

My experience with collectives being limited I am giving them less attention here than they perhaps deserve.

Community in an Urban Setting

People in cities tend to build walls around themselves, so that they are surrounded by strangers. Under these conditions the human qualities engendered by community life tend to erode.

But there have been successful experiments in developing community in urban neighborhoods. An outstanding case was the Hyde Park/Kenwood neighborhood, near the University of Chicago. Black families were starting to move in and there was the beginning of a panic, with white families moving out. At this juncture the Social Order Committee of the 57th Street Meeting of Friends (Quakers) came onto the scene, bringing black and white families into fellowship and building a sense of community. The exodus of white families was checked and a stable community life was achieved.

A similar circumstance arose in an area in Philadelphia that seemed on the verge of becoming a slum. As in Chicago, under Quaker leadership black and white residents were brought together in fellowship, to form a neighborhood community. Powelton Village, as it is called, has been highly successful.

Bert Berlow, of Minneapolis, has been active for years in the field of urban communities but I don't have the specifics on his results.

Clearly, it is possible to develop good community life in urban settings but this requires thoughtful and skillful organizing effort.

Community in the Macrocosm

Thus far I have discussed mainly the dimensions and aspects of the small community—areas in which I have a background of knowledge or experience.

One of the values of good community life, as I pointed out in the paragraphs on "Human Uranium" is the tendency for community values to be projected toward the outside world, as in the case of "The Rural Southern Voice for Peace." While the small community—especially an "intentional" community—does offer an "escape" from typical urban life, it can—and often does—do a lot more than that in terms of social and political involvement.

Rampant individualism, as opposed to a healthy community spirit, threatens to wreck modern society, regardless of the particular form the society takes. I saw this coming in the Soviet Union early in the Stalin era and published an article in *The Christian Register*, "The Bankruptcy of Bolshevism" back in 1937. The Communist movement might have led to a humane and beautiful society had the spirit of community prevailed, but it was corrupted by individualism and finally went down the drain.

We now see the free enterprise system, another system with fine social potential, likewise headed for the sewer, and for the same reason—rampant individualism and the lack of the spirit of community.

America is a prize example. The extreme and growing maldistribution of ownership and income in our country is such that it is only by the astronomical expansion of debt that the buying power of the people can keep pace with producing power—and keep the wheels turning. This is a form of medicine which must be taken in ever-increasing doses—until it kills the patient. As matters now stand, when the borrowing stops we crash. The Great Depression of the 1930's was never solved, but merely postponed through inflation and massive borrowing, fueled largely by war and preparation for war. Growth is put forward as a solution, but perpetual growth is a sure form of suicide.

I will not take space here to set forth economic and political measures which might be effective in achieving a humane and stable society, but I will say that the emergence of a spirit of community throughout society is an essential prerequisite to the successful pursuit of those measures.

This article is based on a transcript of a speech I gave at Carnegie Hall as one of the school people John Gatto had assembled to deliver a message to the citizens of New York about what school could do! Three of John's ex-students plus three school founder/heads spoke. Plus John himself, of course. The entire program was later published as The Exhausted School.

BUILDING COMMUNITY IN A PLURALISTIC SOCIETY
by Mary Leue

Since childhood I have been fascinated with education—or, more properly, with school. The fascination began with the schools I myself had attended, starting, most significantly, with my first grade, which I spent with my grandmother, who had been a teacher in her youth. I remember very clearly the books we read together, the little red spelling frame we used, the abacus we played with, the little, slant-ceilinged room that served as our classroom. It left an indelible impression on me about school. I developed a lifelong love of reading, and during my middle childhood years spent many a happy hour sitting on the floor of the children's reading room in our town's public library. Reading Louisa May Alcott's *Little Men*, and then *Jo's Boys*, started a yearning within me for having this experience myself of actually having my own school, which would run the way I wanted it to run. Actually, this fantasy dovetailed right in with the way I myself had been brought up in a family of six kids and parents who took their role of providing children with wonderful experiences seriously. During my middle childhood and early adolescent years, we all camped, mountain-climbed, sailed, swam, skiied, toboganned, rock-climbed, cooked, weeded gardens, cleaned house, and got read to every night. In fact, so enthusiastic were my parents to do these things with us that they too often forgot to allow us to choose our own activities. I remember more than once hiding in a closet that had a light in it, sitting on the floor and reading one of my precious books while the hue and cry went on all around me to join in the family activity. It's only in looking back, that I can fully appreciate what I received.

Many years later, during the sixties, after all but one of my five kids had reached high school age, I read A.S. Neill's *Summerhill*, and all of the disparate and apparently incompatible ingredients for school that I had had sloshing around inside me throughout the years of my life finally came together into a pretty clear notion of the school I would one day start. It wouldn't be filled with prescribed activities, and yet, the richness would be there—somehow. I wasn't sure quite how.

Here's how it actually happened. We lived in Texas for nine years during the fifties because of my husband's teaching job, and four of my five kids were in public school there. When we moved up north to Albany in 1962 and all five of my kids were now in Albany's public schools, I was faced for the first time with the regimentation and inhumanness of city schools. My fourth child, Ellen, now in third grade, who had blossomed in the relaxed atmosphere of her small second-grade class in Texas, now began to shrink timidly when it came time to head off to school. In fact, her eyesight, which was normal at the beginning of that year, had pulled back to a near-handicap degree of near-sightedness by the following June! I only discovered for myself why this was happening when I was summoned to a parent/teacher conference in the middle of the school year. Ellen's teacher, in this class for the so-called "Academically talented," which the kids themselves called, more accurately, "Animal trained!" turned out to be a tyrannical martinet who ran her classroom as though it were a military establishment!

As a result of this belated realization, the yeast of change began to rise in the dough of my own inner feeling about school. It was high time! I had ignored the effects of public education on my first four, because the problems hadn't been acute. But when my fifth child Mark reached fifth grade, and began to hurt even more than his sister Ellen, I let him persuade me to take him out and teach him at home. It was a big step to have taken, in my own eyes, involving a basic deviation from all the accepted norms of the society. Doing that can be scary, in a status/money-oriented society. The myth prescribes twelve years of maximum striving for good grades in school in order to compete successfully for the glittering prizes.

I know now that it's not real. Why is it so hard for more of us to get it through our heads that schooling is more of a deterrent than an aid? Myths sometimes die hard, I guess, particularly when there is risk involved to people we love! I had to defy that myth in order to find out for myself. Well, it has turned out to be everything I had hoped for. Mark, at 34, is fine, happily married, with two extraordinary kids. They live in a small, western Massachusetts village, in the life of which they are all actively involved. I needn't have worried about Mark's economic future. He is highly successful and totally happy building repairing and selling magnificent stringed instruments.

And he is in no way culturally impaired! The oldest of his kids, Ian, is already, at the age of seven, years ahead of most of his age peers in competence, curiosity, and breadth of understanding and enjoyment of life! They have managed to work out an informal arrangement with Ian's first-grade teacher at the local village school whereby he spends as much time at school as he chooses and the rest at home. Ian is totally self-motivated, reads omnivorously and constantly, writes stories and letters, loves doing arithmetical sums and puzzles, and spends time happily with his father in his shop, learning to work with wood. Madeline, his little sister, at the age of four is as articulate as most kids more than twice her age, and busy, busy, busy all day long, playing with Ian and the day-care kids Helene takes care of during the week.

Taking that first step of allowing Mark to drop out of school, and then taking those that naturally followed from that first one until we ended up with a full-fledged alternative Pre-K through 8th ungraded school which has grown into a community. Having seen the results of our kids' experiences in the school over a period of more than 23 years, there is now no doubt in my mind that any family that wishes a better life for its kids can arrange it, although not necessarily as I did. So that's not the issue I'd like to focus on. There are two issues I'd like to pursue: questions that concern me greatly. I'm not at all sure they can be dealt with separately. One is, is good education possible, in a mass, governmentally-mandated system? John says no. In some ways, I hope it is, at least for the near future. So then, granting hypothetically that the answer to the first question be yes, the question is, can we transform our present school system to provide really good education in the true sense of the word? Can we transform it so that it will do the job it was intended to do — namely, to provide our kids with a setting in which they can thrive, can become *themselves* in the best, most inclusive sense of the word. According to my Webster's Collegiate Dictionary, the Latin word *Educare*, meaning to bring up a child, comes originally from *educere*, to bring forth or out. We aren't there to pour it in, but to draw it forth from the child himself! That cannot be said too often!

Looking at that question of what good education is, I have come to believe that it is impossible to think of "education" in the abstract. For me, it has to do with people—pupils, teachers, parents. And these folks come in all sizes and flavors. One's own experiences inevitably color one's ideas about education, both positively and negatively. I realize also that it is impossible to separate school from the context of our country and its values. School is a mirror of who we are. And we, in turn, are a mirror of what we have learned in school and at home. So my question boils down to how to get hold of the end of the tangle of yarn so as to begin to untangle it. What do we do?

John Gatto has pointed out that the problem with schools at bottom is one of institutions, and that what is really wrong with the institution of school is what is wrong in general with institutions as networks to serve our social goals. Here is his brilliantly provocative reply to a proposal for the enlargement of schooling as an answer to the school crisis, as I have summarized it, drawing from a number of sources for his analysis of the problem:

> A surprising number of otherwise sensible people find it hard to see why the scope and reach of our formal schooling networks should not be increased—by extending the school day or year, for instance—in order to provide an economical solution to the problems posed by the decay of the American family. One reason for their preference, I think, is that they have trouble understanding the real difference between communities and networks, or even the difference between families and networks. Because of this confusion they conclude that replacing a bad network with a good one is the right way to go. Since I disagree so strongly with the fundamental premise that networks are workable substitutes for families, and because from anybody's point of view a lot more school is going to cost a lot more money, I thought I'd tell you why, from a schoolteacher's perspective, we shouldn't think more school but less...
>
> In the growth of human society, families came first, communities second, and only much later came the institutions set up by the community to serve it. Most institutional rhetoric—the proclaiming of what is important—borrows its values from individual families that work well together...
>
> People who admire our school institution usually admire networking in general and have an easy time seeing its positive side, but they overlook its negative aspect—that networks, even good ones, take the vitality from communities and families. They make solutions to human problems mechanical, "by the numbers", when a slow, organic process of self-awareness, self-discovery, and cooperation is what is required if any solution is to stick...

Networks like schools are not communities in the same way that school training is not education. By preempting 50 percent of the total time of the young, by locking young people up with young people exactly their own age, by ringing bells to start and stop work, by asking people to think about the same thing at the same time in the same way, by grading people the way we grade vegetables—and in a dozen other vile and stupid ways—network schools steal the vitality of communities and replace it with an ugly piece of mechanism. Nobody survives these places with his humanity intact, not kids, not teachers, not administrators, and not parents.

The fragmentation caused by excessive networking creates diminished humanity, a sense our lives are out of control, because they are. If we face the present school and community crisis squarely, with hope of finding a better way, we need to accept that schools—as networks—create a large part of the agony of modern life. We don't need more schooling, we need less...

Nearly a century ago a French sociologist wrote that every institution's unstated first goal is to survive and grow, not to undertake the mission it has nominally staked out for itself. Thus the first goal of government postal service is to provide protection for its employees and perhaps a modest status ladder for the more ambitious ones; its first goal is not to deliver the mail. The first goal of a permanent military organization is not to fight wars but to secure, in perpetuity, a fraction of the national wealth to distribute to its personnel...

...If these examples trouble you, think of the New York City public school system where I work, one of the largest business organizations on planet Earth. While the education administered by this abstract parent is ill-regarded by everybody, the institution's right to compel its clientèle to accept such dubious service is still guaranteed by the police. And forces are gathering to expand its reach still further—in the face of every evidence it has been a disaster for all its history.

Particularly over the past century and a half in the United States spokesmen for institutional life have demanded a role above and beyond service to families and communities. They have sought to command and prescribe as kings used to do, though there is an important difference—in the case of ancient kings once beyond the range of their voices and trumpets you could usually do what you pleased, but in the case of modern institutions the reach of technology is everywhere—there is no escape if the place where you live and the family you live in cannot provide sanctuary...

As we approach the 21st century it is correct to say that the U.S. has become a nation of institutions where it used to be a nation of communities. Large cities have great difficulty supporting healthy community life, partly because of the constant coming and going of strangers, partly because of space constrictions, partly because of poisoned environments, but mostly because of the constant competition of institutions and networks for the custody of children and old people, and to monopolize the time of everyone else in between. By reserving young and old from the working life of places, and by reserving the working population from the lives of young and old, a fundamental disconnection of the generations has occurred. The griefs that arise from this have no synthetic remedy and no vibrant, satisfying communities can come into being where young and old are locked away...

A community is a place that faces people at each other over time in all their human variety, good parts, bad parts, and all the rest. Such places promote the highest quality of life possible, lives of engagement and participation. This happens in unexpected ways but it never happens when you've spent more than a decade listening to other people talk, and trying to do what they tell you to do, trying to please them after the fashion of schools. It makes a real difference lifelong if you can avoid that training—or if it traps you...

What gives the atmosphere of remote country towns and other national backwaters a peculiarly heady quality of fundamental difference is not simply a radical change of scenery from city or suburb, but the promise offered of near-freedom from institutional intervention into family life. Big Father doesn't watch over such places closely. Where his presence is felt most is still in the schools, which even there grind out their relentless message of anger, envy, competition, and caste-verification in the form of grades and "classes." But a home-life and community exist there as antidote to the poison.

In John's terms, my daughter Ellen's bad school experience in Albany happened mainly because of this factor of the heightened stakes involved in attempting to teach kids in crowded cities. It's mainly in cities that the acuteness of the problem exists! John says that school needs to be cut down to size, maybe even eliminated altogether in such places! I don't think that is likely to happen—and I'm not sure that would be a such a good idea unless we have a pretty good notion of what we would put in its place! After all, the damage to families and to community has already occurred! Would we be ready to cope with no school, or even with less school, no matter how insane? I'm not sure. City parents, perhaps a majority of them, have become too dependent on school for all sort of functions—baby-sitter, disciplinarian, time-manager, supplier of at least one meal a day—and just plain dumping ground—for that to happen; at least, not in the near future, given the tenor of most people's lives at the present, especially in cities. So I'd like to look at the question—particularly in cities: if we can't sit around waiting for schools to wither away, like the State in the Marxist dialectic, what can we do about the mess we have on our hands? Specifically, what are the ingredients that *could* make a school a good place for kids, at least for now.

Well, to begin with, we could keep in mind that kids are pliant, adaptive and easy to please, naturally curious, filled with bounding energy and natural affection for anyone who truly likes them. So "doing school" should really be the easiest thing in the world! What you would "do" is what's left over when you understood what NOT to do! So you wouldn't preempt half of their total time, you wouldn't lock them up with kids exactly their own age, you wouldn't ring bells to start and stop work, you wouldn't ask kids to think about the same thing at the same time, in the same way, you wouldn't grade them like vegetables, and you wouldn't interrupt their natural, self-chosen activities, nor set them against each other competitively. Actually, you wouldn't even really specify what they are to do while they are in school! It would all be there for them if they wanted it, but never as a prescription! So what does that leave? What do you do?

The question reminds me of an occasion when Betsy and I, both of whom are RN's and direct entry midwives as well as longtime teachers in the school, were attending a birth in the hospital as labor coaches a few years ago. The young nurse who had been assigned to this mother in labor came in to hook up the fetal monitor. We asked her not to do so, and, in fact, not to intervene in any other way in this woman's process that was not absolutely necessary. Birth, we told her, is a natural process, and interventions of whatever kind are more likely to slow down the labor than to accelerate it. She looked astounded and, evidently, felt totally disconfirmed, and exclaimed to us, "But then what *am* I supposed to be doing?" It was a very real question in her mind! I suspect many if not most teachers in the public schools would have a similar question if they were suddenly deprived of all their usual role-centered activities. It doesn't seem to dawn on them that the role-centeredness of their outlook is an artifact of the institutional nature of school, as it is of birth in a hospital. Why do we find it so easy to assume that it is perfectly OK to ask people to adapt to institutional rules and customs rather than the other way around? I suppose the answer is that that is how most of us became habituated to being when we were growing up, and that is also how our parents defined our lives, as well as their own. Time for a change! It's not working! Not that it ever has—but at this juncture, the statistics of disaster are so frequent and so drastic that almost no one can pretend things are OK with city schools and the kids in them!

OK. So can we help teachers and parents to alter their model of what a school is supposed to do? How might we get from where we are now to where we wanted to go, with both teachers and parents? How, and in what order ought changes to occur? Well, one major problem that has been identified by all sorts of studies is the massive failure to educate of mass education. I was very struck a few years ago by a keynote address delivered by a friend of mine, John Potter, to the Small Schools Network, of which he was then the president. John was saying that almost anything is possible if only the institution is small enough so that people deal with each other face-to-face, and so that students never have to feel overwhelmed by the sense of being merely a face in the crowd. But in fact, schools are still consolidating in cities and out in the country as well. They really have to if we are even to make a start on reining in the runaway educational budgets we are currently saddled with! The proposal in New York State is to combine several school districts that have lost population. The teachers' unions, administrators, consultants and the firms that supply school equipment are objecting. After all, education is one of the most lucrative businesses in the country! But it has to happen sooner or later. So can something be done about the size of our schools as creators of mass conformity, in the face of such economic necessity?

Well, yes and no. We can't do much about the overall size of schools per se. But we can begin realizing that the problem of regimentation is not a *direct* result of size, but comes from the nature of institutions in general. Inside every school building there are classrooms and staff rooms, and inside those rooms are groups of people who meet together regularly. We *could* learn to make these face-to-face changes in the direction of community among these small groups of people, if we could fund a will to act So, if a school were too big to be dealt with wholesale, it could be re-defined as a congeries of small, semi-autonomous units manageable by small groups of people of all sizes. Within each of these small groups, the principles of self-governance and full participation in policy-making could be established as a *sine qua non* for the transformation of the status quo. I know this is true, because it is how, for example, the Alternative Community School in Ithaca, New York, a highly successful alternative public high school under the leadership of principal Dave Lehman, has been operating for over 20 years. And the key to Dave's success is real democracy—shared governance in all matters pertaining to the operation of the school.

I don't know quite why, but it seems to me that a lot of professional educators of the alternative persuasion, such as Waldorf or Montessori teachers, who in every other respect have great ideas for teaching children, too often tend to slough off this one crucial ingredient in group process, calling it a "libertarian bias," in contrast with what they call "holistic education." [See the dialogue between Ron Miller and John Gatto on pages 384-400] They focus on spiritually-oriented curricular content and attitudinal compassion *toward* children as the key to good education—which is fine as far as it goes, and in practice, probably often involves a democratic outlook as well—but that never seems to be what they write about. And yet, it is my profound belief that without self-governance, without some form of genuinely democratic process, nothing really works well for very long, and that when it is present, whether or not expressed in a formalized manner, everything else works well. Permitting the unfolding of true selfhood as the sole and proper end of real education involves transforming an institution to a community— and this means allowing for real democracy in action. Of course, that's not a complete proposal for changing our educational system—but it's where I would start. To me a necessary if not a sufficient condition for real change.

And outside the school are hundreds of families who send their kids to it but may not—in fact, probably do not—have much of an idea about what goes on inside their kids' schools. Involving parents in city schools, too often in most schools, is a huge taboo. That is one of the ways we fragment and demoralize families. So I would say that where I would begin to take hold of the end of the tangled institutional ball of yarn which we have created would be in terms of *all* of the people involved in schools—which means beginning to look at a school as a community. Is this possible?

In this connection I am remembering Nat Hentoff's account, in *Our Children Are Dying*, of Dr. Elliot Shapiro's principalship during the nineteen-sixties of P.S. 119, an elementary school in central Harlem with eleven hundred children ranging from pre-kindergarten through sixth grade. I say it might be a good place to start, just because P.S. 119 was such an unlikely place for anything of value to occur. Teachers' salaries were small, the teachers themselves of very varied ability and understanding, the classes were too big and the neighborhood too degraded by racism and abject poverty to permit an ideal atmosphere for any kid in that school. Shapiro himself characterized these children as "dying" because so many of them were going all the way through the school without once experiencing the awakening that occurs when one's innate mental aliveness is being regularly stimulated. So we're not talking about ideal circumstances. What Shapiro did, out of his own outrage against the conditions of the school itself was to allow his families—parents and children both—to organize a strike against the school board for better school conditions. But let me give you a flavor of how it was before the strike. First, a conversation Hentoff had with a teacher named Mrs. Jackson in which she was commenting on Shapiro as a principal:

> ... My first year here I was walking with another teacher who'd been at P.S. 119 a while and we saw him come out of a house on Eighth Avenue that I wouldn't have had the courage to go into without a guard. If then. "What on earth is he doing *there*?" I asked. "Oh," she said casually, "He's looking for a child. He does it all the time." I tell you he was stepping out of there as if he were coming out of his own house. That man will go any place and do anything." She laughed.

Now hear Shapiro himself.

> ... In New York City the United Federation of Teachers is providing a structure of support so that the teacher *can* be lively, energetic and inventive without fear of reprisals ... Let us [also] grant the essential liveliness of our children. How does a teacher make the most of that liveliness, and how can he best avoid dampening it? Suppose, for example, in a social science lesson, the teacher is talking about this being a democratic society. And a kid says, "Teach, we have no heat at home. What

do we do in this democratic society to get heat?" If the teacher doesn't formulate some plan in which the children can participate—picketing or other ways that might change the situation—the children won't buy the lesson. In New York, because of the U.F.T., teachers can work out that sort of plan ... But so far, hardly any New York teachers know the scope of the possibilities in this direction. They don't have a full enough sense of their own strength, through the grievance machinery that's been set up ...

Shapiro was very aware of the problem of the lack of will to make change. Here's a quote:

... There's a lot of Eichmann in everybody. ... I'm not talking about overt viciousness. I mean the strong tendency to go along, to conform. Look, while I've been principal of P.S. 119, in any given year more children are *not* educated than *are* educated. What do I do? Picket my own school? Or do I pick those moments when I can do something effective about changing the situation? But there's always the possibility of corruption. As we let time go on, we ourselves develop a vested interest in keeping our mouths shut. We say to ourselves, this isn't the proper time. But any time will be difficult. What it amounts to is to try to keep yourself as conscious as possible of your basic assumptions so that you don't, in some unconscious way, move in a direction that alienates you from yourself and your hopes without you knowing it.

The size of P.S. 119 was one of the biggest factors in Shapiro's awareness of his relative failure to give his kids what they really needed, despite his deep caring about each of them as a person. And yet, institutions like P.S. 119—and there are hundreds of them in our megopolises—need desperately to work to become real communities, if any real change is going to occur. Can they? Yes, I believe they can, and even that it's not very difficult—nor expensive! The issue for me is not one of "can" but of "will." Do we really have the *will* to make these changes? When most people focus on the issue of making changes, it seems to be easier for them to focus on external matters like length of school day and year, like more money, like accountability by teachers, like doing more and better diagnosing of difficulties, like mandating new curricula to combat racism, sexism, drug usage, teen-age pregnancy, AIDS, and rotten teeth! No, I'm not saying we should ignore these issues—but the process of inner transformation I'm speaking about transcends cultural and racial differences and applies across the lines of socio-economic class belonging, geographical location and population density, because it involves issues about people as individuals: people in groups. The specific presenting problems within each child population will vary widely from one school to another, but the dynamics of personal involvement and awareness are universal; and they underlie all the others. We persist in putting Descartes before the horse! He said, "I think, therefore I am." But we need to begin learning to think with our hearts, not our heads!

I believe that when people (of whatever age) begin to see themselves as significant in shaping policy, in having the right both to define and to satisfy their own inner wants, good things start to happen *from within.* I am quite sure that whatever Elliott Shapiro was able to achieve during his tenure at P.S. 119 came about because of his natural awareness of the essential nature of human relationships as the common ingredient beneath the institutional setting of school, out of his understanding of the dynamics of relationship—in short, out of his understanding of the common currency of day-to-day living in family and in community!

Out of this vessel of Shapiro's understanding came a natural realization of the crucial role of the motivation of children themselves, and of their parents as advocates for their children. This is what created his genius in knowing that they, the entire body of his school families, were the key to the success of the school for everyone—both families and teachers—and thus, for the institution itself, in terms of its true goal of educating children! In these terms, I suspect he was a lot more successful than he himself believed.

Thinking over what Hentoff says about Shapiro's kids and his school in the light of our own, I am struck by several considerations. One is that the issue of whether or not his kids learned to read loomed much larger for him than it does in our school, even though the kids he had were quite similar to most of ours. We had to learn not to worry so much about that issue. I had always believed that since ghetto kids have just one chance to "make it" in our society, what mattered most was the internal "tool kit" filled with 3-R goodies they took with them out into the cold, cruel world. I realize now that what we have to give our kids has very little to do with skills acquisition, but a lot to do with spirit, with an inner fire.

The saying, "Give a man a fish and he will eat for a day; teach him how to fish and he will eat for a lifetime" comes to mind. What we discovered was that what we were doing amounted to teaching our kids how to learn! But even that is a misnomer. We weren't teaching them— they were learning it on their own! We were just giving them the space to find out what they wanted to do. Yes, of course we did and do offer modeling for kids of how to find pleasure and satisfaction in school, as in life. We read to them, rock and hug and joke with them, sing songs, kiss their boo-boos, go on walks, hatch eggs, plant beans, feed chickens, milk goats, play ball games, swim in one of the city's public bathhouse pools, chide them for unfairness to smaller kids—although the latter doesn't happen as often as you might think—help them build ships and boxes, go on trips, and generally do all the lovely, natural things kids and grown-ups do together when they're having fun—including the 3 R's, along the way.

But what really happens in our school is a totally mysterious process which takes place within each kid in a totally unique manner that defies quantification or prediction. It is as though there were a little door inside each one, and only that kid has the key. When the child finally finds it, the door opens spontaneously, and the light inside begins to shine outward. You can actually see it beginning to happen! The child's eyes begin to glow softly; her skin to take on a kind of sheen. Her arms and legs work easily and without strain. Her whole energy system is alive and fully present. She stops being accident-prone or fighting aggressively for possessions, or stealing, or isolating, or whatever the manifestations have been of the absence of Self! She begins to enjoy natural interactions with other kids, to be curious and sustain interest for long periods of time, to become as easily absorbed in solitary as in group activities, to sing and dance, to write poetry and draw pictures, to begin practicing skills because she wants to learn them.

This mysterious process is unique to every kid. Because we deal mainly with terribly vulnerable kids, both lower and middle class, both white and non-white, we sometimes lose a kid before this inner process has completed itself. I used to fret about that, but I don't, any more. I've had enough contacts now with former kids who are now in their twenties and thirties to know that even brief contacts can make a crucial difference in the course of their subsequent lives, whether or not they become members of the so-called literate class. I got a call a couple of weeks ago from a girl named Betty, who had been with us for a year during the mid-seventies. I remember her as about as hopeless a "case" as any we ever had. She was ten when she came to us as a school of last resort—big for her age, dog-faced, marked as retarded and delinquent by the public schools, sullen and unapproachable. She derived most of her fun in life by rebellion and disruption of the activities of other kids, or by organizing them into rebellious gangs. She came from a totally disorganized white ghetto family, and found her own way among us mainly by avoiding the things she didn't want to do—or believed she couldn't—and left at the end of the year, apparently unchanged. Well, I was totally wrong, as I have been about a lot of other apparently "hopeless" kids. "Mary," she said to me. "I've been wanting to say something to you for years and I finally decided I just had to do it. I want to apologize for being so hateful to you when I was at the school. One time when I was really mad, you held me and hugged me and wouldn't let me go and finally made me understand you really cared about me. I've been thinking about those days ever since, remembering how much you cared about me. Those were the good days." I asked her about her life now, and she told me she was married, with four kids, two of them her husband's from a previous marriage, that she was living in Pine Hills, a middle class part of the city.

My point is not that Betty's life is ideal because of her year with us—I'm sure it's not— but that, judging by the warmth and articulateness of her voice and manner on the phone, she has a kind of warm, glowing bubble inside her left over from those contacts, and I am quite sure that in some way or another, she passes on that heritage to her kids. And she's only one of a number of kids who have come back to let us know. I remember another—Birdie—who had been a holy terror when she was with us—the fourth child in a white ethnic family of five. Birdie was apparently the only one with enough energy left to rebel, and she kept us hopping! The others were more passively resistant, only secretly delinquent. Birdie, now a sprightly, charming, articulate young woman, attractively dressed, with shining, well-kept hair, who makes her living as an employee in a business in the city, reminded me of my having offered her a baby bottle at the age of five and a secluded, comfortable spot on a mattress in the kitchen to lie down and suck on it at will. She got me to promise not to tell her mother and father, which I did—but the other kids found out and squealed, and we lost the whole family precipitously! I thought we had lost them forever - but lo! here is Birdie, come back to tell us about the lifelong joy of the recollection of that one shining moment, when she got that precious bottle! All to herself! Evidently, that was what she had needed, demoralized and bedraggled as she was, in a family of five demoralized, bedraggled kids, both of whose parents were deeply depressed and indifferent to the demands of parenting. And the interesting thing to me is, Birdie's brothers and sisters are OK too, not just Birdie herself. They're all married, making a living, raising their kids. No, not spectacularly, but at least as well as most middle class products of our public schools!

So my question is, can we grant that real change is possible, given the will to make it? Has, for example, the fact of that extraordinary dedication to the things that mattered at P.S. 119, spread its transformative influence throughout New York City's schools? No, of course not. There aren't enough Elliott Shapiros and John Taylor Gattos around with the courage and the integrity to do what has to be done for these children trapped inside our city schools. And today the situation is far worse than it was during the sixties! Essential schools, magnet schools, merely syphon off a few kids for salvation. The rest are worse off than ever.

Not all of our country's schools are as desperate as New York City's, or as Los Angeles'—but they are bad enough, and getting worse. Our own small city of Albany is no exception. The head of the Bureau of Attendance and Guidance of our public school system who also serves as our liason with the central office and has been a staunch supporter of our school from almost the very beginning, told Chris, one of our teachers, recently that the percentage of children in serious trouble in Albany is rising rapidly, has already reached 15%. Not much by comparison with the statistics of the megopolises, perhaps, but new to us, an alarming harbinger of the future.

I need to add that it is perfectly apparent to me, as to people like John Gatto and Ram Dass, that no institutional change—not even one in the direction of self-governance—is going to make real change in our society's way of looking at life on our endangered planet so long as we ignore the centrality of humanness—of the heart as the center of every process that involves people—children or adults. This kind of transformation from within is the only real change that can make our continued existence possible. Ecologically as well as demographically, we are 30 years from irreversible damage all over the planet on the scale that exists now in places like Haiti, according to Capitain Cousteau (see below). Are we getting the message? Can we fund a will that will enable us to begin to grapple with the real revolution that has got to happen? No, not someone else—each of us!

Connie Frisbee-Houde is a member of the Free School community in Albany, New York, occasional contributor to ΣΚΟΛΕ, co-editor of both ΣΚΟΛΕ and our new Journal of Family Life, photographer, costume designer and maker, teacher at the Free School, lover of children and cats, and an extraordinary gardener.

OLD RHINEBECK KIDS
by Connie Frisbee-Houde

This summer my pilot husband and I flew our small, 1940's-vintage, two-seater airplane into Old Rhinebeck Aerodrome, New York, to watch the air show of early aviation and old World War I aircraft. The grounds include a number of hangars, a grass airfield, audience seating, a picnic area, a small pond, and wooded areas. We arrived early to eat our lunch at a picnic table next to the pond and a small, people-use-only covered bridge on the edge of the pond. All around the edge of the pond grew beautiful purple loosestrife 5 to 6 feet tall, with a few places where a small group of kids could gather. I had remembered from years before that there had been ducks on the pond. I wondered where they were. Before long, a goose appeared. He must have smelled the food from the picnickers that gather on the grounds before the main events.

This one goose paddled up to the bridge area to see what was happening. A family with two children, 5 and 7 years of age, walked by and the kids stopped to look. They were eating French fries and hot dogs and began to entice the goose to come to eat the pieces of roll from their hands. The goose was a little hesitant, not wanting to come too close, so the kids threw the bread from the hot dog roll into the water for the goose. The water was quite muddy so you could not see the bottom of the pond. Suddenly there appeared a fish after the bread. The father told the children it was a catfish. Apparently the word was out in the fish domain...FOOD! More fish magically surfaced. The kids delightedly began to shout, "Look at the catfish over there! And there!" Because of the excited sounds these two kids were making, a number of other children came running to see what was happening. The catfish lazily came to the surface to see if they could benefit from this noon-time feeding. They would slowly stick their whiskered, large-eyed faces up to the surface, grab the bread, and disappear. The kids were fascinated. It struck me that this was the gathering of the clans—of the catfish and of the children.

The purple loosestrife surrounding the pond helped to create an island of mystery. Not only did more children come, but the ducks I had remembered swam up to the feeding area. One of the children noticed a snake, and the kids again were all fascinated watching and pointing, "Daddy, look at the snake." Then a very interesting thing happened. One of the fathers became fearful for his children and started to tell them not to go near the snake and, by association, the water. The kids stepped back, not sure what to do in their excitement. Some of the braver ones let their curiosity take hold and, in defiance of the warning, stepped closer to find out for themselves about this forbidden fruit. At the same time another father came by who recognized the snake as a harmless water snake. The first father took some time to back off from restraining his kids and creating a fear response in some of the children. The new father began to talk to the kids about what they were seeing, answering their questions. The kids were not held back for long and soon forgot any indication of fear. Next a painted turtle came to investigate what was happening.

Who was watching who? Some of the kids who did not have food to throw or drop in the water began to pick up some of the small gravelly stones that were on the path to throw at the goose, ducks and fish. They wanted so much to be a part of the activity. Very nicely one of the parents told them not to throw stones, and the kids reluctantly stopped. The father who had identified the snake had also noticed that one of the catfish had only one eye and a bruise on his head. He pointed this out to the kids, telling them that this injury may have been caused by a rock. Many of the kids were visibly effected by this possibility, and all the questions just seemed to rush forth, "Could that really happen? How does it feel?" The kids' excitement was so great they forgot about throwing stones.

My husband and I were transfixed watching this community of people that had grown up spontaneously around the little pond, observing the natural happenings. I wonder if at some time the fish were also taking this opportunity to teach their little ones about this occasional food source...to teach them to grab the food and disappear into the mud so they could not be harmed by anything. Were the younger fish just as curious as the kids? Did the younger fish not feel any threat? Were they similar to the children who did feel fear until it was introduced by an adult? What fish game was this? Perhaps the pond was acting as a mirror. Who was seeing whom?

REVIEWS

There Are No Children Here -
The Story of Two Boys Growing Up in the Other
America
by Alex Kotlowitz
Doubleday, 1991

Savage Inequalities
Children in America's Schools
by Jonathan Kozol
Crown, 1991

Reviewed by Joseph Pearl

Joseph Pearl is an Associate Professor in the Department of Applied Behavioral Studies in Education at Oklahoma State University. He teaches courses in educational psychology and human development. Reprinted from Perspective, *the newsletter of the Association for Human Psychology for July, 1992.*

Two recent books about poverty, race, and education have made me think about the relevance of humanistic psychology in solving critical problems plaguing America.

In *There Are No Children Here*, Alex Kotlowitz describes the day-to-day lives of two young African Americans, Lafeyette and Pharoah Rivers, who live in a Chicago public housing project. His book focuses on the period from the summer of 1987, when Pharoah was nine and Lafeyette almost twelve, to the fall of 1989. It's about what living in an environment of poverty, racism, and violence does to the lives and spirits of children.

When Kotlowitz first met Lafeyette Rivers in 1985, he asked him what he wanted to be when he grew up. "'If I grow up, 'd like to be a bus driver,' he told me. If, not when. At the age of en, Lafeyette wasn't sure he'd make it to adulthood."

Kotlowitz's approach to his subject matter is emotional nd personal. He became friends with Lafeyette, Pharoah, and heir mother, and used some of the money he earned from his ook to send both boys to private schools. Though he doesn't xplicitly offer solutions to the problems he details, his own example suggests the efficacy of people getting to know each other on a one-to-one basis, and caring about each other as fellow human beings.

Kotlowitz's example is one that humanistic psychology can enthusiastically endorse. The importance of authentic and caring interpersonal relationships is a central tenet of humanistic psychology. Humanistic psychologists and educators would have a major role to play in any large scale effort to promote such relationships in our society.

In *Savage Inequalities*, Jonathan Kozol takes us with him as he visits the communities and schools of the poor across our country. He paints a horrifying picture: East St. Louis, Illinois, which is 98% black, has had no regular trash collection since October of 1987. Its schools are regularly closed down because of backups in the city's barely functioning sewer system. 75% of its population lives on welfare. Fiscal shortages have forced the layoff of 1,170 of 1,400 city employees during the past 12 years.

A teacher at the University of Southern Illinois describes East St. Louis as "a repository for a non-white population that is now regarded as expendable.:" A reporter for the *St Louis Post-Dispatch*, discussing living conditions in East St. Louis, tells Kozol, "Why Americans permit this is so hard for somebody like me, who grew up in the real Third World, to understand. I'm from India. In Calcutta this would be explicable, perhaps. I keep thinking to myself, 'My God! This is the United States!'" A nine year old boy tells Kozol about his sister, who was raped and murdered and then dumped behind his school.

Kozol is more analytical than Kotlowitz. He focuses on the way public schools are funded, quoting numerous statistics showing the inequity in funding between the schools of the (mostly white) financially well-off and the (mostly black and hispanic) poor. A recent study of the wealthiest and poorest districts of Long Island, New York, for example, showed that differences were large, and had doubled in a five year period: Schools in the wealthy town of Manhasset spent $11,370 for each pupil in 1987. In Levittown, a community of mostly working-class white families, per-pupil spending was $6,900. In poorer Roosevelt, where the schools are 99% non-white, per-pupil expenditure was $6,340. A realtor tells him, "If you're looking for a home, you can look at the charts for school expenditures and use them to determine if the neighbors will be white and wealthy or, conversely, black or white but poor."

Kozol concludes that the first step toward any solution of America's problems with poverty, race, and education must be to fund the schools of children from poor families at the same level as the schools of children from wealthy families (if not at a higher level, he adds, since poor children have greater needs than rich children). He points out that this would require significant sacrifice on the part of the non-poor. They would either have to pay higher taxes or accept lower levels of funding for their own children's schools. In either case, their children would have to compete with the children of the poor on a more even playing field.

Kozol's analysis is emblematic for humanistic psychology. With its emphasis on self-actualization and developing one's own fullest potential, and its tendency to promote quick-fix, feelgood nostrums, humanistic psychology does not easily lend itself to calls for self-sacrifice. In addition, the humanistic psychology community is very much a part of that segment of society—white and well-off—that has benefitted most from the inequity in school funding that Kozol criticizes.

What Kozol's and Kotlowitz's books make clear is that America is in the midst of a crisis. One cannot help but ask, What kind of country is this, what kind of people are we, to allow some of us to have so little while others have so much? Both books bring home an unavoidable conclusion: The way things are now is wrong. It is simply not morally acceptable for a free and democratic country to treat its people this way.

Whether humanistic psychology will be part of the solution or part of the problem remains to be seen.

VIDEO REVIEW:

"Why Do These Kids Love School?" 60 min. $99.50
by Dorothy Fadiman
Pyramid Film & Video
PO Box 1048, Santa Monica, Ca 90406
Call 1-800-421-2304
or send a check or money order

Reviewed by Mary Anne Raywid
(Review reprinted from *The Kappan*, April, 1992.)

Mary Anne Raywid is a professor of education at Hofstra University, Hempstead, N.Y. She describes a film that has powerful lessons to teach, including the simple message that there are schools in this country "where innovation is the norm, mutual respect is the .standard, and children truly enjoy learning." Produced by Dorothy Fadiman in association with KTEH-TV, "Why Do These Kids Love School?" lets you observe, firsthand. the positive results achieved by alternative teaching methods in nine different schools. This documentary offers both tools and inspiration for teachers, administrators, and parents alike.

"There is a chilling assumption that schools are not capable of improving themselves. This remarkable documentation lays that myth to rest once and for all."
—Roland Barth, Harvard University

The title of this article is taken directly from the title of an extraordinary film that has an extraordinary history and makes an extraordinary impact on viewers. Almost everything about "Why Do These Kids Love School?"—its sponsorship, its topic, its length, its distribution, and its amazing success—breaks the mold of "educational films." Many educators have asked, "Why isn't there a film that makes schooling as vivid and appealing as movies manage to make other things?" This film is the answer. Moreover, as one reviewer put it, "This could be the most important media coverage that child-centered education has ever received."

"Why Do These Kids Love School?" is an extremely powerful statement that viewers have described as "moving," "inspiring," and "creating hope." It manages not only to produce a strong emotional impact but also to provide a remarkably intimate look at life inside nine different schools. It successfully conveys a sense of the spirit and personality of the schools portrayed, and it even manages to suggest something of what makes them tick.

The film is the work of a filmmaker who, out of a combination of curiosity and gratitude, set out to make a movie about the school her children had attended. She began with a sense of the discrepancy between the way most children experience school and the joyousness with which her two daughters had experienced it.

And so, Dorothy Fadiman set out to make a documentary about the Peninsula School, a 65-year-old independent, progressively oriented school in Menlo Park, California. As she tells it, the challenge proved so fascinating that she spent several years filming at the school. Eventually, realizing that viewers might attribute the activities and successes of Peninsula to an advantaged population and selective admissions, Fadiman set out to find other schools—public schools—with a similar orientation. She ultimately included in the film portraits of eight additional schools, scattered across the country. "Why Do These Kids Love School?" captures something of the essence of each individual school and identifies some characteristics common to all nine of them.

The film has racked up an amazing array of prizes, but for producer Dorothy Fadiman, who also wrote the script, it remains first and foremost an act of love. Fadiman, the mother of two adult children, has more than a touch of the counterculture and the flower child about her—with the enormous sensitivity and compassion of that era combined with its concern for the vulnerability of the young. There is also a spirituality about her, along with a great deal of intensity. commitment, and dedication. She set out to make a picture that would move and inspire as well as inform. The first question she asks of audiences when the lights go up after a screening is frequently surprising and disarming: "Did it bring tears to your eyes'?" For an overwhelming number of viewers, the answer is yes.

Teachers are accustomed to portrayals of classrooms that make them cringe. Only rarely can professionals in the field find a non educator's understanding of teaching to be terribly penetrating or insightful. How did Fadiman manage it'?

Part of the answer seems to lie in her own unusual capacity to learn. She listens and observes with total absorption—and acts on what she has learned. I will never forget my surprise when, months after our first conversation. I discovered that she had filmed almost every school that I had suggested to her. After the first version of the film was made and we had had several more conversations, she made changes that reflected the advice I and others had offered.

Critics share the enthusiasm of audiences for this film. Since its premiere in May 1990, "Why Do These Kids Love School?" has won a number of coveted awards—in national competitions involving thousands of entries, in one international film festival that drew submissions from 47 nations, in competitions limited to educational films, and in competitions involving a variety of areas. It took the 1990 award for best documentary in a San Francisco/San Jose competition (the Joeys), It took the Blue Ribbon at the 1991 American Film and Video Festival, it earned a Golden Eagle from the Council on International Non-theatrical Events (which means it will represent the U.S. in film festivals abroad), and if won a Silver Apple in the National Educational Film Festival.

Just one of the remarkable things about this film is the way it has been distributed. Since Fadiman produced it herself, with no sales organization behind her, she began distributing it from her home at below-cost prices. However, she was soon assisted by enthusiastic teachers across the country who volunteered to help with distribution within their areas. Today, the film has been purchased by a large number of schools and districts, and it has been bought and distributed by a number of regional organizations. In Hawaii, for example, the Honolulu chapter of the League of Women Voters is in the process of purchasing 50 copies for distribution to that city's elementary schools. The Iowa education department has sought funding to distribute the film in that state. And, after viewing the film, the Kappan editors asked me to write this article to inform their readers about the film.

One of the most unusual attributes of this film is the range of audiences to which it appeals. To mark the beginning of the school year, "Why Do These Kids Love School?" was shown on public television last fall for the second year in a row. It is widely used by parent and civic groups. But it is also used in courses that prepare teacher aides and other paraprofessionals, in teacher preparation courses, and even in courses that prepare experienced teachers to become supervisors. At the same time, the film has been used with youngsters in high school. in junior high, and in the elementary grades as a way of getting them to talk about their school experiences and what they would like them to be.

Just how does a film achieve such broad appeal? First, i tells the story of the Peninsula School, and it traces a Peninsula education from preschool to eighth-grade graduation

Classrooms and activities are shown at each age and grade level—beginning with a toddler's struggle to manage a hose and culminating in a young adolescent's tearful ambivalence about moving on to high school. The other schools portrayed carry the story of child-centered education into the high school. Altogether, the film runs for nearly an hour, though most viewers are surprised to discover that the time has passed so quickly.

Without the use of tedious labels, "Why Do These Kids Love School'?" manages to convey something of significance about the educational process at each level. For instance, a scene in a first-grade science lab shows how observations lead to discovery and how children's ideas can be handled in ways that transmit important affective as well as cognitive messages. There is considerable emphasis throughout on schools, teachers, and parents as cultivators of human beings. Indeed, there is as much to do with the shaping of young lives as with the process of schooling .

It might even be said that this film reveals a powerful hidden curriculum. It evokes considerable thought about what schools are for and why we need them in the first place. In the admiring words of one reviewer, it offers "a gentle reminder that our educational priorities have gotten skewed somehow." Questions of educational mission and of the values we want schools to impart become for many viewers the center of the film. The film places considerable emphasis on freedom, but it also stresses the cooperation and creativity that freedom should yield. Autonomy is one theme, but so is building trust, community, and collaboration .

A second message that the film conveys is that good education is doable. The negative views of education that have characterized the past decade—and the circumstances that gave rise to them—have sometimes made it seem that we are incapable of offering education that is simultaneously effective, high in quality, equitable, and appealing. "Why Do These Kids Love School'?" presents a countervailing (and heartening) point of view. The students and teachers in the nine schools it portrays are "turned on and tuned in."

Moreover, Fadiman was careful to include all kinds of student populations from all parts of the country. While she begins with a small, predominantly white and middle-class independent school, she also shows inner-city public schools whose students are largely minority youngsters from the working class or from the urban underclass. Classroom scenes and interviews were filmed in East Harlem, Minneapolis, and New Orleans, as well as in Lakewood, Colorado, Lowell and Cambridge,

Massachusetts; and Jackson, Mississippi. They illustrate everything from carefully integrated curricula to a focus on individual learning styles and from cooperative learning to unusual roles for students, teachers. and parents.

What is particularly striking about the history of "Why Do These Kids Love School?" is the wide range of purposes for which it has proved effective. When she learned I was writing this article, Dorothy Fadiman wrote to a number of the people who had contacted her and asked them to share with me just how they have used the film. The array of responses was impressive. Here is a brief sampling. One school reported showing it to the school board "to acquaint them with the mission and purpose of the school." Others use it as a consciousness raising experience to stimulate awareness of the distance between the "is" and the "ought to be" and so to demonstrate a need for change. Still others use it for inspirational purposes to generate hope or to heal the wounds of disillusionment. One principal reported that he planned to show it annually to his teachers at the beginning of the school year to heighten dedication and commitment and to help them "rekindle the essential spark."

While it carefully avoids being didactic, the film nonetheless carried substantial freight. It urges child-centered education, considerable individual responsibility for learners, an emphasis on motivation, a personalized and supportive school environment, active engagement of learners with the material to be learned, the centrality of the human community. and a thorough interweaving of the affective, cognitive, and social aspects of development during the .school years.

By virtue of its rich demonstration of these and other educational principles, "Why Do These Kids Love School?" has been used in a variety of professional courses, including classes on instructional methods, educational movements, methods of supervision, students at risk, theories of counseling, alternative education, and child and adolescent development. Even in areas for which the film has little direct application—e.g., school administration—its universal appeal seems to make it useful for sparking discussion of such matters as the kinds of roles played by the educators in the schools depicted, the kinds of scheduling arrangements that these schools require, and the kinds of school organization needed to support and sustain these learning environments.

The usefulness of the film to school administrators is suggested by Thomas Peters, of corporate excellence fame, in his introduction to the film. Peters points out that the schools depicted portray just the sorts of circumstances that "make miracles" in any workplace. Workers are given the autonomy and responsibility to control their own operation, they are encouraged to collaborate with their peers, they are controlled more by a shared set of values and guiding principles than by rules and regulations, and they are made to feel like important and valued contributors to a significant enterprise. The schools depicted manage to establish these conditions for teachers as well as for students.

One reason why such organizational features are present in this group of schools is that all are alternative schools—which have been shown to differ substantially from other public schools with respect to their autonomy within the .system and the way in which they operate as organizations. But alternative schools also typically differ from traditional .schools in what they stand for educationally and in the pedagogy they employ. This is another feature of the film that makes its broad appeal so surprising: lately, alternative education has not had the endorsement of a great many educators in this country. It is not an educational orientation that a great many parents are demanding for their youngsters or that many reformers are urging for schools.

Yet if this film is any test—and I suspect it may be—the features of alternative education enjoy enormous appeal. On the one hand, that should not be entirely surprising, since a great many of these features are currently being urged separately as school improvement measures (e.g., cross-disciplinary study, downsizing, personalization, and learner engagement). On the other hand, it is certainly food for thought that a somewhat marginalized type of schooling should generate such positive response from professionals, parents, and the public.

"Why Do These Kids Love School'?" has powerful lessons to teach, including the simple message that there are schools in this country "where innovation is the norm, mutual respect is the standard, and children truly enjoy learning." But even where its teachings are neither new nor novel, this film manages to present them in enormously attractive ways. My own calling prevents me from concluding that words are superfluous or unnecessary. But this film is a vivid reminder that there are often more direct and powerful ways of getting a point across. For example, a big part of the message of the film was articulated by an esteemed scholar and educational philosopher 30 years ago.

The essence of the curriculum consists not of objective lessons to be learned and courses to be passed, but of the scheme of values, ideals, or life goals which arc mediated through the materials of instruction. The really significant outcome of education is the set of governing commitments—the aims for living that the learner develops. The various subjects of study are simply means for the communication and appropriation of those values.

Dorothy Fadiman's film reframes this message in ways that speak directly to the heart. It is, as one of the people who wrote to me put it, "a beautiful statement on the power of education, the unlimited potential of children, and the importance of teachers."

SMALL SCHOOL NEWSLETTERS:

Living Education
Family Learning Exchange

Reviewed by Chris Mercogliano

There are a number of excellent small desktop journals coming our way these days and we thought this would be a good time to begin reviewing some of them for you.

Living Education is the journal of the Oak Meadow School, a homeschooling center based in Blacksburg, VA. A well-laid out 24 page bi-monthly, the current March/April '95 issue features a very interesting and well-researched historical analysis of the relationship between institutionalized schooling and crime. There are also a number of contributions from children of all ages, including a beautiful and lengthy essay by ninth grader Alysha Turner on the impact of literature on her life to date. A budding young writer herself, she takes us through some of the books and authors that she has been profoundly influenced by. It's enough to make an avid reader out of the stubbornest non-reader.

Subscriptions can be obtained by mailing a check for $18.00 ($33.00 foreign) to Oak Meadow School, P.O. Box 712, Blacksburg, VA 24063.

Another 24 page bi-monthly called *Family Learning Exchange, the Journal of Natural Learning, Family learning, and Homeschooling* states that its purpose is "to support and provide resources and information for families who have chosen to educate their children at home. We believe that our families are the foundation upon which our society is built, and only through building strong families can we hope to build a strong society." This lively magazine is filled with useful information, including a data base of relevant products and resources, reading lists and a national calendar of important homeschooling conferences and events. Featured in the March/April issue is one of the best articles about the mysterious, much misunderstood, and downright mythological subject of dyslexia that I have ever read. A lifelong "dyslexic" himself, the author proposes that what we call dyslexia is not some form of pathology, but rather is a special mode of thinking employed by certain individuals, as well as being their natural reaction to confusion. The magazine is worth getting hold of for this piece alone.

Subscriptions can be obtained by mailing a check for $15.00 to: Flex, P.O. Box 300, Benton City, WA 99320.

"FALSE CHOICES?
WHY SCHOOL VOUCHERS
THREATEN OUR CHILDREN'S FUTURE, "
by the editors of *Rethinking Schools*
Milwaukee, WI
Reviewed by Michael Traugot, editor of the *NCACS News*

Michael Traugot, in addition to being a long-time editor of the NCACS News, *has been a teacher, parent , prefessional tie-dyer and solar technology engineer at The Farm in Summertown, Tennessee, for many years.*

We have published articles about educational "choice" in previous issues of this newsletter, from both sides of the argument, pro and con. I have personally been trying for a long time to get some kind of handle on the situation, to learn enough so that I could arrive at some definitive opinion as to whether and to what extent school choice would be a good idea. I have found it to be a rather complex question, though some advocates of both sides come on like it is really simple.

I know that many members of NCACS [the National Coalition of Alternative Community Schools, from which this review was reprinted] think public and private school choice would be a good idea, both from a general dislike of bureaucracy and government dictation, and because, as "private" schools, they have been doing the actual work of educating kids for years, largely without a cent of government money, while continuing to pay taxes for education which are used by the public schools. It only seems fitting that they should receive some of that tax money for doing the actual job of education. Still, there seem to be compelling reasons not to just go ahead and declare open school choice a reality, without first considering what the results might be for all sectors of society.

In their publication "False Choices: Why School Vouchers Threaten Our Chlldren's Future," the editors of *Rethinking Schools* make the case against all-out public and private school choice better and clearer than I have ever seen it before. The basic plan for school choice revolves around a voucher system. Tax moneys collected for education would be divided up evenly among all students, who would then get to choose—presumably with their parents' help—which schools they wished to attend, public or private. This competition, the "free-market" aspect of the program, would presumably lead to a general increase in quality, as poor schools become "poor" in the other sense, failing to attract students, and therefore funds. They would presumably improve or close down. Public schools are presently prevented from improving, according to this argument, because individual schools cannot hire and fire teachers at will, based on their own judgment, and because they must accept all the students from their district, all of whom are forced to go to that one school system. The prescription for breaking the "gridlock" is, as John Taylor Gatto puts it, to end the "state monopoly" on schooling. Give each student an equal share of the tax money collected for education, allow him/her to attend any school s/he chooses, and allow schools to accept or not accept any students they want; that is the solution, according to school choice advocates.

From "Chris Whittle's Trojan Horse," by Anthony J. Alvarado, printed originally in New York's Newsday *7/13/93, and reprinted in "False Choices,"* Rethinking Schools' *Special Edition, p. 20:*

Financial realities will make it impossible to serve student populations similar to those in the public schools, contrary to Whittle's claims. The poorer the student, and the more at-risk the student, the more difficult and costly the education. The incentive to maximize profits is inherently at odds with the social responsibility borne by the public schools or to choose, subtly, those poor students who can succeed. Deepening the wedge between the educationally advantaged and disadvantaged, between rich and poor, between whites and people of color, is contrary to the American dream. Inventing a system for the best and ignoring the rest rends the social and cultural fabric in a nation struggling to fashion a new *e pluribus unum.*

But, when you read this publication, you hear the other side and begin to wonder. The scenario most feared by the publishers of *Rethinking Schools* (who are dedicated public school teachers in the Milwaukee, WI public school system), is that each child will be awarded a stipend in the form of a voucher, but that the amount of that voucher will not be sufficient for a decent education for any child (some have suggested rates as low as $1000, certainly not enough to provide a good education, unless you have volunteer teachers). This would leave wealthy Americans in a strong position to educate their own children, and those of low income in a terrible position to do so, since they would have no funds to supplement the vouchers. The tax rate for education could easily go down, so that the wealthy would be paying less for education taxes than they are now, plus receiving the amount of the voucher toward sending each of their children to the kind of prep school George Bush attended. A good break for them, at the expense of the poor and middle class, whose tax break on education would be less significant than that of the rich, but whose public schools would no longer receive the amount of money they do currently, which in many cases isn't enough in the first place.

There are many other arguments on both sides of the issue. For example, total choice advocates say that the "free market" system will weed out bad schools and raise the level of education in general. Opponents counter that the "free market" system has already made a mess of our health system, and would make our education system even worse. Total choice advocates say that our public education system is already a mess; opponents counter that at least it represents a commitment by the entire society to educate every child, a commitment that the voucher system would undermine.

Since Clinton and Gore won the election, it seems obvious that the Bush plan for complete public and private school choice will not be instituted, at least on a federal level, during the next four years. However, there will be lots of public pressure at all levels, especially in individual states, to make some kinds of changes in this direction. NCACS members will probably be involved in these efforts, including trying to educate Clinton and Gore to the fact that "private" schools are no longer simply prep schools for the rich. I think it is very important that anyone who joins the fray understand as fully as possible all the consequences of any plan he or she is advocating.

Therefore, I strongly recommend that you read this publication and integrate its information into your personal mental data banks before aligning yourself with one side or the other. And, carry on your educational efforts despite this controversy. It looks like the vast majority of American youth will continue to be educated in public schools, and so the way we can influence the big picture the most is to keep on with our successful educational efforts and publicize the best of what we have to offer to public as well as independent schools.

Reprinted from the National Coalition News, *Winter, 1993, 13-16.*

...her seventy-six years, Mary Leue, mother of five and grandmother of eleven, has been a Maine
...ner, registered nurse, teacher, civil rights and anti-war activist, lay midwife, leader in both
...rnative education and natural childbirth movements, therapist, community organizer, editor, writer,
...top publisher, and bookseller. She has published a number of articles in national and international
...nals of education and psychotherapy, including the *Journal of Orgonomy, Energy and Character,*
...*stic Education Review,* and *ΣΚΟΛΕ,* the alternative education journal that she created eleven years

...n and raised in New England, Mary graduated with an A.B. in history from Bryn Mawr College in
...1. In 1943, she received her graduate nursing degree from The Children's Medical Center Hospital
...ol of Nursing in Boston, Mass. In the early 1950's, she accompanied her husband, then a young
...essor of philosophy, to Denton, Texas, where she raised five children, taught school and did graduate
...k in English literature and education at Texas Woman's University. Mary moved to Albany in the
...y 1960's and began training with several internationally known therapists, in addition to doing
...uate work in psychology at the State University of New York, where she is now a Fellow of the
...luate Program in the Center for Arts and Humanities.

...969, responding to the distress of her ten-year-old son, who was suffering badly in the Albany public
...ols, Mary decided to start The Free School, which is now one of the longest running inner city
...pendent alternative schools in the nation. Influenced by the father of anarchism Prince Pyotr
...otkin, by Mahatma Gandhi, and by Dr. Martin Luther King, Jr., Mary firmly believed that open,
...cratic education should be available to the children of the poor as well as to those of the middle and
...r classes. When she consulted with A.S. Neill, founder of Summerhill, about such a possibility, his
...nse was pure Neill: "I would think myself daft to try."

...969, Mary proceeded to gather an entire group of "daft" individuals who are together to this day,
...g joined her in her vision of living and working in genuine community in a postindustrial world.
...ed by Wilhelm Reich's concept of "work democracy," Mary and the others began creating a series
...all-scale community institutions to both broaden the school's mission and support the health and
...h of community members. She saw clearly from the start that such an experiment would need to
...ts own internal economy and be based on shared, peer-level leadership, and that it would depend on
...ng, emotional honesty for its long-term survival. Finally, the awareness developed in Mary and in
...s that a vital community needs a spiritual basis as well, and what has evolved is multifaceted,
...ng from many diverse traditions.

.A. $15.00   ISBN: 1-878115-11-1   Canada $16.00

uggested)   U.K.   £10.00